THE BOOK OF NUMBERS

COMPILED BY THE EDITORS OF HERON HOUSE

A&W Publishers, Inc.
New York

First published in the United States of America in 1978 by
A & W Publishers, Inc.
95 Madison Avenue
New York 10016
By arrangement with Heron House Publishing Limited

Library of Congress Catalog Card Number: 78-55109

ISBN: 0-89479-028-5

Printed in the United States of America

Editorial Director:	Peter Verstappen
Senior Editor:	Tessa Clark
Research Director:	Esther Piette Runnalls
Art Directors:	Tim Fitzgerald
	Oliver Hickey
Executive Editor:	Michael Brook
Statistical Consultant:	Geoff Dicks
Senior Writer:	Paul Strathern
Illustrator:	Nigel Paige

Writers:	Penny Naylor, Junius Adams with: John Abineri, Robin Cooper, John Cunningham, Carole Hay, Rose Lockwood, Patricia Lyons, Dennis Maddison, Nigel Hinton, Kevin Rose, Kevin O'Sullivan, Marguerite Tarrant
Copy Editors:	Alison Fell, Lynn Greenwood, James McCarter, De Robinson
Editorial Assistants:	Meg Dorman, Kerry Green, Becky Llewellen Maureen Ramm, Maggi Renshaw, Brian Scott
Research Assistants:	Jill Benson, Liz Cashman, Carole Dufrechou, Ellen Frank, Joe Friedman, Ingela Hedlund, Christine Hoover, Beatrice Kernan, Adam Low, Fleur Osmanson, Judie Rosenthal, Carey Schofield, Susan Sickenger, Jamie Somerville, Hilary Whyte

TABLE OF CONTENTS

INTRODUCTION

Many of us are terrified by numbers. Yet, paradoxically, all of us use numbers every day.

- Are my salary increases keeping me ahead of the game?
- How many other people share my views?
- There are 32 children in my child's class and only one teacher. Is that a decent ratio?
- How does my life style compare with others in the States and in other developed countries?
- Is my sex life below average, average or simply spectacular?

We constantly use numbers to compare ourselves and our lives with the lot of others. It's a great competitive sport and we've always been a competitive country.

The Book of Numbers gives you the ammunition to play this game to your heart's content. Back in the 17th century, Sir Thomas Browne said that numbers have "a secret magic" all their own. In the pages which follow we've attempted to take out the mystery while leaving that magic.

Sex, taxes, making money and trying to hold on to it, vacations, crime, the weather and whether or not we are all going to make it – these topics form the very essence of our daily life. They also cover just some of the topics you'll find in the pages of this book.

Whatever the aspect of man in his environment, we've attempted to give you all the available numbers. For numbers are facts and facts are what we all require to draw conclusions.

We've drawn some general conclusions. However, you'll find many facts that are particularly relevant to your own situation, ranging from your economic status compared to the rest of the world to how much vacation you get; from how you like to spend your leisure to how often you're taken to bed. That's the inherent fun of *The Book of Numbers*.

"How do I love thee – let me count the ways".
Elizabeth Barrett Browning, *Portuguese Sonnets*

Even in romance, numbers play a part. How many affairs we've had, how old we were when we lost our virginity, how old the person was with whom we first slept. All of these are based on numbers. Where possible, we've now attempted to tell you how your experience relates to the world at large.

The Numbers Jungle

Numbers frighten most of us, yet they govern our lives from before birth until after death. Numbers can tell you what the odds are of having a child and the odds of it surviving. By the same token, numbers can be used to predict when you are apt to die (it varies widely from country to country) and to indicate what will happen to the estate you leave.

We understand how daunting numbers can seem. Therefore, we've employed a talented team of writers who understand both numbers and people. Each is expert in the fields he covers. All have been told to think of the reader as someone who may not understand numbers and/or is usually frightened by them.

All the Facts Between Two Covers

Now, for the first time, we've assembled the world's most fascinating facts in one book and presented them in a uniform, compact and (we hope) easy-to-understand way. The results will let you compare your own life with other Americans and with citizens of other countries.

Numbers do have one beauty: they represent an absolute and thereby allow us to compare like with like. This is exactly what we've attempted to do in the pages which follow. As a result, you can compare practical matters (how much rent you pay for your apartment – or a steak – compared with a housewife in Paris) and enjoy whimsical facts (the West Germans really *do* drink more beer than anybody else), as well as more weighty matters (for example, how the government spends your money).

How This Book Was Created

The world is not without its share of books on numbers. The United Nations publishes literally hundreds of volumes. So does the United States Government. In fact, most governments are weighed down with numbers. They have to be. You can't make a major governmental decision without them. Private concerns use numbers to make business decisions. Social action groups and lobbyists use them to put forward their case, unions to bargain for their members and to lobby for improved conditions. So the world is full of numbers. With diligent research, good research contacts, and lots of money there is no figure which you could not determine. So why have we bothered to do this book?

The answer is quite simple. This is the first book that takes most of the world's available statistics and puts them on a roughly comparable basis as a single resource. So you can quickly find the facts you want to make interesting comparisons.

You can make these comparisons because our researchers have quite literally circled the globe to bring back answers for you. Our people have waded through statistics at the World Bank in Washington to get financial facts.

We've visited the Danish Institute on Sex for the lowdown on private lives and called on Montreal's International Civil Aviation Organization to find out all about airlines. We've talked to experts to uncover the world's worst airports and Interpol in Paris, Scotland Yard in London and the F.B.I. in Washington to ferret out criminal statistics. These and more than 500 other sources have been tapped, including a wide number of government and United Nations agencies, banks, special research units and other experts in a vast variety of fields.

"A witty statesman said you might prove anything with figures"
Thomas Carlyle, Chartism

We've tried to make the figures in this book as accurate as possible but there are some problems. In the first place, many countries simply don't have adequate statistics. This is particularly true in the less developed world where, in many cases, such rudimentary facts as census statistics are almost non-existent. Rulers often don't even know how many people they rule. Other countries have statistics, but withhold them. For these reasons, we've confined our basic tables to the major industrial countries which produce accurate, roughly comparable facts. These are:

Australia	Japan
Austria	The Netherlands
Belgium	Norway
Canada	Denmark
France	Sweden
West Germany	Spain
Ireland	Switzerland
Italy	United Kingdom
	United States

To a degree, virtually all governments, all over the world, use figures to suit themselves. They do so for a variety of reasons. First, because a politician's primary concern is his own survival, so, when elections loom, figures have an unnatural – albeit predictable – propensity to look good. The increase in the cost of living goes down. The balance of trade looks better. Taxes can be held or cut.

Even where figures do exist, there can be disconcerting problems. These, we've discovered, come in a variety of forms. The first is *when* the figures were compiled. It is patently regrettable, but understandable, that all countries don't conduct the same kind of research at the same point in time. So we've had to make a difficult choice between using older comparable statistics and more up-to-date facts. Please do remember similar facts for different years are not precisely comparable.

Numbers Versus Words
Without going into great detail, there's the problem of research base. Exactly how many people were surveyed? What precisely were they asked? What are the criteria applied to each statistic? We live in a world of numbers but research is conducted on the basis of words. Many responses are subject to widely different interpretations.

Some Troublesome Topics
Some topics have given us far more trouble than others. Three immediately come to mind: personal consumption, sex, and crime.

Quite maddeningly, we know that research exists on how often people change their underwear, yet it's confidential and we haven't been able to get those figures. Some commercial firms have been extraordinarily forthcoming. Others have decided that there's nothing to be gained and much to be lost by releasing their figures. Understandable, perhaps. After all, if you were a pet food company would you want it readily known that the denizens of some countries feed their pets a better protein diet than many citizens in the same country receive? But then, if you were the government concerned, would you want that known?

This explains why we've had trouble coming up with certain consumption facts for various countries.

Sex has presented similar problems. Since Kinsey did his pioneer study back in 1948, an incredible amount has been published on this subject, dear to the hearts of (virtually) one and all. Surprisingly, however, to the best of our knowledge, there are no uniform world-wide statistics. Furthermore, the studies of individual countries show wild disparities in what they set out to do and how accurate they are in going about it. What's more, sex is a private matter. So we are dealing with what people report, not what they do.

This applies equally to other personal matters, including abortion, mental health, and the use of drugs. The world abounds in estimates of illegal abortions, yet no accurate statistics can (or could) exist. It isn't difficult to determine the total number of admissions to mental institutions. It is impossible to determine how many different people have been admitted to mental institutions. Then there's the broader question: what exactly is mental health or illness? By the same token, drug use and drug addiction are complicated matters. Marijuana is relatively socially acceptable in the United States today. In Spain, it used to command a 30-year prison sentence. On a multi-national basis, no one knows how many people have used drugs; so reliable statistics are few and far between.

Finally, and – to our mind – quite incredibly, uniform crime statistics are a major problem. You'd think that to determine how many people were shot in a country would be a simple matter. Nothing could be further from the truth. Selected countries, like the U.S., have these figures. Other countries, like Italy, may not even list them. For example, in Italy, before 1977, if you had shot your wife to defend your honor because she had been sleeping with someone else, you wouldn't have committed an indictable offense.

"Round Numbers are always False"
Dr. Samuel Johnson to Boswell

Perhaps, to a degree, this is true. On the other hand, statisticians will tell you that all figures are rounded. Even a number with three decimal points is rounded from one with five ... or ten (or more). So, yes, our figures are rounded up or down to make them more readily understandable to you, the reader. Whether we've used absolute numbers, or decimal points, we've made sure that the figures in each table are directly comparable.

What's more, the reader should be warned that it's temptingly easy to make oversimplifications on the basis of abstract figures. For example, in Japan in 1976 they had 0.01 fatal accidents for every million man hours worked in their factories. This means a person would have to work eight hours a day for over 30,000 years before he could expect to be killed at his work. A likely tale! Nor does this convey how safety regulations vary in different countries.

What People Say Versus What People Do
In many cases, figures not only have a "secret magic" but a

mystery about them. Italian men say they have extremely advanced ideas about women's liberation, but those attitudes don't translate into action when it comes to helping around the house, as you'll see when you refer to the final chapter. This difference between what people say and do is one of the many paradoxes of *The Book of Numbers*.

Our Credentials

Our work draws on a world-wide data bank including information collected by, amongst others, Gallup International, The Roper Organization and the International Labor Organization.

In addition, we've been helped by a wide variety of multi-national banks and other business concerns, who have been good enough (normally for the first time) to open up their research secrets to us. Much of the book's most interesting data derives from these sources: where you'll find the world's bustiest women, where the use of anti-perspirants is an exception rather than a rule, which countries are car-craziest – and much more.

We hope you'll use *The Book of Numbers* in a variety of ways. First, it will give you answers to many of the world's most interesting questions on a roughly comparable basis. If nothing else, we hope the book will help to settle (or set off) many an argument over an after-dinner drink.

Second, insofar as possible, it lays out all the figures. If you want to link figures on alcoholism to lack of capitalist incentives, be our guest. If you want to link the degree of socialism to economic welfare, the figures are all here.

Third, we hope that, over time, *The Book of Numbers* will become a standard reference work of interest to those who need to obtain accurate facts on a multi-national basis.

The Funny Side of Numbers

On a lighter note, if you want to know where to go to find sexually liberated women or avoid getting robbed or murdered, we've tried to give you the answers.

We doubt that many readers will read *The Book of Numbers* at one sitting. Instead, we've tried to make it a mine of the world's most illuminating and offbeat facts.

People, the land, our environment and how we use (and abuse) it, money, taxes, work, housing, what we do in our hours off, what we eat, our sexual attitudes and habits, what we buy and what we think. We've tried to provide answers in abundance to whatever piques your curiosity.

We're sure we don't have all the answers. We'd like your help in these and other fields. Towards that end, we've included a questionnaire at the back of the book.

This is the first edition of what we hope will be a hardy perennial. We need your help to make this so. In the meantime, we hope that *The Book of Numbers* will be a continuing source of amusing answers.

EXPLANATORY NOTES

We have emphasized the extremes on the tables. The highest figure is outlined in a bold box, the lowest by a dotted box.

We applied average exchange rates prevailing at the time of the data.

COUNTRY GLOSSARY

Benelux: Belgium, the Netherlands, Luxemburg.

E.E.C.:   European Economic Community. Member countries: Belgium; Denmark; France; Italy; Luxemburg; the Netherlands; the Republic of Ireland; West Germany; the United Kingdom.

Great Britain: England; Scotland; Wales. Excludes Northern Ireland.

Ireland: The Republic of Ireland.

Scandinavia: Denmark; Finland; Norway; Sweden. Iceland is also part of Scandinavia but was not included in the surveys used in this book.

United Arab Emirates: Abu Dhabi; Ajman; Dubai; Fujairah; Sharjah; Ummai Qaiwan; Rasal Khaimah.

United Kingdom: England; Scotland; Wales; Northern Ireland.

People

People – where would we be without them? If you're interested in learning more about the world's population, this section is the one for you.

With the first table, we start right at the beginning, with facts and figures about birth rates. You'll be able to see at a glance just where the most productive countries are when it comes to babies, and which are the countries where the birth rate is much lower. The birth rates of some countries are more than double those of others. Can you guess which are which? The table doesn't just stop here. Because when you're born your problems are only just beginning. We've got figures which compare your chances of surviving the first year of life depending on where you happen to be born.

But if you're reading this, then you've already survived. You'll probably find yourself looking with more interest at the other figures in the table. Life expectancy, for example. The figures show just how long you can expect to live in each of the countries on the table. If your own country comes near the bottom of the list, perhaps there's still time to think of moving. By the way, we've got separate figures for men and women. It's common knowledge that women generally outlive men. But by how much? And is this the same everywhere? Our table gives you the answers.

As well as giving the facts on birth rates, this table also shows the death rates for different countries. By comparing these two, you'll be able to get some idea of the rate of population growth. You may be surprised to see that in some countries there are actually fewer live births than deaths. This is an area we look at more closely in a later table.

The next thing you may want to know about population is just how it's made up. And the first question you'll probably be asking depends on your sex. Where are there more men – or women? Our table here has the answers. And we've got good news for the men. In all but three of the countries listed, there are more females than males. If you want specific information, we've got that too. If you're young and fancy free, you might want to know which country to go to in order to find the highest percentage of women between the ages of 15 and 29.

Our next table gives you the facts on one of the most important of all areas of population – how it's distributed. So whatever your inclinations, whether you're the gregarious type or a hermit, this table should have something for you. First of all, we've got the plain facts about population for different countries. And so as to be right up to date, the figures are the estimates for 1978.

This table also shows the population densities of these different countries. In other words, on average, how many people occupy each square mile of the land. And it's when they're put in this way that the figures are especially revealing. If it's wide open spaces you're looking for, you'll find some of the figures are very encouraging. But there are other parts of the world where you'll find very much less elbow room.

No account of population would be complete without looking at the cities of the world. The next table does this. It tells us just how the largest cities of the world are distributed. First of all, on an overall global scale, from which we can make some interesting comparisons between Eastern and Western countries, and between the developed countries and those of the Third World. America and China top the list when it comes to the number of super-cities – those with more than one million inhabitants. But when we include the number of lesser-sized cities, we see that many of the less developed areas are surprisingly well represented in the table.

In the final table in this section, we look to the future. What are the prospects for world population over the next 25 years? Estimates of population growth are never easy to compile because conditions can change so quickly – and unexpectedly. But some general conclusions are inescapable. Populations are growing everywhere. And nowhere more than in the countries where overcrowding is already a problem. In comparison with some of the less well developed Third World countries, the population growth rates of some of the developed nations show signs of easing off. But even here, there's no room for complacency. We can see from the table that, within the next century, many of these countries are likely to have doubled their populations.

Shortage of food is a serious problem today in many parts of the world. There is every likelihood that this problem is going to increase – on a global scale – within the next few decades and become the main focus of political attention.

If you were married and lived in Dublin you'd share a secret with your neighbors. Odds are that one of you would have a baby each and every year. Ireland has turned birth into a booming industry with 22 live births per thousand inhabitants. When you consider that Eire has just three million plus inhabitants and that one million are married, it means a child a year for two out of 15 couples.

Popular myth has it that Catholicism equals conception. Sometimes it's true, sometimes it isn't. Spain is number two in the league with 18 births per thousand, but Italy's birth rate is relatively modest.

Northern Europe has clearly gone on the pill. So much so that wealthy West Germany is actually losing population. There are ten births per thousand population and 12 deaths.

Australians are good at more than tennis and surfing. Clearly they intend to fill up their wide open spaces.

Two out of every 100 German babies die before they reach the age of one, a deplorable record beaten only by their German-speaking neighbors Austria, and Italy with 21 deaths per thousand births.

Japan not only has a baby boom. It is also a country which is a boon for babies. They really look after their little Nippon nippers. Only the Swedes provide better infant care with an excellent low rate of just eight deaths per thousand.

That's half our United States' rate, so there is obviously more to child care than reading Dr Spock. As the chart shows, it's the healthy, highly socialized Scandinavian countries that come out best, along with the Dutch, where subsidized medicine is a womb to tomb affair.

If you want to reach a ripe old age you're far more likely to do so as a woman. There is no equality between the sexes where life expectancy is concerned. In most countries women live at least six or seven years longer than men.

You'd think that the rigors of Scandinavia's climate would take their toll. Nothing could be further from the truth. They all live longer up there. Sweden heads the longevity list for men (an average of 72.2 years).

	U.S.A.	CANADA
	1977	1977
1. Number of live births per 1,000 inhabitants[+]	15	16
2. Deaths per 1,000 inhabitants[+]	9	7
3. Infant mortality rate[o] per 1,000 live births	16	15
	1975	1975
4. Life expectancy (years)[x]		
men	67.9	69.6
women	75.5	75.6
years by which women outlive men	7.6	6.0

U.K.	AUSTRALIA	AUSTRIA	BELGIUM	DENMARK	FRANCE	(WEST) GERMANY	IRELAND	ITALY	JAPAN	NETHERLANDS	NORWAY	SPAIN	SWEDEN	SWITZERLAND
1977	1977	1977	1977	1977	1977	1977	1977	1977	1977	1977	1977	1977	1977	1977
12	17	12	12	14	14	10	22	15	17	13	14	18	13	12
12	8	13	12	10	10	12	11	10	6	8	10	8	11	9
16	16	21	16	12	12	20	17	21	10	11	11	14	8	12
1975	1975	1975	1975	1975	1975	1975	1975	1975	1975	1975	1975	1975	1975	1975
69.6	69.7	68.7	70.1	71.6	70.5	68.3	70.1	70.0	71.5	70.8	71.7	70.3	72.2	70.2
75.6	76.0	75.5	75.8	77.0	76.7	74.3	75.0	75.6	77.3	77.1	77.8	75.4	77.3	75.4
6.0	6.3	6.8	5.7	5.4	6.2	6.0	4.9	5.6	5.8	6.3	6.1	5.1	5.1	5.2

While overall the United States is rapidly growing older, this doesn't mean our men are escaping Father Time. On average U.S. men live to be just 67.9 years old. What's more, though our women can look forward (with dread or delight) to an average of nearly eight more years of sunny retirement in the Sunbelt, they're far worse off in terms of longevity than almost all their counterparts in other countries. The sole exceptions are Austria, West Germany, Switzerland and Spain. When it comes to a one-way ticket to the pearly gates, the German-speakers get there first – notably the Austrians, with a death rate of 13 per thousand population.

Then there's Japan. Their attitude towards death is defer it. Six Japanese per thousand die a year. Half the rate of Belgium, the U.K. or West Germany.

If current trends continue there are going to be a lot of Japanese in Japan.

Sources:

1, 2 & 3 Population Reference Bureau, Washington DC

4 United Nations

+ Estimates for 1977

o The infant mortality rate is the number of infants under the age of one year who died per 1,000 live births.

x Data corresponds to the period 1975-1980, medium variant

Figures rounded up or down

Do men or women make up the larger proportion of the world's population? . . . Every country in our table, except Switzerland, Ireland and Australia has more women than men.

In Austria there are 5.6% more women than men. Male tourists who want plenty of ladies to feast their eyes on should put Vienna at the top of their European itinerary and West Germany with four percent more women.

In the U.S. 51.2% of the population is female. However, just across the border in Canada the population is almost even – the women just win out at 50.1%.

In eight of the countries on the table the largest group of women is between the ages of 15 and 29; in another eight the 45 to 64 age group has the most ladies. In Spain, 11.2% of women fall into both categories. In most countries the largest group of men is between 15 and 29 years-old.

The exceptions are West Germany, where 11.4% of men are between 30 and 44; Sweden (11.8% of men are between 45 and 64 years old); the U.K. with 11.1% of men in both the 15 to 29 and 45 to 64 categories; and Switzerland (11.6% in both the 15 to 29 and 30 to 44 age groups). The highest percentages between 15 and 29 years old are in the U.S., Canada, Australia, Japan and the Netherlands.

Overall, the table shows that in most countries, there are more women than men and most are in a much older age bracket – 45 to 64 against 15 to 29.

Sweden has a high percentage of men

	U.S.A.	CANADA
	1975	1975
1.. Total population (millions)	213.9	22.7
2. Males (millions)	104.4	11.3
3. Males as % of total population:		
0-4 years	4.0	4.5
5-14 years	8.9	9.4
15-29 years	13.6	13.9
30-44 years	8.4	9.1
45-64 years	9.6	9.3
65 and over	4.2	3.7
total	48.8	49.9
4. Females (millions)	109.5	11.4
5. Females as % of total population:		
0-4 years	3.8	4.3
5-14 years	8.6	9.0
15-29 years	13.3	13.6
30-44 years	8.7	9.0
45-64 years	10.6	9.6
65 and over	6.1	4.6
total	51.2	50.1

	U.K.	AUSTRALIA	AUSTRIA	BELGIUM	DENMARK	FRANCE	(WEST) GERMANY	IRELAND	ITALY	JAPAN	NETHERLANDS	NORWAY	SPAIN	SWEDEN	SWITZERLAND
	1975	1975	1975	1975	1975	1975	1975	1975	1975	1975	1975	1975	1975	1975	1975
	56.4	13.7	7.4	9.8	4.9	52.9	61.6	3.1	55.0	111.1	13.5	3.9	35.4	8.3	6.5
	27.5	6.9	3.5	4.8	2.4	26.0	29.6	1.6	26.8	54.6	6.7	1.9	17.3	4.1	3.3
	4.0	5.2	3.6	3.7	3.5	4.2	3.0	5.3	3.9	4.7	4.1	4.1	4.6	3.6	3.6
	8.3	9.2	8.5	7.8	7.9	8.2	8.1	10.1	8.3	7.8	9.0	8.2	9.2	7.1	8.1
	11.1	13.2	10.6	11.5	11.8	12.3	10.5	12.4	11.0	12.5	13.0	11.8	11.4	11.1	11.6
	8.8	9.2	9.4	9.2	9.6	9.3	11.4	7.6	10.0	11.5	9.5	8.3	9.0	9.6	11.6
	11.1	10.0	9.4	11.0	10.9	10.0	9.6	9.7	10.7	9.2	9.6	11.4	10.1	11.8	10.3
	5.3	3.7	5.7	5.9	5.8	5.2	5.4	5.1	4.9	3.4	4.6	5.8	4.5	6.6	4.9
	48.7	50.5	47.2	49.1	49.6	49.2	48.0	50.2	48.8	49.1	49.9	49.7	48.8	49.8	50.1
	28.9	6.8	3.9	5.0	2.5	26.9	32.0	1.5	28.2	56.5	6.8	2.0	18.1	4.2	3.2
	3.8	5.0	3.5	3.5	3.3	4.0	2.9	5.1	3.7	4.5	4.0	3.9	4.4	3.4	3.5
	7.9	8.8	8.1	7.5	7.6	7.8	7.7	9.7	8.0	7.5	8.6	7.8	8.8	6.8	7.6
	10.7	12.4	10.3	11.0	11.2	11.7	9.8	11.9	10.6	12.4	12.4	11.2	11.2	10.6	10.9
	8.6	8.6	9.2	9.0	9.3	8.7	10.3	7.4	10.2	11.6	8.9	8.0	9.3	9.0	10.3
	11.9	9.9	12.3	11.6	11.4	10.5	12.4	9.7	11.8	10.5	10.2	11.6	11.2	12.0	10.6
	8.4	4.8	9.4	8.3	7.6	8.1	8.9	5.9	6.9	4.4	6.0	7.8	6.3	8.3	7.0
	51.3	49.5	52.8	50.9	50.4	50.8	52.0	49.8	51.2	50.9	50.1	50.3	51.2	50.2	49.9

(11.8%) and women (12%) in the 45 to 65 age bracket. West Germany, Denmark and Sweden have the fewest children under four. Nursery school teachers should make for Ireland, Australia or Japan.

In every country on the table there are more women than men in the over 65 age group. Austria tops the list by nearly four percent.

Source:
United Nations

How do you feel about people? Are you a gregarious, sociable type, who enjoys the hustle and bustle of living close to your fellow man? Or do you prefer the peace and quiet of wide open spaces? Whatever your answer, this table will show you where you're most likely to feel at home.

	U.S.A.	CANADA
	1978	1978
1. Estimated number of inhabitants (millions)	219.8	23.8
2. Inhabitants per square mile	62.3	6.7

The U.S. has the highest population estimate for 1978 of the countries in the table. The spacious American landscape is getting more and more crowded. Our country is inhabited by 219.8 million people, an increase of 16 million since 1970. That means about two million more Americans are born each year.

Just across the border in neighboring Canada, there's a completely different picture: with virtually the same area (3.5 million square miles), Canada has a tenth of America's population – a mere 23.8 million. No wonder the crime rate is so much higher in America than in Canada. However, much of Canada's population is concentrated in the South, while vast areas are virtually uninhabited.

America's other neighbors, down in sunny Mexico, are packed in more tightly than either the U.S. or Canada. There's a population of over 65 million, but a much smaller land area.

Japan comes second in the table with 115.1 million. When you consider that its land area only equals four percent of that of the States, this is a startling figure. No wonder the Japanese have mastered the art of miniaturizing everything – from trees to transistors. The people aren't noted for their great size either. None of the other countries in the table approach the two population giants – the U.S. and Japan.

West Germany and the U.K. come next, with populations of 65.4 million and 57.1 million. West Germany, like Japan, has concentrated on developing industry to provide a high standard of living. Tiny Britain actually crams 2.5 times as many people into her borders as vast Canada. But one person in eight actually lives in the great metropolis of London. Maybe that's why the countryside there still seems so pleasantly uncluttered.

Ireland is at the bottom of the table. The small population there is probably partly due to the massive exodus to America during the 19th and early 20th centuries. In fact, the decendants of those millions of emigrants contribute today to the high U.S. population figures.

However, if you break down the figures into inhabitants per square mile, they take on quite a different meaning.

The U.S. may come top of the population table, but it ranks only 13th when it comes to population density. There's a vast population in America providing a huge work force and so much land that there's room for everybody. It's not surprising that the U.S. has traditionally been the first choice of immigrants fleeing the overcrowded nations of Europe.

POPULATION DENSITY

	U.K.	AUSTRALIA	AUSTRIA	BELGIUM	DENMARK	FRANCE	(WEST) GERMANY	IRELAND	ITALY	JAPAN	MEXICO	NETHERLANDS	NORWAY	SPAIN	SWEDEN	SWITZERLAND
	1978	1978	1978	1978	1978	1978	1978	1978	1978	1978	1978	1978	1978	1978	1978	1978
	57.1	14.6	7.6	10.0	5.1	54.3	61.9	3.2	55.8	115.1	65.4	13.9	4.1	36.5	8.4	6.6
	611.4	5.0	237.7	850.7	312.7	257.4	656.8	121.5	491.6	803.7	85.9	1065.3	34.3	189.1	53.2	431.1

Sources:
1 United Nations
2 Heron House estimates; calculated from 1978 population estimates and the land area.

Holland's the country where elbow room is at a premium: with over 1,000 Dutch per square mile, no wonder most of the country's under sea level. Neighboring Belgium comes next. You would never be at a loss for company in that part of the world – "getting away from it all" would probably involve leaving the country.

Japan rates high in both tables. Not only is the population large, but the people are also packed in like sardines. However, the Japanese have made the best use of a potentially difficult situation by intensive cultivation of every available square inch of land. They've also mobilized their massive manpower into a highly efficient technological work force.

Similar sized populations, West Germany and the U.K., also have similar population densities. Italy and Switzerland have very different figures. There are almost eight times as many Italians as Swiss, but when it comes to population density, they're almost neck and neck.

By complete contrast, in Australia, there are only five people per square mile. No wonder they're trying to fill the country with sheep. And in Canada, there are fewer than seven. If you need to be alone at any time, sunny Australia or the chilly northern territories of Canada are the places to head for.

Like Canada, Norway – another northern country – has a low population density. But Norway hasn't had to rely on immigration to populate its empty spaces. Sweden is another northern country with a low population density. There are about 53 Swedes per square mile. Denmark, further to the south, breaks the pattern. There are over 300 people per square mile, so it's positively overcrowded compared to the other Scandinavian countries. However, Denmark is different geographically to its northern neighbors. It is basically a fertile agricultural country with no uninhabitable mountainous areas. Although it is classified as part of Scandinavia, it has more in common with West Germany which it borders to the south.

If you're looking for a happy medium – a country that has neither too few nor too many people – France is the place to go. The French are comfortably distributed: 257.4 per square mile, with a total of 54.3 million in the entire country. That harmonious balance between overcrowding and under population just could contribute to the French *joie de vivre*.

23

	U.S.A.	CANADA
1. Estimated % of population for 1975:		
in urban areas⁺	76.3	78.4
in rural areas	23.7	21.6
2. Estimated % of population for 1980:		
in urban areas⁺	78.5	81.0
in rural areas	21.5	19.0

People may think the country's a nice place to visit – but they prefer to live in town. That's the most obvious conclusion you can draw from this set of figures. Ever since the industrial revolutions in the late 18th century and early 19th century, the general trend has been towards living in cities. And that trend goes on and on. Cities still need more and more industrial workers. They also attract almost all migrant workers, and so their populations increase... and increase.

As far as the greatest concentration in cities is concerned, Australia – surprisingly – tops the list. Forget the popular image of sun-tanned beer-swilling Aussies leading a rugged life in the endless outback; so much of that huge land mass is uninhabitable desert that – in 1975 – 86% of the Australian population was concentrated in the cities. The other 14% were scattered round small settlements and sheep stations.

The Swedes come after the Australians: 83.7% of them have chosen to live among the city lights. This isn't really so surprising, when you think about those Scandinavian winter nights. It's much cosier to live in charming cities like Stockholm, where the warming *schnapps* flows freely.

The third most dedicated urban dwellers are in West Germany. Over 83% of the population lives in cities. The figure is only one percent less for their neighbors in comparatively cramped Denmark.

There are also other countries where a high proportion of the population lives in cities. In the Netherlands, Canada, the U.K., the U.S., France and Japan more than three-quarters of their populations live in cities.

This is understandable in the U.K. and the Netherlands where rural living space is at a premium. However, Canada and the U.S. have vast tracts of fertile and beautiful countryside – much of it comparatively close to the main cities. But the same factors seem to apply here, as in the smaller countries. The big cities attract people like magnets. That's where the action – and the big money – can be found and made.

At the other end of the scale, less than half the population of Norway lives in cities. Many Norwegians still live in small villages and earn their money by fishing or in the timber industry. Norway is a positively rural society, compared with highly industrialized West Germany, where vast numbers of people are needed to man the huge industrial com-

U.K.	AUSTRALIA	AUSTRIA	BELGIUM	DENMARK	FRANCE	(WEST) GERMANY	IRELAND	ITALY	JAPAN	MEXICO	NETHERLANDS	NORWAY	SPAIN	SWEDEN	SWITZERLAND
78.2	86.0	53.0	71.8	82.0	76.1	83.4	55.3	66.7	75.2	63.2	79.4	45.5	69.5	83.7	57.4
21.8	14.0	47.0	28.2	18.0	23.9	16.6	44.7	32.3	24.8	36.8	20.6	54.5	30.5	16.3	42.6
79.1	87.2	54.8	73.9	84.1	78.9	85.3	58.3	69.3	78.5	66.8	81.0	48.5	72.4	86.0	60.3
20.9	12.8	45.2	26.1	15.9	21.1	14.7	41.7	30.7	21.5	33.2	19.0	51.5	27.6	14.0	39.7

plexes that sprang up after World War II. The table on open spaces shows that when it comes to the amount of green space available to each inhabitant, Oslo easily tops the list.

Although Norway is the only country in the table where most of the population lives in rural areas, there are several others where the majority of people prefer not to join the urban rat race. In Austria, Ireland and Switzerland less than six people in ten live in cities. However, these countries are definitely the exceptions, rather than the rule.

The trend towards city living is definitely taking hold. The 1980 figures show that an even greater number of people are city bound, with a corresponding drop in the rural population.

In Australia, the kangaroos will be taking over those wide open spaces, as another 1.2% of the nation's two-legged but pouchless inhabitants head for the bright city lights. In both Sweden and West Germany, about a seventh of the population will be left in the countryside

Source:
United Nations
+Urban agglomerations of over 1,000 inhabitants

while the U.K.'s already crowded urban areas will accommodate almost four-fifths of the British population.

The constant growth of urban population is caused by the fact that more and more people have jobs in large businesses and industries, mainly situated in large cities. The attraction of the fast pace of a city's social life draws hundreds of young people away from quiet country life to racy urban living.

It's certain that the aggravations that accompany city life are going to increase. Apartments may be hard to find now, but just wait until 1980. And commuter trains and subways will be even more crowded. In America, we're already talking of the "megalopolis", as our ever-expanding East Coast cities meet and merge into one gigantic urban sprawl.

The greatest concentrations of big cities are on opposite sides of the world – in North America and China. North America has 30 cities with over a million inhabitants; China has 26. As far as individual countries on our table are concerned, the U.S. has the largest number of great cities. Canada has only three, though this is a significant number for a country with such a small population overall.

Latin America has the next highest total – 21 cities with over a million inhabitants, then Middle South Asia with 16. At first it may seem surprising that this area, with its teeming Indian population of nearly 550 million, is fourth on the list. But the list of large cities of more than 100,000, but fewer than a million people, changes the picture. Here Middle South Asia is surpassed only by North America and Russia. China has so many large cities that only those with over 200,000 people are shown.

The high figure for Latin America shows how the population there tends to concentrate in large cities. The geography of much of Latin America – with its vast areas of virgin jungle, mountains and pampas – cannot support even comparatively small cities. So people abandon the land for the big cities.

	AFRICA	LATIN AMERICA (inc. the Caribbean)
	1975	1975
1. Number of cities in the world:		
with over 1 million inhabitants	10	21
with over 500,000 inhabitants	27	42
with over 100,000 inhabitants+	132	171

	U.S.A.	CANADA
	1975	1975
2. Number of cities per country:		
with over 1 million inhabitants	27	3
with over 500,000 inhabitants	50	8
with over 100,000 inhabitants	175	21

The U.S.S.R. has the most evenly distributed urban population, with only 12 cities of over a million people. This is as many as there are in the U.K. and West Germany combined. On the other hand their 222 cities with over 100,000 inhabitants are by far the highest number in our tables in this category (with the exception of China).

As in Latin America, there are reasons for this. Travel in the U.S.S.R. is strictly

NORTH AMERICA	CHINA	JAPAN	OTHER EAST ASIA	SOUTH ASIA	MIDDLE SOUTH ASIA (inc. India)	WESTERN SOUTH ASIA	EASTERN EUROPE	NORTHERN EUROPE	SOUTHERN EUROPE	WESTERN EUROPE	OCEANIA	USSR
1975	1975	1975	1975	1975	1975	1975	1975	1975	1975	1975	1975	1975
30	26	6	5	9	16	6	7	9	9	12	2	12
58	54	7	8	18	44	12	14	23	19	26	6	40
196	105	78	27	68	183	50	63	80	96	138	15	222

U.K.	AUSTRALIA	AUSTRIA	BELGIUM	DENMARK	FRANCE	GERMANY (WEST)	IRELAND	ITALY	JAPAN	MEXICO	NETHERLANDS	NORWAY	SPAIN	SWEDEN	SWITZERLAND
1975	1975	1975	1975	1975	1975	1975	1975	1975	1975	1975	1975	1975	1975	1975	1975
7	2	1	1	1	3	5	0	5	6	3	2	0	2	1	0
17	5	1	2	1	6	11	1	9	7	5	4	1	5	2	1
58	9	5	5	4	50	54	2	43	78	31	17	3	38	10	7

limited, and all moves are controlled. For example, you need a permit to live in Moscow. As a result the authorities can plan population distribution.

In Western Europe, the U.K. tops the list with seven cities of over a million inhabitants – this is just over a quarter of the U.S. number. West Germany and Italy come next with five each while France has just three.

The two largest cities in the world are New York and Tokyo. Both have more than 17 million inhabitants. Tokyo has grown so large that it has swallowed its next door neighbor, the large port of Yokohama, much as London once swallowed Westminster.

> **Source:**
> United Nations Population Division
> +Over 200,000 for China

Overcrowding and soaring birth rates aren't new. Population problems are older than recorded history. During the pre-history of Europe, for instance, there was a continual migration of tribes from overcrowded Asia which eventually peopled the entire European continent. More recently, the colonization of the New Worlds – like America and Australia – would never have happened without being nudged on by the bulge in the Old.

New nations with plenty of land like a high birth rate: a booming population means a booming work force. A prosperous economy depends on having plenty of people to produce and buy consumer goods.

Until a few decades ago, almost all governments were officially in favor of large families and a high birth rate. However, improved health care and increased life expectancies have changed this picture drastically.

A steady increase of just one percent a year will double a country's population in less than a century, leaving it to beg, borrow or steal twice as much food and fuel.

The table shows that most countries face a crowded future. There are nearly 225 million Americans – and that number is growing. At its present rate of growth, the population will have doubled before the end of the 21st century.

	U.S.A.	CANADA
1. Projected population (millions)		
1975	213.9	22.8
1980	224.1	24.6
1985	235.7	26.5
1990	246.6	28.4
1995	256.0	30.0
2000	264.4	31.6
2. Years taken to double the population	116	77
3. Year when the population will double	2094	2055

Populations in smaller countries are expanding at an even faster rate. At least in America we have 3.5 million square miles of land. If the population doubles, we'll still have only 125 people to every square mile.

Ireland has just over three million people and, by 2041, it'll have twice that number.

Life will be even more crowded in Japan: 115 million Japanese live in just under 144 thousand square miles – over 800 per square mile. Along with the Irish, they're expanding at the fastest rate in the table. By the year 2047, Japan will have to house more than the present population of the U.S. in around a 20th of our area.

None of the countries listed have as big a problem as some Third World nations. For instance the population of Mexico

U.K.	AUSTRALIA	AUSTRIA	BELGIUM	DENMARK	FRANCE	(WEST) GERMANY	IRELAND	ITALY	JAPAN	NETHERLANDS	NORWAY	SPAIN	SWEDEN	SWITZERLAND
56.4	13.8	7.5	9.8	5.0	52.9	61.7	3.1	55.0	111.1	13.6	4.0	35.4	8.3	6.5
57.5	15.1	7.6	10.1	5.1	55.1	62.0	3.3	56.3	117.5	14.1	4.1	37.2	8.5	6.7
58.7	16.5	7.7	10.3	5.2	57.1	62.9	3.5	57.5	122.4	14.6	4.2	39.1	8.8	6.9
60.0	17.8	7.9	10.5	5.2	58.8	64.2	3.7	58.7	126.2	15.1	4.3	41.0	9.0	7.1
61.4	19.0	8.0	10.6	5.3	60.5	65.4	3.8	59.8	129.6	15.6	4.4	43.0	9.2	7.2
62.8	20.2	8.1	10.8	5.4	62.1	66.2	4.0	60.9	132.9	16.0	4.5	44.9	9.4	7.4
+	87	+	+	347	231	+	63	173	69	139	231	69	693	231
+	2065	+	+	2325	2209	+	2041	2151	2047	2117	2209	2047	2671	2209

+*Countries where the population will not double*

(not on the table) has soared from 30 million to over 60 million in the last 25 years. It's expected to double again by the end of this century.

At the other end of the table, the West German population is growing at the slowest rate: by the close of this century, it'll have increased by only seven percent. And there'll only be eight percent more people in Belgium – already very densely populated, with more than 850 people per square mile.

Austria and the U.K. are also expanding slowly. Their population will only be around ten percent larger by the end of the century. Apart from Catholic Spain and Catholic Ireland, European populations are increasing more slowly than those elsewhere in the world. Experts predict that in four of them – the U.K.,

Sources:
1 United Nations
2 & 3 Population Reference Bureau, Inc
1978 estimates

Austria, Belgium and West Germany – the population will never double.

It's true that some countries – notably the U.S., Canada and Australia – still have room to accommodate their growing populations. But as far as population is concerned, no land is an island. Food and energy are exchanged on a worldwide basis, so population is a worldwide problem. Even if we share what we've got, there won't be enough to go round by the end of the century. There could be an international confrontation between the "haves" and the "have-nots".

Number of cities with over one million inhabitants

30 —

Americans seem to be the most gregarious people in the world. The U.S. has 27 cities with over a million inhabitants — more than any other nation. Even 800 million Chinese manage to spread themselves more thinly — there are only 26 million-plus cities in China. People tend to think of Asian cities as overcrowded, but all of Middle South Asia, including India, has only 16 cities of over a million.

Some of the oldest and loveliest cities in the world are in Western Europe. But in this case small is beautiful. Like Russia, Europe has only 12 urban centers with over a million inhabitants. Although you probably don't associate Africa with the word "metropolis", there are ten big-league cities there, almost as many as in Europe.

They really like elbow-room in Oceania. The whole area, including Australia, has got only two million-plus cities.

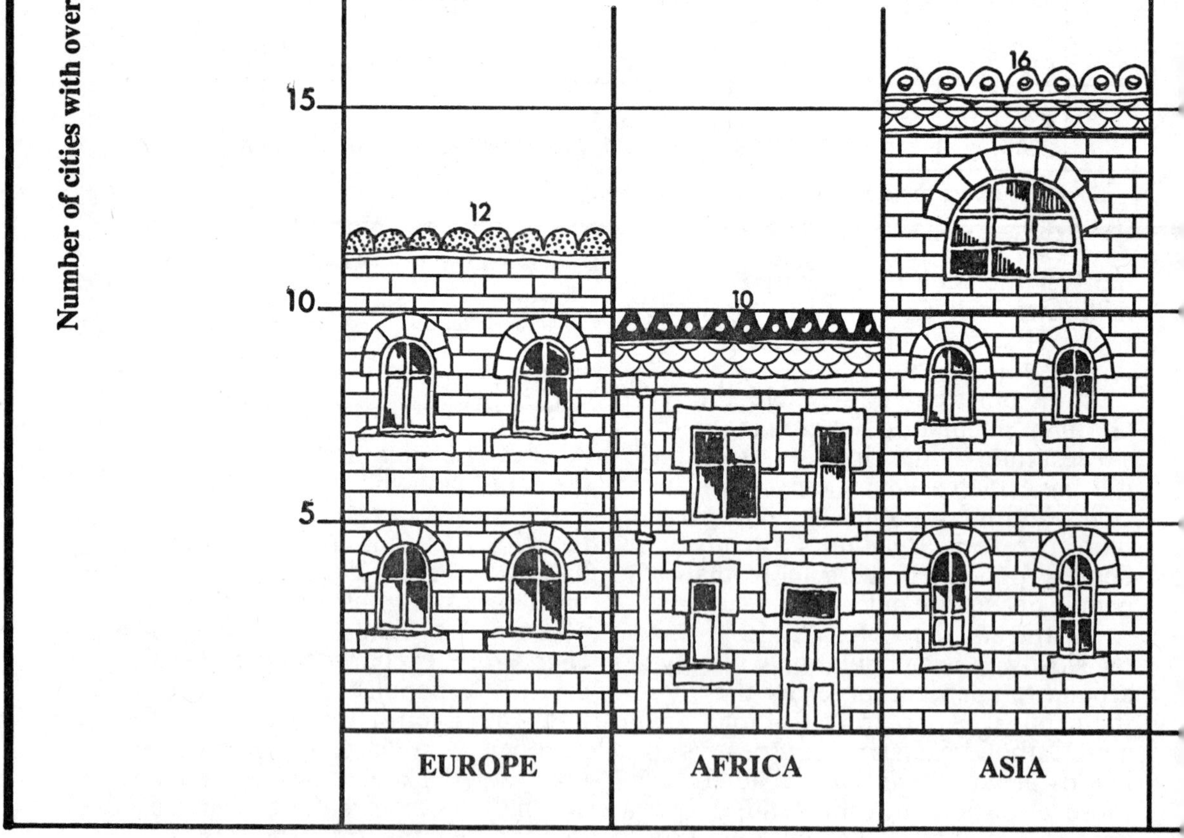

25 —

20 —

16

15 —

12

10

10 —

5 —

EUROPE   AFRICA   ASIA

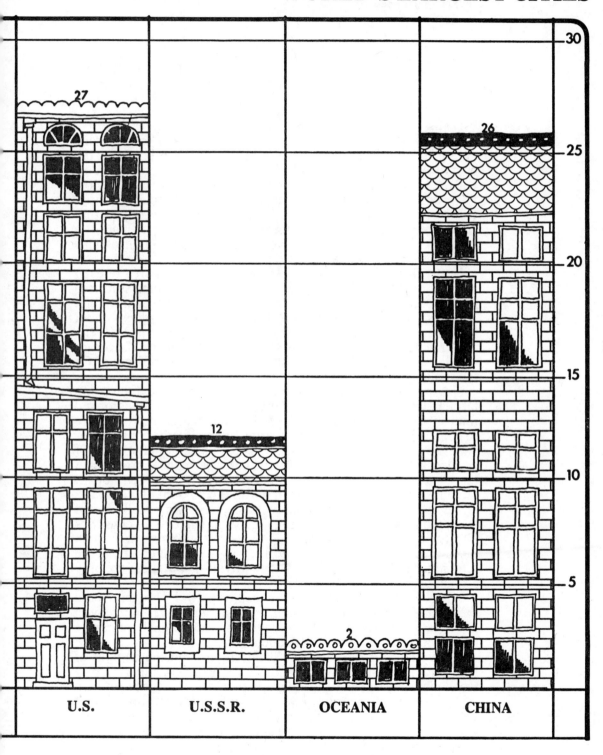

| U.S. | U.S.S.R. | OCEANIA | CHINA |

The Land

Land, labor and capital are the basis of any commercial enterprise, no matter whether it's in the Amazon jungle or the heavily populated Netherlands. Stone age man needed a few tools and the help of some family members in order to sow crops. Most important, however, he needed a patch of land. Land comes first. It is a key form of wealth, and it was for this obvious reason that feudal monarchs assumed the ultimate ownership of all land. It's no coincidence that today's two most powerful countries also have extremely large land areas.

In the first table, you'll find figures for the total area of each country in thousands of square miles. There are some surprises here. For instance, America is not the largest country in the table. Perhaps you know who is on top of the big land league without looking at the table. But what about comparisons? Is the accumulated size of the major European countries larger or smaller than the U.S.? What's the largest country in Europe? Or the smallest for that matter?

Having assimilated this information, you'll find figures on farmland in various countries. Perhaps, you've sometimes longed for a slice of virgin territory. Well, this table will show you where to go. It will also give you information on many other things. For example, the first category has statistics on the total amount of arable land and the amount actually under permanent crop. Then there's a separate breakdown of the two. Have you ever thought of comparing the size of a country with the amount of land it has under cultivation? Norway, for instance, has a very small area of farmland in relation to its overall size. And what about countries like Canada and Australia, which are vast in comparison with those in Europe? They might do very well when it comes to the total number of square miles under cultivation, but these are only a small percentage of their total area.

Where do they have the most sheep or cattle? The figures are there under amount of land under permanent pasture, though you don't get an individual breakdown of the size of each country's herd, you *can* draw your own conclusions.

Following on from this, you'll find figures on the amount of land under forest and woodland. It's worth remembering that wood plays an essential part in many industries. Newspapers are a good example. Everyday we take it for granted that they'll arrive on our doorstep. Where does the wood-pulp come from? Look at the figures and you'll be able to work that out.

Moving on from the land, the next table covers water. And

quite rightly so; for without water there would be no farming. First, we have the figures on the number of square miles of water each country has and then go on to give a breakdown of this as a percentage of the total area of the country. To many of us, water is something that is simply there, yet without doubt it's a major resource. For example, Canadians, who have vast quantities, get most of their electricity from water-generated power.

Perhaps the most revealing figures are those for the amount of water as a percentage of the total area of the country. You'll probably be surprised to find who's on top here. The fact that France has the lowest area as a percentage of total land might explain the French aversion to baths (you'll find figures on that in the "At Home" chapter).

In the same chapter, you'll also find figures on the amount of land under irrigation. Once again, America is on top. But what about the other countries? You might be under the impression that Europe gets enough rain and therefore irrigation isn't necessary. That's not true. Italy, for instance, has large land areas under irrigation. In fact, if you bear in mind the statistics on land size, you'll find that, proportionally, America doesn't irrigate as much as some European countries do.

Then we have a chapter on the amount of land devoted to national parks. And for you city slickers, there are also figures on the amount of open or green space you'll find in the cities. Here we have something for the vacationer. Land might be important when it comes to making a living, but every now and then you want to get out there and simply enjoy it. You'll find it's the New World countries that are way ahead here.

But what about Europe and Japan? These are crowded countries. How well do they do in preserving their countryside from urban encroachment?

And finally what about us city dwellers? No country living for us, but every now and then we do like a stroll through the park. Where would be the best bet? You'll find some of the Scandinavian cities head the list here, though certainly not all of them. If you're the type that gets claustrophobic, there are certain cities you'd be best advised to avoid.

	U.S.A.	CANADA
	1975	1975
1. Total area[+] (square miles — 000s)	3615	3852
2. Land area[0] (square miles — 000s)	3524	3560
as % of total area	97.5	92.4
3. Arable land and permanent crops (square miles — 000s)	807.9[xx]	169.0[xx]
arable land[x]	800.7[xx]	168.7[xx]
permanent crops[‡]	7.2[xx]	0.3[‡‡]
4. Permanent pasture** (square miles 000s)	830.1[xx]	96.9[xx]
5. Forest and wood[++] (square miles 000s)	1175[xx]	1244
6. Other land[00] (square miles — 000s')	710.6	2050

By far the largest country in the world is Russia – a colossal 8.6 million square miles. That's over double the size of the next largest country, China (3.7 million square miles).

The U.S. and Canada are the giants on our table, with over 3.5 million square miles each. And Australia isn't far behind, with nearly three million. But here the similarities end. The U.S. has more than four times as much arable land (land that produces temporary and permanent crops) than either Canada or Australia – over 800,000 square miles.

However, the latter two countries are better off than we are if you compare populations and arable land. Canada, with nearly 24 million people has just over one-tenth as many mouths to feed as the U.S., and Australia has a mere 14 million (less than the combined populations of New York and London).

Europe is a very different story. Everything is about one-tenth the size of the U.S., Canada and Australia. And in countries like Belgium and Denmark, everything is about a hundredth the size.

Europe's empty countries are Norway, Sweden and Spain. But in terms of land usage, Norway's mountains make the country largely a wilderness. Tiny Belgium, with less than one-tenth the area (and over twice the population), has as much arable land under permanent crops. A massive two-thirds of Sweden is forest and wood. Spain's land is much more amenable to cultivation, but on the whole its quality is poor.

The biggest country in Western Europe is France (over 200,000 square miles), with West Germany and the U.K. both about half that size. The U.K. is worst off for farm land: only 27,000 square miles are arable land.

U.K.	AUSTRALIA	AUSTRIA	BELGIUM	DENMARK	FRANCE	(WEST) GERMANY	IRELAND	ITALY	JAPAN	NETHERLANDS	NORWAY	SPAIN	SWEDEN	SWITZERLAND
1975	1975	1975	1975	1975	1975	1975	1975	1975	1975	1975	1975	1975	1975	1975
94.5	2968	32.4	11.8‡‡	16.6	211.2	96.0	27.1	116.3	143.8	15.9	125.2	194.9	173.7	15.9
93.3	2941	31.9	11.7‡‡	16.4	210.8	94.2	26.6	113.5	143.3	13.1	119.0	192.9	158.9	15.4
98.8	99.1	98.6	99.5	98.4	99.8	98.2	98.0	97.6	99.7	82.1	95.0	99.0	91.4	96.3
27.0	177.1xx	6.2	3.2‡‡	10.3	72.6xx	31.1	4.0xx	47.5	21.5	3.2	3.1	80.4	11.7	1.5
26.7	176.4xx	5.8	3.1‡‡	10.3	66.4xx	29.1	4.0xx	36.0	19.1	3.1	3.0	61.1	11.5	1.4
0.3‡‡	0.7	0.4	0.1‡‡	0.05	6.2xx	2.0	0.02‡‡	11.5	2.4	0.1	0.05‡‡	19.4	0.2xx	0.07
44.9	175‡‡	8.4	2.8‡‡	1.1	51.9xx	20.2	14.7xx	20.1	1.7xx	4.9	0.4	42.8	2.7	6.3
7.8	531.7‡‡	12.5	2.3‡‡	1.9‡‡	56.4xx	27.7	0.83	24.3	96.7‡‡	1.2	32.2	57.7	102.0	4.1
13.6	475.7	4.8	3.4‡‡	3.1	29.8	15.2	7.0	21.6	23.4	3.8	83.3	12.0	42.5	3.5

‡‡Non-official sources   xxFAO estimate

Sources:

Food and Agricultural Organization

+Includes areas under inland water bodies 0Excludes areas under inland water bodies

xTemporary meadows for mowing or pasture, land under temporary crops or under market and kitchen gardens or temporarily lying fallow or idle

‡Land cultivated with crops for long periods which need not be replanted after each crop; includes land under shrubs, fruit trees, nut trees and vines, but excluding land under trees grown for wood or timber

**Land used permanently (over 5 years) for both cultivated and wild herbaceous forage crops

++Land under natural or planted strands of trees

00Includes unused but potentially productive land, built-on areas, wasteland, parks, ornamental gardens, roads, lanes, barren land and all other land not already listed

Water, water, everywhere. Yes, most of the surface of the earth is water. Less than 30% of the earth's surface is land and almost all the rest is ocean.

A tiny percentage of the earth's total surface is made up of rivers, lakes and inland seas. And although these areas might be negligible in comparison with the overall surface area of the world, their significance to the countries in which they are found is enormous.

Imagine America or Canada without the Great Lakes, the Mississipi or the St. Lawrence; Egypt without the Nile, or Amsterdam without its canals.

The U.S. is second on the list in terms of total area of inland water with over 91,000 square miles. Much of this is the Great Lakes. Our only other really large area of water is the Great Salt Lake. There are lots of smaller lakes – in the southwestern states and in Minnesota.

The country with the greatest area of inland water is our northern neighbor, Canada, whose lakes and rivers add up to 291,600 square miles – more than three times the total area of the U.K.

Right away, you'll probably think of the Great Lakes again. They're well named. Lake Superior, for example, is the largest freshwater surface in the world, with a total area of 32,000 square miles. Large as they are, they by no means account for most of Canada's inland waterways. For one thing, much of them are in U.S. territory. Lake

	U.S.A.	CANADA
	1975	1975
1. Area of water (square miles – 000s)	91.2	291.6
as % of total area of country	2.5	7.6
2. Irrigated land (square miles)	62,942	1831

Michigan is entirely ours and the Canadian border runs straight through the middle of the others.

Most of Canada's largest lakes are in the North and West. There's Lake Winnipeg, and further up in the wilds there's the comparatively unknown ones – Great Slave Lake, Reindeer Lake, Great Bear Lake and hundreds more.

However, Canada's enormous size means that the lakes and other inland water amount to only 7.6% of the total area of the country, placing it in third position in this category of the table.

Compare Canada's figure with that of the Netherlands – first in this table. Although the Dutch have a mere 2,800 square miles of water, it amounts to more than a staggering 17% of the country's total area.

Australia is third on the table with a total inland water area of 26,600 square miles. However, Australia has few large freshwater lakes and most of its inland water is the seasonal lakes and saltmarshes of the barren interior.

	U.K.	AUSTRALIA	AUSTRIA	BELGIUM	DENMARK	FRANCE	(WEST) GERMANY	IRELAND	ITALY	JAPAN	NETHERLANDS	NORWAY	SPAIN	SWEDEN	SWITZERLAND
	1975	1975	1975	1975	1975	1975	1975	1975	1975	1975	1975	1975	1975	1975	1975
	1.2	26.6	0.4	0.06	0.3	0.4	1.8	0.5	2.8	0.5	2.8	6.2	2.0	14.9	0.6
	1.2	0.9	1.4	0.5	1.6	0.2	1.8	2.0	2.4	0.3	17.8	5.0	1.0	8.5	3.7
	328[+]	5596	15	4	4	2136	1182[0]	0	13733	10204[x]	282	95	10750	202	114

[+] Excludes Scotland and Northern Ireland   [0] Excludes kitchen and market gardens
[x] Irrigated rice areas only

Source:
Food and Agricultural Organization

For its size, Sweden has more than nine times as much water as Australia. Like Finland, Sweden could well be called the Land of Lakes.

France, Japan and Belgium have the smallest percentage of inland water. France, apart from her famous rivers – most of which have their sources in the mountains to the east of the country – has few areas of inland water.

Although smaller than France, the U.K. has nearly three times as much inland water, a lot of it in Scotland or Northern Ireland.

Since the beginning of civilization, people have found it necessary to control and direct their water resources. With 62,942 square miles, the U.S. has more land under irrigation than any other country in the table. It covers more than two-thirds of the country.

There's also a lot of irrigated land in Italy – a total of 13,733 square miles – more than its total area of natural water.

The same is true of Spain, third in the table. We all know that the rain in Spain falls mainly on the plain, but clearly it doesn't rain often enough.

The economies of both Italy and Spain depend very largely upon their agriculture – and they're the driest countries in Europe. It's hardly surprising that some artificial means of directing their water resources is necessary.

Japan and Australia are other countries where widespread irrigation is vital. In Japan, much is in rice-growing areas.

The scarcity of fresh water in Australia's interior has led to a massive irrigation program. It may not be so very long before the bare landscape of Western and Central Australia is transformed.

Belgium and Denmark irrigate less land than any other countries in the world – about four square miles each. That's hardly surprising when you consider that their rainfalls are among the heaviest in the whole of Europe.

The largest countries have the most land set aside for national parks. And the countries with the largest populations (of those on the table) make the most use of their land for recreational purposes.

The U.S. leads the field with over 200,000 square miles devoted to national parks and nature reserves (according to the standards of the I.U.C.N.). That's roughly 1/18th of the total U.S.A. land area, or an area almost as large as France.

Canada is next, with just under half as much land devoted to recreational parks. The other giant, Australia, has one quarter as much or 1/60th the total area. But there are few individual parks in Canada. Divide the total national park land figure by the number of parks, and you'll see that each park covers an average of over 100,000 square miles.

The surprise in this table is overcrowded Japan. There, 37 national parks cover over 9,000 square miles, the same proportion of park land to the total area as in the U.S.

Between them, Sweden and Norway have 41 national parks and reserves. But neighboring Denmark is the lowest country on the table, with about 10 square miles of national park land. Ireland and Belgium have only one national park apiece, as does Switzerland.

Italy has five national parks, but together they cover only 730 square

		U.S.A.	CANADA
		1975	1975
1.	Number of national parks[+]	252	70
	Total area (square miles – 000s) of national parkland	207.1	88.6
	Population (000s) per square mile of national parkland[o]	1.0	0.26
		1972	1972
2.	Green space in cities:	a	b
	Square yards per inhabitant	23	14[x]

miles. The U.K. has 320 square miles of park land. West Germany has approximately the same area as the U.K., with a comparable population, but it has nearly four times as much protected land.

We've divided the national park figures by the number of people living in each country, to find out how many people have to share each square mile of park. In Canada, there are about 260 people for every square mile of national park. But in Belgium there are nearly 700,000 – over 2,500 times as many. There's only about 4½ square yards of national park for every Belgian – just enough room to jog in place or do some jumping jacks.

The Australians are almost as well off as the Canadians, with 280 people for every square mile of national park. Norway has 300 people. The U.S. comes fourth with 1,000 people.

U.K.	AUSTRALIA	AUSTRIA	BELGIUM	DENMARK	FRANCE	(WEST) GERMANY	IRELAND	ITALY	JAPAN	NETHERLANDS	NORWAY	SPAIN	SWEDEN	SWITZERLAND
1975	1975	1975	1975	1975	1975	1975	1975	1975	1975	1975	1975	1975	1975	1975
19	239	4	1	1	10	13	1	5	37	21	15	3	26	1
0.32	50.2	0.43	0.01	0.01	0.96	1.1	0.16	0.73	9.1	0.25	13.2	0.27	2.0	0.07
174.1	0.28	17.5	698.3	433.3	55.2	54.3	190.9	75.6	12.2	55.0	0.30	133.1	4.3	100.2
1972	1975	1972	1972	1972	1972	1972	1972	1972	1972	1972	1972	1972	1972	1972
c	d	e	f	g	h	i	j	k	l	m	n	o	p	q
14	4^x	12	47	2	12	12	21	11^x	1	36	430	9	88	39

a = New York   b = Montreal   c = London   d = Melbourne   e = Vienna   f = Brussels
g = Copenhagen   h = Paris   i = Frankfurt   j = Dublin   k = Rome   l = Tokyo
m = The Hague   n = Oslo   o = Madrid   p = Stockholm   q = Berne

In addition to Belgium, countries with a high ratio of people to national parks include Denmark with over 400,000 citizens for every square mile, Ireland (just under 200,000) and Spain (133,100).

To compare conditions in the cities, we've listed the area of green space available to each inhabitant. Oslo easily tops the table with 430 square yards, more than four times its nearest competitor, Stockholm.

If you live in New York, you fare comparatively well; there are 23 square yards of green space for each inhabitant. This may come as a surprise to many New Yorkers, who can go for days without laying eyes on a piece of grass. London, which prides itself on its parks, has only 14 square yards of park space.

Tokyo is easily the worst off for green space – one square yard per inhabitant.

Sources:
1. International Union for Conservation of Nature and Natural Resources
2. Vision, 1973
0 Heron House estimates
+ This includes all national parks, national nature reserves and equivalent reserves as defined by the IUCN
x National yearbooks

Wonderful, wonderful Copenhagen has a mere two square yards of open green space per inhabitant. (It looks as if the Danes are not keeping up with their northern Scandinavian neighbors ecologically.) The Australians must feel a bit cramped in Melbourne. Each Melbournian is limited to four square yards of green space.

Square yards per inhabitant

400		
350		
30.0		
250		
200		
150		
100		
50		

If you're looking for wide open spaces, don't head for Tokyo. There's only one square yard of green space per inhabitant there. On the other hand the great record of the northern Scandinavians in Olympic distance races is helped by the fact that even city dwellers have got room to practice. For every 430 people in Shiba Park, Tokyo, there's only one in an Oslo park. If you're planning a picnic in Tokyo, spread out a handkerchief, or be prepared to share your rug with someone else.

Between these extremes there's quite a range in the amount of space available to the inhabitants of the world's larger cities. Stockholm with 88 square yards fares well, while New York is one of the less fortunate. No wonder Central Park echoes with the cry, "You're occupying my space."

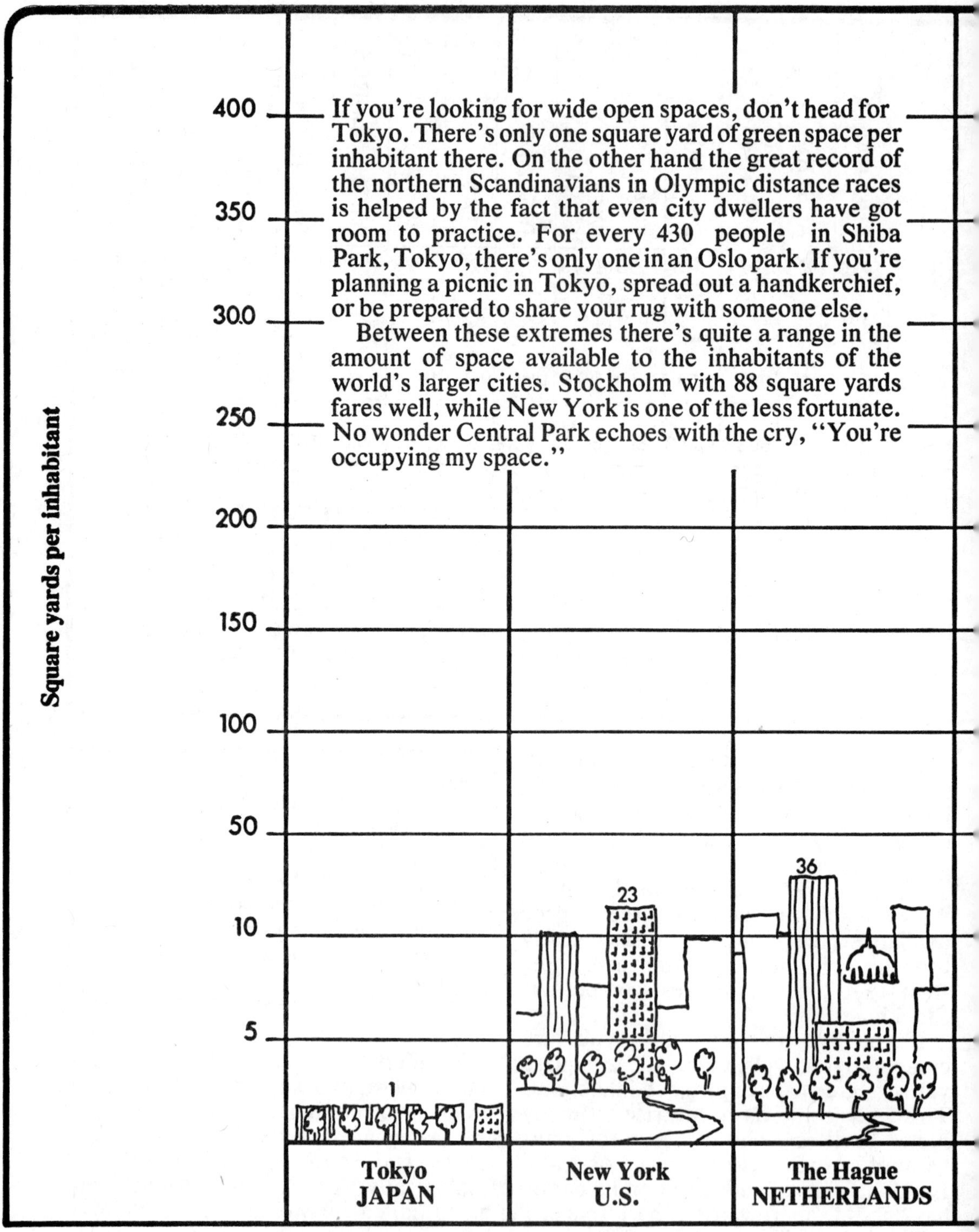

36

23

10

5

1

Tokyo JAPAN	New York U.S.	The Hague NETHERLANDS

GREEN SPACE IN CITIES

Berne SWITZERLAND	Brussels BELGIUM	Stockholm SWEDEN	Oslo NORWAY
39	47	88	430

Man and the Environment

It's often said that we're what our environment makes us. If this is so, it's a good idea to take a careful look at the range of different physical environments we find around the world.

Our first table has got all you'll want to know about the amounts of rainfall and sunshine to expect in a number of the world's largest cities. Whether you're planning a long vacation overseas, or just a quick business trip, it could be worth your while to study these. And if you sell umbrellas for a living, the tables will tell you how many wet days you can count on, per year, for each of the cities. Not only that, it'll tell you which months to avoid if you want to miss getting a soaking.

We'd expect Europe's northern cities to have a higher rainfall than those of the south, and that's borne out by the figures. But if you think that by going south all the way to Australia you'll miss out on the grey skies altogether, you could be in for a damp surprise. Because in Sydney you can expect nearly as many showery days as in Oslo.

The next set of figures looks on the bright side. Where are the sunshine cities of the world? And just how many sunny days can you expect in each of these in a year? The table has all the facts here. And it'll tell you which are the sunniest months, and just how sunny they are.

Having dealt with sunshine and rain, in the next tables we turn our attention to temperature. We've taken some of the major countries of the world, and selected a town in each of them where we might expect to find the lowest temperatures. The table has the mean annual temperatures for each of these towns. And just to help in making comparisons between them, there's other data too. Many factors contribute to the climate of an area, and two of the more important are latitude and height above sea level. With the help of these figures you'll be able to make some interesting meteorological speculations.

The U.S. certainly has some chilly cities, like Duluth. The average temperature there isn't much above freezing point. But you can see it gets pretty nippy in some of those northern Scandinavian towns, too. And if you think that it's hot and sunny everywhere in Spain, you could be in for a surprise. Because there are some towns in Spain where it's not much warmer than in the north of Scotland. To enable you to get some idea of the range of climate in these countries, we've got details of some of the hottest towns, too. Nowhere will you find more striking contrasts than right here in the United States.

Man and the Environment

The next table deals with a different aspect of our environment altogether. Since the arrival of the industrial age, pollution of one kind or another has become a serious problem for most western countries. Nowhere is this more apparent than in the air of our larger cities. We've chosen two measures of air pollution. One measures the accumulation of smoky particles in the atmosphere, and the other provides an estimate of the sulphur-dioxide content of the atmosphere, which is generally associated with heavy industry. The tables are broken down, so you can compare the cities with their suburban neighbors. You'll see that the suburban dwellers don't always get off so lightly. Finally the table enables us to compare the figures over a two year period. And there's good news here. The figures, almost without exception, show signs of improvement.

In the last table we look at the relationship between man and his environment in an entirely different way. We've drawn up a table which offers an original way of seeing how our material environment provides us with the basic needs of life. There's one crude way of doing this, and that's to look at the matter purely in economic terms. How much money does a country's resources generate for each of its members? G.N.P. per capita is the most commonly used measure of this.

But there's another way that we can estimate how well a nation meets the fundamental needs of its people. And that's by making use of what's called the Physical Quality of Life Index. This is explained fully in the text which accompanies the table. Basically this index provides us with a rating which tells us how satisfactorily the members of any country are provided with the necessities of life.

The table shows figures for G.N.P. and P.Q.L.I. for a number of countries. One of the most striking things you'll notice is that the physical quality of life is similar for most western countries, despite some considerable differences in G.N.P. As you'd expect, the low ratings are to be found mostly in the third world countries. Yet in terms of G.N.P. these are by no means always the poorest countries. In some parts of the world, they seem to be getting very poor value for their money.

Who doesn't keep an eye on the weather? Checking to see if we need a coat on our way to work in the mornings. Or an umbrella in the evenings. Or whether it's going to be a good weekend. Or a good day for planting. For some of us, livelihoods may depend on knowing whether the barometer is going up or down.

If you're a duck, take a vacation on a Dutch canal barge. Amsterdam and nearby Brussels are by far the wettest cities on the table. In each of these cities, it rains, an average of 206 days in the year. That's about four days a week.

If you're spending January in Brussels, you'll be lucky to have more than seven days of dry weather during the entire month. And in December, in Amsterdam, you can expect 22 days of rain or snow.

The beautiful city of Copenhagen comes next. If you live with the Danes you'll be wearing your raincoat just about every other day – even more often in December, the wettest month. In Montreal, you can expect 166 wet days in the year. But the Canadian climate is generally so cold that a lot of rain falls as snow in winter.

If you live in one of these cities and are feeling sorry for yourself, take comfort. Things could be worse. In Bahia Felix, Chile (not on our table), it rains, on average, 325 days in the year.

Now where to keep dry? Rome is at the top of the list on the table. It rains only one day in five on their lucky inhabitants (about a third of the rainfall in Brussels). Even in December, the wettest month in Rome, you'll only need your raincoat on eight days in the whole month.

Surprisingly, London is one of the driest cities on our table. It has fewer rainy days than New York, Paris or Sydney, Australia.

Now let's look on the bright side. Where are the sunny spots? Scientists measure the number of hours of bright sunshine for an area by directing sunlight through a lens onto a rotating drum – the

	NEW YORK[x][+]	MONTREAL[+]
1. Days of rain per year[0]	121	166
2. Wettest months	Mar	Jan
days of rain	12.0	18.0[x]
3. Mean hours of sunshine per year	NA	1852
as % of possible hours of sunshine	59	NA
4. Sunniest months	July	July
mean hours of sunshine	66[xx]	253

LONDON	SYDNEY×	VIENNA	BRUSSELS	COPENHAGEN	PARIS	MUNICH	DUBLIN	ROME	TOKYO+	AMSTERDAM+	OSLO+	MADRID	STOCKHOLM	ZURICH
113	150	96.0	206	172	164	127.5	142	68.6	115.0	206	161	84	163	134.6
	Mar/May	July	Jan	Dec	Jan	June		Dec	Sep	Dec	Dec	Mar	Dec	June
11.0**	14.0	9.4	23.0	17.2	17.0	14.0	13.0++	7.9	13.0‡	22.0	17.0	10.0	17.0	13.0
1514	NA	1891	1551	1603	1840	1862	1386	2491	2019	1651	1632	2843	1973	1694
34	NA	42	35	36	52	39	30	54	NA	34	NA	64	44	38
June	NA	July	June	00	June	July	June	July	Aug	May	June	July	June	July
213	NA	266	223	245	243	261	180	334	203	227	244	366	318	238

×Equal to or over a depth of 0.25 millimetres   ××% of possible hours of sunshine
‡No depth specified
**Jan/April/Dec
++Jan/July/Aug/Dec
00May/July
NA not available

length of the burns corresponds to the amount of bright sunshine. The longest burn times are in Madrid, which enjoys an average of 2,843 hours of bright sunshine per year. That's about eight hours of sunshine a day averaged through the year, 64% of the maximum possible. In July, the figure is 366 hours of sunshine for the month.

Rome is second in the sunshine league, with 2,491 hours of happiness a year, or nearly seven hours of sun a day. This is about 54% of the maximum possible, which still means plenty of sun. In July there are nearly 11 hours a day.

If your complexion is delicate and you want to head for the shade, Dublin's the place for you. There, you'll get less than half of the sunshine that they enjoy in Madrid. Dublin sun amounts to less than four hours a day.

London may not have an excess of rain, but it doesn't exactly have a surplus of sun either. The sun shines brightly in London for 1,514 hours a year. That averages out to about four hours a day.

Sources:
Tables of Temperature, Relative Humidity, Precipitation and Sunshine for the World, HMSO
+World Survey of Climatology, Elsevier Scientific Publishing Co.
0Equal to or over a depth of one millimetre

Country	Coldest cities (ft)	Elevation of city (ft)	Length of record (yrs)
U.S.A.[+]	Duluth	610	30
Canada[0]	Saskatoon	1574	30
U.K.	Aberdeen	79	26
Australia	Hobart	177	30
Austria	Salzburg	1427	50
Belgium	Liège	377	30
Denmark	Alborg	10	30
France	Troyes	361	30
Germany (West)	Kiel	46	50
Ireland	Dublin	155	30
Italy	Bolzano	860	9
Japan	Kushiro	108	41
Netherlands	Groningen	16	30
Norway	Vardö	43	40
Spain	Burgos	2808	26
Sweden	Särna	1504	20
Switzerland	Zürich	1539	60

As you'd expect, the coldest cities in the table are in frigid Scandinavian north. Vardo, Norway and Särna, Sweden, both have an annual average temperature at noon of just over 34°F.

North America comes a close second place with Saskatoon, out on the bleak Canadian prairie, at 35.4°F. And Duluth, Minnesota, isn't much better (37.9°F). Aberdeen in Scotland is further north than anywhere else on the table, except for those chilly Scandinavian cities. Yet at 47°F its average temperature is only four degrees less than Burgos down in sunny Spain, where it's almost 3,000 feet above sea level.

The warmest of the cold spots is Hobart, Australia, with a pleasant average of just over 54°F. Kushiro in Japan is about as far north of the Equator as Hobart is south – but it's nearly 3 degrees colder. This is due to the cold Siberian currents from Russia.

But now for the warmest cities. Fort Lauderdale in tropical Florida has an average of over 75°F – almost seven degrees warmer than Brisbane, Australia, which is located well into the tropics. Malmo, Sweden, has the lowest temperature among the warm cities – an average of 45.9°F. Bergen in Norway, and Copenhagen in Denmark don't get too much sun either.

Longitude Latitude	Average temp. (°F)	Warmest cities	Elevation of city (ft)	Length of record (yrs)	Longitude Latitude	Average temp. (°F)
46.47N 92.06W	37.9	Fort Lauderdale	7	30	26.07N 80.08W	75.4
52.07N 106.38W	35.4	Vancouver	38	30	49.17N 123.07W	50.8
57.08N 2.06W	47.0	Torbay	27	24	50.28N 3.30W	51.9
42.55S 147.20E	54.2	Brisbane	134	79	27.03S 153.01E	68.8
47.48N 13.02E	47.0	Vienna	663	50	48.12N 16.22E	48.8
50.38N 20.6W	47.0	Ghent	23	30	51.03N 03.43E	50.4
57.03N 09.56E	44.1	Copenhagen	16	30	55.40N 12.35N	46.9
48.18N 04.05E	48.9	Ajaccio	234	46	41.52N 08.32E	60.7
54.30N 10.08E	45.7	Freiburg im Breisgau	912	30	48.00N 7.51E	50.5
53.22N 06.21E	49.0	Cork	56	27	51.54N 08.28W	50.6
46.31N 11.22E	53.0	Palermo	46	25	38.07N 13.22E	64.9
42.58N 144.23E	51.4	Kagoshìma	16	30	31.36N 130.33E	62.2
53.13N 06.34E	48.5	Eindhoven	66	30	51.26N 5.30E	51.3
70.22N 31.06E	34.1	Bergen	144	49	60.23N 05.20E	46.0
42.41N 03.42W	51.1	Seville	20	30	37.23N 5.59W	65.8
61.41N 13.07E	34.1	Malmo	10	30	53.46N 13.00E	45.9
47.22N 08.31E	46.8	Lausanne	1831	60	46.32N 6.39E	48.9

In the 1940s and 1950s, the city of Pittsburgh, Pennsylvania could be seen from many miles away as a dirty black cloud on the horizon.

As late as in the mid-1950s, London was regularly paralyzed several times each winter by two and three-day pea soupers. The sky would turn dim and dark yellow at noon, and fogs would reduce visibility to 20 yards or less. Nowadays, Pittsburgh is almost sparkling clean. And Londoners spend entire winters without a serious fog.

Pittsburgh achieved its result by imposing stringent controls on smokestack emissions and London by establishing "smoke-free" zones in which no pollution was allowed. Similar steps have been taken in other major industrial cities – also with success – but air pollution still remains a menace. Each year it claims its victims by causing serious illness and even death – especially among children the elderly and people with weak hearts and lungs. This table shows the levels of air pollution in selected cities. And it's worth noting that in almost every case they're going down. The sulphur dioxide figures give an indication of gas pollution, and the suspended particulate figures show how much solid pollution (dust, sand, coal-dust and so on) there is. In most of the cities listed, industrial areas have more sulphur dioxide pollution than residential ones. This is only to be expected. However, there are exceptions. In Prague, the air in the residential suburbs is almost twice as polluted with sulphur dioxide as in the industrial districts. Frankfurt is worse with nearly four times as much sulphur dioxide pollution in the suburban residential areas. The residential suburbs of Frankfurt are easily the worst for sulphur dioxide pollution on our table – even worse than any industrial areas, except in Madrid and London.

	ST. LOUIS	VANCOUVER
The sulphur dioxide count[+] in:		
suburban residential areas		
1973	NA	NA
1974	NA	NA
suburban industrial areas		
1973	NA	NA
1974	NA	NA
The suspended[x] particulate count[+] in:		
suburban residential areas		
1973	112.0	63.8
1974	122.5	64.5
suburban industrial areas		
1973	127.2	78.5
1974	143.5	75.0

LONDON	BRUSSELS	PRAGUE	FRANKFURT	ROME	TOKYO	AMSTERDAM	MADRID	NYKOPING
110.8	102.7	125.8	116.5	22.6	50.9^0	41.5^0	73.3	NA
80.0	84.7	106.8	119.3	16.2	37.4^0	NA	62.6	NA
197.4	123.2	75.4	17.6	57.4	83.3^0	57.0^0	192.7	30.6^0
128.1	102.9	56.0	33.0	107.5	88.4^0	33.7^0	177.7	NA
36.9	31.2	139.0	NA	30.5	72.3^0	NA	72.3	NA
25.7	20.0	134.6	NA	27.5	64.0^0	NA	66.3	NA
46.8	28.7	NA	NA	53.1	77.1^0	NA	303.5	NA
29.7	23.6	120.8	NA	60.3	63.2^0	NA	306.8	NA

NA not available

Madrid has the highest level of sulphur dioxide pollution in industrial areas. London comes second (despite strict regulations) and then Rome.

It is said that you can barely breathe on a bad day in Tokyo because of car fumes. They do have street corners where you can stop for a blast from an oxygen machine. However, on our table, the figures for Tokyo are only average.

Madrid has the dubious honor of being most polluted by suspended particulates, which makes it the most polluted city on the table. St. Louis comes second. It's

Source:
World Health Organization
[+]Micrograms per cubic metre in 24 hours (arithmetic mean)
[0]Micrograms per cubic metre in one hour
[x]Dirt: sand, dust, coal dust, etc

the only American city that can come close to European competition.

Which cities have the lowest levels of solid pollution? London and Brussels, both high in sulphur dioxide, are the lowest in suspended particulates.

	U.S.A.	CANADA
1. GNP per person[+] (US $)	7890	7510
2. Physical quality of life index[0]	94	95

Money isn't everything. And at last even the statisticians have come to realize this. The richest country in the world isn't necessarily a pleasant place in which to live. We know how to measure the wealth of a country, but how do we measure its "quality of life"?

Recently, the Overseas Development Council (a world-renowned Washington organization devoted to the improvement of conditions in under-developed countries) worked out a "Physical Quality of Life Index". This combines life expectancy, infant mortality and literacy rates in a single figure – and thus provides us with an insight into how people's basic human needs are being met in any given country. The ratings run from one to 100.

The G.N.P. only shows the annual wealth per capita generated in a country. For example, although the G.N.P. per person in Kuwait is nearly $15,500 – almost double ours – the P.Q.L.I. figure is only 74, compared with 94 for the U.S. On the simplest level, this shows that in spite of the massive wealth generated by the citizens of Kuwait, the physical quality of life there is considerably lower than ours in the United States.

The tables give the P.Q.L.I. ratings and also the G.N.P. per person. Thus we can see at a glance how much real value people are getting for their money.

Sweden has the highest P.Q.L.I. rating – 97. And it comes second in G.N.P. per person. But what about the Swiss? Their G.N.P. per person is highest but their P.Q.L.I. rating is only 95 – about average. However, only two points separate Sweden and Switzerland – which shows how high the P.Q.L.I. ratings are amongst the countries on the main table. Between them are three, the Netherlands, Japan and Denmark, all equal at 96. It's interesting to see how the G.N.P. figures differ for these countries: in Japan, for instance, it's just under $5,000 per person whereas in Denmark it's nearly $7,500 – a substantial difference.

Spain and Norway are lowest. Next lowest in the P.Q.L.I. are the Italians, and then come six countries which all have a rating of 93 – including affluent West Germany, and Ireland, which has the lowest G.N.P. on the table. There seems to be little correlation between the P.Q.L.I. and the G.N.P. – take the figures for the U.S. and the U.K.: the per person G.N.P. for the U.S. is nearly twice that of the U.K. – but they both have P.Q.L.I. rating of 94.

The accompanying list is full of surprises. The P.Q.L.I. figure for the U.S.S.R. is almost equal to that of Spain – the lowest in the main table. South Africa – with a G.N.P. per head approximately half that of the U.S.S.R. – has a P.Q.L.I. rate of 48, a mere seven points higher than India. And India has a G.N.P. per person only one-tenth that of South Africa. In Gabon, West Africa, they have a G.N.P. per head of $2,500 – but their P.Q.L.I. is only 21, just over half India's. So all that money must be going into the pockets of a select – and very wealthy – few.

PHYSICAL QUALITY OF LIFE

U.K.	AUSTRALIA	AUSTRIA	BELGIUM	DENMARK	FRANCE	(WEST) GERMANY	IRELAND	ITALY	JAPAN	NETHERLANDS	NORWAY	SPAIN	SWEDEN	SWITZERLAND
4020	6100	5330	6780	7450	6550	7380	2560	3050	4910	6200	7420	2920	8670	8880
94	93	93	93	96	94	93	93	92	96	96	91	91	97	95

	U.S.S.R.	ARGENTINE	INDIA	SRI LANKA	SOUTH AFRICA	GABON	KUWAIT
1. GNP per person[+] (US $)	2760	1550	140	200	1340	2590	15,480
2. Physical quality of life index[0]	91	85	41	82	48	21	74

Source:
Overseas Development Council,
Washington DC
[+]Preliminary 1976 World Bank data
[0]Composite of life expectancy, infant
mortality and literacy figures, each rated
on an index of 1 to 100

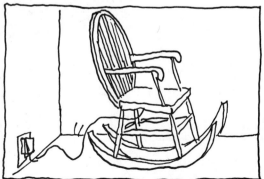

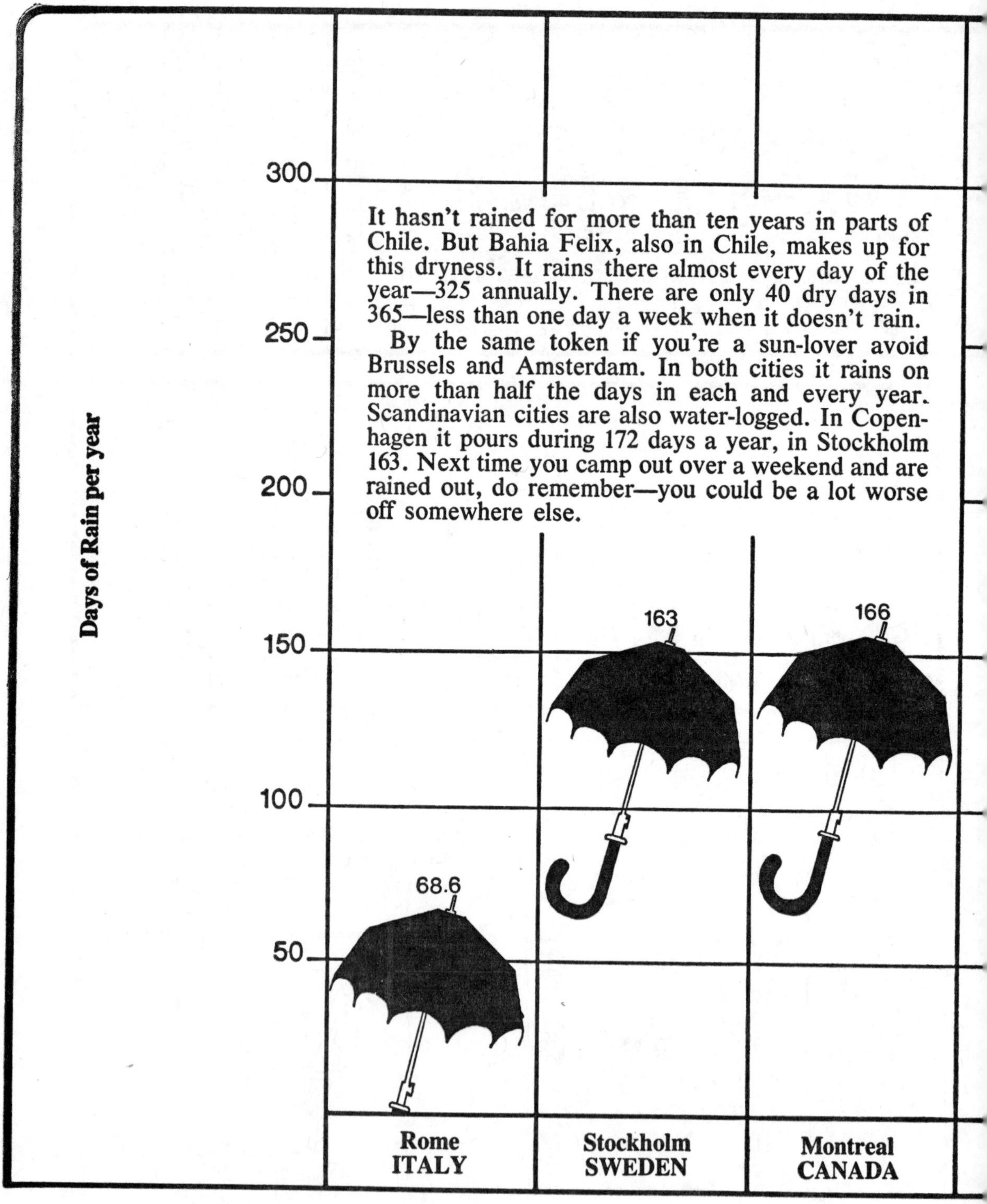

Days of Rain per year

300 —

It hasn't rained for more than ten years in parts of Chile. But Bahia Felix, also in Chile, makes up for this dryness. It rains there almost every day of the year—325 annually. There are only 40 dry days in 365—less than one day a week when it doesn't rain.

250 —

By the same token if you're a sun-lover avoid Brussels and Amsterdam. In both cities it rains on more than half the days in each and every year. Scandinavian cities are also water-logged. In Copenhagen it pours during 172 days a year, in Stockholm 163. Next time you camp out over a weekend and are rained out, do remember—you could be a lot worse off somewhere else.

200 —

163

166

150 —

100 —

68.6

50 —

| Rome ITALY | Stockholm SWEDEN | Montreal CANADA |

DAYS OF RAIN

			325
	206	206	
172			
Copenhagen DENMARK	Brussels BELGIUM	Amsterdam NETHERLANDS	Bahia Felix CHILE

People and Money

There's one thing that no one can do without and that's money. For better or worse, we're all involved in the old game of making money to make the world go round. So read on and find out who the richest people are, who has the most diamonds, or for that matter, who spends the most on steak.

In the first table you will find statistics on per capita income, and interesting they are too. Americans, for instance, don't, on average, earn more than the people of most other countries. In fact, the statistics show that to be wealthy, economic might is not everything. The figures support the idea that small is beautiful. Of course it helps if you produce oil, like the United Arab Emirates, or provide facilities for gambling, like Monaco.

Having looked at the table on per capita income, you'll find statistics on the G.N.P. of various countries. And the word to bear in mind here is "gross" if you'll pardon the expression. Before, we were looking at individual wealth, now it's national wealth, and that includes everything that is produced from automobile engines to Big Macs. America is in a league of its own here, followed a long way behind by the post-war boom economies of West Germany and Japan.

But bear with us and look at the next table – you'll find the plot thickens. Don't be put off by the title, "International Gold and Reserves". It's simply another way of posing the same question – who's got the most money? And just as people worry about how much they've got tucked away in the bank, so nations worry about how much they have in their reserves, whether it's in gold, dollars or Japanese yen.

Of course, in these matters there comes a time of reckoning. For you and me, it's the bank statement, but for each individual country, it's the balance of payments, and this is what the next table deals with. Who's spending beyond their means? Who's putting money aside for a rainy day? Look carefully at the statistics and you'll be able to draw some interesting conclusions.

But bear in mind one very pertinent factor – inflation. The figures in this table are evidence that no country is immune to the effects of rising prices. In fact, this, above all else, is the thorn in the side of economic progress.

Want to take out a mortgage? You'll find that inflation affects your chances of getting one – and the interest you'll have to pay on it. Interest rates have gone up in most Western countries in the last seven years. There are, however, certain anomalies. For example, why has West Germany's interest rate dropped? A look at the tables might give you an answer. And you don't have to be an economic expert to figure this one out.

Perhaps you've noticed that all the tables so far, except the first one, have dealt with what is termed, in economics, the macro-picture, i.e. the country as a whole. Now we take a look at how people are doing on an individual basis: how does the financial situation vary from the inhabitants of one country to another? Where would you be best off?

And just to remind us who's who in the per capita income league, we've introduced some more up-to-date figures. These only cover the major economic countries of the West so if you want to remind yourself about how people in Liechtenstein, say, are doing, you'll have to refer to the first table again.

But, for those of us who like to imagine we're hobnobbing with the rich, we have a couple of tables on gold, diamonds, furs and expensive cars. Which country do you think buys the most Rolls Royces in a year? And, for that matter, who's likely to be wrapped in sable?

Then we come back to the world of everyday living. Have you ever wondered how your cost of living compares with that of people in other countries? This table will show you just that. The next table gives basic food prices. Where can you buy the cheapest pound of coffee or cheese? Or for that matter, the most expensive egg? Perhaps you feel you already know. Read on and see if your suspicions are confirmed.

The next two tables deal with household expenditures and savings accounts. One table gives a breakdown of the various items on which people spend their money, and the other shows the level of savings on a national and per capita basis. This brings us full circle and reintroduces us to the macro-figures again. For example, you can make an interesting comparison of savings figures with inflation rates: see how much that nest egg you put away ten years ago is worth by today's standards.

The final table deals with socio-economic groups. It tells you what percentage of the working population is in the professional and executive category; what percentages are white-collar, skilled, or unskilled workers.

	U.S.A.	CANADA
	1974	1974
National income per person (US $)	5941	5672
Countries in order of wealth	8	9

Which are the richest countries in the world? If you think America comes anywhere near the top of the list, you're wrong. As might be expected, the tiny oil-producing Arab nations around the Persion Gulf head our wealth parade. The United Arab Emirates, with a population of around 800,000 and a land area one-ninth the size of Texas, has a per capita income of $16,000 – almost three times that of the U.S. Qatar and Kuwait aren't far behind. But before you start envying the Arabs, ask yourself if you'd really like to live in Abu Dhabi (if it drove you to drink you'd be out of luck – alcohol is prohibited).

The richest country in Europe is the dot-sized principality of Liechtenstein (all 20 square miles of it) with an income of $8,000 for every inhabitant. Liechtenstein derives much of its income from printing postage stamps which are seldom used for mailing anything. Instead they're sold to stamp collectors around the world. The principality also serves as nominal headquarters for many foreign corporations which register there to avoid being taxed in their home countries.

Switzerland, with $6,340 per capita, is the second richest European country. The Swiss export watches, dairy products and chocolate bars. They also have a thriving tourist industry, but their principal import is money. Untold billions in foreign funds lie on deposit in Swiss banks, making the country one of the great financial powers in the world.

After the Swiss come the Swedes, who enjoy $6,151 per capita. Sweden is a highly industrialized nation with extensive natural resources. Not only do the Swedes earn a high income, they're also covered by one of the most comprehensive social welfare systems in the world. Citizens of a welfare state *can* be hard-working.

The famous gambling tables of Monte Carlo – and perhaps the presence of glamorous Princess Grace – attract enough gamblers and tourists to give the people of Monaco the fourth largest per capita income in Europe – $6,000.

Finally, we come to the U.S. – number eight on the world-wide list, with $5,941 per capita. It's curious that this figure should be so low, since our Gross National Product is more than $7,000 for every man, woman and child. Perhaps government spending and the reinvestment of profits by large corporations account for much of the disparity. The Canadians are close behind us in ninth place.

A real oddity on our list is country number 13, New Caledonia. It's a small group of South Pacific islands, discovered by Captain Cook and now administered by France. When its 100,000 inhabitants aren't busy basking in the tropical sun, they mine their mineral resources, including gold and silver, and cultivate something equally precious nowadays – that brown gold called

	AUSTRALIA	ANDORRA	BELGIUM	DENMARK	(WEST) GERMANY	KUWAIT	LIECHTENSTEIN	LUXEMBOURG	MONACO	NEW CALEDONIA	NORWAY	QUATAR	SWEDEN	SWITZERLAND	UNITED ARAB EMIRATES
	1974	1974	1974	1974	1974	1974	1974	1974	1974	1974	1974	1974	1974	1974	1974
	5460	5000	5044	5403	5462	9900	8000	5050	6000	5400	4912	12500	6151	6340	16000
	11	16	15	12	10	3	4	14	7	13	17	2	6	5	1

Source:
United Nations

coffee. The New Caledonians have become so prosperous that they're now good customers of the Rolls-Royce Company.

The tiny state of Andorra (190 square miles), tucked away in the Pyrenees between France and Spain, is 15th in prosperity. Tourism is one of Andorra's principal sources of revenue: 500,000 tourists pass through the country every year.

The table shows that industrialization and technical expertise are no guarantees of wealth. Three great industrial powers, the U.K., France and Italy are all conspicuously missing from the list. And Belgium, another industrial nation, barely qualifies. The top half of our table is dominated by fairly small countries.

Finally, high income *per se* doesn't always mean affluence. To find out which country has the most buying power, you'll have to consult the table on taxation. It may be that those happy-go-lucky New Caledonians are the richest of all.

What does Gross National Product mean? It's a cash figure for the value of everything that a country produces or earns each year – from nuts and bolts to the tourist trade. So the figure for the Gross National Product (or G.N.P. as it's usually called) is the measure of the real economic strength of a country.

It's commonly known that the U.S. is the largest economic power in the West, but our sheer magnitude is staggering. The U.S.'s G.N.P. is the equivalent of its four closest free-world competitors combined (Japan, Germany, France and the U.K.) – more than $1.5 trillion. That's the equivalent of over $7,000 a year generated for every man, woman and child in the U.S., or nearly $200 per head for the entire population of the world. And the U.S.'s G.N.P. is growing at a rate of nearly five percent – more rapidly than all the other countries shown except for Japan's and Ireland's.

Next come the two boom economies of two nations defeated in the Second World War: Japan, with a G.N.P. of nearly $500 billion, and West Germany with just over $400 billion. Both these countries obviously benefited from a fresh start after the war. Compare their figures to those of the U.K., one of the victorious nations. Formerly second only to the U.S., the U.K. is now producing about half as much as either Germany or Japan.

But the U.K. is, in some ways, a special case. Since the war, Britain has shed the burdens and the benefits of an empire. Membership of the E.E.C. has meant that it has to break into tough European markets instead of relying on Commonwealth members to buy their goods. These factors, plus a reputation for industrial inefficiency, strikes and outmoded business attitudes have helped cause the U.K.'s industrial deterioration.

France comes after Japan and Germany, but ahead of the U.K. For years, France suffered from appalling labor relations, an internal Communist threat, unstable governments and the loss of an empire. But with de Gaulle the country began to enjoy increasing stability and prosperity.

Italy has not yet found its de Gaulle. In fact, its political and industrial unrest is on the upswing. There may be an economic boom in the northern cities – Milan and Turin – but the south of Italy is still one of the most backward and poverty-stricken areas in Europe.

Next comes Canada. Canadians rival the U.S. in terms of production

		U.S.A.	CANADA
		1975	1975
1.	Average annual GNP (US $ – billions):	1,509	151.7
2.	Average rate of economic growth (%):		
	1964 – 74	3.3	5.2
	1975	−1.8	0.6
	1976	6.0	4.9
	1977	4.9	2.3

U.K.	AUSTRALIA	AUSTRIA	BELGIUM	DENMARK	FRANCE	(WEST) GERMANY	IRELAND	ITALY	JAPAN	NETHERLANDS	NORWAY	SPAIN	SWEDEN	SWITZERLAND
1975	1975	1975	1975	1975	1975	1975	1975	1975	1975	1975	1975	1975	1975	1975
214.9	76.2	35.5	59.4	35.0	304.6	408.8	7.6	164.1	495.2	76.3	26.2	95.6	64.6	51.5
2.4	4.7	5.1	4.8	3.8	5.2	4.1	3.9	4.7	8.8	4.9	4.3	6.5	3.4	3.3
−1.8	0.5	−2.0	−1.9	−0.7	−1.3	−3.2	−0.5	−3.7	2.1	−1.1	3.3	0.8	0.6	−7.0
1.2	3.5	5.2	2.3	5.0	5.2	5.6	3.0	5.6	6.3	4.6	6.0	2.1	1.5	−2.1
0.6	2.0	3.5	2.8	1.0	2.3	2.4	5.3	1.8	5.7	2.5	4.5	2.4	−2.3	3.5

efficiency: $6,000 per head of population. Compare this with the U.K.'s $4,000 per head. And Canada, with all those natural assets in the far north, is certainly a country to watch in the 1980s. But partly because of its relatively small population, its G.N.P. is only a tenth of the U.S.'s.

Spain may be the land of the siesta, but it's actually producing nearly half as much as the U.K.

Ireland has easily the lowest figure in the table – just $7.5 billion. That's only a third of the figure for Norway. But Ireland's rate of economic growth is now second only to Japan's.

The 1973 oil crisis made a nasty dent in everyone's figures. In most places the growth rate went into the red. Only Japan and Norway sustained a positive rate of over one percent during the worst of the recession. This was due to cheap Japanese exports and the beginning of Norway's North Sea oil bonanza. Switzerland was hit worst of all, with a negative rate of seven percent in 1975.

What are the prospects for the future?

Sources:
1. *World Bank Atlas*
2. Organization for Economic Co-operation and Development

Along with Japan and Ireland, the U.S. has a healthy rate of expansion. (Nearly five percent.) And Norway's rate, like that of the U.S., will probably continue to grow. With a G.N.P. of only $26 billion – just about half that of Switzerland or Belgium – Norway is still a long way from being a world economic power. But if North Sea oil revenue is put to good use, the country could lead the field in its growth rate.

Things don't look too rosy for its Scandinavian neighbors. Sweden's growth rate, never high at the best of times, is now minus 2.3%. And Denmark's G.N.P. is barely growing at all. But at least Denmark is doing better than the U.K. With a growth rate of just over one half of a percent, Britain's economy still isn't out of the woods.

The wealth of nations can be measured by the same method you'd use for private individuals: find out how much money there is in the bank. Governments usually refer to their bank accounts as reserves. Reserves are mainly held in "hard" currencies – which once meant American dollars. Until just a few years ago, money from every other country was measured against them. Today though, other currencies such as the Swiss franc, German mark and Japanese yen are more stable. However, gold is still the ultimate standard of value. The worth of a country's paper money may fluctuate, but its gold reserves will always retain full value. Like your house, a country's gold reserves are its security.

In 1970, America was the world's leading money power with $14,487 million in reserve funds. By 1977 we'd slipped to fourth place with reserves of $19,831 million. That might seem like a healthy increase in reserves, but it isn't. The table shows that the last seven years tell a dramatic story. In 1970, West Germany was the second richest nation on the table with $13,610 million in international reserves and Japan was sixth with $4,840 million. Today, Germany is tops with $39,744 million in its coffers, Japan is next with $23,247 million and the U.K. comes third at $21,044 million. We're a lowly fourth. These figures show how economic power has shifted in the last decade.

International reserves (US $ – millions)	U.S.A.	CANADA
1970+	14,487	4679
in gold (as % of total reserves)	76	17
1975+	15,873	5323
in gold (as % of total reserves)	71	17
1976+	18,291	5834
in gold (as % of total reserves)	61	15
1977+	19,831	4605
in gold (as % of total reserves)	61	20

However, currency is still largely paper – no matter how secure it may seem at the moment. Economic crises can cause even the hardest currency to soften in the space of a few months. So it's important to see what percentage of a country's reserves is in the form of gold. America tops the table at 61% (down from 76% in 1970). Other countries with substantial gold reserves are France, Belgium, Italy, the Netherlands, Switzerland, Austria and Canada. By contrast, the three countries with the highest international reserves don't have much gold in their coffers. West Germany weighs in with a respectable 13% or $5,167 million in gold, but Japan and the U.K. each have only four percent of their reserves in gold: $930 million for Japan and $842 million for Britain. (The American figure is $12,000 million in gold reserves).

However, someone with a lot of money in the bank isn't necessarily rich. He may have debts that are larger than his bank

GOLD AND INTERNATIONAL RESERVES

U.K.	AUSTRALIA	AUSTRIA	BELGIUM	DENMARK	FRANCE	(WEST) GERMANY	IRELAND	ITALY	JAPAN	NETHERLANDS	NORWAY	SPAIN	SWEDEN	SWITZERLAND
2827	1693	1751	2847	484	4960	13610	697	5352	4840	3241	813	1817	761	5132
48	14	40	52	13	71	29	2	54	11	55	3	27	26	53
5456	3254	4437	5794	876	2586	31017	1531	4771	12808	7105	2236	6086	3075	10422
16	9	19	30	8.5	33	15.5	1	71	7	31	2	10	7	33
4224	3164	4403	5198	914	9796	34747	1834	6700	16579	7375	2226	5321	2487	12972
20	9	19	33	8	42	14	1	50	5	30	2	11	9	26
21044	2382	4242	5758	1669	10188	39744	2371	11601	23247	8060	2198	6685	3666	13821
4	14	21	31	5	42	13	0.9	30	4	29	2	9[0]	7	26

Source:
International Monetary Fund
+End of year
0November 1977

balance. The U.K. is a case in point. Although third richest in reserves, it has had to do a lot of international borrowing to bolster the pound and offset its balance of payments deficit. If its debts were paid – at least $10 billion – it would be much further down the list. The U.K.'s gold reserves have dwindled from 48% in 1970 to four percent today, so its economic outlook isn't as rosy as its bank balance might suggest.

France's fortunes have wavered since the upheavals of the late 1960s. In 1970 its reserves – mainly in gold – stood at $4,900 million. By 1975 it had built up more foreign currency reserves. However, the 1977 table shows France down to seventh position, although a good percentage of its reserves is still in gold.

The Scandinavian countries are at the bottom of the table. In 1977 Norway was lowest with $44 million in gold, Denmark second with $83.4 million and Sweden third with $257 million. Their positions have held stable over the years. These countries are among the wealthiest in the world on a per capita income basis, so there must be a lot of cash in day-to-day circulation. Certainly, judging by the figures, the Scandinavians aren't gold-diggers. Well, reserves aren't everything. For example, you can bet your bottom dollar that after the U.K. has paid its debts, it will no longer hold its position in third place.

Ireland is the poorest country on the table when it comes to gold reserves, with less than one percent in gold – only about $21 million. Japan is rich in foreign currency but has a low four percent of its reserves in gold.

Goldfinger knew what he was doing when he went shopping for $12 billion in the coffers of Fort Knox.

We hear a lot about the balance of payments when people diagnose the state of our economy. If a country exports more than it imports, the result is a profit for the country – and the balance of payments is a positive figure. If a country, like a store, stocks (imports) more than it sells (exports) it's in deficit and the balance is negative. So the balance of payments is a financial account of a country's overseas trade.

Balance of payments (US $ – millions):	U.S.A.	CANADA
1972	- 5824	–388
1973	+6892	+107
1974	+1168	–1540
1975	+17,738	–4719
1976	+3507	–4230

Imports mean consumer items and raw materials brought in from outside the country. Exports mean goods sold abroad. But something known as "invisible exports" is another factor to consider. These are services – such as banking, insurance and tourism. Though no actual goods are exchanged, the money paid for these services comes into the country.

As you can see, many of the countries on our table had a surplus (or positive) balance of payments in 1972 – the exceptions were Norway, Denmark, Canada, Ireland, Austria and the U.S. We had the biggest deficit – a colossal debt of $5.8 billion. The reason for this was the enormous expense of the Vietnam War. When we withdrew from Vietnam in 1973, the balance shot up to $6.8 billion.

The oil crisis caused by the 1973 Yom Kippur War lies behind many of the changes in figures on our table. The Arab countries embargoed oil as a result, and the effect on the world was catastrophic.

Our figures reflect this. Price rises began to bite into the spending power of people in the West in 1973 and 1974. The U.S., Switzerland, the Netherlands, West Germany and Belgium were the only countries who managed to avoid going into deficit. Even though the U.S. didn't go into the red, its 1973 surplus of just $6.8 billion fell to about a billion dollars – a 83% reduction. By the end of 1974, only West Germany still had a steadily growing surplus.

Look at what happened to Japan, a country that relies totally on imported oil. In 1972, Japan had a trade surplus of $6.6 billion. By 1973, the booming Japanese export economy was running at a deficit of over $130 million. And in 1974, this had plummeted to a deficit of $4.6 billion. Italy went from a healthy surplus of $2.2 billion to a deficit of $6 billion in those two years. Just like Japan, Italy has no internal oil resources.

The U.K. was easily the worst hit of all countries on the table. After two years of the oil crisis, a $385 million trade surplus had crashed to a $7.8 billion deficit.

It would be interesting to compare these figures with the balance of payments in oil-rich, exporting countries. If

BALANCE OF PAYMENTS

U.K.	AUSTRALIA	AUSTRIA	BELGIUM	DENMARK	FRANCE	(WEST) GERMANY	IRELAND	ITALY	JAPAN	NETHERLANDS	NORWAY	SPAIN	SWEDEN	SWITZERLAND
+385	+561	−187	+1142	−63	+297	+748	−136	+2266	+6624	+1290	−59	+653	+269	+220
−1804	+474	−329	+1153	−464	−691	+4372	−235	−2510	−136	+2342	−365	+569	+1215	+279
−7829	−2614	−457	+911	−981	−5942	+4722	−686	−6039	−4693	+2061	−1116	−3231	−933	+171
−3717	−582	−335	+705	−492	−3	+3896	−70	−530	−682	+1658	+2456	−2927	−1640	+2587
−2502	−1391	−1486	−299	−1906	−6033	+3396	−250	−2856	+3680	+2385	−3728	−3728	−2428	+3497

Source:
International Monetary Fund

Iran were shown, we would see that it was one of the main beneficiaries from the oil price rise. In 1972, it had a trade deficit of $380 million (almost exactly the same as the British surplus for that year). In 1973, this deficit was transformed into a $150 million surplus. In 1974 the surplus suddenly rose to a gigantic $12 billion.

What are the general trends in our table? The U.K. has gradually recovered from its record deficit. Though the negative figure of $2.5 billion for 1976 is still far from healthy, the British did break even in 1977.

Other countries haven't managed to stage a similar recovery – although no one else had quite so far to go. The figures for all the Scandinavian countries show an increasing decline in their balance of payments. There are many reasons for this. Neither Sweden nor Norway is a member of the Common Market, and as a result, both countries have been cut out of their traditional markets and they're beginning to feel the pinch now that the E.E.C. tariff barriers are going up. Denmark, on the other hand, *is* a member of the E.E.C. Norway does have the hope of selling North Sea oil to improve their exports: the Norwegians are expected to find themselves the wealthiest people in Europe by the year 1982.

France, Canada, Spain and Austria still have to halt the slide in their balance of payments. France and Canada are worst off but France improved in 1977. And the U.S. economy has also taken a steep downturn. Some people think we may have to devalue the dollar to improve our foreign trade balance. Devaluation would mean that imported raw materials cost more. But it would also mean that our goods would be cheaper overseas.

Now for the success stories. Japan, West Germany and Switzerland have the best records. Switzerland, as always, has a large invisible exports surplus. But West Germany and Japan have won through by the sheer strength of their economies. Japan weathered the oil crisis despite a couple of bad years. And West Germany seems to be able to maintain a pretty stable trade advantage. In 1977, Japan's surplus was about $17 billion.

Inflation goes up, up, up. And the value of the currency goes down, down, down. When prices rise, wages rise too. Then prices go up again. Soon we're caught in a vicious circle.

In the U.S. – and many other countries – inflation has been the most troublesome economic problem for the past half-dozen years. The rising rate of inflation has wiped out most increases in pay. It continues to undermine the standards of profit for consumers and labor as well as for businesses.

The rate[+] of inflation (%):	U.S.A.	CANADA
1964-75	4.7	4.8
1970-75	6.3	7.3
1975	9.1	10.8
1976	5.8	7.5
1977	6.5	8.0

Inflation also goes hand-in-glove with higher rates of unemployment. Economies running at full tilt tend to be inflationary, while those that keep inflation to a minimum often do so at the expense of full employment. Thus any severe anti-inflationary measures often come at the expense of those who can't get work or lose their jobs.

By the standards of some European countries, the U.S. has kept its inflation rate within acceptable single digit limits. But for most Americans, it's still too high. Maintaining the rate below seven percent has been one of the Carter administration's chief priorities.

The rate of inflation world-wide was given a sharp boost by the quadrupling of oil prices by the O.P.E.C. in 1974. This affected nearly every major Western industrial economy. In the Netherlands, all Middle Eastern oil imports were cut off for a time, and Italy was forced to introduce rationing. Soon the whole world was feeling the bite. As the table shows, inflation started to spiral.

The exceptions? West Germany's post-war economic miracle rode out the storm and its inflation rate actually decreased in 1977 to a level lower than it had been from 1964 to 75. Switzerland's dropped to an almost non-existent 1.3%: all that new Arab money went into Swiss bank accounts.

Of the major Western industrial countries, the U.K. was worst hit by inflation between 1970 and 1975. Its rate leapt a record 11% after the oil crisis and reached an astounding 24% during 1975 (15% higher than the U.S. in the same year). Ireland followed close behind at 21%.

Italy was also badly hit by the oil price rise. It started to recover in 1976, but inflation began to spiral again in 1977. With high unemployment and lack of confidence in the economy – as well as the government's inability to deal with increasing political unrest – the economic prospect in Italy looks bleak indeed.

In 1975, the Western industrial nations began a concerted effort to bring down inflation. Everywhere except Spain and Sweden things improved, though with varying degrees of success. Spain's economy was adversely affected by the

U.K.	AUSTRALIA	AUSTRIA	BELGIUM	DENMARK	FRANCE	(WEST) GERMANY	IRELAND	ITALY	JAPAN	NETHERLANDS	NORWAY	SPAIN	SWEDEN	SWITZERLAND
6.9	5.6	4.9	5.1	7.5	5.6	4.1	7.7	5.8	7.9	6.1	5.9	8.2	5.7	5.2
13.0	10.2	7.3	8.4	9.3	8.8	6.1	13.3	11.3	11.5	8.6	8.2	12.1	8.0	7.7
24.2	15.1	8.4	12.8	9.6	11.7	6.0	20.9	17.0	11.8	10.2	11.7	16.9	9.8	6.7
16.5	13.5	7.3	9.2	9.0	9.6	4.5	18.0	16.8	9.3	8.8	9.1	17.6	10.3	1.7
15.9	12.3	5.5	7.1	11.1	9.5	3.9	13.6	19.3	8.0	6.7	9.1	24.5	11.4	1.3

Source
Organization for Economic Co-operation and Development
+Annual average rate of increase

political unrest which accompanied the transformation from dictatorship to parliamentary government after Franco's death in 1975.

If the U.K. was the country worst hit in the first half of the 1970s, it has also made the greatest strides in the world-wide battle against inflation. Heavy cuts in public spending, wage restraint and the exploitation of North Sea oil brought the U.K. inflation rate down to below ten percent in early 1978.

Australia's inflation rate is still dangerously high. Its traditional markets in the U.K. and other E.E.C. countries are being cut off by rising tariffs. Until it finds new markets for its exports it will have trouble reducing its inflation rate.

Sweden's figures also point to an uncertain future. By keeping its traditional neutrality, it has not joined the E.E.C. As a result, it is losing ground in many traditional European markets.

Norway voted not to join the E.E.C. But the development of off-shore oil has contributed to the health of its economy.

Which countries are doing well? The world needs a Switzerland – a stable, invisible safety deposit box for its savings that somehow escapes the pressures of the world's economic ups and downs. As long as the Swiss continue banking everyone else's money, they won't have much to worry about. West Germany too has managed to ride out the world economic recession. When you compare the size and complexity of the German economy with the comparative simplicity of the Swiss, you can see that in hard economic terms it is the Germans who have done best of all. Austria has also survived well. Even though it's not in the E.E.C. and can never become a full member for treaty reasons, its economy is tied to that of West Germany.

The Japanese economy is buoyant but its inflation figures are far from excellent – especially compared to West Germany's. Japan made a killing in exports when inflation hit the Western economies. But now Western economies are taking measures to protect themselves against the unlimited flow of underpriced Japanese products.

When we think of banks we often think of getting a loan – but banks are also heavy borrowers. And when banks borrow, they turn to the central government bank: the Federal Reserve system in the U.S., the Bank of England and similar monetary sources in other countries.

Rate of interest at end of:	U.S.A.	CANADA
1965	4.5	4.7
1970	5.5	6.0
1975	6.0	9.0
1976	5.2	8.5
1977	6.0	7.5

The interest rate that the government charges the banks is a crucial figure for the whole economy: it's the base upon which the whole pyramid of other interest rates is built. This figure is generally referred to as the minimum lending rate, but its official title in the U.S. is the Federal Reserve discount rate.

During the economic uncertainties of the recent past, the minimum lending rate in the U.S., as elsewhere, has tended to fluctuate several times in the course of a single year. Whether the rate moves up or down depends a great deal upon how much the government is trying to attract foreign investment capital. Other factors being equal, investors are most eager to lend where they can get the highest return for their money. The disadvantage for the borrower, of course, is that he must pay more for the privilege of using the money.

In times of economic strength, a country tends to lower its minimum lending rate. But a nation that is having problems – a heavy deficit in its balance of payments – will probably offer a high rate of interest as part of its attempt to attract foreign capital. Thus the minimum lending rate is one reliable guide to the general health of a country's economy.

Minimum lending rates often don't vary up or down by more than a fraction of a percentage point. But such a seemingly small shift can still make a costly difference. Investments affected by the change in the rate often run to tens or hundreds of millions of dollars. An adjustment upwards of a half percent means an extra $50,000 in the interest payments on a $10 million loan. When interest rates make a soaring leap of nine percent as they did in Italy between 1975 and 1976 – it means $900,000 extra interest added on to the original $10 million borrowed.

Italy with a rate of 11.5% wins the dubious distinction of having the highest minimum lending rate for 1977. But even that figure is a significant drop from the 1976 rate of 15% – the highest figure in the whole table. These punishing interest rates give some indication of the massive economic problems the Italians have had to contend with in recent years. Only 1976 figures for Ireland (14.7%) and the U.K. (14.2%) begin to approach Italy's lending rates.

The second highest lending rate figure

INTEREST RATES

U.K.	AUSTRALIA[+]	AUSTRIA	BELGIUM	DENMARK	FRANCE	(WEST) GERMANY	IRELAND	ITALY	JAPAN	NETHERLANDS	NORWAY	SPAIN	SWEDEN	SWITZERLAND
6.0	4.8	4.5	4.7	6.5	3.5	4.0	5.9	3.5	5.5	4.5	3.5	4.6	5.5	2.5
7.0	6.3	5.0	6.5	9.0	7.0	6.0	7.3	5.5	6.0	6.0	4.5	6.5	7.0	3.7
11.2	8.5	6.0	6.0	7.5	8.0	3.5	10.0	6.0	6.5	4.5	5.0	7.0	6.0	3.0
14.2	8.7	4.0	9.0	10.0	10.5	3.5	14.7	15.0	6.5	6.0	6.0	7.0	8.0	2.0
7.0	9.7	5.5	9.0	9.0	9.5	3.0	6.7	11.5	4.2	4.5	6.0	8.0	8.0	1.5

in 1977 is for Australia. Since Australia doesn't have an official government lending rate, the numbers here are based on rates for short-term government bonds, which give a roughly equivalent figure. The rate of 9.7% reflects Australia's recent trade problems: higher tariff barriers set up by the European Economic Community have cut her off from many of her traditional markets.

France (9.5%), Belgium (nine percent) and Denmark (nine percent) follow Australia. All three countries had to wrestle with both high unemployment and balance of payments deficits. Though they were not struck by the recession of 1975-6 as hard as the U.K., Ireland and Italy, their recovery has been slower and less complete.

Three countries stand out for their markedly low interest rates – particularly Switzerland with an eye-catching 1.5%. After Switzerland, West Germany (three percent) and Japan (4.2%) have the lowest lending rates.

Compared with world-wide lending rates, the U.S. looks comparatively healthy with a 1977 figure of six percent –

Sources:
Bank of England
International Monetary Fund
+No official interest rate. The figures shown are the rates on short term government bonds for the average period involved.

the same as in 1975. But it's a jump of over three-quarters of one percent since 1976, and reflects the country's growing balance of payments problem.

On the whole, interest rates all over the world have been rising and don't seem likely to return to 1965 levels in the foreseeable future. In most countries (though not the U.S.), rates peaked in 1976 when the world-wide economic recession was at its worst. In 1977, only Switzerland, West Germany and Japan had lower lending rates than in 1965 – another trustworthy indication of the persistent economic strength of these nations, based in the first case on international banking services, and in the latter two, modern industrial and manufacturing methods.

	U.S.A.	CANADA
	1976	1976
National income		
per household (US $ – 000s)	23.7	22.1
per person (US $)	7683	6646

National income figures are designed to show how much a country produces in goods and services in a year. It's a systematic way of looking at all the manufacturing, servicing, buying and selling that's done. It's usually expressed in money terms as the simplest and most direct way of covering a wide variety of economic activities. The per capita income is the national income divided by the population and the household income is the same figure divided by the number of households. Just because a country has a high per capita income, however, don't assume that everyone has the same amount of money to spend. It's only an average figure and doesn't show how that money is spread among the population. The wealth may be in the hands of a very few – as it is in Spain, for instance – and the gap between rich and poor may remain considerable.

It may come as a shock to find that the U.S., considered by most people to be the richest country in the world, is only third in the per capita income figures with an average income of $7,683. We're in third place for household income as well. This position is even more surprising when you consider that we're certainly the richest country on the list in terms of natural resources. The Swiss, who come top of both tables here, have proved that it's not what you've got, it's what you do with it.

We used to associate the Swiss with cuckoo clocks, skiing, chocolate and cheese, but these days they have a reputation as serious and respected bankers. It's this, more than anything else, that puts them right at the top of our table. From all over the world, money has found a home in the secret and inviolate vaults of the Swiss banks. The fabled "gnomes of Zurich" have obviously been taking care of their own interests, too. Today, the Swiss enjoy a per capita income of $9,349 and an income per household of $26,551.

Sweden comes a close second. The Swedes have some of the richest ore deposits in the world which they have no trouble turning into cash. They also have abundant timber and one of the highest agricultural yields per acre in Europe, so they don't have to spend their money abroad. All this adds up to a handy $9,000 per person.

With Norway and Denmark coming fourth and fifth in the table, it's clear that the Scandinavians know how to make money. Denmark has a healthy $7,448 per capita income and it's fairly certain that Norway's figure of $7,494 is more likely to go up than down now that the North Sea Oil is flowing steadily. Generally speaking, the Scandinavians feel that things have improved in the last five years and whatever problems the future holds, it doesn't look as if money is going to be one of them.

INCOME

U.K.	AUSTRALIA	AUSTRIA	BELGIUM	DENMARK	FRANCE	(WEST) GERMANY	IRELAND	ITALY	JAPAN	NETHERLANDS	NORWAY	SPAIN	SWEDEN	SWITZERLAND
1976	1976	1976	1976	1976	1976	1976	1976	1976	1976	1976	1976	1976	1976	1976
11.5	23.4	15.9	21.4	20.3	19.8	19.0	10.3	9.2	15.3	20.9	22.1	11.4	23.8	26.5
3871	6752	5437	6927	7448	6512	7336	2524	2936	4424	6336	7494	2874	9000	9349

Sources:
Government sources

After all the talk about Britain's gloomy economic situation, it probably comes as no surprise to see that the U.K. comes only fourteenth in the league. The per capita income in the U.K. is $3,871, only about half of the U.S. figure, and the income per houshold is $11,536. British figures are well under half of those for the most affluent countries and that means only Italy, Spain and Ireland are less well off than the British. They're right down there with the countries that are traditionally regarded as the underdeveloped, poor cousins of Europe.

Right at the bottom end of the scale comes Italy, Spain and Ireland. These are primarily agricultural countries, with no great banking houses to invite foreign capital and very little industrial development in relation to the population. The small slice of the economic cake that these countries have been able to get is reflected in their per capita income figures. Italy has $2,936 per person, Spain $2,874 and Ireland comes right at the bottom with $2,524. Ireland's figure is only just over a quarter of the Swiss figure. The vicious circle that such poverty sets up has been seen in all three of these countries. Having very little at home to swell the coffers, they've been forced to export their most valuable asset

– manpower. Many of their workers have emigrated and helped to enrich the rest of the world.

The most interesting disparities between per capita and household incomes occur at the bottom of the table. The household income for Italy, for instance, is $9,200 which is lower than either Spain or Ireland ($11,496 and $10,323 respectively.) In the per capita table, Australia comes eighth and Canada ninth but in the household table they have changed their position to fourth and sixth. West Germany which is in sixth place in the per capita income table has, with a household income of $19,073, dropped to 11th in the household table.

Before you rush off to live in Switzerland or Sweden, it might be worth checking with the cost of living table. After you've paid for the *fondue* or *smorgasbord* will there be enough money left for the rent, not to mention the *schnapps*? It looks as though the best deal might still be in the U.S. Though no longer the richest country in the world, the cost of living here is still comparatively modest.

If "diamonds are a girl's best friend" it's no surprise to find that the U.S. – where the song was written – has the most women with best friend baubles. Here 44% of women over the age of 15 own diamond jewelry. And that figure doesn't even include diamond engagement rings.

The Canadians and West Germans are second with 25%. Again, the Canadian figure doesn't include eng-agement rings.

Spain and Belgium rank next, with 20% each, closely followed by the U.K. with 19% – an average figure. Nearly one out of four U.K. women owns a diamond.

Pity the poor girls of Italy: a mere 13% of women over 15 own diamonds.

The top country for average retail price figure is Japan at $818. While comparatively few Japanese women manage to get their hands on a diamond, when they do it's a whopper of a sparkler.

Belgium is second highest in this list. The average price there is $551 – after all, Antwerp is the diamond market of the world. But there's a very feminine reservation: 53% of Belgian ladies who were asked were unable (or unwilling) to give the price of their diamonds. And this vagueness may well be true of other countries. The lowest average figures are for the U.K., where the average price is a mere $193. All the most reliable facts about diamonds are probably in the figures for the total number of pieces of diamond jewelry sold. Here, the U.S. is way ahead: we bought over six million pieces in 1976.

When you compare the number of pieces of diamond jewelry sold each year, as shown on this table, with the country by country female population aged 15 years and over, some fascinating facts emerge. If diamonds were dispersed evenly (and we all know this ain't necessarily so) about one in twelve U.S. women would receive a piece of such

	U.S.A.	CANADA
	1976	1976
1. Diamonds:		
women over the age of 15 who own diamond jewelry (%)[+]	44	25
average retail price (US $) of a piece of jewelry[+]	240	351
total number of pieces of diamond jewelry sold (000s)[+]	6,227	400
2. Gold:		
made into jewelry (lbs - 000s)	147.5	26.9
made into medals, medallions and coins[o] (lbs)	1,543	
made into official[x] coins (lbs)	3,086	24,471

DIAMONDS AND GOLD

	U.K.	AUSTRALIA	AUSTRIA	BELGIUM	DENMARK	FRANCE	(WEST) GERMANY	IRELAND	ITALY	JAPAN	NETHERLANDS	NORWAY	SPAIN	SWEDEN	SWITZERLAND
	1976	1976	1976	1976	1976	1976	1976	1976	1976	1976	1976	1976	1976	1976	1976
	19	NA	NA	20	NA	16	24	NA	13	18	18	NA	20	18	NA
	193	NA	NA	551**	NA	451	338	NA	451	818	NA	NA	NA	716	NA
	420	NA	NA	64	NA	359	1,388	NA	395	862	73	NA	315	495	NA
	++43.2	9.7	4.9	14.6	3.7	53.8	79.4	NA	390.2	104.5	5.3	1.8	100.3	4.0	24.0
	++882	NA	221	661	NA	221	6,614	NA	12,566	2,204	661	NA	6,614	1,323	1,984
	++6,614	221	62,611	6,614	NA	882	NA	NA	1,323	NA	441	NA	NA	NA	7,496

++Includes Ireland   NA not available

**This figure is only approximate, as 53% of people questioned were unable or unwilling to give prices

jewelry each year. Comparable figures for some other countries are: Canada 16.5 women, U.K. 37 and France 47.4.

The other, perhaps more traditional, indicator of wealth is gold. And in the figures for the amount of gold made into jewelry, the U.S. comes a paltry second to poor crisis-ridden Italy where nearly 400,000 pounds of gold was used.

The U.S. figures are still substantial with a good 147,500 pounds melted or beaten down. And in Spain and Japan, over 100,000 pounds of gold was devoted to these end products. The U.K. had just over 43,000 pounds.

Sources:
1 Market Research Surveys
2 Consolidated Gold Fields Ltd, London
+Excludes diamond engagement rings
0Not official government issue
xOfficial government issue

The lowest figures may say something about European taste. Norway is lowest in the table, with just about 800 pounds of gold devoted to jewelry. Next come Denmark and Sweden, each with just about 4,000 pounds.

If you're thinking of trading in your car and have sixty thousand dollars to spare, you could treat yourself to a Rolls Royce. Or why not keep out the winter chills with a sable coat – a mere snip at about eight to 12 thousand dollars. Most people find such luxury isn't quite their style – if only because they can't afford it. The figures in this table show the countries where those with a few thousand to fritter away are only too eager to give house-room to such status symbols. The figures for sable (winter warmth for people who like to be pampered) are for the number of raw sables *imported*, rather than sold. Not all that fur necessarily finds its way on to the backs of the ladies in the countries concerned – some coats will be exported. But any country whose furriers find it worthwhile to import sable *must* house a fair proportion of the well fleeced.

We've read in the press that the U.K. has been suffering from economic difficulties. Even so, 1,450 people in the U.K. still manage to ride high in the comfort of a Rolls. And those 5,700 imported raw sables must help a few of them to keep out the economic draughts.

It seems that a lot of the wealthy in the U.S. also like to sink their money in a Rolls. A thousand of us opted for luxury English-style, rather than something home-grown.

We seem to have a passion for sable,

	U.S.A.	CANADA
	1977	1977
1. Number of cars bought:		
Panther de Ville	3	0
Rolls-Royce	1000	64
Aston Martin (V8 and V8 Vantage)	90+	0
2. Number of raw sables bought+	76,700	NA
as % of all sables bought	76.7	NA

too. We imported 76,700 raw pelts to be made into coats. These must grace the backs of quite a few lucky people.

The Swiss also seem to favor sable, although not as much as we do – they imported 9,400. At least a few Alpine ladies must be defying the weather in a truly chic fashion. But when it comes to Rolls Royces, it looks as if those thrifty Swiss just aren't interested. They bought no Rolls Royces at all during 1977.

The Arabs have no problem as far as running a Rolls is concerned – most of them shouldn't have to go too far to get gas. It's not surprising that 173 lucky Arabs go for a rather more opulent "ship of the desert" than a camel. Understandably, oil-rich sheiks just aren't interested in buying sable for their wives.

The people of New Caledonia don't go for sables either. They're in the tropics, and are sitting on a gold mine of minerals.

WEALTH INDICATORS

U.K.	ENGLAND	NEW CALEDONIA	AUSTRIA	BELGIUM	DENMARK	FRANCE	GERMANY	IRELAND	ITALY	JAPAN	HONG KONG	MIDDLE EAST	NETHERLANDS	SWITZERLAND	OTHERS
1977	1977	1977	1977	1977	1977	1977	1977	1977	1977	1977	1977	1977	1977	1977	1977
4	NA	0	1	0	0	1	2	0	0	0	2	5	NA	2	NA
1450	NA	93	0	12	1	70	70	82	55	0	0	173	NA	0	NA
90[+]	NA	0	0	0	0	0	0	0	0	30[+]	0	0	NA	0	NA
NA	5700	NA	500	NA	NA	400	1200	NA	1000	2400	600	NA	1000	9400	1100
NA	5.7	NA	0.5	NA	NA	0.4	1.2	NA	1.0	2.4	0.6	NA	1.0	9.4	1.1

[+] Estimates   NA not available

Sources:
1 Aston Martin Lagonda Limited, Rolls-Royce Motors Limited, Panther Cars Limited
2 Sojuzpushnina, Moscow
[+] A total of 100,000 raw sables were sold by auction in Russia in 1977. Calculations were based on invoicing and shipping instructions: it was assumed that home consumption of sables in Europe is higher as some dressed skins and ready-made coats are sold back from the U.S.

They have substantial revenue from coffee, too. In 1977, 93 New Caledonians chose to travel to work in nothing less comfortable than a Rolls Royce – compensating them for the discomfort of the tropical heat.

On the other hand, the millionaires of Japan just aren't interested in Rolls Royces. And even when it comes to sables they only bought a moderate 2,400 pelts. Perhaps that famous oriental asceticism dies hard – even for millionaires.

Canada bought a respectable 64 Rolls, according to our table, but no sable at all. (But then, Canadians have plenty of sable of their own, plus other furry things.)

You might think a Rolls is costly, but the Panther de Ville costs about $35,000 more than a Rolls. Only 20 were produced in 1977. Five of these found their way to the Middle East, four to the U.K. and three to the U.S.

Ninety Americans plumped for an Aston Martin along with 90 Britons. The Japanese bought 30: so what *have* they got against the Rolls?

If you work in New York, and your boss tells you you're being transferred to Germany with a whopping 30% increase in salary, don't celebrate – consider quitting instead. Your standard of living will actually drop by 29%. That's what these fascinating figures show. This data is compiled by the ultimate international organization – the United Nations. Their personnel people use it to equitably determine salary rates amongst professional and higher categories of staff all over the world. It's a professional lifestyle cost of living index which is radically different (and we believe much better) than your normal cost of living rating.

There are a number of reasons why this is so. A normal cost of living index is generally more accurate for low income families and is based on a limited number of basic cost factors (meat, bread, etc.). Not so the U.N. data. Instead it's based on a comparable 300 items for each of their 164 countries. And the expenditure on those items (the kinds of things an upper middle class family of three buys) is actually researched amongst their own staff. Secondly, all living standards are expressed in one currency – U.S. dollars – then adjusted for local currency fluctuations, so the index deals with comparable data. Finally the figures are constantly reviewed and are adjusted no less than three times a year. Those shown are for the end of June 1978. For convenience they're indexed to New York.

So much for the background. What do the figures say? The first big surprise is that, today, New York is actually much cheaper than 11 other major cities. Only

	NEW YORK	MONTREAL
	1978	1978
Cost of living[+]	100	80

Ten of the World's Least Expensive Cities	
New York, U.S.	100
1. Moscow, U.S.S.R.	50
2. Colombo, Sri Lanka	50
3. Belize, Belize	60
4. Alexandria, Egypt	65
5. Valletta, Malta	65
6. Cook Islands	70
7. Bratislava, Czechoslovakia	70
8. Tarawa, Gilbert Islands	70
9. Kingston, Jamaica	70
10. Mexico City, Mexico	70

Dublin, Rome and Montreal are less expensive when you take in decent rented accommodation, public transport, gasoline, automobile costs, liquor and other items. A combination of high salaries and comparatively low living costs have combined to produce the comfortable and much-envied "American way of life". The figures certainly prove just how lucky we are. In the E.E.C.'s headquarter town, Brussels, you'd need 61 cents added to every dollar you earn today just to stand still. In Geneva you'd very nearly have to double your salary to level peg, while in Tokyo you'd need $21,000 to equal a $10,000 New York salary's purchasing power.

If you're thinking of fleeing to an exotic tropical country, don't necessarily flee to Zaire to save your bucks – it's almost twice as expensive as New York. On the

COST OF LIVING

	LONDON	SYDNEY	VIENNA	BRUSSELS	COPENHAGEN	PARIS	BONN	DUBLIN	ROME	TOKYO	THE HAGUE	MADRID	STOCKHOLM	GENEVA
	1978	1978	1978	1978	1978	1978	1978	1978	1978	1978	1978	1978	1978	1978
	102	105	145	161	153	142	159	97	90	210	156	100	135	182

Source:
United Nations
+Based on index rating of 100 for New York

Ten of the World's Most Expensive Cities

New York, U.S.	100
1. Tokyo, Japan	210
2. Geneva, Switzerland	182
3. Kinshasa, Zaire	180
4. Brussels, Belgium	161
5. Manama, Bahrain	159
6. Bonn, Germany	159
7. The Hague, Netherlands	156
8. Copenhagen, Denmark	153
9. Muscat, Oman	150
10. Djibouti, Djibouti	150

The two real bargain cities of the world are shown on the other table – Moscow and Colombo (in Sri Lanka – as if you didn't know). Obviously accommodation is a large part of the equation. In Moscow, while rents may be low, you don't choose your apartment – it's chosen for you. So here our diplomatic cost of living presents a relatively false picture. In either city we think you would find that doubling what your dollar can buy is cold comfort when there's not much choice of what to spend it on.

other hand, from a cost of living standpoint, Jamaica's a rather attractive choice.

The price of food varies greatly from country to country. What's more it doesn't always differ as you'd expect.

Americans have always eaten a lot of steak. But an even better place to go for steak is Australia. There a sirloin costs only 94¢ a pound. Along with the Portuguese and the Canadians, we have to pay around twice the Australian price. Our steak averages around $1.97 a pound. Even so it's a lot more expensive in most other countries.

The place not to go if you want a cheap steak is Japan. A pound of sirloin will set you back $7.75 a pound. That's enough to turn the most dedicated carnivore into a vegetarian overnight. Small wonder that an unusually high percentage of Japanese eat mainly vegetarian meals.

If you can't eat steak, how about fish? Unfortunately, and unexpectedly, it's a similar story in Japan. Fresh fish costs an average of just $4.92 a pound. That's almost twice what it costs in Portugal and Italy – the next most expensive countries in the table! These high prices are surprising. All these countries have long coastlines, and are renowned for their excellent fish dishes. In fact, fish is one of the major sources of protein in Japan.

For good inexpensive fish, head for Holland. It has easily the cheapest fish on

The cost (US $) of:	U.S.A.	CANADA
	1976	1976
boned sirloin[+]	1.97[‡]	2.02[‡]
fresh fish[+]	1.56	1.42
white wheat bread[o]	.82	.65
potatoes[+]	.13	. .08
1 egg	.08	.08
cheese[+]	1.81	1.65
pasteurized milk[x]	.23	.29
butter[+]	1.40	1.16
sliced smoked bacon[+]	1.86	1.86
onions[+]	.21	.21
oranges[+]	.45	.27
sugar[+]	.23	.18
coffee[+]	2.20	2.46

the table – 72¢ a pound. Denmark is a near number two at 81¢.

You'd expect fish to be less expensive in countries with long coastlines than in countries with no coastline at all. Yet though fish is reasonably inexpensive in the U.K. ($1.32 a pound), it's even cheaper in land-locked Austria ($1.13).

A very good general indicator of relative food costs is to look at the price of the major sources of calories in most countries – bread and potatoes. They're still the staple diet in many countries in our table, with a few regional exceptions.

As far as the price of bread goes,

	U.K.	AUSTRALIA	AUSTRIA	BELGIUM	DENMARK	FRANCE	(WEST) GERMANY	IRELAND	ITALY	JAPAN	NETHERLANDS	NORWAY	PORTUGAL	SWEDEN	SWITZERLAND
	1976	1976	1976	1976	1976	1976	1976	1976	1976	1976	1976	1976	1976	1976	1976
	2.38	.94	3.80	4.30	3.65	3.34	5.26	2.09	3.00	7.75	NA	3.55	1.75	5.52	3.37
	1.32	1.09	1.13	2.00	.81	1.95	1.44	1.03	2.45	4.92	.72	1.21	2.63	1.77	2.18
	.39	.52	1.14	.87	1.09	.80	.94	.40	.57	.84	.57	.87	.15	1.34	.70
	.20	.23	.07	.17	.25	.22	.20	.14	.22	.20	.20	.19	.11	.21	.17
	.06	.10	.12	.11	.11	.10	.09	.08	.09	.07	.08	.16	.07	.13	.14
	.92	1.01	1.36	1.79	2.04	NA	2.33	1.17	3.81	1.75	1.62	1.32	1.10	1.92	2.54
	.15	.18	.18	.18	.22	.18	.19	.12	.18	.44	.19	.14	.09	.17	.26
	.87	.89	1.46	1.72	1.65	1.72	1.61	.94	2.00	2.16	1.57	1.15	.82	1.13	2.42
	1.45	2.52	.68	1.68	NA	1.48	1.68	1.21	.28	3.10	NA	3.75	.26	3.05	1.87
	.25	.28	.16	.23	.47	.31	.29	.27	.21	.25	.25	.50	.08	.59	.33
	.27	.19	.28	.36	.40	.36	.38	NA	NA	.37	.32	.46	NA	.42	.36
	.45	.15	.23	.27	.07	.25	.29	.21	.29	.38	.28	.30	.27	.36	.33
	2.60	NA	2.81	2.95	3.54	NA	4.06	NA	2.68	NA	2.61	2.80	NA	2.81	2.49

‡With bone   NA not available

Portugal is the cheapest country at 15¢ a large loaf. Ireland, home of the famous soda bread, is also low on the table. Sweden, on the other hand, is worst off. Bread costs $1.34 a large loaf – more than three times the price of Irish bread.

Once the Irish were the greatest potato growers and eaters in the world. But the potato blight came, and there was widespread famine, and a mass exodus. A century later, Ireland is no longer the home of the cheapest potato. The best places to make Irish stew these days are Austria, Canada and Portugal.

Milk, eggs and cheese are staple ingredients in most North American diets. In the U.S. we have to pay a lot more, at 23¢ a pint for our milk – yet we also drink much more. Our cheese is only slightly more expensive than the average – though Switzerland, Germany and Italy pay much more. Finally our eggs are among the world's most reasonable.

Source:
Bulletin of Labor Statistics
+1lb weight
0Large loaf
xPint

	U.S.A.	CANADA
	1976	1976
Household expenditure (%) on:		
food, drink and tobacco	15.3	18.5
rent, fuel, furnishings, household goods and health	28.7	36.6
education, recreation, personal effects and financial other services;	18.8	22.9
car and other transport	30.3	15.0
clothing and footwear	6.9	7.0

Where do all those hard-earned dollars go? Mostly on food and rent. This is true of 15 out of the 17 nations studied. Six spend the most on food, and eight on rent. Norway spends equally on both. With less than four percent of its land under cultivation, it has to import most of its food. Groceries consume three dollars out of every ten spent by the average Norwegian housewife. But that's including tobacco and liquor.

The U.K. and Ireland also have to import a lot of food, which drives the prices up and adds to the high grocery bill. In the U.K., almost one in every three dollars goes for food, drink and tobacco. Ireland, which has a whopping 43.6% expenditure on food, tobacco and drink, spends 11.9% of that figure on alcohol, or nearly four percent of their total household budget. That's under half their expenditure on clothing.

You might expect the French, with their renowned cuisine and wines, to be next on the table. But the Italians beat them to it. A higher percentage of lira goes for *fettucine* and *linguine* than francs go for truffles and *foie gras*. The Italians spend $37.2 out of every hundred they earn, on food. Almost six percent of that goes on liquor.

Ireland and Italy are the big spenders in the food and drink category, with most other countries spending between 24% and 33%. There's a big drop in the figures for North America. Canadians spend only 18.5% in this category. And the U.S. spends even less – only 15 cents, out of every dollar earned in income, get spent on food, drink and tobacco. This doesn't mean we don't eat as well as the French or Italians. We just produce more. Both the U.S. and Canada are more than able to fill their own food requirements. Given a topography that ranges from Arctic to sub-tropical, and efficient transportation and marketing systems that can get Florida oranges to Anchorage supermarkets, it's clear why North America has a unique spending pattern.

Where do we spend the bulk of our incomes? Not surprisingly – on transportation. And a major portion of our transportation bill goes for cars. The U.S. is the most mobile nation in the world (see table on automobiles). An automobile is regarded as more of a necessity than a luxury. A whole sub-culture of services and activities has grown up around the car – drive-in

HOUSEHOLD EXPENDITURE

	U.K.	AUSTRALIA	AUSTRIA	BELGIUM	DENMARK	FRANCE	(WEST) GERMANY	IRELAND	ITALY	JAPAN	NETHERLANDS	NORWAY	SPAIN	SWEDEN	SWITZERLAND
	1976	1976	1976	1976	1976	1976	1976	1976	1976	1976	1976	1976	1976	1976	1976
	31.0	24.9	27.5	28.3	31.1	25.9	28.1	43.6	37.2	31.0	26.4	30.9	33.5	28.5	26.0
	26.6	28.5	32.2	37.8	30.0	34.3	32.1	20.9	27.7	29.2	35.1	30.9	27.1	31.8	31.7
	20.1	16.0	16.0	12.2	20.8	21.0	17.0	14.7	15.1	15.8	18.9	17.2	20.8	18.4	23.5
	13.5	21.0	12.2	14.2	12.1	10.7	11.9	11.1	10.9	13.5	9.9	11.6	9.4	14.0	12.6
	8.8	9.6	12.1	7.5	5.8	8.1	10.9	9.7	9.1	10.5	9.7	9.4	9.2	7.3	6.2

Source:
Euromonitor

movies, drive-in restaurants, drive-in banks, drive-in churches, even drive-in funeral parlors. To support this culture we spend almost one out of every three dollars we earn on our cars – and other means of transportation.

Apart from the U.S., only the Australians spend a significant chunk of their incomes on transportation. Twenty-one percent of their incomes goes towards getting around their vast, sparsely populated country.

Most of the other European countries on the chart spend an average of about 14% on transportation – a much lower rate than the Americans or Australians.

An overall look at the table shows a definite pattern for most countries – the cost of eating and maintaining a roof over the head accounts for about 60% of the total earning expenditures. Belgium spends the most with the combined costs of these two categories totalling over 66%. The cost of housing in Belgium is unusually high – not surprising in a country averaging 1,000 people per square mile.

Most of the householders surveyed spend between 15% to 20% of their total outlay on personal needs, recreation and educational expenses. Again the exception is Belgium, this time with the lowest expenditure (12.2%). Presumably, the overcrowded Belgians don't have enough elbow room to indulge in recreation – or enough money left over after buying the groceries and paying the rent.

Clothing expenses come at the bottom of everybody's list. The French, surprisingly, maintain their famous chic while spending less money on clothing than most countries on the table. The Austrians hand over considerably more for their clothing expenses.

With the myth of Diamond Jim Brady and other "last of the big spenders", it might be assumed that Americans don't save their dough. After all, we're a consumer society. We're strung out on credit. And we're in hock up to our ears making payments on the new decorator, freezer and the latest model car.

	U.S.A.	CANADA
	1975	
Savings (US $):[+]		
total (billions)	813.4	NA
average per person	3780	NA

But it ain't necessarily so. Americans certainly enjoy spending what they earn. And they're great ones for investing in the latest wildcat oil company or a cactus-studded patch of desert in the Arizona sun. But they save money too in old-fashioned savings accounts, for a conservative seven or eight percent a year. In fact, after the Swiss, the Belgians and the Japanese, Americans save more per capita than any other people on the table.

Theoretically, the Swiss are the biggest savers of all, putting away twice the average (or $8,280). Why not? With the Swiss franc the most stable currency in the world, why shouldn't they just hang on to what they've got. In truth, however, not all the money in Swiss savings accounts belongs to the Swiss. Switzerland is the world's safety deposit box. More banks are registered in Zurich than in any other city in the world. The Swiss also have a famous system of numbered bank accounts. With only a number, the owner remains unknown. This particular method of banking is popular with people who want to keep their financial affairs to themselves (nervous despot rulers of foreign states, for example, who want to put something aside for a rainy day, or tax-dodgers or criminals). Even if the tax officers catch you, they can't get your money if it's in a numbered account – especially if no one but you knows it's there.

Japan is second highest on the table, with average savings per head of just over $5,600. This is no great surprise. The Japanese economy is in a boom period and the Japanese work hard to stay on top. At the same time, the Japanese haven't quite developed the consumerism of the West. But there's an historic reason as well. After the war ended, most people in Japan literally had nothing. Many Japanese are old enough to remember this, and such memories die hard. Against such nightmares, money in the bank is the future assured.

The Germans are a curious contrast: they save less than the average on our table. Probably one reason for this is that Germans have not forgotten the notorious inflationary collapse of 1923 when German money became utterly worthless. It took a basket of paper currency to buy a *bockwurst* or a piece of *brot*. Entire savings accounts were suddenly wiped

	GREAT BRITAIN[0]	AUSTRALIA	AUSTRIA	BELGIUM	DENMARK	FRANCE	(WEST) GERMANY	IRELAND	ITALY	JAPAN	NETHERLANDS	NORWAY	SPAIN	SWEDEN	SWITZERLAND
	1976	1976	1976	1976	1976	1976	1976		1976	1976	1976	1976	1976	1976	1976
	115.0	33.4	20.9	38.0	15.0	274.1	180.3	NA	89.4	63.5	26.6	11.6	109.4	51.0	52.6
	2055	2447	2787	3847	2957	2868	2931	NA	1591	5628	1931	2874	1685	3434	8280

NA not available

Source:
International Savings Bank Institute
[+]In banks and savings institutions at the end of 1976
[0]Excludes Northern Ireland

out. Like Americans, (who saw the banks close during the Depression) Germans learned to be wary of banks the hard way. Today, Germans prefer to save by investing in objects whose value won't vanish in an economic crisis. This will probably change as the memory of 1923 fades, and the Deutschmark becomes stronger and stronger.

The U.K. is well below average on this table, with just over $2,000 of savings per capita. Lack of confidence in the pound and accompanying economic difficulties are probable reasons for the small average savings. Traditionally the British think of themselves as a saving nation. But their wages don't always stretch far enough to include a savings account.

The British save even less than the French, who are notorious for preferring to keep their savings under their mattresses or in holes in the ground in the hardest currency of all – solid gold. The Gauls have never been ones to trust their wealth to the local bank. But, as many French learned during World War II, holes in the ground can be a risky way to save. If the head of the family was unlucky enough to be killed, no one else knew whether the gold was under the vegetable garden or the hay.

The worst savers on the table are the Italians. They average around $1,600 a head – about a third less than Americans. The Italians traditionally prefer to invest in land. And with the tumbling lira, many Italians are taking their savings across the border to Switzerland.

Just higher than the Italians are the Spaniards – the only other people with average savings of under $1,700. Spain's relative poverty accounts for this figure – incomes are low and prices are getting higher, leaving few pesetas to stash away in savings accounts. The Netherlands comes next lowest. It throws an unusual light on the thrifty Dutch – especially when you consider the good savings record of their neighbors, the Belgians. Perhaps the Dutch just prefer to keep their cash in diamonds.

When Scott Fitzgerald told Ernest Hemingway: "The rich are different from you and me", he was making a class distinction in terms of money. There are other ways of defining class. In most countries a poverty-stricken poet or artist would be granted higher class status than a materially secure auto worker. The table looks at how people earn their living across the world and places them in four categories: professional and executive; white collar workers; skilled workers; and unskilled workers and manual laborers. The figures only refer to heads of households.

There isn't any doubt as to which country wins for the highest number of professional and executive workers – the U.S., home of "the man in the gray flannel suit", is way out front with 24%.

Almost an identical number of us (23%) are white collar workers. That's the third lowest figure on the table. On the other hand, the figure for skilled workers (33%) is the second highest of the countries shown. In other words, well over half the population falls into either the professional and executive or the skilled worker category.

The Canadian figures closely parallel the situation in the U.S. There's a slightly lower percentage (20%) in top-level jobs, and four percent less skilled workers.

Next to North Americans, the Scandinavians boast the largest number of executive and professional workers, with nearly one in six heads of households in

	U.S.A.	CANADA
	1976	1977
Working population ^{0} **divided into social classes:**		
A professional and executive^X (%)	24	20
B white-collar workers‡ (%)	23	26
C skilled workers** (%)	33	29
D workers^{++} (%)	16	17

jobs with status. But the figures show a surprisingly broad base of unskilled labor when you consider that Scandinavia is a relatively affluent area. In Sweden, 39% of family heads (35% in Norway and 33% in Denmark) are unskilled laborers.

In the U.K. things are better balanced. While 15% rise into the professional and executive class and 27% stick to unskilled or semi-skilled work, 55% opt for skilled manual work, office jobs or small business enterprises.

Italy has more unskilled workers and laborers than any other nation in Europe.

In Ireland, life also seems to be a matter of brute strength – at least for the 45% of household heads who make their money by their muscle. Many of them move temporarily to the U.K. to earn higher wages in the British construction industry. Only four percent of Italians and seven percent of Irish make it into the top category of teachers, doctors, management executives and so on. Earning one's bread by the sweat of one's brow has always been a feature of Italian and Irish life. Only 18% of Italian workers fall

	U.K.	AUSTRALIA	AUSTRIA	BELGIUM	DENMARK	FRANCE	(WEST) GERMANY	IRELAND	ITALY	JAPAN	NETHERLANDS	NORWAY	SPAIN	SWEDEN	SWITZERLAND
	1970	1971	1970	1970	1970	1970	1970	1970	1970	1976	1970	1970	1970	1970	1970
	15	16	9	5	16	9	5	7	4	11	8	16	14	16	13
	26	23	41	35	28	32	44	29	18	29	44	21	36	27	47
	29	37	18	21	23	24	29	19	23	37	26	26	32	17	27
	27	15	27	39	33	30	24	45	52	20	20	35	15	39	15

Source:

"Survey of Europe Today", *Readers Digest*, 1970

[+]Heron House estimates based on I LO figures

[0]Heads of households

[x]People in professions and specialist occupations; employers of ten or more people; em employees at top management or senior executive level

[‡]Employers of less than ten people; self-employed; non-manual workers and non-manual employees of supervizory or lower grade

[**]Skilled manual workers; self-employed semi-skilled workers

[++]Semi-skilled and unskilled manual employees; self-employed laborers

in the scope of the second category on the table: white collar workers. (This category includes small employers, self employed non-manual workers and non-manual employees of a supervisory or lower grade.) Another 23% find work as skilled manual workers and self-employed, semi-skilled workers.

Spain is one of the poorer, less industrialized countries in Europe, yet 14% of Spanish heads of households find their way into some professional or administrative position. Though more than 50% of Spain's income comes from the agricultural products which fill the nation's dinner plates and pull in foreign currency, a mere 15% of Spanish heads of family are manual employees.

Judging by the table the Germans have a pretty hard time making it to the top. In 1970 only five percent of them reached the upper echelons of management and the professions. They appear to have a comfortable middle class with 44% in the ranks of small employers, self-employed or white collar workers. Another 29% earn their living as skilled manual, or self-employed semi-skilled, workers.

Number of cars bought

	1,400
	1,300
	1,200
	1,100
	1,000
	900
	800
	700
	600
	500
	400
	300
	200
	100
	1

We hear a lot about the U.K.'s economic troubles, but the British like to suffer in comfort. They bought 1,450 Rolls Royces in one year, more than anywhere else in the world.

Americans were the next biggest customers for these instant status symbols. One thousand were sold in the U.S. That's still only one for every 200,000 people, so it can hardly be called a fad.

No prizes for figuring out who's next. Those Middle East oil sheikhs bought 173 Rolls Royces. At least the gas is cheap there.

Ninety-three went to New Caledonia. Just in case you're wondering, that's a Pacific island where the natives must be doing something right.

Ireland isn't a very prosperous nation, but 82 Rolls Royces were bought there. Somebody must be finding those pots of gold the leprechauns hide.

Only one lonely Rolls ended up in Denmark. Either the Danes just aren't interested, or they prefer to spend their kroner on local luxuries like aquavit.

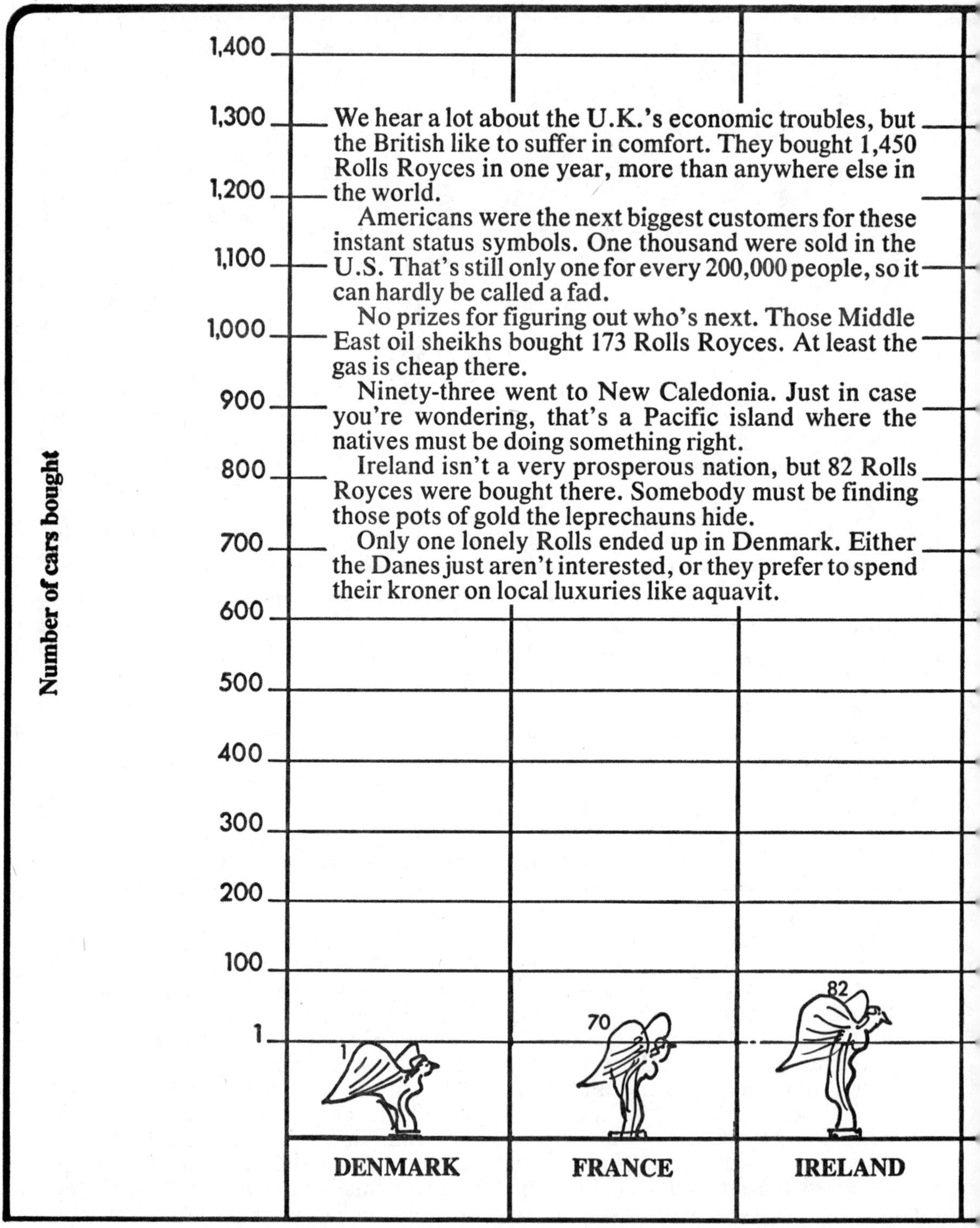

1

70

82

DENMARK	FRANCE	IRELAND

ROLLS ROYCES

NEW CALEDONIA	MIDDLE EAST	U.S.	U.K.
93	173	1,000	1,450

Where the Money Goes

"Government spending reaches new high" scream the headlines. But what does that really mean? Government budgets are written in figures so huge they seem almost meaningless. When you've only thousands to deal with, it's relatively easy to figure out if you'll have enough money to buy a new car next year. But how *does* one decide if it's worth spending $24 billion on a new missile program?

However, if you want to know what your government is up to, you should at least try to comprehend these colossal sums. And it's not really that difficult to think big – as you'll see if you look at the tables in this chapter.

The first table deals with government expenditure. And instead of using those mind-boggling billions we've split the figures up into percentages. This way you can see at a glance what your government's priorities are – as well as how other governments choose to spend their money.

The first list of percentages is for government defense spending. This is something a lot of us question. Why waste all those billions on defense? Do we really need so many intercontinental ballistic missiles, nuclear defense systems, and all that sophisticated arsenal of weaponry? Well, perhaps if the world was a better place we wouldn't. But at the moment world peace seems to be maintained in part by fear – fear of what the other guy can do to you. Every time the U.S. comes up with something new like the neutron bomb, Russia feels obliged to devise something equally awesome. And vice versa.

But the two super powers are the only big spenders in this field. Surprisingly little is spent on defense by most other governments. At least, so it appears. The average for the countries on our list is around ten percent. The U.S., however, shells out a quarter of its budget on military purposes. Still, even ten percent of a multi-billion dollar budget is an awful lot of money – especially when it could be spent on something positive and useful.

Some may look at defense spending in another way – that it's the price we pay for freedom and independence with the government of our choice. So, you could say that most countries use that ten percent of their national budget on giving teeth to democracy – since all the countries in our list are democracies of one kind or another.

Now let's see what else the government squanders our money on. Besides defense, we've also got percentages for government spending in the following categories: health, social welfare and security; public works and housing; law and order, police and justice; public debt; finance; and "other spending".

Surprisingly, almost every country spends more for health, social welfare and security than anything else. The U.S. government is the biggest welfare spendthrift of all with almost half the national budget in this category – 13% more than socialized Sweden, for instance.

Other big figures are for education and public works – and also that anonymous category "other spending", which accounts for over half the government spending in Spain and Belgium. Some countries seem to spend nothing at all on certain activities. Actually this means they don't want to specify the amounts they disburse and put them under "other spending", or turn them into budgets for something totally different. Spain, for instance, is loath to reveal how much she spends on her police, and our own C.I.A. budget has never been disclosed.

Now that you know (almost) how governments of different countries spend their money, it's interesting to find out how much they pass on to the rest of the world. The next table deals with foreign aid, and it shows how generous certain countries are to each other.

Obviously, countries with bigger budgets and a bigger G.N.P. can afford more money. For this reason, we've split up our figures to show spending in terms of percentage of the G.N.P., which gives a picture of the generosity of governments in terms of how much they can actually afford. The table shows how much different countries really care about the rest of the world, especially those less fortunate than themselves.

There's a catch here, however, foreign aid isn't always altruistic. There are often strings attached – such as friendship treaties, trade agreements and so on. Foreign aid doesn't necessairly mean a country wants to be helpful but that it desires to have its influence felt in the world. Today, we no longer have empires, and dominance is a subtle matter of "spheres of influence" and "economic interdependence". So you'll have to decide whether these figures really represent government generosity, or just disguised self-interest!

GOVERNMENT EXPENDITURE

The way a government spends all those hard-earned dollars, pounds, francs or marks that its citizens pay in taxes is one indication of what sort of government it is.

However, figures can be misleading, and those in the table show that the U.S. spends the most on defense – almost a quarter of the national budget. It seems that America is the most militaristic of all the countries represented. This assumption is more or less correct. But look at the next column. According to this, we must also be the biggest welfare state: a whopping 43.7% of our outlay goes to health, social welfare and security. We aren't the biggest welfare state. Many other countries have more comprehensive health and welfare systems than we do, even though they spend less of their budgets on them. The U.K., which lays out 32.5% of its budget for health and welfare, and Sweden (30.4%) both offer much more extensive welfare coverage to their people.

As you look at this table, bear in mind that every country has a slightly different way of reporting its expenditures. For instance, funds the U.S. reports under welfare might be put under the category of community development and housing by another country. In some cases, governments will say they have no expenditures in certain categories. This doesn't mean they spend nothing on the activity. Instead, the expenditure is listed elsewhere. Some nations don't like to be too specific: about half the budgets of Belgium, Spain, Denmark, Norway and Italy are listed under the heading "other expenditure."

In general, most governments spend the highest percentage of their budgets on health, social welfare and security. Australia, the Netherlands and France are exceptions: they spend more on education. And those secretive countries we just mentioned blow it all on "other".

The Australians are the biggest splurgers on education, over 30%. The West Germans (5.2%) and the Danes (8.1%) appear to have low figures for education.

Government expenditure (%) on:	U.S.A. 1976	CANADA 1976
defence	24.6	9.0
health, social welfare and security	43.7	26.9
public works, transport	4.8	3.6
education	5.1	NA
agriculture	0.7	NA
community development, housing	1.5	NA
law and order, police, justice	0.9	NA
public debt	NA	NA
finance	NA	20.8
other	18.7	39.6

	AUSTRALIA[+]	AUSTRIA[+]	BELGIUM	DENMARK	FRANCE	(WEST) GERMANY	IRELAND	ITALY	JAPAN	NETHERLANDS	NORWAY	SPAIN	SWEDEN	SWITZERLAND
U.K.														
1976	1976	1976	1976	1976	1976	1976	1976	1976	1976	1976	1976	1976	1976	1976
10.6	14.0	3.73	7.2	6.4	18.0	20.6	4.4	6.4	6.5	8.2	9.9**	14.9	10.1	20.4
32.5	23.7	25.2	19.8⁰	32.0	17.5	36.6	29.9	8.0	19.3	19.2	26.5**	NA	30.4	18.0
4.7	19.2	26.5	NA	1.5	5.8	7.1	3.6ˣ	2.2	15.9	7.3	12.5**‡	10.3	4.8	18.2
12.5	30.5	9.2	NA	8.1	25.5	5.2	13.5	11.6	12.9	21.6	11.4**	15.3	14.0	9.7
2.0	3.4	2.4	NA	1.1	3.7	1.2	7.1	2.2	NA	4.5	NA	5.3	4.3	9.1
10.7	1.3	0.5	NA	NA	5.3	1.3	NA	NA	NA	6.6	NA	NA	4.9	NA
1.9	NA	3.5	NA	2.3	NA	NA	3.7	0.8	NA	11.3	NA	NA	4.0	NA
9.3	NA	19.5	7.2	NA	NA	NA	20.2	NA	NA	6.7	NA	NA	5.0	NA
1.3	NA	NA	NA	0.1	NA	NA	NA	10.6	16.0	NA	NA	NA	7.0	NA
14.5	7.9	9.4	65.8	48.5	24.2	28	17.6	41.8	29.3	14.6	49.7**	54.2	15.5	24.6

NA not available   ⁰*Includes education*   ˣ*Transport only*   ‡*Communications*
**1978 budget estimates*

But these figures are incomplete – both countries have large, well-equipped school systems. Similarly, the U.S. figure of 5.1% is low because it represents only federal money. Most of the funds for American schools come from state and local taxes.

Next to the U.S., the West Germans and Swiss spend the highest proportion of their budgets on defense. These large military expenditures are understandable. West Germany is right in the front line should a Third World War ever start in Europe. And Switzerland has her traditional neutrality to defend.

Uncle Sam is a piker about doling out money in agricultural programs. Our figure is 0.7% – lowest of all the countries

Sources:
Europa Publications Ltd
[+]National statistical offices

reported. The Swiss are the big butter and egg men here (9.1% of the budget goes to agriculture), followed by the Irish (7.1%) and the Spanish (5.3%). The Netherlands, at 4.5%, is fourth in this category.

We're positive misers, too, in paying for law and order. Less than a cent of every U.S. tax dollar goes to courts and law enforcement agencies. (Only Italy, at 0.8%, spends less.) However, these figures refer to the federal budget – state and local governments pay for most of our policemen and judges.

International aid is global charity on a grand scale with rich countries spending from small to colossal sums of money to help poorer ones.

But countries are as human as the people in them. Strings are often attached to the aid – trade agreements, mutual cooperation pacts, or treaties of alliance. In other words, international aid is often tied to performance clauses.

Aid given through United Nations' organizations is an exception. The United Nations administers their funds independently and its agencies set up and develop schemes of their own.

This is why we have two tables. One gives total governmental development contributions to international aid, the other lists contributions to United Nations' agencies. Sheer size of aid is not the real measure of generosity. The real indicator is the country's contribution as a percentage of its G.N.P.

In 1976, the U.S. gave more than $4.3 billion. But we're by far the largest and richest country in the table with a G.N.P. of $1.5 trillion. So the amount we give in aid is only 0.25 percent of our G.N.P.

Sweden and the Netherlands are the most generous countries in terms of percentage of G.N.P.: both give more

	U.S.A.	CANADA
	1976	1976
1. Governmental development aid (US $ – millions)	4334	886
as % of GNP	0.25	0.46
2. Countries in order of:		
% of GNP allocated to development aid	12	7
per capita GNP	4	3
3. Extra amounts needed (US $ – millions) to equal Sweden/Netherlands	9659	694
4. Government contributions to UN agencies (US $ – millions):	327.0	119.2
as % of development aid	7.5	13.0
5. Government food aid contribution (US $ – millions):	1288	189.6
as % of development aid	30	21

than 0.8 percent. That's $720 million from the Netherlands and $608 million from Sweden. Both countries give around a fifth of their contributions through United Nations' organizations.

Norway is next, giving more than 0.7 percent of its G.N.P., about a third of which goes to United Nations' organizations (the highest proportion shown on our table).

France comes fourth in terms of real generosity. It gives over $2 billion in aid –

	U.K.	AUSTRALIA	AUSTRIA	BELGIUM	DENMARK	FRANCE	(WEST) GERMANY	NEW ZEALAND	ITALY	JAPAN	NETHERLANDS	NORWAY	FINLAND	SWEDEN	SWITZERLAND
	1976	1976	1976	1976	1976	1976	1976	1976	1976	1976	1976	1976	1976	1976	1976
	835	385	39	340	214	2146	1384	53	226	1105	720	218	51	608	112
	0.38	0.42	0.10	0.51	0.56	0.62	0.31	0.43	0.13	0.20	0.82	0.71	0.18	0.82	0.19
	10	9	17	6	5	4	11	8	16	13	1=	3	15	1=	14
	16	9	13	8	6	10	7	15	17	14	11	5	12	2	1
	963	370	292	207	99	693	2276	48	1173	3439	–	34	180	–	373
	51.7	16.4	6.9	24.5	69.1	20.7	76.2	6.7	9.3	75.2	114.4	71.9	13.8	124.4	25.4
	6.0	4.0	18.0	7.0	32.0	0.96	5.5	13.0	4.0	7.0	16.0	33.0	27.0	20.5	23.0
	33.3	35.8	1.1	17.6	22.5	50.2	90.5	2.7	20	8.1	45.2	14	10.0	25.	13.7
	4.0	9.0	3.0	5.0	10.5	2.0	6.5	5.0	9.0	0.7	6.0	6.0	20.0	4.0	12.0

second only to the amount given by the United States.

The U.K. is tenth in terms of percentage contribution from its G.N.P. Even so, the U.K.'s percentage of contributions is higher than that of the U.S. – which has traditionally been considered generous with its aid. The U.S. is generous only in the actual amount given. Canada gives almost twice the percentage we do. In terms of "percentage" generosity, only Japan, Switzerland, Finland, Italy and Austria give less. Along with these countries we surely qualify as the Scrooges of international aid. In order to equal the generosity of the Swedes and Dutch, the U.S. would have to give over three times what it presently does.

Source:
Organization for Economic Co-operation and Development

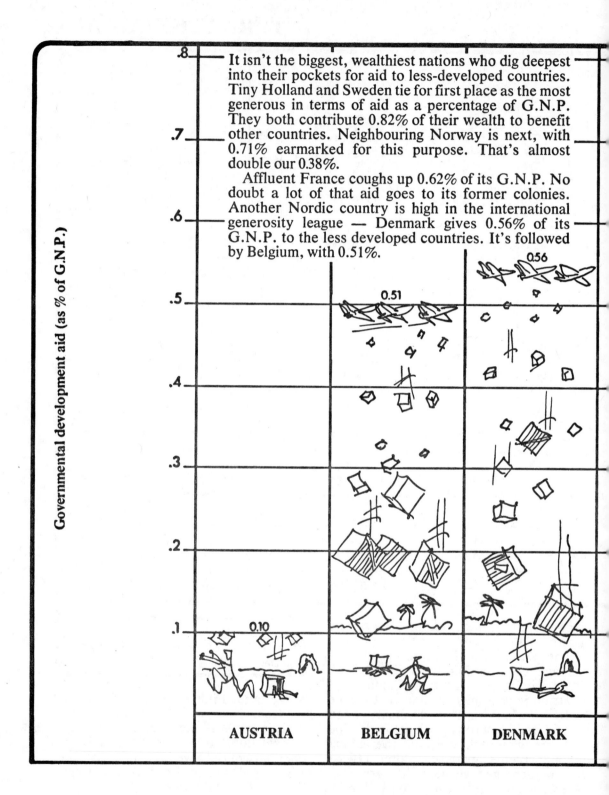

Governmental development aid (as % of G.N.P.)

It isn't the biggest, wealthiest nations who dig deepest into their pockets for aid to less-developed countries. Tiny Holland and Sweden tie for first place as the most generous in terms of aid as a percentage of G.N.P. They both contribute 0.82% of their wealth to benefit other countries. Neighbouring Norway is next, with 0.71% earmarked for this purpose. That's almost double our 0.38%.

Affluent France coughs up 0.62% of its G.N.P. No doubt a lot of that aid goes to its former colonies. Another Nordic country is high in the international generosity league — Denmark gives 0.56% of its G.N.P. to the less developed countries. It's followed by Belgium, with 0.51%.

.8

.7

.6

0.56

.5

0.51

.4

.3

.2

.1

0.10

AUSTRIA **BELGIUM** **DENMARK**

| FRANCE | NORWAY | SWEDEN | NETHERLANDS |

The Taxman Cometh

Have you ever wondered if there's anything you can be absolutely sure of in this fickle world of ours? Well, one thing is tax. Some people – usually the very poor and the shrewd rich – manage to get away without paying income tax, but you'd have to be a complete recluse to avoid the sales tax (or V.A.T. as they call it in Europe). Then, of course, there are death duties, gift taxes, excise taxes. Read on and find out what your friendly taxman has in store for you. You might as well, you'll end up paying him anyway.

The first table shows tax revenue per capita in U.S. dollars. In other words, the total sum of money raised in taxation is divided by the number of people in the population. And remember this includes both direct and indirect tax, i.e. both income tax and sales taxes. So if you've sometimes wondered if anyone could possibly shell out more than you do, here's your chance to find out if it's true.

Moving on, you'll find the next figures in this table show what percentage of the total revenue is raised by income tax. Perhaps you are under the impression that having paid your dues to society, the money you put in the bank is yours and no one else's. Well, if you look at the figures, you might be rather shocked. Not one single country raises 50% of its revenue by direct means. Or put another way, having paid your income tax, there's still a lot more to pay.

What about tax raised on personal income as a percentage of G.N.P.? These figures are also on this table. And remember G.N.P. is a way of showing the monetary value of everything that has been produced in a year from pins to canned tuna, and automobiles to sky-scrapers. These statistics, then, will show how much G.N.P. the government is taking in the way of income tax, so you can see what your contribution is towards the country's economic well-being.

The next figures follow directly on from this and show the total tax revenue as a percentage of the G.N.P. This includes both direct and indirect taxation as well as social security. It will probably come as quite a surprise when you find out how much the friendly social security people are salting away each year!

Having digested all this, would you like to know the actual rates of income tax in various countries? The first figures in this table show what percentage of a single person's income goes in taxes. In the same table, you will also find figures on what percentage social security takes, and then a total of these two as a percentage of the average income. For those of you who're married and – in this instance – it's married with two children, there are other figures. You can draw your own conclusions about whether it's better to be single and pay more tax, or married and pay less. Presumably, that depends on how much it costs to support a family. You can also compare rates and will probably find, no matter how much your tax bite hurts, that you're not paying the highest. Still, the table might cause you to consider emigrating – to the country with the lowest tax rate, of course. Which is? Have a look and find out.

And talking of finding out, have you given much thought to the problem of inheritance tax? As they say, people come and people go, but the taxman he always cometh – bless his little heart. In fact, many more people end up paying inheritance today, than, say, 25 years ago. Not just because the government has possibly raised the rates, but simply because people own more. For example, far fewer people owned a house before World War II, and if they did, it certainly didn't cost $35,000 or $50,000.

If you look at the table, you'll find it's divided into three categories. The first one shows what percentage you would pay the taxman on a $10,000 inheritance and what you'd have left after that, the second on $100,000 and the last one on a million. You'll probably be quite surprised at the number of countries that don't even have an inheritance tax on the first $20,000, or for that matter, those that do! For millionaire readers, this interesting information is worth the price of the book.

Sales taxes are the hardest to avoid: impossible really, unless you want to give up smoking, drinking and just about everything else. If not, you can't help but feed coffers, seeing as just about everything you're likely to buy has sales tax or V.A.T. slapped on top of the basic purchase price.

The next table gives a breakdown of the tax revenues raised from the sale of tobacco and liquor. And if you sometimes wonder what percentage of the total revenue raised by the government comes from taxes on these two items, you'll find figures on that, too. The information's all there, but perhaps you'd rather leave it for another night. Anyone for a drink?

Nobody loves them. But almost everybody has to pay them.

The difference between taxes and other forms of revenue is that taxes are "unrequited". A lot of money goes out – but few tangible goods come back, except in the case of direct welfare or other government payments. What does come back, theoretically, are a lot of social services. Roads, schools, and social service programs of many types. We also pay billions to finance the government bureaucracy, including thousands of civil servants in the Bureau of Internal Revenue.

		U.S.A.	CANADA
		1974	1974
1.	Tax revenue per capita (US $)	1925	2213
2.	Tax on personal income:		
	as % of total tax revenue	33.96	34.95
3.	as % of GNP	9.82	12.16
4.	Total tax revenue as % of GNP:		
	including social security	28.93	34.79
	excluding social security	22.77	31.61

Although taxes are collected for the benefit of all tax payers, the amount paid by each individual is by no means equal to the benefit received. A millionaire industrialist pays much more towards the building of a highway than a small shopkeeper – but they're both entitled to use the road (or hospital, or public swimming pool). On the other hand, for taxes on consumer goods and services, the poor and the rich get docked the same amount.

There are two main classes of taxes – direct and indirect.

Direct taxes are essentially the taxes you pay to federal and state governments. They include individual income tax, levied on personal net income, usually when it rises above a certain basic minimum.

There are four main categories of indirect tax: on consumer goods, including customs duties on many imports; on consumer durables (cars, appliances and other consumer goods); on intermediate goods and production factors (including raw materials), and on certain legal and financial proceedings, such as stock transactions and capital gains. Few stones are left unturned by our alert friends in the taxation bureau.

Who pays the most taxes? The long-suffering Scandinavians cough up the most money – Norwegians, Danes and Swedes each pay an average of more than $2,600 per year, with Sweden at the top of the list with $3,036. The West Germans, the Dutch, the Belgians and the Canadians come next. They are assessed at well over $2,000.

Americans are comparatively well off, paying a per capita average of under $2,000. If you're pathological about the tax collector, the best place to live is Spain. The Spanish pay an average of

U.K.	AUSTRALIA	AUSTRIA	BELGIUM	DENMARK	FRANCE	(WEST) GERMANY	IRELAND	ITALY	JAPAN	NETHERLANDS	NORWAY	SPAIN	SWEDEN	SWITZERLAND
1974	1974	1974	1974	1974	1974	1974	1974	1974	1974	1974	1974	1974	1974	1974
1215	1473	1668	2109	2789	1902	2326	716	860	945	2321	2605	461	3036	1998
35.17	40.07	24.20	29.36	53.37	10.83	30.49	22.92	15.24	24.17	27.61	27.49	12.93	45.05	34.72
12.51	10.89	9.23	11.19	24.91	4.06	11.47	7.43	4.86	5.36	12.48	12.44	2.43	19.90	9.10
34.56	27.18	38.14	38.13	46.68	37.50	37.64	32.43	31.86	22.18	35.18	45.27	18.83	44.21	26.11
29.47	27.18	28.41	26.11	44.00	21.77	24.39	28.65	18.55	17.60	27.76	32.09	10.42	35.68	18.81

$461 per person. But then they don't earn much.

The figures for taxes on personal income as a percentage of total taxation show how much of the per capita tax revenue is levied in the form of direct income tax. The results largely echo those of the previous table. The people who provide the highest proportion of tax revenue tend to pay a higher percentage of it as income tax. The Danes are at the top of the list – over 53% of the taxes they pay are as income tax. The Swedes are second, paying 45%. The Spanish pay less than 13%. And the French lowest, less than 11% – although they rank ninth in amount of tax revenue per capita.

The next figures on this table show what percentage of the taxes paid by the citizens of each country contribute to the Gross National Product. In Sweden, income and other personal taxes account for almost 20% of the entire GNP. Spain's figure is under three percent.

Source:
Organization for Economic Co-operation and Development

This table shows how much of your paycheck goes to Uncle Sam, and how much people in other countries pay in taxes to their governments. American rates are about average – although married couples with children are given more tax credit than in some other countries.

The Danes have the worst deal. In Denmark single people turn over an average of 43% of their paycheck. If you are a Dane earning $100 a week, you'd take home only $57, losing nearly half what you earned to the government. Even if you were married and had two children, you'd still give 38% of your salary to the state. That's the same rate a single person pays in Sweden – the second highest rates on the table. If you were a married Swede with two children, you'd get a bit of a better deal, paying 33%.

Where does it pay to have marriage and a family? Austria gives a whopping average tax credit of 12% to married couples with children (compared to the average tax rate for single persons). Germany is next with ten percent, followed by the U.S. and Ireland with nine percent and the U.K. with eight percent. Surprisingly, two of the most family-oriented countries in the world – Italy and Spain – offer no tax credit for families regardless of their size.

	U.S.A.	CANADA
	1974	1974
1. Tax paid by a single person:		
average rate of taxation on personal income (%)	20	19
social security rate (%)	6	2
total (%)	26	21
2. Tax paid by a married couple with two children:		
average rate of taxation on personal income (%)	11	14
social security rate (%)	6	2
total (%)	17	16

At 33% average single tax rate, West Germany and Norway run a close fourth place on the table. The U.K., where everybody complains about high taxes, is only sixth on the table.

For an accurate comparison, tax rates should be compared to wage rates and the cost of living index for each country. Higher wages and lower tax rates in the U.S. mean more money in the pocket than in most European countries. When it comes to buying groceries and paying rent, it's take-home pay that counts. A primary school teacher in the U.S. earns about twice as much as one in the U.K. or

TAX RATES

U.K.	AUSTRALIA	AUSTRIA	BELGIUM	DENMARK	FRANCE	(WEST) GERMANY	IRELAND	ITALY	JAPAN	NETHERLANDS	NORWAY	SPAIN	SWEDEN	SWITZERLAND
1974	1974	1974	1974	1974	1974	1974	1974	1974	1974	1974	1974	1974	1974	1974
25	21	13	12	39	8[x]	19	20	5	10	15	25	3	36	12
6	–	13	11	4	8	14	4	7	4	20	8	4	2	10
31	21	26	23	43	16	33	24	12	14	35	33	7	38	22
17	16	1	10	34	NA	9	11	5	5	11	20	3	31	9
6	NA	13	11	4	8	14	4	7	4	20	8	4	2	10
23	16	14[‡]	21	38	8	23	15	12	9	31	28	7	33	19

[x] Does not take account of communal taxes (ie Taxe d'Habitation)
‡ Tax credits wholly or partially cancel out the tax liability

Source:
Organization for Economic Co-operation and Development

Germany, and pays five to seven percent less in taxes.

Which country is best in terms of keeping your income in your pocket? In Spain a single person pays only seven percent of his total earnings. But he doesn't get a tax break if he's married with two children.

The Italians have the second-lowest tax rates. Single people pay only 12% of their wages, but get no relief if they're married with two children. Low-paid workers with heavy family expenses pay the stiffest penalty – a fact which may contribute to social unrest. Italy also suffers from a marked discrepancy in wages. The top of the wage scale isn't particularly high compared to other countries – but the lower end of the scale is very low. A primary school teacher in Italy earns a mere 25% of an American doing the same job.

Inheritance taxes aren't easy to calculate or compare. Most countries have systems which allow for innumerable deductions and exceptions before tax is payable. This can reduce the amount considerably. And many people (perhaps the wisest) leave such small sums that no tax has to be paid on them.

Different rates of tax may apply depending on who inherits the money. Generally, the tax system favors close relatives. More duty may be payable if an estate is left to distant relatives, or friends. Our table shows minimum inheritance taxes. In many cases, the amounts are much higher.

Which countries demand the highest death taxes? Look first at the tax payable on the lowest of the figures in our table – an estate worth $10,000.

In the U.S. you don't pay anything on an estate of $10,000 – something to remember when you're on your last shopping spree.

Japan and Canada have the highest levels of inheritance tax (11%) with Spain (ten percent) close behind. If a Japanese or Canadian leaves $10,000 to his children, they'll end up with $8,900 after paying taxes to the government.

In Australia, Denmark, Ireland and the U.K. (as well as the U.S.), no tax is paid on estates worth $10,000.

It's a different story if you leave a $100,000 estate. This figure isn't as large as it seems, since it's tax based on the value of the whole estate, not just cash in the bank. A small business could be worth that. Or a home with furnishings.

In the $100,000 range, the Swedes pay the highest rate of inheritance tax, an astonishing 53.5%. If a successful Stockholm businessman dies and leaves $100,000 to his wife, she'll end up with only $46,420. With the cost of living what it is in Sweden, she'll need every kroner of it.

The U.K. comes second with a death duty of 35%. This may be less than Sweden, but it still means that only $65,000 is left from a $100,000 inheritance. In other words it costs $35,000 for family assets or business to be passed on to the next generation. American beneficiaries pay 15.6% and end up with $84,400. Canadians are even better off: they pay 11% and are left with $89,000.

Ireland is at the top or bottom of the league, depending on whether you're the heir or the tax collector. In the Old Sod you keep every penny of the $100,000 left to you. Other countries with low death duties are Switzerland (4.5%) and West Germany (six percent). In these countries there's little difference between tax

Inheritance tax[X] (as % of total estate) paid on:	U.S.A.[+]	CANADA[°]
$10,000	0	11.0
amount left (000s)	10.0	8.9
$100,000	15.6	11.0
amount left (000s)	84.4	89.0
$1,000,000	33.4	19.0
amount left (000s)	666	810

U.K.	AUSTRALIA	AUSTRIA	BELGIUM	DENMARK	FRANCE	(WEST) GERMANY	IRELAND	ITALY	JAPAN	NETHERLANDS	NORWAY	SPAIN	SWEDEN	SWITZERLAND
0	0	2.5	3.0	0	5.0	3.0	0	5.0	11.0	9.0	8.0	10.0	7.5	3.0
10.0	10.0	9.8	9.7	10.0	9.5	9.7	10.0	9.5	8.9	9.1	9.2	9.0	9.3	9.7
35.0	7.0	7.0	10.0	15.7	20.0	6.0	0	16.0	24.2	15.0	30.0	13.0	53.5	4.5
65.0	92.9	93.0	90.0	84.3	80.0	94.0	100.0	84.0	75.8	85.0	70.0	87.0	46.4	95.5
65.0	26.3	12.0	17.0	29.9	20.0	12.0	29.1	45.0	52.5	17.0	35.0	19.0	53.5	6.0
350	737	880	830	701	800	880	708	550	475	830	650	810	464	940

rates on small and medium estates.

On estates of $1,000,000, the inheritance tax rate in the U.S. more than doubles to 33.4%. That means you'd pay a whopping $334,100 if you were lucky enough to die a millionaire. Canadian millionaires do somewhat better, paying a mere $190,000 for the privilege of passing on – a difference of $144,000.

The most striking contrast between progress rates of inheritance tax is found in Switzerland and the U.K. In Switzerland, inheritance tax is paid at a low rate regardless of the size or value of the estate. In the U.K., tax is minimal on small estates – then soars.

A U.K. estate worth $1,000,000 is taxed at a rate of 65%. If an Englishman dies and leaves his $1,000,000 castle to his heirs, only $350,000 will remain to be shared out after tax.

Switzerland is at the low end of the table; inheritance tax on $1,000,000 is just six percent, up only three percent from the tax rate on $10,000. This means that a Swiss left a $1,000,000 estate pays only $60,000 in tax – almost $600,000 less than his U.K. counterpart. Inheritance taxes

Sources:
Official government documents
×1978 figures
Figures are illustrative calculations, by Heron House. They show how much inheritance tax would be paid if the entire estate were left to the spouse and/or children – the lowest-rated category.
+State death tax, unified rate schedule
0In Ontario

are a way of dividing a country's wealth among more of its people, and Switzerland's considerable riches are shared comparatively equally in the first place. In the U.K. a much higher proportion of money and property is in the hands of relatively few individuals.

Whatever the reason for inheritance taxes, the contribution they make to a country's total tax revenue is small. In the U.S., where just over 33% of a $1,000,000 estate goes in tax, inheritance taxes account for about 1.4% of the total federal tax. Even in the U.K. it only amounts to about 1.3% of the total tax income – a very low figure.

It hurts to see what a big chunk the government takes out of your paycheck every week, but what you don't see can hurt too. When you go to spend your pay you'll be giving away a percentage of every dollar in indirect or "hidden" taxes. Included in the price of every bottle of liquor, pack of cigarettes or gallon of gasoline is a substantial tax for Uncle Sam. (He even makes you pay for the bubbles in your champagne – sparkling wines are taxed at a higher rate than still wines.)

	U.S.A.‡	CANADA‡
	1977	1977
VAT+ or sales⁰ tax rates:		
standardˣ	4-5	7-8
reduced‡	na	5.0
highest**	7.0	10.0

In the U.K. and the European Common Market countries they use a system called Value Added Tax or VAT for short. This tax is added to consumer items at each stage of production. For instance, when a steel mill buys iron ore a tax is levied on the ore and then a tax on the finished steel, then a tax on whatever is made from the steel, and so on.

When you buy something in France, you hand over 23 cents of every dollar to the government. Why France should take such a huge bite is hard to fathom, but perhaps it's because Frenchmen are such notorious income tax evaders. Bad luck, *Messieurs*, but you can't win against the taxman.

If you don't like paying taxes, move to Alaska, New Hampshire or Oregon, where they have no sales tax at all. Or perhaps you'd prefer sunny Spain, which taxes purchases at a lowly two percent. The Spanish know how to keep those tourists pouring in – a Bacardi and Coke costing 25 cents instead of $1.50 makes for much happier holiday spirits. After Spain, the U.S., where state sales taxes average four percent to five percent (except in the three states just mentioned) takes the smallest bite out of every consumer dollar. The tourist-minded Swiss are also lenient with retail purchasers – their sales tax is 5.6%.

Canada (seven percent to eight percent) and the U.K. (eight percent) are the only other countries to show any mercy for shoppers. All the others in the list have sales taxes well above ten percent.

One trouble with the sales tax, from the point of view of economists and social planners, is that it puts an unequal burden on the poor. Income taxes are graduated, with the rich paying the largest percentage of their income and the poor the lowest, or none at all. But sales taxes hit everyone the same. A lowly French chambermaid buying a cheap pair of slippers has to endure the same 23% tax bite as a multi-millionaire industrialist buying silk or brocade curtains for his 50-room chateau.

To soften this inequity, many countries impose a reduced rate of taxation on

U.K.	AUSTRALIA ‡	AUSTRIA	BELGIUM	DENMARK	FRANCE	(WEST) GERMANY	IRELAND	ITALY	JAPAN	NETHERLANDS	NORWAY	SPAIN	SWEDEN	SWITZERLAND
1974	1974	1977	1977	1977	1977	1977	1977	1977	1977	1977	1977	1977	1977	1977
8.0	15.0	16.0	18.0	18.0	23.0	11.0	16.37	18.0	15.0	14.0	20.0	2.0	17.65	5.6
na	2.5	8.0	6-14	15.0	7.5	5.5	4.5	1-35	5.0	4.0	na	22.0	na	1.8
12.5	27.5	18.0	25.0	na	33.33	na	30.26	35.0	30.0	18.0	na	33-110	60.0	8.4

na not applicable   ++*Sales tax*

Sources:
Government documents
+Sales tax on consumer goods or services at each stage of production or distribution; a VAT-registered individual or company can claim rebate on VAT paid in the course of business.
0Not rebatable; US figures are illustrative as an additional sales tax is levied by certain cities and counties.
xGeneral rate applied to sale of most consumer goods and merchandise
‡Applied in some countries on certain goods, e.g. food in France
**Highest rate applied to "luxury goods", e.g. cookers, cameras, radios, etc.

necessities such as food, or exempt them entirely from taxes.

Another way to even things out is to soak the rich – via special taxes on luxury items. Spain which is lowest in standard sales tax, has the highest luxury taxes of all: a whopping 33% to 110%, depending on the item being purchased. They go particularly heavy on imported automobiles. A $60,000 Rolls Royce, for example, would cost you $126,000 in Madrid. (No wonder you don't see too many of them around the city – nor for that matter many Cadillacs either.) Sweden is also very high. At 60% a $12,000 mink coat would sell for $19,200 in Stockholm.

This table is all about booze and cigarettes – how much they cost and why.

Take cigarettes, for instance. On average, the cost of manufacturing a pack of cigarettes runs between 18 and 35 cents. In Spain, France and Italy, costs are even lower (Spain produces 20 cigarettes for about only eight cents). Norwegian cigarettes are the costliest to manufacture at 68 cents a pack. If you buy cigarettes in any of these countries, the prices you'll pay will vary widely.

Taxes on tobacco are an important source of revenue to all nations' governments.

Where are cigarettes cheapest? In Spain you can buy a pack for just 22 cents. Japanese cigarettes are cheap as well, about 52 cents – six cents a pack less than in Italy.

Prices in the U.S. vary from state to state and city to city because of differences in local taxes, but they average 55 cents a pack, a low price compared to other countries.

A pack of cigarettes costs about a dollar in the U.K., which is average for our list – although this doesn't stop the British complaining about the price.

Perhaps those British moaners should try visiting Denmark. Here the average pack of cigarettes costs a colossal $2.42.

		U.S.A.	CANADA
		1974	–
1.	Tax revenue[+] (US $ – millions) from the sale of:		
	tobacco	6250	NA
	liquor	8428	NA
2.	Tax revenue[+] (as % of total revenue) from the sale of:		
	tobacco	1.53	NA
	liquor	2.07	NA
		1978	1978
3.	Average retail price (US $) of a pack of 20 cigarettes[0]	0.55	0.67
	excluding taxes	0.19	0.23
4.	Estimated tax as % of the retail price	55-75	55-75
5.	Average retail price (US $) of bottle of Scotch whisky[x]	7.43[++]	7.78
	excluding taxes	4.60[++]	2.64
6.	Estimated tax as % of retail price	38[++]	66

In Norway, the second most expensive country in our list, cigarettes cost $1.96. Sweden charges $1.49. Then comes West Germany at $1.29 and Belgium at $1.22.

In Ireland, nearly eight percent of national revenue is supplied by smokers, almost double the rate for the next country in the list – the U.K.

Who pays the most for another pleasure in life – Scotch? Again, the poor

LIQUOR AND TOBACCO TAXES

	U.K.	AUSTRALIA	AUSTRIA	BELGIUM	DENMARK	FRANCE	(WEST) GERMANY	IRELAND	ITALY	JAPAN	NETHERLANDS	NORWAY	SPAIN	SWEDEN	SWITZERLAND
	1974	–	–	1974	–	1974	1974	1974	–	1974	–	1974	–	1974	1974
	2998	NA	NA	317	NA	1386	4087	175	NA	2390	NA	184	NA	547	162
	2589	NA	NA	228	NA	1461	2723	265	NA	3468	NA	342	NA	976	168
	4.40	NA	NA	1.54	NA	1.39	2.83	7.96	NA	2.30	NA	1.78	NA	2.21	1.78
	3.80	NA	NA	1.11	NA	1.46	1.89	12.06	NA	2.78	NA	3.30	NA	3.94	1.30
	1978	1978	–	1978	1978	1978	1978	1978	1978	1978	1978	1978	1978	1978	1978
	1.00	0.62	NA	1.22	2.42	0.42‡	1.29	0.78	0.58	0.52‡	1.16**	1.96	0.22‡	1.49	0.82
	0.30	0.22	NA	0.34	0.31	0.11	0.37	0.30	0.15	0.26	0.36	0.68	0.08	0.52	0.28
	70	55-75	NA	72	87	73	71	62	74	50	69	55-75	55-75	55-75	55-75
	8.04	9.77	9.84	6.69	16.18	7.60	7.81	8.88	4.97	10.16	6.79	17.37‡	10.62	15.49‡	17.14
	1.77	4.88	NA	2.87	NA	2.88	4.37	NA	2.43	5.99	NA	NA	5.31	NA	NA
	78	50	NA	57	NA	62	44	NA	51	41	NA	NA	50	NA	NA

‡ NA not available ++ For New York 00 For Ontario
‡ State monopoly ** A pack of 25 cigarettes

Norwegians seem heaviest hit by the taxman. They pay $17.37 for a bottle compared to $17.14 in Switzerland and $16.18 in Denmark. We Americans get off cheaply at $7.43, while our Canadian neighbors pay $7.78. In the U.K., where Scotch is actually produced, the price averages $8.04 a bottle. Thirsty Scotsmen have to travel to Italy if they want Scotch. There it's only $4.97 a bottle.

Sources:
1 & 2 Organization for Economic Co-operation and Development
3, 4, 5 & 6 Confidential industry sources
+ All taxes levied on production, sale, leasing, delivery of goods, etc.
0 Popularly-priced brand
X Standard brand; 26 ounces

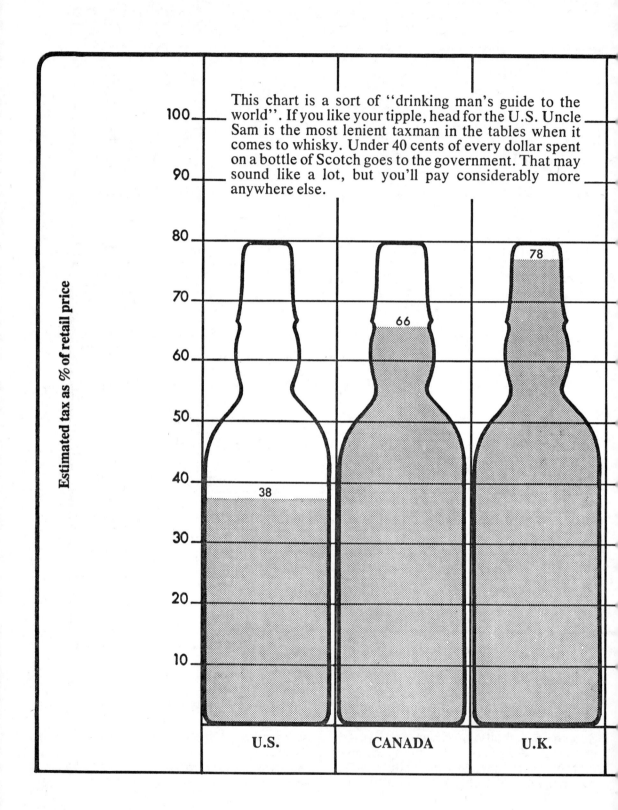

Estimated tax as % of retail price

This chart is a sort of "drinking man's guide to the world". If you like your tipple, head for the U.S. Uncle Sam is the most lenient taxman in the tables when it comes to whisky. Under 40 cents of every dollar spent on a bottle of Scotch goes to the government. That may sound like a lot, but you'll pay considerably more anywhere else.

100

90

80

78

70

66

60

50

40

38

30

20

10

U.S.   CANADA   U.K.

TAX ON WHISKY

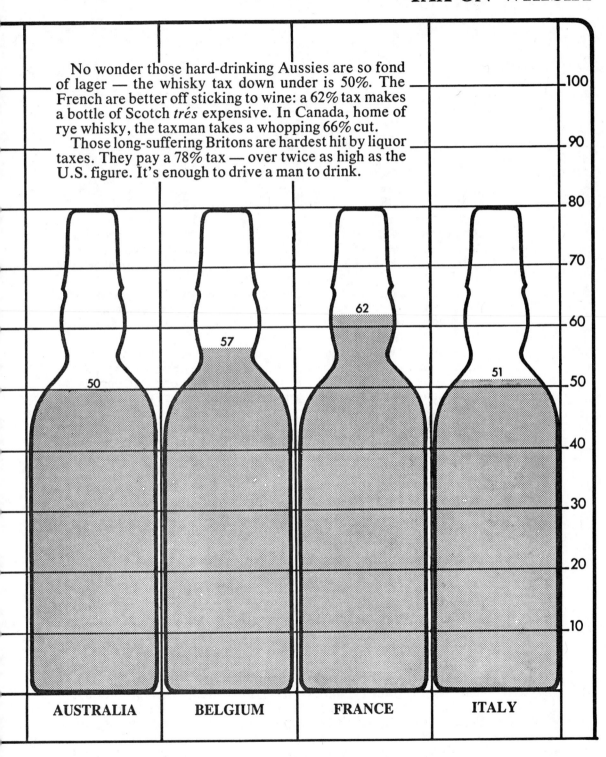

No wonder those hard-drinking Aussies are so fond of lager — the whisky tax down under is 50%. The French are better off sticking to wine: a 62% tax makes a bottle of Scotch *trés* expensive. In Canada, home of rye whisky, the taxman takes a whopping 66% cut.

Those long-suffering Britons are hardest hit by liquor taxes. They pay a 78% tax — over twice as high as the U.S. figure. It's enough to drive a man to drink.

| AUSTRALIA | BELGIUM | FRANCE | ITALY |

50 57 62 51

100 — 90 — 80 — 70 — 60 — 50 — 40 — 30 — 20 — 10

At Work

If there's one thing that's virtually as certain as taxes and death, it's work. Most of us spend more of our lives working than involved in any other single activity. So it's a subject worth finding out about. This chapter shows you, around the world, who works, and at what and for how much. It also gives all sorts of comparative data, so, if you're foot-loose and fancy free with top secretarial skills, you may well read the working chapter with special interest. Even if your primary aim in life is to avoid work, there's still a few useful facts – you can find out where unemployment is highest, for instance.

Our first table shows what people do in the way of work in the 17 countries we cover. For example, how many people work on the land, compared with those who work in manufacturing, in mines or in construction.

The table also gives you an insight into the working priorities each country has and its stage of development. For instance, it's interesting to see that the U.S. is now a service oriented society. Sixty-seven percent of the work force are employed in some form of service. So two out of every three of us are busy waiting on one another while the third guy is producing the goods.

The next table gives you facts on the total workforce and divides it into three revealing categories. First, it shows how many people are wage earners and salaried staff – in other words how many work for someone else. Next, it shows how many people are employers or are self-employed – that is, how many bosses there are, and how many prefer to remain their own boss. And then it shows how many people are unpaid family workers – mostly family members and dependents who help out around a business or farm but receive no specific remuneration.

Now that you know how many people work and what they actually do in the way of work, it's interesting to know how many people there are in each country who can't get work. That's what the third table in the chapter is about. It has quite a few shocks. For example, here in the U.S., the world's largest and strongest economy, we have the highest rate of unemployment amongst all countries covered.

Then there's the question of productivity – how much each individual worker produces. In other words, in raw cash terms, how much does each worker actually contribute, on average, to the total earnings of his country? That's what the next table is all about. This isn't an easy topic to discuss. All kinds of factors play a part – worker efficiency, industrial plan efficiency, management planning, incentives and (in some cases) restrictions on the number of hours which can be worked.

Causes aside, the results speak for themselves – they show that, in many ways, America is by no means the most efficient country in the world today.

Mention steel production at a cocktail party and you're apt to encounter complete silence. But steel is the basis of the West's industrial might, so the figures in the following table on steel production and consumption are an important indicator of the relative strength of various countries' economies. As in almost all of our tables, there are one or two surprises here. And the accompanying text provides some interesting insights.

One of the reasons we work is to go on vacation. So we've included some interesting comparisons on paid vacation days. But one of the most basic reasons most of us work is to earn money. *That's* what the next tables are all about. Where can you get the highest average earnings per hour? Where are people paid the least? And the accompanying text also shows you how to get an idea of how much this cash is worth in terms of actual spending power.

The next table breaks down these overall figures by comparing the earnings in different countries for six different occupations. Here, for instance, you'll find out how much a female textile worker in New York earns in comparison with a construction worker, and also how much she earns in comparison with her counterparts in Madrid or Zurich.

No chapter on employment would be complete without an account of industrial strife – strikes. Which people are most strike-prone? Where do most workers go on strike? And which countries lose the largest number of working days through strikes? The section which follows has all the details.

Finally ,we've tables which profile how safe it is to go to work and also how much you'll have squirrelled away when you retire in any of the countries on our list.

We've divided types of work into several sections to compare how many people do what type of work in which countries. The categories are divided broadly by agriculture, mining, manufacturing, utilities, construction and services – with a catch-all category called "other".

Most of the countries on the table are industrial nations. But in Ireland one person in every four lives off the land or sea – the highest figure in that category on the table. Almost as many Spaniards are country-dwellers. Compare these percentages with the U.K., where about one person out of every 38 in the workforce farms or fishes for a living. Or the U.S., where a scant four percent of the workforce supplies enough food, fish and timber to support the entire country. That means that one U.S. farmer or fisherman feeds about 62 people.

After Ireland and Spain, Italy, Austria and France have the highest percentage of the workforce engaged in agriculture, fishing and forestry. They've got more open land than most of the other countries on the table. In France and Italy the agricultural tradition has maintained in several areas, while industrialization has developed elsewhere.

Mining and quarrying occupy few workers in all the countries on the table. (The list would change dramatically if South Africa and Zaire were included.)

	U.S.A.	CANADA
	1975	1975
1. Total working labor force[+] (000s)	84,783	9171
2. Percentage of working labor force[+] employed in:		
agriculture, hunting, forestry, fishing	4.0	6.1
mining, quarrying		1.4
manufacturing	29.0	20.9
electricity, gas, water		1.1
construction		6.5
services[o], others	67.0	64.0

But roughly a third of the workforce of the countries listed is involved in manufacture – producing the volumes of hard and soft goods that have changed the nature of our values and our ways of life.

Switzerland has almost half of the workforce involved in manufacture, power industries and construction. (The rest are either herding their Swiss Brown over the edelweiss or minding everyone else's money in the banks.) West Germany has 36% involved in manufacturing – roughly one in every three workers. We all know what they're up to – making sure the post-war economic miracle survives into the 21st century.

In the U.K., Austria, Belgium, France, Italy and Sweden, about three in ten workers are employed in manufacturing. The lowest figure on the table

LABOR FORCE: ACTIVITIES

	U.K.	AUSTRALIA	AUSTRIA	BELGIUM	DENMARK	FRANCE	(WEST) GERMANY	IRELAND	ITALY	JAPAN	NETHERLANDS	NORWAY	SPAIN	SWEDEN	SWITZERLAND
	1975	1975	1975	1975	1975	1975	1975	1975	1975	1975	1975	1975	1975	1975	1975
	24632	5726	2943	3748	2332	20764	24828	1030	18818	52230	4535	1694	12692	4062	2784
	2.7	6.7	12.5	3.6	9.8	11.3	7.3	24.5	15.8	12.7	5.0	10.2	22.1	6.4	7.9
	1.4	1.4	1.2	1.0	0.1	0.9	1.4	1.0	1.8	0.3	0.2	0.7	0.8	0.5	
	30.9	23.6	30.1	30.1	22.7	27.9	35.8	20.4	32.6	25.8	24.0	23.8	26.7	28.0	45.0
	1.4		1.2	0.9	0.6	0.8	1.0	1.4	NA	0.6	1.0	1.0	0.7	0.8	
	7.1	8.8	11.9	7.9	8.1	9.1	7.7	6.9	9.8	9.2	9.6	8.7	10.0	7.1	
	56.5	59.5	43.1	56.5	58.7	50.0	46.8	45.9	40.0	51.5	60.1	55.6	39.7	57.1	47.1

NA not available

for manufacture is Ireland – consistent with the high Irish rate of fishing and agriculture. Surprisingly, in industrial Japan, only one in four in the workforce is involved in manufacturing – ten percent less than in West Germany.

Neither Canada nor Denmark employs a lot of people in manufacturing. But many Canadians and Danes work in the service industries – covering everything from wholesale and retail sales to restaurants, banking, social services and tourism. In Canada two out of every three workers are employed in a service industry.

But the percentage in the U.S. is even higher. Sixty-seven percent of the U.S. workforce provides a service of some kind. This may be an indication of the growing "softness" of the U.S. and other economies (as compared to the "hardness" of manufacturing actual goods). But it also could be evidence of a world economic trend away from essentials to "luxuries" of one sort or another. First you need food. Then you need autos, detergents and appliances. Then you need services that make life a little easier and more indulgent – like having a hamburger delivered to your door.

Source:
Organization for Economic Co-operation and Development

+Civilians only; excludes members of the armed forces
OWholesale and retail trade, catering, business services, etc

111

Most people work, and most people work for someone else. Are you a boss, or a mere cog in the machinery? Self-employed, or a wage-slave?

The first category in our table deals with the total number of people at work (excluding members of the armed forces). Not surprisingly, the U.S. tops the table. There are a lot of potential workers in a population of over 200 million. Of course, capital has to be added to this potential – in the form of equipment and know-how, to transform it into economic wealth.

What better proof of this than the second-ranking country on the table – Japan? It wasn't until the post-war years and the introduction of modern technology that the vast labor force there was equipped to create material prosperity.

Of course, modern methods of production involve highly organized workforces directed towards a common goal. And that's the antithesis of self-employment.

The highest proportion of people who work for someone else is in the U.K., where 92.2% of the workforce are employees. One of the criticisms of British society today is that fewer and fewer people work for themselves, and more and more are employed by the government.

It's harder to explain why the U.S. should be second on the list (90.3% employees) – notably since we're reputed to be a nation of rugged individualists. We certainly don't have the same huge proportion of government workers as the U.K. The explanation for our low number of bosses and self-employed is probably that most U.S. businesses today are corporations. Even the smallest business or partnership is apt to incorporate if it becomes at all successful. When this happens owners become employees of their own corporation.

Sweden comes third in the employee sweepstakes. Not much doubt why – it's their socialist welfare state. All that government involvement in the life of the nation means mountains of paperwork. And that means thousands of workers, in the form of government clerks, to keep the bureaucratic wheels moving.

The Italian, more than anyone else on our table, likes to be his own boss. More than one in five Italians are self-employed in a business or profession. This figure reflects the way of life in much of Italy,

	U.S.A.	CANADA
	1975	1975
1. Total working civilian[+] labor force (millions)	84.7	9.1
2. Total working civilian[+] labor force divided into:		
wage earners; salaried staff (%)	90.3	88.9
employers; self-employed (%)	8.7	9.5
unpaid family workers[o] (%)	1.0	1.6

LABOR FORCE: STATUS

	U.K.	AUSTRALIA	AUSTRIA	BELGIUM	DENMARK	FRANCE	(WEST) GERMANY	IRELAND	ITALY	JAPAN	NETHERLANDS	NORWAY	SPAIN	SWEDEN	SWITZERLAND
	1975	1975	1975	1975	1975	1975	1975	1975	1975	1975	1975	1975	1975	1975	1975
	24.6	5.7	2.9‡	3.7	2.3	20.7	24.8	1.0	18.8	52.2	4.5	1.6	12.6	2.3	2.7
	92.2[x]	85.7	80.5	83.2	81.4	80.9	84.2	70.8	72.4	69.8	84.5	84.4	69.8	89.3	NA
	7.8[x]	14.0	19.5	13.1	13.8	19.1	10.1	29.2	21.4	18.0	15.5	11.8	30.2	10.4	NA
	NA	0.3		3.7	4.7		5.7		6.2	12.0		3.8		0.3	NA

[x] This figure is slightly inflated, as the number of unpaid family workers is not available
‡ Includes armed forces.   NA not available

where there are still plenty of small shops and independent craftsmen. Japan (18%) is second on the list of self-employed workers, in spite of the fact it is now the home of gigantic industrial corporations. Japan, like Italy, still has many small tradesmen – peddlers, operators of small food stands and shops, etc. Australia, Denmark and Belgium also have high proportions of the self-employed.

It's an obvious conclusion that the North American way of life is actually eliminating the small businessman and other self-employed workers.

The third category of workers is people who work without pay. These are mostly family members and dependents who help out around a business or farm and don't receive any specific remuneration. Spain tops the table here with a combined figure of 30.2% for self-employed plus unpaid family help. Think of all those small bars and cafes in Spain, open till all hours, with everyone from Grandma to

Source:
Organization for Economic Co-operation and Development
+Excludes members of the armed forces
0People who assist in the operation of a business or farm, and who have worked at least one-third of the period covered

the kids lending a hand. Japan is second with a combined figure of 30% and Ireland close behind with 29.2%. All three countries have strongly conservative family traditions. Italy is next – about one in three of the self-employed has a family member working without pay. The combined Italian total is 27.6%. This is followed by Austria (19.5%) and France (19.1%).

Australia and Sweden have the lowest number of unpaid workers – about three per thousand in the working population. The U.S. figure is ten per thousand, and in Canada, 16 per thousand are unpaid.

		U.S.A.	CANADA
		1975	1975
1.	Unemployment:		
	Total unemployed (000s)	7,830	694
	Unemployed as % of labor force	8.3	7.0
	Unemployed men as % of male labor force	7.6	7.3
	Unemployed women as % of female labor force	9.3	6.4
2.	Youth unemployment (15-24 year olds):		
	1970	9.9x	10.3
	1973	9.8x	9.7
	1975	15.2x	12.2
	1976	14.0x	12.5

The world trade recession has caused the most feared of all economic diseases – high unemployment, and in the U.S., we have suffered worst of all. Over eight percent of the total labor force was out of work in 1975. That's nearly one person in 12 without a job. In a country the size of the U.S., that's nearly eight million people out of work.

The proportion of people unemployed in Ireland is almost as high as it is in the U.S. But there the situation is different, because Ireland has always relied on emigration to solve the worst of its unemployment problems.

Third in our table comes Canada, where unemployment is running at seven percent of the total labor force. Canada, the U.S. and Ireland are way ahead of the other countries on our table. Canada, for instance, has double the British unemployment rate. Although the British believe that unemployment is their major problem, the U.K.'s unemployment rate of just under 3.4% is below average for the countries listed.

A surprise on this table is Italy's low figure. At 3.3% it's even fractionally lower than the U.K.'s. But there's a hidden factor here. The Italians traditionally have a large migratory labor force. Many Italian workers head for the factories of Germany, Switzerland or other parts of Europe, and work there for several years before returning to Italy. If you take these workers into account, Italy's low figures aren't so impressive.

A similar situation exists in Spain. There the rate of nearly five percent is high enough – without taking into account migrant workers in Paris factories and London hotels who aren't shown in the figures.

The country with the lowest unemployment rate is Switzerland. However,

U.K.	AUSTRALIA	AUSTRIA	BELGIUM	DENMARK	FRANCE	(WEST) GERMANY	IRELAND	ITALY	JAPAN	NETHERLANDS	NORWAY	SPAIN	SWEDEN	SWITZERLAND
1975	1975	1975	1975	1975	1975	1975	1975	1975	1975	1975	1975	1975	1975	1975
866+	254	52	168	121	889	1,074	90	654	1,000	206	40	625	67	10⁰
3.4+	4.2	1.7	4.2	4.9	4.0	4.1	8.0	3.3	1.9	4.3	2.3	4.7	1.6	0.4⁰
4.4	3.4	1.4	3.1	4.7	2.7	3.7	8.6	2.8	2.0	NA	1.8	4.8	1.3	NA
1.6	5.7	2.2	6.3	5.1	6.1	4.6	6	4.6	1.7	NA	3.0	4.2	2.0	NA
2.7‡	2.5	1.4**	NA	NA	1.5	0.3++	NA	10.2⁰⁰	1.9	NA	NA	2.3	2.8ˣ	NA
2.9‡ xx	3.8	1.4**	NA	NA	2.9	1.0++	NA	12.6⁰⁰	2.2	NA	NA	6.7	5.3ˣ	NA
7.4‡ xx	8.9ˣˣ	1.4**	NA	NA	7.6	5.8++	NA	12.8⁰⁰	3.0	NA	NA	10.5	3.6ˣ	NA
13.1‡ xx	9.0	1.4ˣˣ**	NA	NA	9.9ˣˣ	5.2++xx	NA	14.4⁰⁰xx	3.1	NA	NA	12.5	3.6ˣ	NA

+ Registered wholly unemployed excluding school leavers ⁰ Registered wholly unemployed
ˣ 16-24 year olds ‡ Under 25 year olds — labor force 16-24 year olds
** Under 30 years old — labor force 15-29 year olds ++ Under 25 years old — labor force 15-24 year olds ⁰⁰ 14-24 year olds ˣˣ OECD estimates NA not available

its figure of less than half of one percent only takes account of the registered wholly unemployed. The Swiss employ migrant labor too. But when these people are out of work the Swiss government doesn't support them. So they're not registered as unemployed.

Sweden has the second lowest unemployment rate — just over 1.5%. Austria comes next with a rate of only 1.7%. These countries use immigrant labor which isn't included in national figures. On the other hand immigrant labor *is* included in the U.K. figures.

As far as unemployment among the young is concerned, Italy has the highest rate. But the U.S. also has a high proportion of out-of-work young, notably in the black community. The U.K. is third on this list.

Source:
Organization for Economic
Co-operation and Development

Labor productivity figures are one way to measure workforce efficiency. If you look at the overall production of a country, you can see how much wealth its people actually create. Our figures show how much the members of a country's working population earn for their country each year.

With characteristic Swiss efficiency, each worker there produces an average of $18,500 worth of goods a year. And this in a country with little heavy industry, and few raw material resources. Most of this revenue comes from what's called "invisible earnings" – money generated without producing tangible goods. Banking and tourism, for instance, are both cost-efficient and capable of earning a lot without employing lots of labor – especially if planned with Swiss know-how.

In Switzerland, tourism brings year-round profits because it caters not only to the winter tourist who enjoys skiing and winter sports, but also the summer visitor captivated by the scenery.

And the wealthy; wherever they obtained their money, often deposit it in Zurich banks, secure in the knowledge that Switzerland has a high level of political and social stability.

In most statistics, America tops the league in terms of overall production, but our workers produce only $17,790 worth of goods a year – about four percent less than the Swiss.

This may be because some elements of our workforce – for instance, migrant farm workers or the urban poor – don't have high productivity levels.

Next in terms of labor productivity is the Netherlands ($16,820) followed by Canada ($16,540) and West Germany, close behind at $16,460.

Holland and West Germany are known for their efficient industries, arising from the modernization which followed World War II. Canada has enjoyed a steady and undisturbed growth rate, helped by rich mineral and fuel resources available for export. Furthermore, all three have prosperous agricultural industries.

Sweden is also high in this table. It's sixth, with $15,900. Modern industrial methods, good labor relations, social stability and an efficient farming industry all play their parts in this high figure. Belgian workers are only $50 behind the Swedes. Norway and Denmark also do well. Their workers produce over $15,000 worth of goods every year.

France comes next with $14,660 – surprisingly low, considering France's

	U.S.A.	CANADA
	1975	1975
1. National economy[+] (US $ 000s) per person employed	17.79	16.54
2. Comparison of national economy[0]	131	122
3. Comparison of 1975 national economy with 1970[X]	105[‡]	114[*][*]

	U.K.	AUSTRALIA	AUSTRIA	BELGIUM	DENMARK	FRANCE	(WEST) GERMANY	IRELAND	ITALY	JAPAN	NETHERLANDS	NORWAY	SPAIN	SWEDEN	SWITZERLAND
	1975	1975	1975	1975	1975	1975	1975	1975	1975	1975	1975	1975	1975	1975	1975
	8.72	13.30	12.06	15.85	15.01	14.66	16.46	7.37	8.72	9.48	16.82	15.46	7.53	15.90	18.50
	64	98	89	117	111	108	122	54	64	70	124	114	56	117	137
	104	NA	118	108[++]	111	118	116	121	111	127	118[00]	120	NA	106	109

NA not available   ‡Total private economy   **Excluding public administration
++1972 figure   001974 figure

present economic prominence. However, France is recovering from previous decades of economic difficulty and its figures are improving year by year. Only Japan, Ireland and Norway are moving upward at a greater rate.

Ireland, with $7,370 annual production per worker, is at the bottom of the list, while Spain at $7,530 is little better. In both countries more than a third of the working population is employed in agriculture – more than any other European country. Not only do relatively few people work in industry, but farms are comparatively small. Both countries are unsuitable for large-scale mechanized farming, although the picture may soon change. Spain proposes to join the Common Market, and massive foreign investment is pouring into Ireland.

Britain and Italy are near the bottom of the table, tied at $8,720 annual production per person.

The reasons for Britain's poor productivity are said to be unimaginative management, outdated machinery and

Sources:
1 International Labour Organization
2 & 3 Heron House calculations based on ILO figures
[+] Ratio of output (GNP) to input (civilian employment).
[0] Index of 100 as the average of the specified countries.
[x] Index of 100 – GNP or GDP per employed person

the fact that more than half the working population is employed in service industries – more than anywhere else in the world except America. Britain's industrial muscles have grown a bit flabby, and the British can no longer rely on cheap raw materials from their Empire.

A high percentage of Italy's workforce is in manufacturing, but its worker-management relations are appalling. It's a land of contrast. Modern Italy is concentrated in the north, while in the south life has hardly changed since the last century.

There would be no modern industry without steel. It's the foundation of our present industrial system and the chief basis for our high standard of living. The U.S., as you'd expect, is the leading steel producer (128 million tons). Perhaps the U.S.S.R. makes almost as much but we don't know – for security reasons the Russians refuse to release any reliable statistics.

	U.S.A.	CANADA
	1976	1976
1. Total crude steel production (tons — millions)	128.0	14.4
2. National consumption (tons — millions)	141.5	13.5
3. Steel consumption per capita (lbs)	1316	1173

Japan is the second largest producer (118.3 million tons) on our table, a difference of just about ten million tons. This might seem like a lot, but in the overall figure it's not.

Japan probably has the most efficient steel industry in the world and, therefore, is able to capture a large part of the world market. The Japanese produce almost twice as much as they consume (118.3 million tons compared with 65.7 million tons consumed). This isn't true of the U.S., which has to import around 12 million tons a year.

Germany comes next in terms of crude steel production (46.7 million tons), followed by France (25.6 million tons). The U.K. is in fifth place with 24.5 million tons. The German steel industry is thoroughly modernized and almost as efficient as the Japanese. It's the old story. Both countries were completely devastated at the end of World War II and had to rebuild, making use of the most modern methods and equipment available. The U.S., France and the U.K. are barely managing to hold their own in the steel market. U.S. industry is hampered by rising labor costs and outdated, deteriorating manufacturing plants. We can't produce steel as cheaply as the Japanese, even though they import much of their iron from us.

The efficiency of a country's steel production can be estimated by adjusting the population figures. For instance, Canada has just over one inhabitant for every nine of ours. Multiply Canada's steel output by nine and you get 129.6 million tons – showing that the Canadian steel industry has a per capita production almost identical to the U.S.'s (128.0 million tons). If the U.K. were the same size as the U.S., theoretically it would produce about 98 million tons a year. By the same calculation, the Germans would produce 163 and the Japanese a whopping 236 million tons a year. Japan is by far the largest steel exporter – 52.6 million tons annually. Of the other countries on the table, only West Germany exports any significant quantity of steel: 6.3 million tons.

High steel consumption indicates that a country is heavily industrialized. The table shows that the U.S. has the most

	U.K.	AUSTRALIA	AUSTRIA	BELGIUM+	DENMARK	FRANCE	(WEST) GERMANY	IRELAND	ITALY	JAPAN	NETHERLANDS	NORWAY	SPAIN	SWEDEN	SWITZERLAND
	1976	1976	1976	1976	1976	1976	1976	1976	1976	1976	1976	1976	1976	1976	1976
	24.5	8.6	4.9	13.3	0.8	25.6	46.7	.06	25.8	118.3	5.7	1.0	12.0	5.6	0.6
	25.2	7.8	3.0	5.2	2.5	25.8	40.4	NA	23.8	65.7	5.0	1.9	11.4	6.6	2.1
	899	1146	805	1023	983	979	1314	NA	851	1166	736	968	637	1614	650

NA not available

industry, followed by Japan, West Germany, France, the U.K. and Italy. Countries with the lowest steel consumption tend to have the least industry: Spain, Switzerland and the Netherlands, for example, where you'll find fewer landscapes marred by ugly smokestacks and cooling towers.

The heaviest consumers of steel are the Swedes, who run through 1,614 pounds per person every year. The U.S. is next at 1,316, followed by West Germany. Canada, Japan and Australia are the next three countries on the consumer table. High consumption of steel generally indicates a high standard of living. Much of the steel used in the U.S. for instance, goes into cars, washing machines, toasters – and girders for high-rise buildings. However, some nations with low steel consumption still have a high standard of living – Switzerland, for example. The nature and quantity of a country's exports must also be considered. The Swedes export a lot of cars and heavy machinery – not all of those 1,614 pounds stay at home. And Volvos use more steel than Swiss watches.

Source:
British Steel Corporation
+Benelux (Belgium, the Netherlands & Luxemburg)

Paid vacation[+] days per year:	NEW YORK 1976	TORONTO 1976
bus driver[o]	20	15
automobile mechanic[x]	10	10
plant manager[‡]	15-25	20
secretary[**]	10	10

Every time you open your newspaper these days you're apt to encounter another article on the coming of the four-day week — and what are we all going to do with all that extra leisure? There's only one problem — chances are that you'll be reading that newspaper in your coffee break at work. U.S. citizens along with Canadians share the dubious distinction of having less vacation time than most of the world.

Obviously, how many vacation days depends on a variety of different factors: how long you've been employed, what your qualifications are, your age and, in some countries, whether or not you're married. The Union Bank of Switzerland has done a brilliant job of specifying exactly identical people and then comparing their benefits in 41 different countries around the world. We've extracted the table from this data.

Overall, it paints a depressing picture of the pressures of our North American work-oriented society.

Take any category of employment and we still have far fewer vacation days than most others round the world. New York City's bus drivers are better off than their buddies in some other cities though.

Sydney, with its strong unions, leads all the 41 cities covered. Drivers there enjoy a lavish seven weeks vacation.

If you're a qualified auto mechanic in any one of the North American sample cities (New York, Toronto, Montreal, Chicago, Los Angeles or San Francisco)

you ought to feel clutched. Your paid vacation time is clearly out of sync with the rest of the world. In fact, at just ten days paid leave per year, you're right at the bottom of all 41 cities. As the data shows, that can also be the case in Spain.

If you're a white-collar plant manager (with plenty of years with the firm) you'll average three to five weeks in New York, your counterpart in Chicago averages only three weeks, in Los Angeles or San Francisco only two to three weeks.

Clearly Germany is the leader on our table with over 5½ weeks as average paid leave for plant managers.

While on the subject of Germany, its also interesting to compare that country with its next door neighbor Austria. You'd think they'd be roughly similar or that, if anything, those waltzing Austrians would have more time off. Not a bit of it. The exact opposite is true. Compared to Germany, Austrians come out badly right across the board. For example, given two managers performing similar jobs, the German can enjoy a 40% longer vacation. On the other hand neighboring Belgium and Holland display remarkably similar patterns.

PAID VACATION DAYS

LONDON	SYDNEY	VIENNA	BRUSSELS	COPENHAGEN	PARIS	DUSSELDORF	DUBLIN	MILAN	TOKYO	AMSTERDAM	OSLO	MADRID	STOCKHOLM	ZURICH
1976	1976	1976	1976	1976	1976	1976	1976	1976	1976	1976	1976	1976	1976	1976
15	35	20	21	24	26	24	17	26	20	22	20	30	20	15
17	20	18	20	24	26	19	15	15-24	14	21	20	20-30	20	15
20-25	20	20	24	24	26	28	15	25	20	22	20	25	27	25
20	20	15	20	24	26	23	15	20-24	20	20	20	30	24	15

When it comes to all 41 countries our West Coast cities are right at the bottom of the table. Who's at the top? Al Manamah in the Arab Sheikhdom of Bahrain – with eight weeks of vacation.

Secretaries are equally lucky in Bahrain. A 25-year-old single secretary with five years experience also gets exactly the same vacation as her boss – eight weeks.

A New York secretary with the same skills ought to be typing out her resumé to work in Spain, France, Italy or Denmark. She'd double or triple her paid days off. In fact, if she just moved to Chicago she'd average an extra five days a year on the company. You'd think California would be big on time off. It's not. Secretaries in Los Angeles and San Francisco average about 2½ weeks paid vacation leave.

London secretaries get four weeks on average – at least she does better than her Dublin counterpart.

For most of the world the disparity between the time off given to executives and to their employees is quickly becoming equal; as is the time off that blue collar workers earn when compared with their office worker counterparts. However, the big two-week gap between what a North American or Swiss executive has off and a secretary are still glaring anachronisms. Even in Ireland people have come to accept that all workers deserve roughly equal vacation time. While in Spain slaving behind a typewriter can merit one week's vacation more than the boss.

In general the Latin countries – France, Italy and Spain – are well above average on vacation days. Given more time maybe we'd all be Latin lovers.

Source:
Union Bank of Switzerland
+ Working days
o Works on public transportation, ten years' experience; 35 years old, married, two children
x Qualified, five years' experience; 25 years old, single
‡ 100 people work for him, long experience; 40 years old, married, no children
** Secretary to head of department, shorthand, typing and one foreign language, five years' experience; 25 years old, single

121

		U.S.A.	CANADA
1.	Total average earnings in manufacturing industries (US $ per hour)	1975 4.81	1975 4.97
2.	Highest earnings (US $ per hour)[0]	6.42	6.72
3.	Lowest earnings (US $ per hour)[x]	3.19	3.26
4.	Ratio of: highest earnings to the average	1.33	1.35
	lowest earnings to the average	0.66	0.66
	highest earnings to the lowest	2.01	2.06

It's worth looking at this table in conjunction with those on inflation and taxation and also the tables comparing the cost of living in various countries in the world. The figure showing how much someone is paid gives no precise indication of the value of what he or she actually earns until you've taken into account the figures from the other tables.

For instance, the Spaniards have easily the lowest average hourly earnings. Their $1.82 is well below half the norm. But they pay very low taxes, and many things are cheaper in Spain than elsewhere. So although Spanish workmen are still lowest in the table, these factors help to close the gap. The opposite is true when you come to the top end of the table.

Danish workers top the list with an average hourly wage of only just under $6. That's nearly $240 a week. And in Sweden they earn on average just ten cents less per hour. But those high-earning Scandinavians pay high taxes too – well over 30% in both Denmark and Sweden. And prices are high: in 1976 Swedes had to pay about $6 for a pound of sirloin steak. Their large earnings don't buy as much as you might think.

Neither Sweden nor Denmark have been doing well economically. These high figures reflect how inflation (with high wages always chasing high prices) has hit them.

The U.S. and Canada follow Denmark and Sweden. Surprisingly, the Canadians – with an average of $4.97 per hour – are ahead of U.S. workers by 16 cents. That adds up to over $6 more a week.

Norway, the other Scandinavian country in our table, comes next. There, they earn an average $4.76 per hour, just a fraction less than in the U.S. And although they pay high taxes (an average of 39% of the paycheck for a single person) the North Sea oil bonanza, which is about to arrive, means things are looking up for the Norwegians.

West Germany is comparatively low on the table. Average earnings there are equal to those of the Netherlands – but lower than Switzerland and the other countries mentioned so far. The reason – once again – is inflation.

Spain is the only country with wages below $2 an hour ($1.82). Ireland is next lowest with an average wage of $2.44.

Italy comes next with an average hourly figure of $2.75, only four cents

U.K.[+]	AUSTRALIA[+]	AUSTRIA[+]	BELGIUM	DENMARK	FRANCE	(WEST) GERMANY	IRELAND[+]	ITALY	JAPAN[+]	NETHERLANDS	NORWAY[+]	SPAIN	SWEDEN[+]	SWITZERLAND[+]
1975	1975	1975	1975	1975	1975	1975	1975	1975	1975	1975	1975	1975	1975	1975
2.79	5.66	3.42	3.92	5.83	2.80	3.94	2.44	2.75	3.28	3.93	4.76	1.82	5.73	4.01
3.28	6.13	4.18	6.09	7.50	3.38	5.20	3.08	4.49	4.49	5.11	5.50	2.42	6.46	5.32
2.21	5.15	2.01	2.71	4.82	2.15	2.91	2.01	2.16	1.92	3.66	3.96	1.08	4.88	3.94
1.18	1.08	1.22	1.55	1.29	1.21	1.32	1.26	1.63	1.37	1.30	1.15	1.33	1.13	1.33
0.79	0.91	0.59	0.69	0.83	0.77	0.74	0.82	0.78	0.58	0.93	0.83	0.59	0.85	0.98
1.48	1.19	2.08	2.22	1.56	1.57	1.79	1.53	2.08	2.34	1.40	1.39	2.24	1.32	1.35

lower than the average wage in the U.K. Most Italian workers in the manufacturing industries in the north, earn more than their counterparts in the U.K. – the Italian figure takes into account wages earned in southern Italy, which are often on a par with those in Spain.

It's interesting to see that in France – where there's a minimum wage law ($2.20 per hour in 1977), – the lowest rate of pay is smaller than in the U.K. (where there is no such law). Although the U.K. has the fourth lowest average earnings, the gap between lowest and highest wages is comparatively narrow. In many other countries, there is a large difference between the highest and lowest average wage. Top wage earners get more than twice as much as the lowest in the U.S., Canada, Austria, Belgium, Italy, Japan and Spain. This invariably reflects an even greater disparity between wages and salaries. In these countries, there tend to be extremes of wealth and poverty.

Sources:
International Labour Organization
[+]Heron House estimates
[0]Includes petroleum refineries and chemical, paper, beverage, tobacco, iron and steel, rubber products, and printing and publishing industries
[x]Includes textile, clothing, footwear, leather, and wood furniture industries

	New York	Montreal
	1976	1976
Net earnings (US $) of:		
an automobile mechanic[+]	9725	10,397
a construction worker[0]	12,075	11,277
a toolmaker/lathe operator[X]	8644	13,201
a female textile worker[0]	5322	6420
a department manager[‡]	20,065	18,920
a bank teller[**]	9653	6888[++]

If you want to earn a higher-than-average salary, go to Zurich. The Swiss score three firsts in the six occupations shown on the table, two seconds and one third. In New York, in the land of opportunity, only the department manager and the construction worker earn the highest rates. If you are a female textile worker in New York, you'd make more if you worked in Zurich, Sydney, Copenhagen, Montreal, Stockholm or Oslo.

London is well below average, right across the board – in fact, it's at the bottom of the table for department managers and bank tellers.

Overall, Dublin pays the lowest wages of the cities listed, scoring lowest for auto mechanics, lathe operators and female textile workers. Irish salaries never range higher than third from the bottom of the list. Londoners come next, earning less in all but one category than equivalent workers in Madrid.

One of Zurich's firsts is the salary paid to an automobile mechanic – more than $10,400 per year. Montreal comes a close second with $10,397. New York is only third – $9,725. After these three cities there's a big drop of $1,416 a year till you get to Sydney.

In the U.K., an auto mechanic earns under $4,000 a year – less than half the salary paid his counterpart in Australia.

Dublin auto mechanics are the worst off, earning only $3,205. Mechanics in Milan and Madrid don't do much better. They both earn around $3,500 a year. Even these salaries are generous compared with a mechanic's pay in Manila in the Philippines (not on the table) – just over $1,000 a year.

The same pattern is reflected in the construction industry. If you're a hard hat your best bet is New York, where you'll earn $12,075. A Parisian construction worker gets $3,027. He's the odd man out in the Paris figures – Parisian salaries for the other occupations are further up in the table.

For lathe operators, Montreal is tops at over $13,201. Zurich is next with an income of $12,486. Then there's a drop to Sydney (just under $9,000) and New York, fourth on the table at $8,644. The lowest salaries are paid in Dublin and Milan, where lathe operators earn from $4,000 to just over $4,500.

The next category produces at least

124

AVERAGE SALARIES

London	Sydney	Vienna	Brussels	Copenhagen	Paris	Dusseldorf	Dublin	Milan	Tokyo	Amsterdam	Oslo	Madrid	Stockholm	Zürich
1976	1976	1976	1976	1976	1976	1976	1976	1976	1976	1976	1976	1976	1976	1976
3915	8309	5449	6454	7578	5360	5814	3205	3549	5192	5588	7267	3397	7219	10465
3859	7396	4648	5311	7859	3027	5024	3340	3430	5363	5765	8523	3867	7718	8607
4587	8879	8009	7520	8068	6947	6845	4199	4540	7314	6488	8117	4907	8364	12486
2679	6573	3436	4270	6560	4059	3552	2415	2518	4314	4549	5944	3369	6324	7023
6985	13366	11878	12668	12718	16376	15416	7732	8382	18184 00	12870	11775	7144	10857	19045
4824	8893	7976	8869	8803	6905	8506	6172	8528	12407	7663	8255	4903	8817	14188

++Without complete bank training
00Bank employee

one surprise. Women in New York are well down the scale, earning just $5,322 a year – seventh of the 17 cities. Again, Zurich scores highest in this category.

If you look at the figures for department managers, you'll see that there's an enormous disparity between the New York salaries of over $20,000 and the skimpy U.K. figure of $6,985. Management is given a higher priority in the U.S. – the salary is a work incentive.

Bank tellers are laughing all the way to the bank in Zurich, where they earn more than $14,000 – way ahead of the rest of the field. Their New York counterparts come a poor second at $4,535 less. And banking isn't a funny business at all in London, where tellers earn a meager $4,824, barely enough to keep them in bowlers and pinstripe suits. Perhaps they should follow the example of their Irish colleagues whose recent strikes closed the banks for several months.

Source:
Union Bank of Switzerland
+25 years old, single; completed apprenticeship, five years' experience
025 years old, single; unskilled or semi-skilled
×35 years old, married, two children; skilled, ten years' experience
‡40 years old, married, no children; head of a production department (100 employees), many years' experience
**35 years old, married, two children; completed training, ten years' experience

Strikes in North America have many features which make them as distinctive as the continent we inhabit. For openers, when our people walk out they tend to stay out for a good long time. In the U.S., the average number of working days lost per man on strike is just under 18 and in Canada the time out is over four working weeks.

Compare these with our continental cousins and you get some idea of the size of the difference. In Austria, the average worker is out for just a day and a half – barely long enough to shuss down a mountain and buy a candy bar before the dispute is over.

As the table shows, strikes outside the U.S. – almost without exception – are far shorter in duration. Only Ireland and Sweden exceed a two working week average and, in each case, that figure is based on a small data base.

Speaking of the data base, we believe there are several important caveats to bear in mind when using the table. In the first place it only represents one year which, given the cyclical nature of labor disputes and (importantly) of labor contracts/negotiations, can and does distort the overall picture. Holland is a good example. In 1975, the latest year for which we have comparable figures, just 4,639 days were lost; in 1976 the figure was over three times that at 13,984.

Then, too, it depends on who is striking. If it's the coal miners, as it was in

1978, the number of workers can be massive and the "ripple" effect on the whole economy severe.

But big numbers aren't needed to cause big disruptions. If a country is highly dependent on tourism for example, as the U.K. and Spain are, and ten air traffic controllers walk out because they don't like the smile on the computer's face, the economy may go into a tail-spin. One result? A lot of other workers (such as hotel employees) are laid off.

Given all these qualifications, the table does highlight some fairly interesting facts. Compare the U.S. to Canada, for example. With just over ten percent of the work force of the U.S., Canada manages to rack up over one-third of our number of lost man days. Something in the order of one out of 20 Canadians walks off the job compared to one in about 50 U.S. workers.

But the percentage of participants in labor disputes in North America is small

	U.S.A.	CANADA
	1975	1975
1. Number of disputes	5031	1171
% versus U.S.[+]	–	23.2
2. Workers involved (000s)	1746	506.4
3. Man working days lost (000s)	31237	10909
4. Average number of workers per dispute[+]	347	432

U.K.	AUSTRALIA	AUSTRIA	BELGIUM	DENMARK	FRANCE	(WEST) GERMANY	IRELAND	ITALY	JAPAN	NETHERLANDS	NORWAY	SPAIN	SWEDEN	SWITZERLAND
1975	1975	1975	1975	1975	1975	1975	1975	1975	1975	1975	1975	1975	1975	1975
2282	2432	NA	243	147	3888	NA	151	3601	3391	5^0	22	2807	86	6
45.4	48.3	NA	4.8	2.9	77.3	NA	3.0	71.6	67.4	0.1	0.4	55.8	1.7	0.1
808.9	1398	3.8	85.8	59.1	3814	35.8	29.1	14110	2732	0.27^0	3.3	504.3	23.6	0.32
6012	3510	5.5	610.2	100.1	5011	68.7	295.7	27189	8016	0.48^0	14.5	1815	365.5	1.7
354	575	NA	353	402	980	NA	193	3918	806	54	149	180	275	54

NA not available ^{0}*In 1974 there were 17 disputes, 2,979 workers involved and 6,854 days lost. In 1976 there were 11 disputes, 15,255 workers involved and 13,984 days lost.*

compared to certain other countries on the table. Italy is a notable example. There, workers involved in disputes are equal to 73.7% of the employed – very nearly three out of four workers. Australia has the dubious distinction of being in the number two slot, with the equivalent of just under one in every four workers involved in a dispute; France comes next with just under one in five.

All in all, a far cry from Switzerland and the Netherlands, where those walking out wouldn't keep a revolving door busy for half an hour.

If Italy and France are big on strikes, they also tend to have a lot of strikers per dispute. That figure is just under 4,000 workers in Italy, 1,000 in France. The Japanese are in third place with just over 800 workers out per dispute.

The U.K. has long been regarded as a strike-plagued society and some of the figures shown on the table support this reputation–but others don't.With a work

Sources:
International Labour Organization
+Heron House estimates

force that's just 28.7% as large as ours, the U.K. manages to rack up 45% as many disputes as the U.S., and the percentage of total workers who hit the bricks is bigger. But the average number involved in a strike is little different and the average British worker is out for about 7½ days.

That's where Italy's chronic woes show how glaring her problems are: with just over one-fifth of our work force she racks up very nearly 90% of our lost days.

Finally, if you don't believe in crossing picket lines, head for Holland or Switzerland – the Dutch are clearly too busy making money to spare the time. As for the Swiss – when did your banker last man the barricades?

How safe are you at work? Obviously this depends on the kind of job you have: you're safer working in an office or cream cheese factory than on a construction site. The table on the right shows three potentially dangerous occupations (manufacturing, construction work and mining) and compares fatal accident rates in different countries for these occupations. To show how much progress each country is making in on-the-job safety, figures for two years – 1967 and 1976 – are given.

Not surprisingly, the figures show that fatal accidents occur more often in the building trades than in manufacturing, and that mining is even more dangerous. Obviously there can be tremendous variations within each of these occupations: you'll be safer in a mattress factory than in a steel mill or digging an open pit mine, rather than working a mile-deep tunnel. Taking the figures as a whole, mining is about seven times as dangerous as factory work.

Japan has the best figures for safety in the factory: 0.01 fatal accidents for every million man hours worked in 1976. That means you'd have to work eight hours a day for over 30,000 years before you might expect to be killed.

The Japanese are very safety-conscious in their factories. However, this figure is impressive in a country with so much heavy industry. You'd be more

	U.S.A.	CANADA
	1967	1967
Fatal accident rates for:		
manufacturing	0.03^0	0.12^x
construction	0.19^0	0.96^x
mining and quarrying	0.51^0	$3.09^\ddagger$
	1976	1976
Fatal accident rates for:		
manufacturing	0.03^0	0.10^x
construction	0.16^0	0.75^x
mining and quarrying	0.31^0	$1.72^\ddagger$

than 30 times as safe working in Japanese industry than on a mining job, and six times safer than you'd be in a West German factory.

On the whole, the U.S. comes off well in its safety figures. Our industrial accident rate is holding steady at 0.03 per million man hours of work in manufacturing industries – not as good as the Japanese, but better than most other countries listed. Between 1967 and 1976, we reduced on-the-job construction fatalities from 0.19 to 0.16. This is still higher than in some countries, but then they don't build as many high-rise buildings as we do. Mining accidents have declined more dramatically – from 0.51 to 0.31 in nine years.

Canadian accident rates are much

U.K.	AUSTRALIA	AUSTRIA	BELGIUM	DENMARK	FRANCE	(WEST) GERMANY+	IRELAND	ITALY+	JAPAN	NETHERLANDS+	NORWAY	SPAIN+	SWEDEN+	SWITZERLAND+
1967	1967	1967	–	–	1967	1967	1967	1967	1967	1967	1967	1967	1967	1967
0.04x	NA	0.36x	NA	NA	x++0 0.12	+0 .08	0.09‡	+0 0.04	0.04⁰	+0 0.02	0.08‡	+0 0.02	0.04⁰	+0 0.07
x00 0.16	NA	NA	NA	NA	0.48x	+0 0.20	0.14‡	+0 0.29	0.29⁰	+0 0.06	0.43‡	+0 0.07	0.12⁰	+0 0.24
x** 0.52	0.79x	0.50x	NA	NA	+0 xx 0.23	+0 0.32	1.08‡	+0 0.18	0.59⁰	NA	0.47	+0 0.20	0.31⁰	NA
1976	1976	1976	NA	NA	1975	1975	1975	1974	1976	1975	1975	1975	1975	1975
0.04x	NA	0.18x	NA	NA	x++ 0.10	+0 0.06	0.09‡	+0 0.03	0.01⁰	+0 0.02	0.06‡	+0 0.03	0.03⁰	+0 0.05
00 0.15x	NA	0.62x	NA	NA	0.46x	+0 0.14	0.09‡	+0 0.25	0.06⁰	+0 0.04	0.17‡	+0 0.09	0.08⁰	+0 0.25
x** 0.32	0.71x	0.52x	NA	NA	+0xx 0.16	+0 0.18	0.65‡	+0 0.16	0.33⁰	NA	0.16	+0 0.43	0.20+	NA

0 Per million man hours worked   x Per 1,000 persons employed, excluding uranium mining
‡ Per 1,000 wage earners   ** Excluding Northern Ireland and quarrying
++ Including mining and quarrying   00 Excluding Northern Ireland
xx Excluding quarrying   NA not available

higher than ours in all categories. Even though they almost cut their mining accidents by half between 1967 and 1976, they will have nearly two mining fatalities per thousand wage earners. Part of the reason for this is that most of Canada's mines – it's the world's largest producer of zinc – are in newly opened up areas of the frozen north where conditions are treacherous.

Austria is the worst country for industrial accidents among manufacturing workers. Even though the Austrians halved their rate from 1967 to 1976, they're still at the top of the table with 0.18 fatalities per thousand employees . French and Canadian factories are second (0.10 fatalities per thousand employed).

Sources:
International Labour Organization
+ Heron House estimates

The U.K.'s figures for mining and quarrying have improved noticeably: they've dropped from 0.52 per thousand employees in 1967 to 0.32 in 1976. Its other figures have remained fairly static.

Most countries on the table have improved their safety records, with one dire exception: in Spain, mining fatalities have more than doubled – from 0.20 per million man hours worked in 1967 to 0.43 in 1976. The figures for accidents in the manufacturing and construction industries have also increased – though not as dramatically.

	NEW YORK	TORONTO
	1976	1976
1. Retirement age	65	65
2. Annual pension for a single person (US $):[+]		
minimum	1217	1658
maximum	4368	2821
3. Annual pension for a married couple (US $):[+]		
minimum	1825	3316
maximum	6552	5381

An old joke has it that, "Money may not buy happiness, but at least it allows you to be miserable in comfort." Sad to say, age often brings poverty, and while there may never be an elixir that will rejuvenate our bodies, most people will settle for enough money to live in security and perhaps with enjoyment after retiring.

Is your government pension worth waiting for? If you want the highest benefits, live in Milan or Vienna – the Italian and Austrian governments provide pensions giving you a maximum of four-fifths of your highest-earning years. Of course, you pay all your working life for this eventual nest egg. In all state pension systems, workers, employers and government contribute to the retirement funds.

When governments began taking responsibility for those who were too old to work, everyone usually received the same basic weekly or monthly amount. Now, with such vast numbers of people involved, at such a wide range of salaries, most countries have differential benefits.

In some countries, retirement benefits are designed to help mainly the lower income groups. This is true of our own Social Security system. A couple living in New York and earning $35,000 a year in 1976 would have paid Social Security contributions on only $15,300 of their income and would collect annual benefits of $6,552 upon retirement. This isn't much of a pension for someone used to relative affluence. For many Americans, however, Social Security payments represent only a supplementary income which they receive in addition to a company or union pension.)

Other countries pay much larger retirement benefits than we do. In Stockholm, Sweden, for instance, a retired couple can receive up to $10,888, and in Düsseldorf, Germany, $9,948.

Many countries adjust their retirement benefits to inflation and the cost of living, but for more affluent old age you should look not to the government but the private sector. With almost all unions pressing for higher pensions, and large corporations offering lavish pensions to lure promising executives many people's prospects are improving.

	LONDON	SYDNEY	VIENNA	BRUSSELS	COPENHAGEN	PARIS	DUSSELDORF	DUBLIN	MILAN	TOKYO	AMSTERDAM	OSLO	MADRID	STOCKHOLM	ZURICH
	1976	1976	1976	1976	1976	1976	1976	1976	1976	1976	1976	1976	1976	1976	1976
	60/65	60/65	60	65	67	65	65	65	60	55/60	65	67	65	60/65	65
	1253	NM	1981	1723	2636	1712	NM	1041	1014	1113	3475	2768	V	2250	2412
	NMx	2642	6530	V	4140	4032	9948	1145	12728	2782	V	4914	V	9569	4823
	1997	NM	2834	2371	3202	2568	NM	1766	1174	1209	5004	3918	V	3870	3617
	NM	4388	6530	V	5280	4830	9948	2006	12880	2878	V	5953	V	10888	7235

NM no minimum   NMx no maximum   V varies (see notes below)

Source:
Union Bank of Switzerland
⁺These figures can vary according to individual circumstances. For further details see notes below.

RETIREMENT BENEFIT QUALIFICATIONS

New York Based on the average of the 17 contributory years with the highest earnings in accordance with the maximum earnings which are creditable for social security.

Toronto Determined by financial circumstances at the time of retirement, not on previous earnings.

London The basic retirement benefit is independent of previous earnings.

Sydney Determined by financial circumstances at the time of retirement, not on previous earnings.

Vienna Determined by the length of insurance coverage. After 45 years, benefits reach 79.5% of the average earnings during the five years before retirement.

Brussels For a single person, about 60% of average earnings during the years contributions were made. For a married man, about 75%.

Copenhagen Determined by financial circumstances at the time of retirement, not on previous earnings.

Paris Contributing for 37.5 years gives a maximum regular retirement pension of about 50% of the creditable earnings during the ten covered years with the highest earnings.

Dusseldorf Determined by the number of years insured.

Dublin Fixed amount, not dependent on earnings.

Milan Maximum benefits equal about 80% of the average covered earnings of the three years with the highest earnings out of the last five years before retirement.

Tokyo Determined by the number of contributory months and the amount of previous earnings.

Amsterdam Fixed amount, not dependent on earnings.

Oslo Determined by previous earnings and the number of years of coverage.

Madrid Determined by the amount of contributions and the number of years they were paid into the scheme.

Stockholm Minimum benefits equal the national pension received by everyone over the age of 65. The supplementary pension depends on previous earnings and the number of covered years. The maximum is 60% of average earnings 15 years with the highest income.

Zurich Determined by the number of years insured and the average earnings for the years contributions were paid.

National economy (US $-000s) per person employed

	U.S.	CANADA	U.K.
	17.79	16.54	8.72

The popular image of the hard-working, efficient Swiss may be true. Each industrious worker in Switzerland produces $18,500 worth of goods annually. It's not all cuckoo clocks and chocolate, of course. Switzerland is banker to the world.

U.S. workers run the Swiss a close second when it comes to high productivity. Each one, on average, generates $17,790.

Australia, like North America, is a young, vigorous country. This is reflected in its productivity figure of over $13,000 per head.

Despite Japan's booming economy, each worker there generates only slightly more wealth ($9,480) than his British counterpart in the U.K.

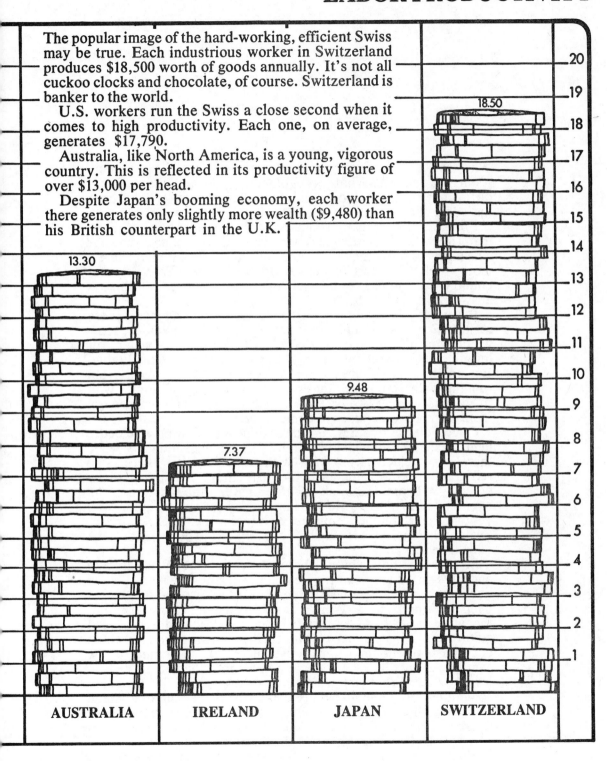

AUSTRALIA	IRELAND	JAPAN	SWITZERLAND
13.30	7.37	9.48	18.50

At Home

What sort of a roof do you have over your head? How many rooms are under it? What sort of plumbing and appliances (if any) do you have in them? How much does all this cost you? These are just some of the questions answered in this chapter.

For a start, how many rooms are there in most houses? How many households live in one room, in two – in five or more rooms? The answers to all these questions are in the first table. There's more, too. What sort of houses do we live in? Tract houses, country mansions, one-room apartments? Again, this is answered in the first table.

But we still have no idea of the standard of living inside these homes. For this, we need to know about basic amenities. How would you like to live in a home without running water, for instance? Not too many do, as you can see from the next table. But still the numbers are greater than you might think. Apart from running water, we have figures on the percentage of homes with fixed bath or shower or flush toilet – which gives a general indication of the standard of domestic living.

Once you have water, the next thing you'll want is electric light. Remember the last blackout? Life changes radically when there's no electricity. And without electricity there's no refrigerator or washing machine. Are these two items really essential? From the look of the figures, the answer is an overwhelming "yes". Most households can live quite well without a telephone, however. Only in the U.S., Canada, Switzerland and Sweden do half or more of the households have telephone service.

So now we know what the homes in various countries are like and have an idea of how they're equipped. But how many people live in each one? The next table shows the average number of people per household. What's most surprising here is how *little* the figure varies from country to country – despite differences in culture and living standards. The average for the countries we've covered is about three per household. Only in Ireland is the average marginally over four, and no country has an average of less than 2.5. What conclusion can we draw from this? Is there something about human beings which makes them naturally tend to live together in groups of three? That's the great thing about figures – they're just facts. You can always draw your own conclusions – so long as they fit the figures, of course.

Next we have a table on home ownership. How many people own their own homes? How many rent and how many live in homes provided by their government or employers? Home ownership used to be for the rich – but from the look of the figures that's no longer true. In more than half the countries we've covered, at least half the population live in houses of their own. Though in affluent Sweden, an exception, only a third of the population owns their own home. Home ownership is obviously becoming a matter of life style and convenience, rather than simple affluence.

There are other aspects to housing also. Rent, for instance. You're always meeting people who say how cheap it is to live in various cities. Now you'll be able to check up on their statements – we've got the facts for you. We've taken some of the largest cities in all of the countries listed and given the figures for renting different sizes of apartment, both furnished and unfurnished.

But even if it appears comparatively expensive to rent an apartment, it may still turn out to be worth your while to stay in the city of your choice – especially if local wages are higher. The next table shows what percentage of household expenditure goes on rent, power and fuel. This gives more of an idea of how much it actually costs people to live in their homes.

And what about those lucky few who can afford to have a little hideaway in the country or on the beach? We also have figures on the number of people in the listed countries who own second homes. And here there are a few more surprises. Having a second home also seems to be more a matter of life style and availability, rather than money. It's the countries with the wide open spaces and remote rural areas that tend to have second homes. Owning a second home turns out to be very much a Scandinavian habit. They easily lead the field here.

Last of all, we have a table which shows the number of new houses going up in the listed countries. This also shows figures for the relative age of houses – broken down into the percentage of houses built before World War I, built between the wars, and the percentage of houses built after World War II. And as an added indicator of housing conditions, we've given a list of the percentage of people who are considered to be ill-housed in the various countries.

Although home sweet home can mean anything from a 50-room château to a tin shack, most people in the world live in houses that are somewhere between these extremes.

Most homes in most countries on the table have four or five rooms. Canada is an exception: the highest proportion of Canadians live in a seven-room house.

In France, over 11% of the population live in only a one-roomed dwelling and over 20% in two-roomed dwellings – a figure beaten only by Denmark's 22.5%.

In the U.S., 64% of us live in a house of our own, with at least a bit of land. Only four people in a hundred live in an attached or "row" house – the kind that's so familiar in Europe. Only 28% of us are apartment-dwellers.

	U.S.A.	CANADA
	1975	1977
1. Homes (%) with one room	1.0	1.3
two rooms	2.0	2.6
three rooms	10.0	9.6
four rooms	21.0	16.2
five rooms	25.0	23.7
six rooms	20.0	20.1
seven rooms or more	21.0	26.5
	1976	1977
2. Type of home as % of all homes		
detached house	64.0	59.0
attached house	4.0	8.0
apartment or flat	28.0	33.0
other[o]	4.0	NA

In the U.K., almost three-quarters of the population live in one-family houses and less than a quarter in apartments. Fifty percent of British houses are attached and 23% detached.

France tops the table for apartment living, with a whopping 78% housed in apartments. West Germany is next in the number of people living in apartments, followed by Austria, Spain, Belgium and Sweden, each with over 50% of their inhabitants living in apartments.

The housing patterns of any country are inclined to follow that country's traditions. In European countries, farmers always lived clustered together in small villages. When the rural populations emigrated to the big cities, they looked for similar cheek-by-jowl housing. In other countries – the U.S., the U.K. and Canada – farmhouses were on or near the fields. People moving to the cities wanted separate houses of their own.

However, population density doesn't force people into apartments. In Japan three-quarters of the people live in individual houses. And the figure for the crowded Netherlands is 58%.

DWELLINGS

	U.K.+	AUSTRALIA	AUSTRIA+	BELGIUM+	DENMARK+	FRANCE+	(WEST) GERMANY+	IRELAND+	ITALY+	JAPAN	NETHERLANDS+	NORWAY+	SPAIN+	SWEDEN+	SWITZERLAND+
	1975	1971	1975	1975	1975	1975	1975	1975	1975	1973	1975	1975	1975	1975	1975
	0.7	1.9	2.7	1.1	3.3	11.3	3.4	2.1	1.3	6.3	0.8	4.0	5.7	4.3	3.9
	3.6	3.7	7.3	3.8	22.5	20.3	8.8	5.9	8.5	17.6	4.2	9.5	9.7	7.8	8.9
	9.8	6.9	21.4	6.2	30.6	27.0	20.8	16.5	22.3	20.3	11.8	22.8	19.7	13.8	19.0
	28.3	17.3	31.3	19.6	23.8	23.0	31.6	31.8	33.5	18.4	18.9	26.4	25.0	16.8	29.5
	36.2	37.8	17.5	33.5	10.4	10.5	16.5	19.5	25.2	13.9	29.7	17.5	21.6	23.8	19.7
	13.5	20.2	8.4	25.7	6.3	4.4	13.0	13.8	6.3	10.2	19.3	10.0	8.8	21.7	9.2
	7.9	12.2	11.4	10.1	3.1	3.5	6.0	10.4	2.7	13.3	15.3	9.8	9.8	11.8	9.8
	1974	–	1974	1974	1974	1974	1974	1974	1974	1973	1974	1974	1974	1974	1974
	23.0	NA	28.0	17.0	50.0	17.0	22.0	27.0	18.0	65.0	18.0	45.0	12.0	36.0	33.0
	50.0	NA	5.0	23.0	11.0	2.0	5.0	55.0	9.0	12.0	40.0	7.0	23.0	8.0	5.0
	23.0	NA	64.0	56.0	31.0	78.0	69.0	11.0	65.0	23.0	36.0	46.0	61.0	56.0	62.0
	4.0	NA	3.0	4.0	8.0	3.0	4.0	8.0	8.0	NA	6.0	2.0	4.0	NA	NA

NA not available

Sources:
National statistical offices
+Euromonitor
0Trailers, mobile homes, etc.
Figures do not always total 100 as percentages
have been rounded up or down.

Every man's home may be his castle. But what does every man's castle require to make it a decent home? The first thing he needs is a roof over his head. But after he's got a roof what else does he require? Television? The family silver? Genuine Aubusson tapestries? Perhaps the most important – and basic – facility in his home is running water.

Ninety-nine percent of the households in many of the countries listed have running water. This means that every house has its own well, rainwater catchment or else it is connected to a municipal water main.

In Austria, Belgium, France and Italy, more than 90% of all households have piped water. At the bottom of the list are Ireland and Spain. In Ireland, only 86% of all households have piped water. In Spain, the figure is a low 68%. This means that nearly one in every three households in Spain has to rely on the water bucket for its water supply. This can be a real hardship – as you know if you've tried to live in a waterless cabin in the woods.

After running water, what else do you need in your humble castle? How about a bathtub or shower stall? If you look at the table, you'll see that most households have baths and showers – though not as many as have running water. The top countries in bath facilities are Canada, Australia, the Netherlands and Sweden – where 98% of all households have a fixed

	U.S.A.	CANADA
	1975	1975
1. Homes equipped with piped water (%)	99	99
	1975	1977
2. Occupied homes with fixed bath or shower (%)	96$^+$	98$^+$
	1975	1975
3. Occupied homes equipped with flush toilets (%)	98	97

bath or shower. In the U.S. four in every hundred households do not have bathtubs or showers. That's roughly three percent of over two hundred million people – over six million who go without baths. (Fortunately, U.S. citizens use more antiperspirants than just about any other people in the world.)

Compared to the running water statistics, the rate for bathtubs and showers is often surprisingly low. The lowest figure is Spain's – less than half of all Spanish households have a fixed bath or shower. This means that roughly 18 million Spaniards have to wash out of the sink or have a bath in a tin tub. The Italians aren't much better off.

The big question is: why do over 36% of all Belgian households have no fixed bath or shower? And why over 33% in France and Austria? None of these countries are low when it comes to

	U.K.	AUSTRALIA	AUSTRIA	BELGIUM	DENMARK	FRANCE	(WEST) GERMANY	IRELAND	ITALY	JAPAN	NETHERLANDS	NORWAY	SPAIN	SWEDEN	SWITZERLAND
	1975	1975	1975	1975	1975	1975	1975	1975	1975	1975	1975	1975	1975	1975	1975
	99^0	99	92	93	99^0	97	99^0	86	92	99	99^0	99	68	99^0	99^0
	1975	1971	1975	1975	1975	1975	1975	1975	1975	1973	1975	1975	1975	1975	1975
	97	98^+	66	63	90	66	94	80	50	73^{x+}	98	75	46	98	85
	1975	1975	1975	1975	1975	1975	1975	1975	1971	1975	1975	1975	1970	1975	1975
	99^0	98	90	99	99	80	96	79	96^+	35	99	87	71^+	98	97

^{x}Bathrooms

running water – and none have large areas of rural poverty. They do have many old buildings, homes, apartments and farmhouses, built centuries before the invention of the water pump.

Another essential, for a home with running water, is a flush toilet. As you'd expect from the hygiene-conscious countries in our list, the figures are again high. In fact, more houses have flush toilets than fixed baths and showers. At the top of the list are the Netherlands, Denmark, Belgium and the U.K.: 99% of households have flush toilets. Only five countries on the table have less than 90% of households with flush toilets. These are Spain, Ireland, Norway, France and Japan. Even these countries have figures of over 70% – with the sole and surprising exception of Japan. Why do only 35% of Japanese households have flush toilets? A question for the sociologists.

Sources:
Euromonitor
$^+$National statistical offices
^{0}Heron House estimates

Electricity, refrigerators, washing machines and telephones – now we're getting down to basics when it comes to home requirements. Running water, bathtubs and flush toilets are alright as far as they go. But in a society weaned on electric tooth-brushes, frozen gourmet foods and drip-dry clothes, we need another standard of household comparison.

It's no surprise to find that electricity is almost universal in the households in the countries on the list. In fact more households have electricity than running water – which just goes to show that more people would rather watch T.V. than bathe.

Ninety-nine out of every hundred households in almost all the countries in the table have electricity. There are only three exceptions. In Spain, 96% of the households have electricity. And in Ireland and Japan, the figure is 98%.

Once you've got electricity, you might as well have a place to chill your beer (except in the U.K., where they prefer their brew lukewarm). Life is so much more enjoyable if you've got a fridge. Ice cubes, ice cream, frozen fish croquettes, crisper lettuce, unsour milk – these are just some of the reasons to have one. Ninety-nine percent of the households in the U.S. and Canada wouldn't be able to cope without a refrigerator. In Australia, almost as many consider it vital to have somewhere to keep those cans of lager.

	U.S.A.	CANADA
	1975	1975
1. Homes equipped with electric lighting (%)	99	99
	1976	1976
2. Households owning refrigerators (%)	99	99+
3. Households owning washing machines (%)	83	82
	1976	1976
4. People with telephones as % of population	70	57

In most of the other countries on the list, around 90% of the households have refrigerators. But in the U.K., only 85% have fridges and in Norway the figure is 84%. Perhaps it's so cold there electricity isn't needed to chill food.

In Japan, more than one in four households does *not* have a refrigerator.

But the lowest country on the list is Ireland. Less than half the Irish households have a refrigerator. And in Spain, one out of every three households drinks warm *sangria* and keeps its left-over *paella* in the cupboard.

After the fridge, the next home essential is the washing machine. It's not the U.S. that heads this list, but the spick and span Dutch. In 85% of Dutch households there's a washing machine. The West Germans run a close second; there, 84% of all households have washing machines. And in the U.S., where so many house-

	U.K.	AUSTRALIA	AUSTRIA	BELGIUM	DENMARK	FRANCE	(WEST) GERMANY	IRELAND	ITALY	JAPAN	NETHERLANDS	NORWAY	SPAIN	SWEDEN	SWITZERLAND
	1975	1975	1975	1975	1975	1975	1975	1975	1975	1975	1975	1975	1975	1975	1975
	99+	99	99	99	99+	99	99+	98	99+	98	99+	99+	96	99+	99+
	1975	1976	1975	1975	1975	1975	1975	1975	1975	1976	1975	1975	1975	1975	1975
	85	96	89	86	92	88	91	49	91	71	95	84	69	91	91
	71	68	70	75	60	69	84	62	79	61	85	75	68	80	51
	1975	1975	1975	1975	1975	1976	1975	1976	1976	1976	1975	1975	1975	1975	1976
	38	39	28	29	45	26	32	14	26	41	37	35	22	66	61

wives say they'd leave home if they didn't have a washer, only 83% have one.

The U.K. is about average on this list. Seventy-one percent of all British households have washing machines. Lowest of all on the table is Switzerland. Half of all Swiss housewives send their laundry out or wash it all by hand. The Danes are second lowest at 60%. And the third lowest is Japan with 61%.

There are people who say they'd simply die without a telephone in the house. Yet it's surprising how many households still don't have them in some of the most communications-sophisticated countries in the world. Well below half the households in many countries on the table have telephones. Even in the U.S., where Alexander Graham Bell invented the infernal talking machine, only 70% of all households have a telephone.

Sources:
1, 2 & 3 Euromonitor
4 United Nations
+Heron House estimates

In Canada there are telephones in over half of all Canadian households. In most other countries on the table, less than half the households have a phone. The U.K. is about average with almost 40%.

Ireland is the lowest on our table – only one household in every seven has a phone. Even Spain has more than Ireland. But the loquacious French are surprisingly low at a mere 26%. The same figure maintains in Italy – only one household in four has a phone. Could be that people with Gallic and Latin temperaments feel restricted when they can't express themselves with their hands.

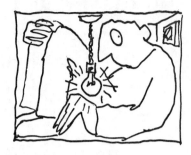

Household size depends upon where you come from. America is the land of couples, with 31% of us living in twos. Germany tops the table for singles, with 28% of its people living alone – as many as live in two-person households.

The largest households are in Ireland, where 31% of people live in households of five or more. Ireland also has almost the lowest number of single-person households. Spain comes after Ireland, with an average of four per dwelling.

Why do people in these countries live together in larger units? For one thing, in Catholic countries families are usually larger and they stay together longer. Children in more affluent countries are likely to take on jobs or training that involve leaving home. In agricultural countries such as Ireland and Spain, they're more likely to stay and help with the work at home. The same is true of older people: in poorer countries their famililies care for them at home. The extended family of aunts, uncles and cousins is a tradition which lingers. In more affluent societies, the elderly often spend their latter years in nursing homes or communities.

The U.S., the U.K. and Switzerland are in the lead when it comes to small-sized households and space to accommodate them. All three average fewer than three people in a household and just

		U.S.A.	CANADA
		1977	1977
1.	Average number of people per household	2.9	3.1
		1977	1977
2.	Households (%) consisting of:		
	one person	21	17
	two people	31	28
	three people	17	18
	four people	16	19
	five or more people	15	18
		1970	1971
3.	Average number of people per room	0.6	0.6

0.6 people per room. The Canadians, with an average household size of 3.1 people – and almost two rooms per person, obviously have space to spare. Among the affluent countries, Japan must be feeling the squeeze with an average household of 3.4 people and 0.9 people per room.

The overall impression from this table is that, as countries get richer in terms of G.N.P. per capita (see G.N.P. table) households get smaller. Technological advances breakdown both tradition and the extended family. The smaller, nuclear family becomes more prevalent. And, of course, as people get richer, they buy more – including more breathing space.

	U.K.	AUSTRALIA	AUSTRIA	BELGIUM	DENMARK	FRANCE	(WEST) GERMANY	IRELAND	ITALY	JAPAN	NETHERLANDS	NORWAY	SPAIN	SWEDEN	SWITZERLAND
	1977	1971	1977	1977	1977	1977	1977	1977	1977	1975	1977	1977	1977	1977	1977
	2.9	3.5	2.9	3.1	2.7	3.0	2.6	4.1	3.1	3.4	3.3	2.9	4.0	2.6	2.8
	1977	–	1977	1977	1977	1977	1977	1977	1977	1977	1977	1977	–	1977	1977
	20	NA	25	17	24	21	28	15	12	14	15	18	NA	26	21
	31	NA	27	30	30	28	28	22	20	17	27	24	NA	30	29
	19	NA	18	21	19	19	18	17	23	20	19	21	NA	19	19
	16	NA	15	15	17	15	15	15	21	27	20	19	NA	16	15
	14	NA	16	16	10	17	11	31	24	22	20	18	NA	9	16
	1971	1971	1972	1970	1970	1973	1972	1971	1971	1973	1970	1970	1970	1970	1970
	0.6[+]	0.7	0.9[+]	0.6[+]	0.8[+]	0.8[+]	0.7[+]	0.9[+]	0.9[+]	0.9	0.7[+]	0.7[+]	0.9[+]	0.7[+]	0.6[+]

NA not available

Sources:
Euromonitor
[+]National statistical offices

Once upon a time, most young American couples dreamed of the day when they would own their own home.

Today, values have begun to change. With the enormous increase in the price of land (especially urban land) and the high rate of property taxes, apartment living and house rentals, in both the cities and the suburbs, have come into their own.

Conversely, it is appropriate that Ireland – still rural in most areas – heads the list when it comes to home ownership. Centuries of British rule and absentee landlords prevented most people from owning their land or their homes. With the Republic came a slump in land prices which made land ownership a possibility for greater numbers of people. Approximately seven out of every ten Irish homes are owned by the people who live in them.

Historically, the passion for land applies – in a different sense – to the colonial settlers of Australia and Canada, where two-thirds of the population live in their own homes.

In the States, nearly 65% own their own homes, ranking fourth highest in the world. After World War II, the introduction of prefabricated housing made home ownership possible for many who had previously been unable to afford it.

	U.S.A.	CANADA
	1974	1977
1. Home owners as % of population	64.6[+]	65.4[+]
2. Tenants as % of population	35.4[+]	34.6[+]
3. Free housing provided by state or company	0	0
	1976	1976
4. Average monthly rent[‡] in big cities (US $)[x]:	a	b
for average-priced furnished 4-room apartment	1600	816
for average-priced unfurnished 3-room apartment	699	458
normal local** rent	299	229

In the U.K., the figures fall in about the middle of the countries on the table. The population is almost evenly divided between home owners and renters. There is extensive council housing in Britain where many houses and apartments are owned by local governments and rented at subsidized rates.

Do the millions of renters get what they pay for? The normal local rent (estimates based on middle to high rents) is as low as $36 a month in Vienna. The normal local rent in London – the next lowest city in the table – is three times as high, but the rents in both cities are still comparatively

U.K.	AUSTRALIA	AUSTRIA	BELGIUM	DENMARK	FRANCE	(WEST) GERMANY	IRELAND	ITALY	JAPAN	NETHERLANDS	NORWAY	SPAIN	SWEDEN	SWITZERLAND
1976	1971	1972	1970	1970	1973	1972	1971	1971	1973	1971	1970	1970	1970	1970
53.3[+]	67.3[⁰]	49.4[⁰]	55.9[⁰]	47.0[⁰]	45.5[+]	33.5[⁰]	70.8[+]	50.8[+]	59.2[+]	35.4[+]	52.6[+]	57.2[+]	35.2[⁰]	28.5[⁰]
46.7[+]	27.3[⁰]	45.1[⁰]	44.1[⁰]	48.6[⁰]	44.3[+]	66.5[⁰]	26.8[+]	44.2[+]	34.4[+]	64.6[+]	42.4[+]	24.7[+]	51.6[⁰]	68.4[⁰]
0	5.4[⁰]	5.5[⁰]	0	4.4[⁰]	10.2[+]	0	2.4[+]	5.0[+]	6.4[+]	0	5.0[+]	18.1[+]	13.2[⁰]	3.1[⁰]
1976	1976	1976	1976	1976	1976	1976	1976	1976	1976	1976	1976	1976	1976	1976
c	d	e	f	g	h	i	j	k	l	m	n	o	p	q
470	740	539	460	311	466	488	263	297	1998	406	454	378	385	725
253	307	237	155	197	320	311	225	175	999	167	291	189	205	342
100	247	36	217	197	255	235	177	175	151	157	255	203	193	180

a = New York b = Toronto c = London d = Sydney e = Vienna f = Brussels g = Copenhagen h = Paris i = Dusseldorf j = Dublin = k = Milan l = Tokyo = m = Amsterdam n = Oslo o = Madrid p = Stockhom q = Zurich

low. Vienna, like London, has thousands of government-owned apartments.

The highest, normal, local rents are in New York, with Paris and Oslo running a close second. It's not surprising. In crowded New York, renters pay a premium for space.

For those who want a large, furnished apartment, New York is not the place to go. A medium-priced, furnished, four-room apartment will cost $1,600 a month compared to a mere $263 in Ireland. Citizens of Tokyo pay an even greater premium for space – $2,000 a month for an average-priced, furnished four rooms.

Sources:
[+]National statistical offices
[⁰]United Nations
[x]Union Bank of Switzerland
[‡]Rent is defined as payments for rented dwellings, implied rental value of rent-free or subsidized housing and owner-occupied dwellings.
[**]General estimates based on middle to high rents.

The song tells us that those old bare necessities will come to us. It's a pity, but that's just wishful thinking. Those necessities don't come to you – you have to go out and get them. So how much today do we have to set aside from our household incomes to cover the cost of rent (or mortgage repayments), fuel and power?

	U.S.A.	CANADA
	1974	1976
1. Households (%) who own a second or vacation home	4.1+	6.8
	1976	1976
2. Expenditure on rent^X, fuel and power as % of household expenses	11.1	19.0

The Swedes are at the very top of the table – 20.9% of their income is swallowed up by these essential items. The Canadians are very close behind with 19% – just under one-fifth of their family budget. Both Sweden and Canada are northerly countries and although their summers are hot they are also short. They have to endure long cold, dark winters, and so need to spend more on keeping their dwellings and themselves, warm and comfortable.

The British might not have to suffer Siberian blizzards, but even Julius Caesar complained of their endless grey, damp, chilly winters. He wasn't too impressed by their summers, either. So it's not surprising that they're third on the list when it comes to paying out for keeping a roof over their heads and Jack Frost outside the door.

However, the 18.4% they spend on rent, fuel and power really puts them in the luxury league compared with the Irish. With virtually the same climate to contend with, the Irish spend only ten percent of their money on providing themselves with a warm place to live. Either rents are very much cheaper or

they must all be huddling together for warmth round peat fires.

Here in the U.S., you can pay your rent and the bills for the fuel and power needed to keep your house comfortable and still have 89.9% left of your budget for household expenses. This low expenditure on these items reflects our wealth in natural resources, but it must also have something to do with our climate. While in some parts of the U.S. it's possible to spend as much on keeping cool in summer as on keeping warm in winter, many areas have ideal outdoor weather for much of the year.

The Norwegians, whose country extends up to the edge of the Arctic, have to spend 14.2% of their family income on the basic necessities of shelter, warmth and lighting which places them seventh on the table with the French. It's not for nothing that Norway has been called the "Saudi Arabia of the North", and their careful development and exploitation of their North Sea oil and gas resources certainly seems to be paying dividends. Not only are Norwegian families better off than most others in the family income

U.K.	AUSTRALIA	AUSTRIA	BELGIUM	DENMARK	FRANCE	(WEST) GERMANY	IRELAND	ITALY	JAPAN	NETHERLANDS	NORWAY	SPAIN	SWEDEN	SWITZERLAND
–	–	1976/7	1970	1974	1975	1977	–	–	–	1971	1973	1975	1974	–
NA	NA	6^0	3.3	8.3	9.6	3.0^0	NA	NA	NA	0.2	18	7.4	14	NA
1976	1976	1976	1976	1976	1976	1976	1976	1976	1976	1976	1976	1976	1976	1976
18.4	15.0	17.9	14.1	13.1	14.2	16.0	10.0	13.9	13.7	13.5	14.2	14.1	20.9	17.5

NA not available

groupings, but more of them (18%) own a second or vacation house which places them in first place on that table.

The French are not nearly so well-off, but nor are they so poor as they would often have us believe. They spend 14.2% of the household budget on rent (or mortgage), fuel and power, but only 9.6% of French families believe in putting what surplus cash they have into a second or vacation home.

The Netherlands, though among the most prosperous countries in Europe, manages to keep the cost of rent, fuel and power very low indeed. The Dutch, for some years, have suffered acutely from a housing shortage but an enlightened government policy and careful husbanding of housing resources has brought the possibility of adequate accommodation within the reach of all. Still, the Dutch are not particularly interested in owning second or vacation homes. As the table indicates only a minute 0.2% spend their surplus cash in this way, whereas in Spain, one of the poorer countries in Europe, 7.4% of Spanish families own a second or vacation house.

Sources:
1 National statistical offices
2 Euromonitor
+US Bureau of Census
0 Institut für Markt und Sozialanalysen
x Rent is defined as payments for rented dwellings, implied rental value of rent free or subsidized housing and owner-occupied dwellings, including mortgage repayments

Although we in the U.S. appear to have more money left over than anybody else to spend in pursuit of the "good life", we don't seem to bother that much with a second or vacation home. In 1974, only 4.1% of American families spent their surplus income in this way.

Everyone these days has complaints about the high cost of living and the great difficulties in making ends meet. According to this table, though, people in most countries spend well under one-fifth of their household budget on those essentials – rent, fuel and power. That leaves plenty of money for the other essential, food.

Americans are the best-housed nation in the world. Right? Wrong. Two out of every hundred of us still live without a flush toilet, three without a bath or shower, one without electricity and one without running water.

The cleanest, best-lit countries are the U.K. and the Netherlands. Virtually all their dwellings have electricity, and a bathroom or toilet. The not-so-sanitary French have electric light, but 20% are without toilets and 34% without bathrooms.

Japan has more primitive facilities than any other country in the table – 65% of their homes lack a flush toilet, 27% have no bath or shower. The Japanese have never been squeamish about bodily wastes. They collect it, compost it, and use it to maintain the fertility of their fields – an old trick they learnt from the Chinese. (It's ecologically sound too.) Don't look for too much modern plumbing in Spain, either. Twenty-nine percent of Spanish homes have no toilet, 54% no bathroom.

Baths aren't terribly popular in Europe judging by our figures. Fifty percent or more of the homes in Spain and Italy have no bathroom, nor do a third of those in Austria, Belgium and France.

You'd expect the U.S. to be a world leader in building new housing, to judge from all those new housing developments in many of our major cities. That's not the case: we're behind most other nations. Japan is tops, with 18.7 new houses per thousand population. Our figure is 9.4. Most European countries build more new homes relative to population than we do.

Japan easily takes the prize for having the largest number of recently-built

	U.S.A.	CANADA
	1973	1973
1. New dwellings+ (000s)	1981	248.9
per 1,000 inhabitants	9.4	11.2
	1976	1977
2. Housing (%) built:		
before World War I	37	29
between World War I and World War II		
after World War II	63	71
	1975	75/77
3. Houses (%) without:		
flush toilet	2	3[0]
electric lighting	1	1[0]
fixed bath or shower	3	2[0]
piped water	1	1[0]

U.K.	AUSTRALIA	AUSTRIA	BELGIUM	DENMARK	FRANCE	(WEST) GERMANY	IRELAND	ITALY	JAPAN	NETHERLANDS	NORWAY	SPAIN	SWEDEN	SWITZERLAND
1973	1973	1973	1973	1973	1973	1973	1973	1973	1973	1973	1973	1973	1973	1973
315.4	149.1	44.2	61.1	55.6	517.6	714.2	24.0	181.3	2030	157.2	44.8	348.5	97.5	83.3
5.6	11.4	5.9	6.3	11.0	9.9	11.5	7.9	3.3	18.7	11.7	11.3	10.0	12.0	12.9
1974	–	1971	1970	1970	1968	1972	1971	1971	1973	1971	1970	1975	1975	1970
31	NA	40	35	29	51	28	45	18	22	21	25	42	15	55
27	NA	15	28	24	17	14	20	12		25	20		18	
42	NA	45	37	47	32	58	35	70	78	54	55	58	67	45
1975	71/75	1975	1975	1975	1975	1975	1975	1975	1975	1975	1975	70/75	1975	1975
1	2[0]	10	1	1	20	4	21	4	65	1	13	29[0]	2	3
1	1[0]	1	1	1	1	1	2	1	2	1	1	4[0]	1	1
3	2[0]	34	37	10	34	6	20	50	27	2	25	54[0]	2	15
1	1[0]	8	7	1	3	1	14	8	1	1	1	32[0]	1	1

NA not available

houses: 78% of their homes were built after World War II.

The oldest housing is in France (where more than half the homes are pre-World War I) and Ireland (45%).

If Japan takes the prize for the world's biggest housing program, the award for the classiest plumbing goes jointly to the U.K., the U.S., Canada, Australia, Sweden and the Netherlands.

Sources:
1 United Nations
2 National statistical offices
3 Euromonitor
[+] Houses, flats, apartments, suites of rooms
[0] National statistical offices

Average monthly rent for furnished four-room apartment $

2,400 —

2,200 —

The cost of keeping a roof over your head isn't a big worry in Dublin. At least, not if you live in a furnished four-room apartment. The rent is only $263. It's almost double that in London, where the cost of comparable accommodation is $470.

2,000 —

The cost of a four-room apartment in Zurich leaps to $725. That's close to the rent in Sydney ($740). Toronto's in about the same bracket, with rent taking a bite of $816 out of your income.

1,800 —

If you cross the border into the U.S., there's an enormous 100% increase in the cost of an apartment. The rent in New York skyrockets to $1600 a month. But the Japanese rent-payer is even more hard-pressed. After coming up with nearly $2000 a month, there can't be much left over for *sukiyaki*.

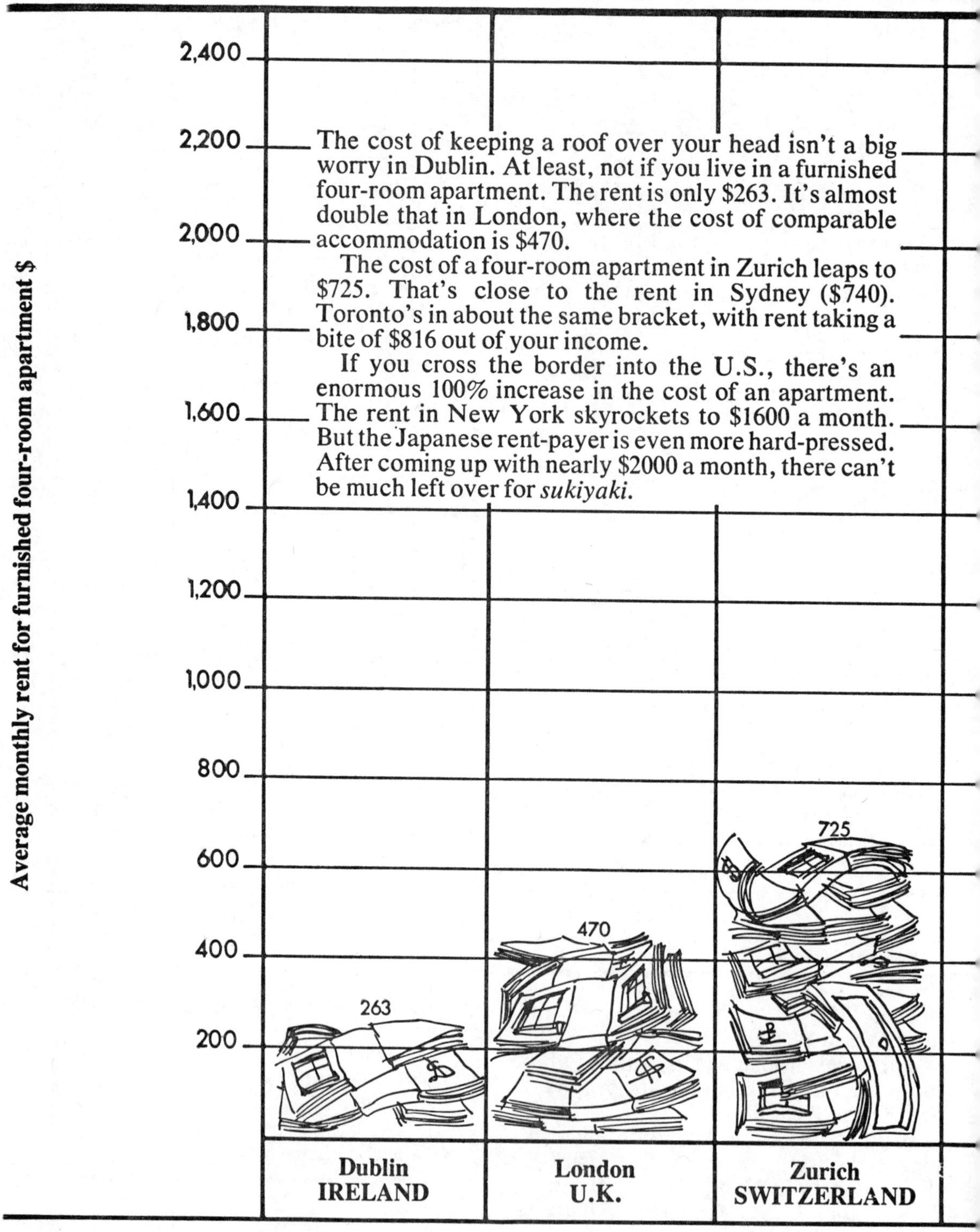

1,600 —

1,400 —

1,200 —

1,000 —

800 —

600 —

725

470

400 —

263

200 —

| Dublin | London | Zurich |
| IRELAND | U.K. | SWITZERLAND |

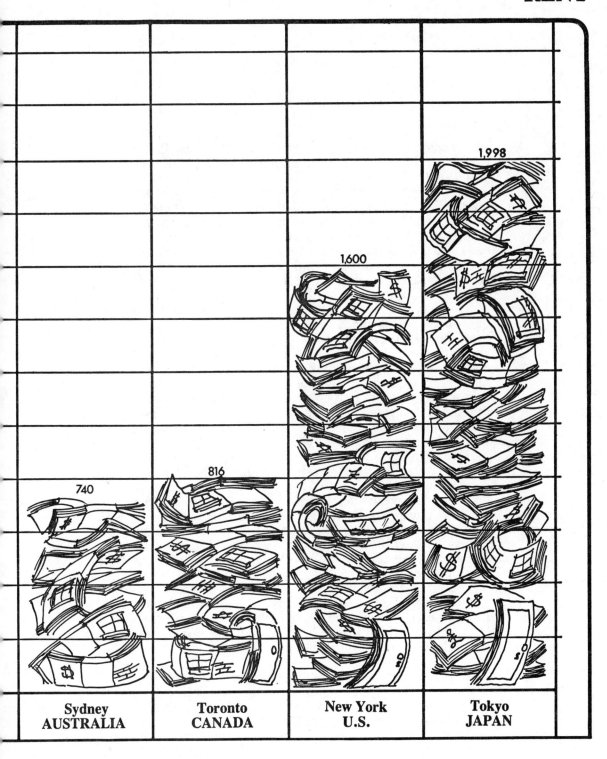

1,998

1,600

816

740

Sydney **AUSTRALIA**	Toronto **CANADA**	New York **U.S.**	Tokyo **JAPAN**

At Play

In this chapter, we'll be taking a look at the ways we find to amuse ourselves. They vary surprisingly from country to country, as you'll see.

First there's the subject of leisure activities, right across the board. That takes in a wide field of possibilities – everything from propping up those tired feet and unwinding in front of the T.V. to putting on your dancing shoes and going to a party. And we got some very different responses according to nationality. Like to hazard a guess as to what *your* fellow countrymen prefer to do after a hard day's work? Check it out against the section on favorite leisure pursuits.

As you may have guessed, a lot of the responses to the above question were the same. And that brings us to the next figures, those on television ownership. No doubt about it – in just one generation that electronic miracle has changed our life styles to an enormous degree. We've taken a long hard look at the one-eyed monster, both from the point of view of program content and also its popularity in different countries. An important topic, and one that crops up again and again. Are our children growing up in a television-addicted society? Is most of what you see just drivel? Read this section and take a viewpoint.

Here in the U.S., we own more T.V. sets and spend more of our time watching them than any other nation in the world. We've done an in-depth study of U.S. leisure time activities, however, and have discovered that the No 1 popular interest in America is not T.V. but sports. That's not too surprising in a country which has made professional sports a major industry. Don't think America is a cultural wasteland, however. Figures on museum attendance, theater-going, and other such activities suggest quite the opposite.

Of course, the mention of the U.S. and entertainment in the same breath brings us to America's gift to the world in this field – the movies. As befits the home of Hollywood, we take a keen interest in the silver screen. But you may be in for some surprises about the rest of the world. Who, for example, actually produces the most movies each year? And which nation do you think actually has the most theater seats for avid movie fans?

One thing this chapter points out is the great interest in sports in many nations. So we looked at the "big time" in that field – the Olympics. You may be surprised to see how certain nations – notably the U.K. and East Germany – have fared against those giants of international competition, the U.S. and the U.S.S.R.

Then we turned our attentions to the sport of golf. Golf has come a long way since its origin in ancient Scotland. The whole world has taken to the sport in a big way – especially the U.S.

Next we take a look at the distinctly more glamorous – you might even say decadent! – leisure pursuits of gambling and champagne drinking. You can probably guess why we've linked the tables of those two high-living activities. After all, what better way to celebrate a successful bet than with a bottle of bubbly?

On a less frivolous note, we examined the reading habits of many nations – and exploded some popular myths in the process. It's not true that Americans seldom read, nor is it true that when they *do* read they prefer books of fact to books of fiction. In this section, we also examine the current state of the struggling newspaper industry.

Then there's another aspect – book production. Our table here provides a basis for some thought-provoking speculation on the state of a nation's culture. We look not just at the number of books produced, but also the main types of books each country publishes – another indicator of cultural patterns.

And where do a lot of books end up? In libraries, of course. Our table on these worthy institutions offers some real shocks. For instance, which European nation has a mere 31 libraries to serve its entire population?

While we're on the subject of literacy as a way of enjoying yourself, let's not forget a time-honored form of communication. That's letter writing. To get a good idea of how much time each nation spends with pen in hand, we looked at mail traffic figures. And found a link between a fondness for book reading as a national pastime and volume of mail.

Another popular form of entertainment is listening to music. That's especially true in both the U.S. and in the U.K., homes of the Beach Boys and the Beatles, Aaron Copland and Benjamin Britten. In fact, a look at the relevant section in this chapter will show you just where record sales are booming.

One of the most eye-opening tables is the one on museums. A look at that section should shatter any cultural snobbery you might have felt regarding the New World!

What do Americans do in their spare time? The number of television sets we own might lead you to think that watching T.V. is our favorite pastime. That's true, but the chart shows that while 38% of those interviewed said that T.V. was of greatest interest, an even larger number – 43% – said they were very interested in sports. That brings us back to T.V. While many sports events draw big gates, these crowds are dwarfed by the millions who watch sports on the tube.

There's no denying the enormous popularity of the television. A total of 88% of respondents admit to being either very or moderately interested in watching T.V. while only three percent claim no interest whatsoever. (Even more people – 15% – have no interest at all in sports.)

At the other end of the spectrum the figures show that the five subjects in which the fewest people have a high degree of interest are classical literature, ballet and symphony (tied at seven percent), modern art (five percent), and last, opera, at four percent. A fair guess would have it that these folks include the three percent who don't watch T.V.

There's a strange pairing slightly up the table: the 11% high interest mark is jointly shared by detective story readers and modern dance lovers.

After sports and T.V., Americans' favorite ways to unwind are by listening to popular music, not rock but M.O.R. – which stands for middle of the road or "easy listening" music – what Frank Sinatra and Andy Williams do so well. This is probably why we have such a wide variety of F.M. and A.M. stations blasting out music for every taste.

Despite the apparent lack of interest in highbrow music such as operas and symphonies, there's still hope for American culture – 44% of us show high or moderate interest in the theater.

This figure is all the more significant since, until recently, vast numbers of Americans only had limited access to the theater. In recent years, Broadway has been challenged by smaller theaters springing up all over the country. Still, there's no denying that the legitimate theater takes a back seat to the movies with 64% of Americans claiming high or moderate interest.

In the world of literature, fiction leads in popularity, closely followed by non-fiction. The latter varies from learned books by eminent college professors to the tome you're now reading.

It's difficult to make a connection between the fact that the same number of people say they are moderately interested in novels and non-fiction books as claim to be moderately interested in sports. Maybe that figure represents all the wives who like to curl up with a book while their hubbies are out playing golf or watching sports on T.V.

Where will you find the fewest Americans? That's easy – at the opera house. Sixty-seven percent of us say we have no interest in opera.

LEISURE ACTIVITIES

Activities	High	Moderate	Low	None	Don't know
American leisure activities/interests[+] (1977)		Degree of Interest			
Television	38	50	9	3	0
Sports	43	32	8	15	1
Movies	21	43	20	16	0
Novels	22	30	17	31	1
Non-fiction books	17	35	17	31	1
Live theater	18	26	17	37	1
Traditional art	12	29	17	42	1
Modern dance	11	24	15	49	1
Detective fiction	11	23	21	46	0
Poetry	8	20	20	51	1
Classical literature	7	19	21	52	1
Ballet	7	15	17	60	1
Modern art	5	18	19	56	1
Opera	4	12	17	67	1
Symphony	7	18	17	57	1
Rock music	12	20	14	53	0
Other popular music	25	50	11	13	0

Source:
Roper Reports, 1978—1
[+]The question asked: "Here (on a card) is a list of some different kinds of interests people have. Would you go down that list, and for each one tell me whether it is something in which you are highly interested, moderately interested, not very interested, or not interested at all?"

What do you like to do after a hard day's work? Stretch out in front of the television set, play a few sets of tennis or maybe relax over a drink with some friends? A look at the table suggests your answer may well depend on your nationality. Our culture has a strong influence on how we unwind.

When Americans were asked how they like to spend an evening, a staggering 46% opted for – you guessed it – the television set.

The Italians at 25% are Europe's most dedicated television addicts. They rate television high on their list of favorite leisure activities – day or evenings. They're also Europe's most gregarious nation – 18% gave socializing as their preferred way of enjoying themselves.

The Americans and Spanish aren't far behind in liking parties and visits with friends– 16% and 17% respectively. In the U.K., a mere seven percent of Britons ranked socializing high on their list of favorite activities. Nearly as many people prefer pottering about at home: they're probably the ones with the neat gardens and shiny cars. The French come top of this category with seven percent.

Compared with the other figures, those for sports are also low. Charging around a football field or swinging a tennis racquet just aren't many people's ideas of fun.

The French, Austrians and West Germans are the most active people on the

	U.S.A.	U.K.
	1974	1975
1. Favorite leisure pursuit (%):[+]		
watching television	46	23
reading	14	16
sport (as participant)	5	8
house and vehicle maintenance	3	6
parties; entertaining; visiting friends	16	7
	1975	1974
2. Government expenditure on culture[x] (US $ — millions)	128.3[0]	67.8
as % of total expenditure	0.03[0]	0.2

table. One out of ten people in these countries lists a participant sport as his or her favorite diversion.

The Germans are the bookworms of the world. Twenty-one percent of them prefer reading to any other pastime – more than in any other country. They're avid for culture of all kinds – music, the performing arts, going to museums and art galleries. This shows on the table giving the amounts that various nations spend on culture. West Germany is in a class of its own. It spends a staggering $763.8 million a year on cultural activities. Germany's postwar economic growth has enabled her to spend vast sums on cultural activities while hardly cutting into the national budget – the money spent on culture is only one

	AUSTRIA	BELGIUM	DENMARK	FRANCE	(WEST) GERMANY	ITALY	NETHERLANDS	NORWAY	SPAIN	SWEDEN	SWITZERLAND
	1975	1975	–	1975	1975	1975	1975	–	1975	1975	1975
	13	18	NA	14	15	25	18	NA	19	21	18
	14	13	NA	13	21	11	17	NA	12	15	16
	10	7	NA	10	10	7	8	NA	6	8	7
	4	6	NA	7	4	3	6	NA	3	6	6
	16	14	NA	14	13	18	13	NA	17	13	13
	1974	1974	1974	1974	1974	1974	1974	1974	–	1974	–
	51.9	178.0	101.3	189.1	763.8	141.3	60.7	23.2	NA	81.4	NA
	1.0	2.2	1.4	0.5	1.0	0.7	0.5	0.6	NA	0.7	NA

NA not available

Sources:
Europe: Euromonitor
US: The Gallup Organization Inc.
[+]The question asked (Europe): "What is your favorite leisure pursuit?" In the US the question was: "What is your favorite way of spending an evening?" The US figure for sports participation is therefore probably comparatively lower than the one for Europe, and those for television watching and entertaining probably higher.
[0]US Information Office, London
[x]Creative and performing arts, museums, art galleries, etc.
Totals do not add up to 100 as categories have been extracted from a more extensive questionnaire.

percent of West Germany's total public expenditure. Tiny Belgium allots twice that percentage for similar activities – but this only amounts to $178 million. The Germans may be champion art subsidizers, but the Belgians are there trying.

At the other end of the scale, Americans are hardly in the public expenditure race. The most powerful nation in the western world spends a barely noticeable 0.03% of government money on culture – $50 million less than Belgium.

T.V. has changed our lives more than anything else in the past 30 years. Gone are the days when a family would sit around the fireplace reading, talking or playing games. Today, we sit in front of the T.V. and only talk during commercials. We spend more time with Walter Cronkhite and Johnny Carson than we do with our own friends. For many of us, life without T.V. would be quite unimaginable.

Where has T.V. taken the firmest hold? Right here in North America, of course. In America we have 571 sets for every thousand people. Placed end to end, those sets would stretch twice around the world. There are 1.7 people to every T.V. set. That's a lot of two- (and three-) set families. We have more color sets, more channels to choose from, and more hours of programming.

The Canadians come second with one set for every 2.7 people, closely followed by the Swedes with 2.8. Next comes the U.K. – one for every 3.1 people.

Even in Spain – which has the lowest number of sets of any of the countries on the table – you're never far from a T.V. There are about 5.7 people to a set. Ireland and Italy are also low in the T.V. watching stakes. It's tempting to see these figures simply reflecting the relative lack of affluence or larger households in those countries. More likely, they've got better things to do with their spare time.

	U.S.A.	CANADA
	1974	1974
1. Television sets per 1,000 inhabitants	571	366
2. People per television set	1.7	2.7
	1977	1974
3. Type of program as %[+] of all programs:		
information	15.7[x]	27.5
education	43.3[x]	25.8
entertainment	34.8[x]	44.0
programs for special audiences[o]	6.2[x]	2.8

When the T.V. viewer turns on his set, what sort of programs does he have to choose from? You might think there would be more programs devoted to entertainment than to anything else, but that's not the case. In most countries, fewer than 20% of broadcasting hours are devoted to entertainment. U.S. figures are high – 34.8% – and the fun-loving Canadians are even higher with 44%. Except for Canada and Italy, all countries give more broadcasting time to education than to either information (news, documentaries and so on) or entertainment programs. Of course, few educational broadcasts take place during peak viewing times. In Japan though, more than 60% of broadcasting time is taken up with education of one kind or another – just another example of the

U.K.	AUSTRALIA	AUSTRIA	BELGIUM	DENMARK	FRANCE	(WEST) GERMANY	IRELAND	ITALY	JAPAN	NETHERLANDS	NORWAY	SPAIN	SWEDEN	SWITZERLAND
1974	1973	1974	1974	1974	1974	1974	1974	1974	1974	1974	1974	1974	1974	1974
315	226	247	252	308	235	305	178	213	233	259	256	174	348	264
3.1	4.4	4.0	3.9	3.2	4.2	3.3	5.6	4.7	4.3	3.8	3.9	5.7	2.8	3.8
1975	–	1975	1974	1974	1972	–	1974	1974	1975	–	1974	1974	1975	1974
20.0	NA	27.4	23.4	19.6	18.5	NA	30.7	32.9	16.2	NA	26.7	21.7	23.1	21.7
56.4	NA	51.1	57.2	40.9	53.3	NA	33.6	21.9	60.1	NA	30.8	25.6	36.4	31.3
15.5	NA	8.6	8.3	10.7	19.6	NA	11.0	10.4	23.4	NA	19.9	21.8	17.1	19.7
8.1	NA	8.1	8.8	14.1	6.4	NA	24.8	15.0	–	NA	12.1	15.0	14.8	14.3

NA not available

businesslike Japanese philosophy. In the U.K., the figure is 56.4%.

The Italians have fewer educational programs than anyone else. They don't go in for entertainment either. Only about ten percent of viewing time is devoted to dramas and serials, quiz shows, music, sports, etc. You'll find more news information programs on Italian T.V. than anywhere else. That's understandable in a country undergoing social and political turmoil. Italians look to T.V. to tell them what's going on – and events are happening almost too fast to follow.

The percentage of time the U.S. devotes to news and documentary programs is much smaller. After education, most T.V. time is given to entertainment. Many of these programs are shown around the world.

Sources:
1 Organization for Economic Co-operation and Development
2 & 3 Heron House estimates
+Totals do not always add up as some categories have been excluded
0Women, children, religious groups, etc
xIndustry estimates

Canada and the U.S. score quite low when it comes to programs for special audiences (religious programs or programs for minorities). It's surprising. We both have great ethnic diversity in our populations. Italy, Spain and Ireland, all strongly Catholic countries, have the largest number of special interest programs. In Ireland, these account for almost a quarter of all broadcasting time.

The U.S. is known as the home of Hollywood. But, perhaps more accurately, Hollywood might be known as the home of the U.S. For the better half of a century, the Hollywood Dream Machine has churned out celluloid icons for us to adore and emulate.

We're the most film-fixated people in the world. We've got nearly 17,000 cinemas, with a total seating capacity of over seven million. That means we could take the entire populations of Norway and Ireland to the movies on a rainy day. And that's not even counting our 4,000 drive-in cinemas!

The U.K., on the other hand, has just over 1,500 movie houses, with a capacity of nearly one million. That's about average for the list.

But look at the figures for seating capacity per thousand population. Here the U.S. is actually deprived. Spain is at the top of the list with 74 movie seats per thousand population. Next comes Belgium with half that amount, and then Australia and Norway each with over 35 seats per thousand. The Japanese, surprisingly, have just over ten seats per thousand population. And the Brits have a meager 17. But the U.S., despite our 17,000 movie theaters has just under 30 seats per thousand. Maybe that says we're staying home to catch our favorite films on T.V.

If we're the most film-fixated people in the world, it follows that we go to the movies the most often. Wrong. The Italians go twice as often as we do. And the Spanish go three times for our every two visits.

In the U.K. the average person sees an average of only 2½ films each year. But, after all, they've got such good, inexpensive theater.

The Japanese have the distinction of seeing the least number of films a year – just under two. This is peculiar because they make twice as many films annually as the Italians, and nearly three times the U.S. If the Japanese built more movie houses they'd have the seats to sell, so people would pay to see the 405 films made every year – and everyone would go home enriched and happy after enjoying home-produced entertainment.

France, not the U.S., comes after

	U.S.A.	CANADA
	1977	1973
1. Number of movie theaters	16,829	1135
2. Seating capacity (000s)	7167	650.9
per 1,000 inhabitants	29.8	28.7
3. Annual attendenance (millions)	1066	89.0
per capita	5.0	3.9
	1974	1975
4. Number of long$^+$ films produced	156^{x0}	41‡

	U.K.	AUSTRALIA	AUSTRIA	BELGIUM	DENMARK	FRANCE	(WEST) GERMANY	IRELAND	ITALY	JAPAN	NETHERLANDS	NORWAY	SPAIN	SWEDEN	SWITZERLAND
	1974	1972	1974	1972	1974	1974	1974	1974	1974	1974	1973	1974	1974	1974	1975
	1535	976	645	728	367	5844	3114	240	5924	2468	380	448	5178	1199	521
	973.0	478.4	NA	359.0	128.0	1817	1189	NA	NA	1107	NA	142.0	2600	NA	195.8
	17.4	36.9	NA	37.0	25.4	34.6	19.2	NA	NA	10.1	NA	35.5	73.8	NA	30.1
	138.5	NA	23.7	32.8	19.9	178.5	136.2	NA	546.1	185.7	26.5	17.9	262.9	25.4	27.0
	2.5	NA	3.2	3.4	3.9	3.4	2.2	NA	9.8	1.7	2.0	4.5	7.5	3.1	4.2
	1975	1970	1975	1973	1974	1974	1975	1975	1975	1974	1975	1975	1975	1975	1975
	70‡	11‡	6ˣ	17‡	22ˣ	234‡	81‡	2**	203**	405‡	16ˣ	14ˣ	105**	14**	15**

ˣ Released or shown commercially for the first time by censor   ‡ Production completed   ** Approved

Japan when it comes to film-making. The French turned out 234 films in 1974. In Italy, in 1975, they made over 200. The reason the U.S. ranks a poor fourth may be because of the frugal budgets and elaborate procedures of the Hollywood film-makers. In Europe and Japan, cineasts turn out first-rate films with skeleton crews – not multi-million epics with casts of thousands.

In the U.K., where the film industry is said to be in very bad straits, they still made 70 films for exhibition in cinemas during 1975. Ireland is at the bottom of the list – they only made two films in 1975. (Maybe all the potential film-makers were in the pubs, or writing poetry at home – contributing to Ireland's list of great writers.) The figures for numbers of films produced don't include films made solely for T.V.

Sources:
1, 2 & 3 United Nations
4 United Nations Educational, Scientific, and Cultural Organization
⁰ Confidential industry source
⁺ For commercial exhibition in cinemas, duration 37 minutes and over.

It's a long time since 776 B.C., the year when the ancient Greeks held the first athletic contests on the plains of Olympia. The Roman Emperor Theodosius abolished the Games in A.D. 393 after Greece lost its independence, and it was 1500 years before they were revived in 1896. Except for lapses during the two world wars, they've been held at four year intervals ever since.

The tables on the right show how different countries have fared in the Games. However, not all the countries listed have been competing for the same length of time. Only four – the U.S., the U.K., Australia and Switzerland – have never missed an Olympic Games. They've participated in all 19 – something which deserves a medal in itself. At the other end of the scale, East Germany has only competed three times as a separate nation. Considering how many medals they take home, they've certainly made up for lost time.

The U.S. has won by far the most medals in the Summer Olympics: 628 gold, 473½ silver and 413 bronze – more than 1,500 altogether. (If you're wondering about that half medal, it means they tied with another country.) The other giant of the sports world the

	U.S.A.	CANADA
1. Number of Olympic Games[+] in which country has taken part	19	18
2. Medals won at Summer[0] Olympic Games		
gold	628	26
silver	473½	43
bronze	413	53
total	1514½	122
3. Medals won at Winter[x] Olympic Games:		
gold	30	12
silver	38	7
bronze	27	14
total	95	33

U.S.S.R. (not on the table), is in second place with a total of 670, including 238 gold medals. This is still an impressive record: Russia came into the Olympics later than other countries and has competed only 11 times against our 19. However, if you compare the average number of medals won in each Olympics, the U.S. still comes out the overall winner. Our average figure is 79, compared with 62 for Russia.

The U.K. comes next – and her record is impressive. With only a quarter the

U.K.	AUSTRALIA	AUSTRIA	BELGIUM	DENMARK	FRANCE	(WEST) GERMANY	IRELAND	ITALY	JAPAN	NETHERLANDS	NORWAY	SPAIN	SWEDEN	SWITZERLAND
19	19	18	17	18	18	16	10	17	13	16	18	12	18	19
160½	62	18	35	28½	140	135½	4	124	73	38	40	1	127½	40
198	51	27	48	58	152	181	3	115	64	42	30	6	122	63
168	65	34	43	51	157	178	6	106	63	53	31	4	152	53
526½	178	79	126	137½	449	494½	13	345	200	133	101	11	401½	156
5	0	22	1	0	12	25	0	10	1	9	50	1	25	15
4	0	31	1	0	9	20	0	7	2	13	52	0	23	17
10	0	27	3	0	12	23	0	7	1	9	43	1	26	16
19	0	80	5	0	33	68	0	24	4	31	145	1	74	48

‡*East and West Germany competed as one country up to 1964 (as an 'All German' team 1956-64). From 1968 they competed as separate teams and East Germany has won a total of 19 medals in the Winter Games, 181 in the Summer Games: 7 and 69 gold; 5 and 57 silver; 7 and 55 bronze.*

population of the U.S. or Russia, the U.K. has won a total of 526½ medals.

The Germans have 494½ medals to their credit for the 16 years they've been competing in the Summer Games. This includes 135½ gold medals – about the same average per contest as the U.K. East Germany has competed separately since 1968.

No prizes for guessing that the Scandinavian and Alpine countries are well in front when it comes to the Winter Olympics. The Norwegians are first –

Source:
International Olympic Committee archives
+Summer and Winter Games
⁰19 Games, 1896-1976
×12 Games, 1924-76

they must learn to ski before they learn to walk. Despite its tiny size, Norway has won more winter Olympic medals than any other country. At 145, their total is higher than those of Russia or America, who both have 60 times its population.

	U.S.A.	CANADA
	1974	1974
Number of:		
public and private courses	11,956	1,127
golfers (000s)	11,000	1,750
teaching professionals	11,000	1,200

The origins of golf are obscure. The Scots claim to have invented it, but they have their rivals. A game called *kolf* was played in Holland in medieval times.

Be that as it may, golf was well established in Scotland by the 15th century, when James II issued a decree that "fute-ball and golfe be utterly cryed down." The reason? They encouraged people to miss their archery practice. That ancient regal decree seems to have had little effect on either sport. And archery is hardly flourishing today.

James II also considered golf an "unprofitable sportis." Times have certainly changed. The top pros in the U.S. win hundreds of thousands of dollars annually. Not to mention the billions of dollars spent every year on golf equipment and greens fees.

By the end of the 15th century, James IV became addicted to the sport and changed royal policy. A bill for "golf clubbis and ballis" was found among his equipment. Scottish royalty also provided the first recorded woman golfer – Mary Queen of Scots. She was charged with playing golf in the fields around her castle just a few days after her husband's murder. It looks as though hitting a golf ball has always been an escape from matrimonial difficulties, as many golf widows, or widowers, will confirm.

Golf spread from Scotland as soon as the Scots laid down their swords and taught the game to the Sassenachs, south of the border in England. Today, the major golf-playing country is the U.S. By 1974 there were nearly 12,000 public and private courses. The U.S. even boasts a thriving association of professional golf-course architects.

The U.K., the home of golf, comes second, with nearly 2,000 courses. Australia is next with 1,345. If you look at the number of golfers in Australia, you'll see that there's one course for every 261 players. In the U.S., over 900 players have to share the average course. But in Italy, there are only 181 players per course. Your best bet is Austria, with one course for every 150 golfers.

Both Canada and Japan (more than 1,000 courses each) take golf seriously. The Japanese figure is impressive – 40 years ago you could count Japan's golf courses on the fingers of one hand. Today golf is the big boom sport in Japan. The only trouble is that there are over 4,300 golfers for every course – and there isn't the available space to allow for enough courses to meet the demand.

The Norwegians evidently have better things to do than play golf. There are only seven courses in the entire country.

U.K.	AUSTRALIA	AUSTRIA	BELGIUM	DENMARK	FRANCE	(WEST) GERMANY	IRELAND	ITALY	JAPAN	NETHERLANDS	NORWAY	SPAIN	SWEDEN	SWITZERLAND
1974	1974	1974	1974	1974	1973	1974	1973	1974	1974	1973	1974	1974	1974	1974
1,982	1,345	16	13	44	111	103	238	49	1,045	25	7	47	132	27
682.2	350.6	2.4	5.0	14.5	154.1	25.6	70.0	8.9	4,500	7.6	3.4	25.0	55.7	7.0
NA	486	7	16	21	182	125	65	80	924	32	7	212	101	60

NA not available

Source:
"Census of World Golf", *Golf Digest*, February 1975

Many golfers would consider this a criminal waste – so much beautiful countryside without a fairway in sight.

Belgium, Austria and the Netherlands come after Norway. The Dutch may have been playing *kolf* for centuries, but they lack staying power. Maybe too many golf balls were lost in the canals. Or, possibly, golf just doesn't appeal to the Flemish temperament: Belgium, with many Flemish citizens, has only 13 courses.

As you'd expect, the U.S. has more golf players than any other country – more than 11 million of them. That's the equivalent of the populations of Norway and Denmark added together. Over one in every 20 Americans plays golf.

Japan comes next with 4½ million golfers. Nearly one in every 25 Japanese spends a large proportion of his leisure time swinging a club and worrying about his handicap. Canada comes third, with 1¾ million golfers. One in every 15 Canadians play golf – an even higher proportion of golfers than across the border in the U.S.

The U.S., Japan and Canada are way ahead of the rest of the field. The U.K. is fourth, with nearly 700,000 golfers. In the U.K., only one person in 85 plays golf.

It's interesting to see the number of pro's per country. They're the expert professionals who teach golf at various courses and enter for professional tournaments. According to Jack Nicklaus, one of the greatest golfers playing today, there are at least a hundred professional golfers on the golf tournament circuit who, ten years ago, would all have been better than anyone else in the world.

In the U.S. we have 11,000 professionals one for every thousand golfers. The Canadians are second on the table, with 1,200 pros. The U.K. figure isn't available, but there's at least one professional to every course – which puts the U.K. figure around the 2,000 mark.

Professional golfers in Austria and Norway must be pretty lonely – there are only seven of them in each country.

Almost everyone likes to gamble from time to time, but for most of us this doesn't go much beyond the Saturday night poker game or occasional bet on the ponies. That's a long way from the casinos of Las Vegas or Monte Carlo.

Some people take gambling more seriously than others. Here in the U.S., there's a lot of flirting with lady luck. Americans spend a lot more on gambling than anyone else in the world. We each gamble to the tune of about $177 a year, or nearly $4 a week. Since this figures includes children, we can assume that the real figure for adults is even higher. Or else there's a lot of school kids squandering their lunch money in crap games.

Why such a high figure? Well, for one thing, compared to many other nations, we've got a lot of money to spend on leisure activities like gambling. Of course, gambling is concentrated heavily in states like Nevada, where huge establishments cater for thousands of eager gamblers 24 hours a day. These glittering "pleasure palaces" obviously increase the appeal of gambling excursions for many.

The U.K. comes second in the table. Each Briton gambles away over $99 a year. There's no equivalent of Reno or Las Vegas in Britain, but the Brits make up for that with horse racing. Even the Royal family are devotees of the thoroughbreds.

"Going to the dogs" is a popular pastime in Britain – bets on greyhound racing account for a large percentage of that $99. It's a pretty safe bet that the British are just as interested in gambling as we are in the U.S. In fact, gambling is legal throughout Britain, unlike the U.S. But there is a much lower average income there, and so the total amount of money spent on betting per person is less.

As in most areas of life, the Swedes have a liberal approach to this sometimes controversial pastime. The average Swede spends approximately $65 on gambling, just a little more than his French counterpart. But there's more temptation in France, from the National Lottery to the Longchamps races.

Members of Gamblers Anonymous might try moving to Austria, where they squander a mere $6.90 each per year. Or perhaps Switzerland, where they channel their gambling instincts in other directions – such as banking.

Even if you never manage to break the bank at Monte Carlo, you'll still feel like celebrating from time to time. That's when a bottle of champagne comes to mind. No prizes for guessing where they knock back the most – France. They go

	U.S.A.	CANADA
	1974	–
1. Money spent on gambling (US $) per person per year	177.0^0	NA
	1977	1977
2. Champagne (bottles) imported[+] (millions)	4.8	1.4

U.K.	AUSTRALIA	AUSTRIA	BELGIUM	DENMARK	FRANCE	(WEST) GERMANY	IRELAND	ITALY	JAPAN	NETHERLANDS	NORWAY	SPAIN	SWEDEN	SWITZERLAND
1975	–	1975	1975	1975	1975	1975	–	1975	–	1975	1975	1975	1975	1975
99.7	NA	6.9	17.5	18.2	59.4	42.8	NA	17.6	NA	21.2	48.7	12.4	65.0	16.2
1977	1977	1977	1977	1977	1977	1977	1977	1977	1977	1977	1977	1977	1977	1977
7.3	0.4	0.2	6.8	0.4	124.5 x	4.0	0.1	7.3	0.2 ‡	1.4	0.07	0.3	0.3	2.3

x Home consumption figures   ‡Includes sparkling wines

through a staggering 124.5 million bottles a year. That's about 2½ bottles for each man, woman and child.

Of course, France is the producer of the world's finest champagne. And at the rate they're downing it, we're lucky any gets out the country at all. On this front, no other country approaches France. The next largest number of champagne consumers is in the U.K. where they drink about 7.3 million bottles. That might sound paltry, compared with those effervescent Frenchmen, but look at it another way, corks pop all over Britain about 20,000 times a day.

In the U.S., we get through 4.8 million bottles of imported champagne a year, rather a low figure compared to the size of our population. But then we do drink a lot of domestic bubbly from California and New York State.

Norway is the land where champagne is least popular. One big factor here is the fact that large parts of Norway are dry, so no one drinks alcohol. The lucky Norwegians who *are* allowed to crack open a bottle of something prefer to drink their native *aquavit*.

Sources:
1 Euromonitor
2 Government trade offices
+ Champagne imported from France
0 Gambling in America, Commission on the Review of the National Policy Toward Gambling

In Ireland, they only import about 100,000 bottles of champagne each year. Per head of population, that's far more than we drink in the U.S. The Irishman is fond of his Guinness stout, but the Irish like to blend the best of both worlds in the land of misty mountains. They mix Guinness with champagne and call it Black Velvet.

It looks as if the Japanese prefer to stick to *sake*: they drink only 200,000 bottles of imported champagne a year. The Austrians drink the same amount. If you enjoy the high life, think twice before heading there, because Austria also ranked lowest on our table on gambling. Those rugged Austrians are probably too busy scaling Alpine peaks to be bothered with such frivolous pastimes.

Americans are the worst-read people of all the nationalities on our table. In the U.S. three-quarters of all adults don't seem to read a single book from one year to the next. Probably, we're just too busy with other leisure activities, ones that don't tax the eyes with small print. (However, almost everyone reads magazines and newspapers – see table on newspapers.) T.V. is our most popular national pastime, far ahead of reading. Even those who despise T.V. aren't necessarily driven to the printed word. In this country there are plenty of things to do that don't require literacy – from watching ball games, hockey matches and movies to relaxing at home with a stiff Martini.

Our nearest rivals as non-readers are the Italians. Only a third of them ever read a book from cover to cover. There's a bit more interest in Spain – 48% of Spaniards read books, 52% don't. The U.S., Italy and Spain form a kind of anti-literacy league. More than half the people in these places never read a book.

The best read people on our list are the Swiss. Only 19% of them fail to read at least one book per year. And only one Dane out of four is a non-reader. In the U.K., the figure is 29% – in other words nearly a third of the population never reads a book. But more than one British adult in five does pick up a book every day. The British are closely followed by the Danes and Swedes – one in five of whom reads a book daily. The daily reading norm for all the countries listed is 15% – so about one adult in seven reads a book every day, except in Spain and Italy. Only one Italian in 9 reads daily and in Spain the figure is one in 14.

The most revealing figure on this table is the number of books a person reads each year. The Danes are the most enthusiastic readers: they average 5.7 books a year – roughly one book every two months. Britain, with 5.5 books a year, is next, and Sweden, with 5.2, is in third place. The Netherlands, who read 5.1 books a year, comes next. The French and Swiss are also reasonably

	U.S.A.	CANADA
	1971	1975
1. People who, in a year, read books:		
never (%)	74[+]	45[0]
daily (%)	NA	NA
2. Average number of books read per person per year	NA	NA
	1975	–
3. Retail sales of books (US \$ – millions)	4591[‡]	NA
4. Expenditure on books (US \$) per capita	21.46[‡]	NA

U.K.	AUSTRALIA	AUSTRIA	BELGIUM	DENMARK	FRANCE	(WEST) GERMANY	IRELAND	ITALY	JAPAN	NETHERLANDS	NORWAY	SPAIN	SWEDEN	SWITZERLAND
1974	1974	1974	1974	1974	1974	1974	1974	1974	1974	1974	1974	1974	1974	1974
29	48[x]	33	45	25	38	34	40	68	NA	27	30	52	28	19
21	NA	12	13	20	14	18	NA	9	NA	15	13	7	20	14
5.5	NA	2.6	3.4	5.7	4.9	4.8	NA	1.9	NA	5.1	4.3	2.8	5.2	4.5
1975	–	1975	1975	1975	1975	1975	–	1975	–	1975	1975	1975	1975	1975
540.5	NA	62.0	83.0	42.5	320.0	400.5	NA	215.5	NA	120.0	24.7	84.4	110.6	75.0
9.66	NA	8.23	8.17	4.34	6.09	6.47	NA	3.79	NA	8.86	6.19	2.38	13.52	13.98

NA not available

avid readers. They turn the pages of just under five books a year. Italians are right at the bottom of the ladder – they read less than two books a year. The Austrians (2.6) and Spanish (2.8) are just above.

Americans may not read books, but we certainly buy them. On average we spend around $20.00 a year on books – more than twice as much as readers spend in any country except Switzerland and Sweden. In Switzerland, the figure is nearly $14.00 and in Sweden, about $13.50. The British certainly read more books than the Americans or the Swiss and Swedes, but they spend less than half as much on them as the average American – possibly because of the U.K.'s excellent public library system.

Sources:
Euromonitor
[+]Gallup Organization Inc
[0]Leisure Survey of the Secretary of State
[x]Australian Embassy
[‡]Confidential source

		U.S.A.	CANADA
		1974	1973
1.	Number of daily newspapers	1798	121
2.	Estimated circulation (000s)	62,156	5207
	copies per 1,000 inhabitants	293	235

John F. Kennedy was famous for speed reading his way through ten or fifteen newspapers a day. The average American is less well informed. On average, there are only 293 daily newspaper copies printed for every thousand people. That means about one for every three inhabitants.

Sweden has the highest rate of copies per thousand on the table. Over half the population buys a newspaper every day. There the rate is 536 newspapers purchased for every thousand people – one paper for every two people. Japan is next on the list with 526 newspapers purchased for every thousand people. If newspaper sales are an indication of being well-informed, the Swedes and the Japanese are the most up-to-the-minute people on the table.

The British come next, they buy 443 dailies per thousand – or one paper for every 2.3 people. Considering the way newspapers are left lying around, or given to someone else when finished with, it means most of them must see the newspaper every day.

In some countries readers share newspapers as an established procedure. In the Netherlands, Austria, France and other countries, many cafes have newspaper racks with a selection of the daily papers hanging over poles for the customers to read over their daily refreshments. These countries have slightly lower rates of purchases per thousand people. But the fact that their figures aren't so high doesn't mean that they're not keeping up with the news. They're just taking it in small, civilized doses.

The lowest figures are for Spain. Only 96 Spaniards buy a newspaper each day for every thousand inhabitants. That's a rate of only one in ten people who feel it's important to know what's going on. But the Spanish figures are four or five years old – from a time when the press was firmly controlled by Franco's government. Since then, Spain has undergone dramatic changes – Franco's death, the coronation of the king and the restitution of democracy. Presumably the Spanish are buying the newspapers more often nowadays – and finding it more worthwhile.

Today, people want the news fast – and that's how we get it on T.V. and radio. With satellite communications, videotape, and instant replay, we see the news almost as it happens – even when it's taking place on the other side of the globe. This must be worrying newspaper journalists and circulation managers.

The result is an almost universal decline in newspaper readership. In the U.S. there were 310 copies bought per thousand just a decade ago – compared to 293 in 1974. And the U.K. figure was 479 per thousand in 1965. On the other hand, the Italian figure has risen since 1965. Then it was 113 per thousand, compared

NEWSPAPERS

U.K.	AUSTRALIA	AUSTRIA	BELGIUM	DENMARK	FRANCE	(WEST) GERMANY	IRELAND	ITALY	JAPAN	NETHERLANDS	NORWAY	SPAIN	SWEDEN	SWITZERLAND
1974	1973	1974	1974	1974	1973	1974	1974	1974	1974	1973	1974	1974	1974	1974
109	58	30	31	51	103	320	7	79	180	93	75	115	111	92
24800	5126	2316	2416	1792	11458	17872	729	6963	57820	4175	1567	3396	4362	2535
443	386	308	247	355	220	289	236	126	526	311	391	96	536	391

Source:
United Nations Educational,
Scientific, and Cultural Organization

with the 1974 figure of 126. But the Italian rise is an exception – perhaps it bears witness to Italy's recent unending series of newsworthy crises.

The number of daily newspapers printed also indicates readership trends. France, West Germany and the U.K. all have about the same populations – but in West Germany there are three times as many newspapers. Perhaps this is explained by the fact that in France and the U.K., the journalistic action tends to focus on the capitals of Paris and London. Whereas in West Germany, the press tends to be more evenly distributed among the large cities. Instead of reading just *The Times* or *Le Monde*, West Germans, depending on where they live, may subscribe to *Die Frankfurter Allgemagne, Die Zeit, Die Welt* or others. And this variety seems to be good for the newspaper market.

In general, things don't look too good for the newspaper industry. With ever more sophisticated T.V. techniques, video cassettes that tape programs for replay even when you're not at home, and other new technology, some experts believe that in 20 years time newspapers as we know them may have become a thing of the past.

Data on book publication can be read as an informal profile of a nation's culture. We all know about China, for instance, and Chairman Mao's *Little Red Book*. In the countries studied, there's a bit more variety. This table shows what kinds of books people like to read and which subjects are studied. It should be kept in mind, however, that our figures are for 1974. Book production is a growing industry and up-to-date figures would be somewhat higher.

The U.S., with almost four times as many inhabitants as West Germany, publishes 10,000 *fewer* books a year. The figure in the table includes government publications, university theses and juvenile fiction, without which the total number would be 28,143.

Number of titles+ published	U.S.A.	CANADA
	1974	1974
generalities	908	428
philosophy	1033	150
religion	1612	220
social sciences	7014	1656
philology	319	291
pure sciences	2523	338
applied sciences	4833	827
arts	2519	937
literature	4992	1131
geography/history	2390	605
Total	68,600[0]	6583

The greatest number of books in the U.S. are in the field of social sciences. But even with over 7,000, we're still short of the West Germans by 4,000 titles.

In keeping with the spirit of that great American phenomenon – the bestseller, our second most popular kind of book is called, somewhat ambiguously, "literature". Most of the 5,000 or so "literary" tomes we publish annually are novels and stories. Presumably this includes everything from murder mysteries to pornography – although not comic books.

Books on applied science run "literature" a close third. We publish only slightly fewer books of applied science than we do of literature – though we can't be sure as many people actually *read* the scientific books. The West Germans publish about the same number in the applied science category. Little wonder the U.S. reaped the benefit of so many prolific German scientists during and after the war.

In the arts, the U.S. ranks third, with about 2,500 books. West Germany comes first, and the U.K. second. Canada ranks relatively high in this field with sixth place. Next to the social sciences and literature arts is the highest . The Canada

U.K.	AUSTRALIA	AUSTRIA	BELGIUM	DENMARK	FRANCE	(WEST) GERMANY	IRELAND	ITALY	JAPAN	NETHERLANDS	NORWAY	SPAIN	SWEDEN	SWITZERLAND
1974		1974		1974		1974	1974	1974	1974	1974	1974	1974	1976	1974
714	NA	81	NA	187	NA	3176	29	279	634	151	139	2170	NA	127
762	NA	177	NA	181	NA	1017	12	355	648	293	93	711	NA	238
784	NA	165	NA	189	NA	1894	31	434	613	343	226	1102	NA	553
4891	NA	1054	NA	1110	NA	11583	115	1802	5465	1239	1557	4347	NA	1766
518	NA	68	NA	177	NA	1366	4	171	514	685	302	487	NA	236
2744	NA	598	NA	550	NA	2284	23	409	1148	600	531	1059	NA	904
3770	NA	819	NA	1091	NA	4998	110	741	6362	701	799	2041	NA	1658
2623	NA	407	NA	396	NA	2715	59	629	1828	452	237	1082	NA	916
5149	NA	599	NA	1470	NA	7318	198	2449	6007	2197	1281	5355	NA	1480
2355	NA	455	NA	608	NA	3261	41	644	1833	538	378	1670	NA	679
24310	NA	4423	NA	5959	NA	39612	622	7913	25052	7199	5543	20024	6990	8557

⁰Includes government publications, university theses and juvenile fiction   NA not available

Arts Council is well known both for its generosity in subsidizing arts projects in Canada, and for encouraging a wide variety of projects by young artists. It shows in their thriving book trade in this field, and in their reputation for arts.

As the home of more Nobel Prize-winning scientists than any other country, it's no surprise that the English publish the most books in pure science. If only they could get together with the Japanese – who top the list in applied science – they might work to each other's benefit. The Japanese would have a fresh source of scientific ideas. And the British could put some of Japan's efficiency into practice.

Source:
United Nations Educational, Scientific, and Cultural Organization
+First editions only

Spain ranks fifth overall, publishing over 20,000 titles annually. They come second in that undefined category of "general" works, and third in both religion and literature. The Spanish have always had a rich literature. And they're deeply religious too. In the field of religious works, they produce only 500 fewer books each year than in the entire United States.

	U.S.A.	CANADA
	1974	1971
1. Number of public libraries (000s):	8.3	0.7
per 100,000 inhabitants[+]	4	4
2. Number of volumes in public libraries (millions)	387.6	26.2
3. Average number of books per public library (000s)	46.5	37.7
4. Number of registered borrowers (000s)[+]	NA	NA

When Andrew Carnegie turned some of his profit from steel into public libraries, his idea was to bring books to the common man. His endowment did a lot for literacy and scholarship in many places. But the ratio of libraries to population in the U.S. is still surprisingly low: one U.S. public library per 25,000 people – a reason a lot of folks may stay home to watch T.V.. Nonetheless, virtually every town and city in the country has a public library, with almost 50,000 volumes to browse through. The average Canadian library has a respectable 38,000 volumes.

Italy claims almost 9,000 public libraries – more than the U.S. But each has an average of only 2,000 volumes. Even with 16 libraries per hundred thousand people there are fewer than 32,000 books per hundred thousand, or roughly one book for every 30 people.

Norway claims 11 libraries per hundred thousand, each with about 21,000 books. West Germany and Spain equal the U.S. in the proportion of libraries to population. But West Germany has about 17,000 books per library, less than half as many as the U.S.

On the surface, the U.K. and Ireland are the big winners in the book sweepstakes. But the figures are somewhat misleading. The U.K. has an unusual public library system that makes comparisons practically impossible. With a large number of mobile libraries, the total number of libraries is magnified out of proportion. Many of the 239 libraries per hundred thousand of population are tiny trailers carrying a rotating stock from a larger central library.

Sweden and Denmark have excellent libraries. Sweden has five for every hundred thousand people – or one for every 20,000. The average size of a Swedish library is over 73,000 volumes. Denmark, with the same number of libraries, averages more than 130,000 volumes.

Japan has the lowest proportion of libraries to population on the table – less than one for every 100,000 Japanese and the average number of books is 4,300. France has about the same number of libraries as Japan.

The most interesting figures on the table are for Ireland. The Republic has only 30 libraries. But each library has a remarkable average of 165,000 volumes.

	U.K.°	AUSTRALIA	AUSTRIA	BELGIUM×	DENMARK	FRANCE	(WEST) GERMANY	IRELAND	ITALY	JAPAN	NETHERLANDS	NORWAY	SPAIN	SWEDEN	SWITZERLAND
	1977	1974	1974	1974	1974	1973	1974	1974	1974	1974	1974	1973	1974	1974	1974
	135.0	0.9	0.4	1.6	0.3	0.8	2.5	0.03	8.7	0.9	0.4	0.5	1.4	0.4	1.9
	239	6	6	16	5	2	4	1	16	1	3	11	4	5	29
	125.5	11.5	4.4	20.5	32.7	37.4	43.0	5.1	17.0	38.8	17.9	9.4	8.7	30.5	NA
	0.93	13.5	10.3	12.7	130.3	44.7	17.2	165.3	2.0	4.3	43.7	21.0	6.1	73.4	NA
	16,928	NA	635.3	NA	NA	NA	90.8	720.8	2944	3756	2292	621.2	943.4	NA	NA

NA not available

Sources:
United Nations Educational, Scientific, and Cultural Organization
[+]Heron House estimates
[°]Library Association. Figure includes mobile libraries, prison libraries, etc.
[×]National statistical office

We're told that letter writing is a dying art. But a lot of letters still get sent through the mail – and each year the number goes up. Why is this, in an age when more and more people rely on the telephone?

We may send fewer long, gossipy, personal letters to distant friends, but we still send postcards when we go on vacation. Then there are Christmas cards, and birthday cards, and Mothers Day cards... We also send more and more business letters.

Which countries make the most use of their mail service? Where do people send and receive the most letters? That's what this table is all about.

The U.S. is easily the world's most mail-happy nation. Nearly 90 billion separate pieces of correspondence pass through our postal system each year. Yet the Post Office is still able to live up to its proud boast: "Neither rain, nor sleet nor snow nor dark of night shall stay the mail on its appointed rounds."

Statistics may not show how many flat feet mailmen have incurred delivering the letters, postcards, merchandise samples, parcels and junk mail we get. They do show that somebody stamped 422 pieces of mail for every man, woman and child in the U.S. That's a lot of letters per person – but Switzerland beats us to it in this category. There, every inhabitant, (save St. Bernards) sends or receives ten pieces of correspondence a week. Every burgher, large or small, is in the 500-a-year bracket – in mail that is.

	U.S.A.	CANADA
	1973	1975
1. Total mail[+] handled[0] (billions)	89.9	5.0
2. Domestic mail handled[0] (billions)	87.6	4.7
3. Foreign mail handled[0] (millions)	2279	234
4. Mail per person [x]	422	227

Such a heavy volume of correspondence can't be credited entirely to politicians depositing their money in unnamed bank accounts. However, banking and insurance are two of the country's major interests and involve extensive correspondence.

The Italians are at the other end of the scale. Including ransom notes, they average only about two pieces of mail a week. Obviously their strong point is talking, not writing.

The Irish postal workers appear to have less to do. They only deal with about 460 million pieces of mail a year for the entire country. About 157 million are from foreigners.

Norway, with a population roughly the size of Ireland's has a similar approach to writing letters. Norwegians make better readers though. The average inhabitant of Norway receives twice as many letters a year as his Irish counterpart. Maybe he just can't afford to mail as many.

However, in total amount of foreign mail received and sent, we have to take a back seat to the world-trade-conscious West Germans.

U.K.	AUSTRALIA	AUSTRIA	BELGIUM	DENMARK	FRANCE	(WEST) GERMANY	IRELAND	ITALY	JAPAN	NETHERLANDS	NORWAY	SPAIN	SWEDEN	SWITZERLAND
1975	1974	1973	1975	1975	1975	1975	1974	1975	1975	1975	1975	1975	1975	1975
10.4	2.6	1.8	2.3	1.3	11.8	17.8	0.46	6.6	13.4	3.8	0.96	4.5	2.5	3.0
9.2	2.3	1.3	2.0	1.2	11.0	11.3	0.3	5.7	13.2	3.4	0.8	3.8	2.3	2.7
1139	303	389	279	125	777	6470	157	816	198	456	81	727	215	384
186	200	240	255	260	227	292	153	120	121	292	240	128	312	500

Probably because of its position as a leading European industrial power, West Germany handles almost three times as much foreign mail as we do even though it's population is smaller.

The U.K. is third when it comes to foreign correspondence.

Even though memories of the British Empire are now confined to the occasional television series, mailmen are still kept busy trying to decipher the British "public school scrawl".

These are average figures. In reality, mail delivery isn't usually spread out evenly over the year, particularly in western countries where Christmas provides the postal system with its greatest challenge.

Modern technology has made certain aspects of the postal service much easier. For example the sorting, cancellation and mislaying of those 90 billion letters circulated yearly in the U.S. is no longer done by hand.

And there is a hope that one day Farley's Law (that the further the mail has to go the sooner it will be delivered) will be disproved.

Source:
United Nations
[+] Includes air mail, ordinary and registered mail, postcards, printed matter, merchandise samples, small packets, phonopost packets. Except in the U.S., it excludes ordinary parcels, insured letters and parcels.
[0] Received and sent
[x] Heron House estimates

The U.S. buys 276 million record albums every year. (We also take home 114 million pre-recorded tapes.) On average every man, woman and child in the U.S. buys one L.P. and half a tape every year – and this figure doesn't include single records or E.P.s. Nevertheless, we're pikers compared with the U.K. – home of the Beatles and the Rolling Stones. They buy 106 million L.P.s annually – almost two for each person in the country.

Third in this list is Japan, where over 90 million L.P.s are sold every year, closely followed by West Germany (80.5 million). Who buys the fewest records? Norway, where they purchase only about two million followed by Austria (2.6 million), the Danes and the Swiss (three million each). It seems Scandinavians don't go for sounds.

The real story, however, isn't in total sales but in L.P. records sold per person.

The U.K. again comes out on top – almost 2,000 records are sold each year per thousand inhabitants. Next comes Canada, where the figure is 1,800. Australia – home of the Beachcombers – is third. The U.S. is fourth in this category, with 1,300 records bought per thousand people, about the same as Sweden and West Germany.

The Italians – well-known for bursting into song at the least provocation – buy the fewest records of all – 200 per thousand inhabitants. In the land of opera they obviously prefer to do their own singing in the bathtub or shower.

Austria, home of Wolfgang Amadeus Mozart, is second lowest. They sell just 300 L.P.s per thousand people.

The Spanish figure (500) includes singles and E.P.s as well as L.P.s, so it may be the Spanish who are the worst customers of all for long-playing records They're busy tuning up their guitars and voices to serenade their señoritas. A stereo set under the balcony just wouldn't have the same effect.

One reason we come off poorly in record sales is that the U.S. is heavily into tapes. We buy 540 pre-recorded tapes per thousand inhabitants – by far the highest figure. The British come next at 320 per thousand. Combine the record-buying figures with the ones for tape purchases, and the Brits are still world champion recorded music buyers.

	U.S.A.	CANADA
	1974	1974
1. Total sales of records (millions):	276.0[o]	40.8[x]
per 1,000 inhabitants[+]	1300	1800
2. Number of classical records manufactured as % of all records	5.2	N A
3. Total sales of pre-recorded tapes (millions)	114.0[o]	NA
per 1,000 inhabitants[+]	540	NA

RECORD AND CASSETTE SALES

	U.K.	AUSTRALIA	AUSTRIA	BELGIUM	DENMARK	FRANCE	(WEST) GERMANY	IRELAND	ITALY	JAPAN	NETHERLANDS	NORWAY	SPAIN	SWEDEN	SWITZERLAND
	1974	1973	1973	1973	1972	1974	1973	–	1974	1974	1973	1973	1974	1974	1972
	106.0^X	22.0^X	2.6^0	10.6^0	3.0^0	54.6^0	80.5^0	NA	9.1^0	90.5^X	NA	2.1^0	$16.0^{X‡}$	10.7^0	3.0^0
	1900	1600	300	1100	600	1000	1300	NA	200	800	NA	500	500	1300	500
	10.0	9.0	25.0	NA	7.0	NA	13.0	NA	NA	9.0	16.0	NA	NA	NA	NA
	18.0^X	NA	1.2^0	1.0^0	1.2^0	7.5^0	9.7^0	NA	7.7^0	NA	NA	0.8^0	7.7^X	1.8^0	1.5^0
	320	NA	160	100	240	140	160	NA	140	NA	NA	200	220	220	230

NA not available ^{0}*Sold* ^{X}*Produced*   ‡*Includes singles and EPs*

The U.S. comes in second with Canada close behind.

Austria, second from the bottom in total record sales, comes top in the classical league: twenty-five percent of all records manufactured are classical. That's a lot of Mozart and Strauss. The Netherlands places second in the classical sweepstakes, 16% of their production is classical. West Germany, home of *von Karajan* and the Berlin Philharmonic, comes in third with 13%. In the U.K. only about ten percent of records made are classical and, in Australia, nine percent. It seems that Americans are rock freaks rather than classical enthusiasts: only 5.2% of all the records they manufacture are classical.

The newest trend in the recording industry is the shift to tapes instead of records. It's well under way in the U.S. and U.K.

Source:
EMI Ltd
+Heron House estimates

The figures for museums and museum attendance show one thing clearly. The number of museums in a country isn't necessarily related to the age and depth of the country's culture. The U.S., with just 200 - 300 years of history to commemorate, has by far the most museums – almost 2,000 – or roughly one for every 100,000 people. Over 300 million visitors attended these museums. That's an average of 1½ visits for every man, woman and child in the country. If the visits were spread evenly among the 2,000 museums, each could count on 156,000 visitors.

	U.S.A.	CANADA
	1975	1975
1. Number of museums	1994	708
2. Number of visitors (millions)	312.0[+]	55.0
per museum (000s)[+]	156	77

Some of the success of American museums is due to the show-biz marketing of their treasures. The grand old Metropolitan Museum of Art in New York, which has one of the two or three greatest art collections in the world, has been packaged "for the people". Visitors crowd the steps below the Met's august doors.

Another reason museum attendance is so high in the U.S. is that many inherently rootless Americans are almost desperate to ally themselves with a sense of culture and history. There's no doubt that the polyglot and diverse origins of the American people have something to do with this. Digging out family "roots" is a perennial American pastime. While new minority groups regularly join in the hunt, the search for the past is practically as old as European settlement.

We also try to immortalize our past almost as soon as it occurs by encapsulizing our memorabilia inside museum cases. In addition to our many fine art museums, we have Pilgrim museums, Shaker Museums, baseball museums, cowboy museums, goldrush museums, museums of science and industry, jazz museums, rock and roll museums, automobile museums, space museums and many more.

Americans have also managed to gather some of the greatest works from other countries and cultures. Thanks to the great wealth and discerning taste of some American collectors, many of our museums are straining at the seams with treasures from the Renaissance, ancient Egypt and Greece, 18th and 19th century Europe, and the dynasties of the Orient.

The closest competitor to the U.S. in numbers of museums is Japan. An average of about 23,000 visitors attend each museum, with one for every 950,000 people. The Japanese have far more museums than their European counterparts. Perhaps, in the face of rapid and disruptive industrial change, they wish to preserve the art and crafts of their rich and ancient culture.

In terms of annual visitors, Canada follows the U.S. with 55 million – almost double the entire Canadian population. Unless the Canadians are the most museum-going people in the world, a high

	U.K.	AUSTRALIA	AUSTRIA	BELGIUM	DENMARK	FRANCE	(WEST) GERMANY	IRELAND	ITALY	JAPAN	NETHERLANDS	NORWAY	SPAIN	SWEDEN	SWITZERLAND
	1975	1975	1975	1975	1975	1975	1975	1975	1975	1975	1975	1975	1975	1975	1975
	950	69	108	210	245	871	574	15	734	1183	369	177	546	314	225
	15.7	2.1	3.6	4.2	7.6	1.2	17.5	1.5	32.9	28.0	4.4	3.0	3.1	11.2	5.7
	16	31	33	19	31	1	30	100	45	23	12	17	5	35	25

percentage of their museum visitors must be Yankee tourists.

With 950 museums, the British have immortalized everything from Victorian teapots to the Tower of London. Yet museum attendance in the U.K. is lower than in Italy and West Germany.

Some of the other European attendance figures are surprisingly low. The Netherlands, with a rich and prolific art history, ranks ninth, with only 369 museums. Over four million people visit Dutch museums each year. That's an average of about 12,000 visitors to each museum.

Austria, Belgium, Ireland, Norway and Sweden also have relatively few museums, although the average number of visitors to each museum varies widely – from 19,000 in Belgium to 100,000 in Ireland.

Italy, rich in art and history, has an abundance of museums with an average museum attendance of 45,000. France has the worst record. With 871 museums packed with mind-boggling art treasures, an average of only 1,000 visitors go to each museum annually. When you factor out the millions who tread the halls of the Louvre, the *grande dame* of French museums, that leaves a lot of museums to enjoy in privacy.

Source:
United Nations Educational, Scientific, and Cultural Organization
+Heron House estimates

MUMMIES BOY

This table is about vacation habits in different countries. Where do the most people go abroad? Where do they prefer to stay at home? Where do they simply do without any vacation?

More Swedes take vacations than any other nationality on our table – 84% of them. That's over ten percent more than their Scandinavian neighbors in Norway. Here 73% spend the long winter nights browsing through colored brochures and planning their vacations – ready to get up and go as soon as the summer arrives. The Norwegian figure is closely followed by that of Italy, 72% of whom take vacations.

Denmark has the next highest figure which completes the Scandinavian trio. If you want to set up a tourist agency, go to Scandinavia.

Only 63% of Britons take vacations. This is about average for the countries in our table – exactly the same percentage as in Belgium and West Germany. But it's a big surprise to find that only 58% of Americans go on holiday.

The Spanish are at the bottom of the vacation table – only 32% take a vacation. That's understandable, sunny Spain is a major tourist attraction, and most of us think that every day there must seem like a holiday.

Holland follows Spain. Only 40% of Dutch take vacations. It's hard to believe. Over-crowded Holland is one of the wettest countries in Europe.

Australia has the third lowest figure

	U.S.A.	CANADA
	1977	–
1. People (%) who take a vacation	58	NA
2. Percentage of people taking a vacation who:		
go abroad	30	NA
stay in their own country	70	NA

(50%). Of course, if you're living in Sydney you can go to Bondi Beach any weekend.

The other figures on this table show where people go when they do go on holiday. Who prefers to go on holiday in their own country? Who likes to get up and go abroad? The Swiss top the table when it comes to vacationing abroad –74% of them leave their home country at least once a year. Switzerland isn't exactly large – and it's also near lots of interesting places. Paris, Brussels, Vienna or Rome are all just 300 miles across the border.

The West Germans, famous for their wanderlust, are the next most dedicated foreign travelers. Sixty-eight percent of West Germans who take a vacation prefer to take it abroad. They usually head for the sun – that's one reason why beaches in Italy, Spain and Greece always have so many well-tanned West Germans in residence. And hard-currency German Deutschemarks go a long way in Mediterranean countries.

Two Scandinavian countries come next. In Norway, 53% of vacationers go abroad; in Denmark the figure is 50%.

U.K.	AUSTRALIA[0]	AUSTRIA	BELGIUM	DENMARK	FRANCE	(WEST) GERMANY	IRELAND	ITALY	JAPAN	NETHERLANDS	NORWAY	SPAIN	SWEDEN	SWITZERLAND
1975	1976	1975	1975	1975	1975	1975	–	1975	–	1975	1975	1975	1975	1975
63	50	59	63	71	53	63	NA	72	NA	40	73	32	84	69
33	15	47	49	50	36	68	NA	28	NA	49	53	28	38	74
67	85	53	51	50	64	32	NA	72	NA	51	47	72	62	26

The Swedish figure is comparatively low. Only 38% of Swedes who take vacations go abroad. There are two main reasons. Sweden is a large and beautiful country and many Swedes prefer to spend their vacations in their own lakeside cottages, or puttering about the lakes in boats. Also, Sweden is a long way from European holiday areas.

The Swedes aren't the most dedicated stay-at-homes on the table – not by a long way. Eighty-five percent of vacationing Australians don't go abroad. The reasons are obvious. The Swedes may be a thousand miles from the Mediterranean – but many Australians have to travel that far before they leave their native shores.

The Spanish and Italians come second in the stay-at-home stakes. Who can blame them? Many people travel hundreds of miles for the sunshine and scenery they have on their doorsteps.

The U.S. comes next: 70% of us prefer to stay at home. Like the Spanish, we have scenery and sunshine on our doorsteps; and like the Australians anywhere but home is a very long way off. There are lots of places to see in the U.S., whatever kind of holiday you want.

Source:
Euromonitor
+Industry estimates
0Australian Tourist Board

Once a year they pack their suitcases, stop the milk and the papers, board the cat and – where *do* all the tourists go?

You'll find a lot of them gazing at the Colosseum, floating on Venice's canals in gondolas and studying the old masters in Florence museums. Italy gets more foreign visitors than any other country. There were nearly 38 million of them in 1976. These tourists outnumbered the entire population of Spain, Egypt or Poland. They left more than $2.5 billion behind them, or about $67 apiece.

	U.S.A.	CANADA
	1976	1976
1. Foreign arrivals at frontiers (millions)	17.5	14.1
comparison with 1975 (%)	+11.6	−5.1
2. International tourist receipts (US $ millions)	5860[+]	1641[+]
comparison with 1975 (%)	+20	+7

The second biggest crowds were to be found exploring the Prado, climbing the steep cobblestoned streets of Toledo or lounging in the sun at the Costa del Sol. Thirty million tourists opted for Spain that year – not as many as went to Italy, perhaps, but then they did spend more money – over three billion dollars, or over $102 each. When the price is right, tourists shell out more money. In Spain prices and sales taxes are low.

The third most visited country was the U.S. We had 17.5 million foreign visitors in 1976 – more than the combined populations of Ohio, Indiana, Illinois and Wisconsin. When they weren't gazing out at the Grand Canyon, riding up in elevators to the top of the Empire State Building or taking a tour of the Universal Studios in Hollywood, all these visitors were busy spending money: $5.86 billion of it, to be precise, or $334 apiece. That's a lot more travelers' checks than in any other country. America's a big place, and lots of tourist dollars went to airlines and car rental companies. Nonetheless, the amounts spent show that America – like Spain – gives good value for the tourist's dollar. We may think we're plagued by inflation, but New York is less expensive for visitors than London, Paris or Tokyo. So stop and think about those European bargains.

An astounding 14.4 million tourists chose tiny Denmark as their vacation spot in 1976 – that's almost three times the entire Danish population. Denmark's visitors spent $803 million – that's over $55 each. Denmark's quiet charm and pleasant scenery are the big draws here: there's still a real fairy-tale charm about the land of Hans Christian Andersen.

But all those tourists didn't take the opportunity to visit nearby Sweden or Norway. Those two countries welcomed fewer tourists than almost any other

	U.K.	AUSTRALIA	AUSTRIA	BELGIUM×	DENMARK	FRANCE	(WEST) GERMANY	IRELAND	ITALY	JAPAN	NETHERLANDS	NORWAY‡	SPAIN	SWEDEN	SWITZERLAND
	1976	1976	1976	1976	1976	1976	1976	1976	1976	1976	1976	1976	1976	1976	1976
	10.1	0.5	11.6	NA	14.4‡	13.4	NA	1.2	37.7	0.8	NA	0.4‡	30.0	0.8	NA
	+14.1	+3.1	+4.1	NA	-3.6	+3.1	NA	+0.1	+4.5	+12.4	NA	+13.2	−0.4	+4.3	NA
	2889	306⁰	3131⁰	959⁰	803⁰	3613⁺⁰	3211⁰	200	2525	312⁰	1061⁰	395⁰	3083⁰	353⁰	1679
	+17.3	+9.7	+3.2	+9	+7.7	+4.1	+12.8	−0.5	−2.0	+23.8	−4.2	+7.7	−9.4	+3.2	+4.4

⁺OECD estimates ⁰Figures refer to receipts registered in foreign currency grouped regionally according to the denomination of the currency. These figures do not correspond exactly to the amount of receipts from visitors coming from certain countries. ×Includes Luxembourg ‡Excludes Scandinavian citizens

Source:
Organization for Economic Co-operation and Development

nation in our table. Apparently the legendary beautiful blondes don't make up for the very high prices.

Japan didn't attract many foreigners either. This is probably accounted for by a combination of high prices and the language barrier. But the Australians may be wondering why they're so unpopular. Let's face it – they just live in the wrong neighborhood! They've got a California-style climate and great surfing beaches, but after paying the air fare you can't even afford swimming trunks.

When it comes to counting up tourist bucks, the Irish leprechauns must be trying to figure out what happened to the pot of gold. They made a measly $200 million. But that does work out at $166 spent by each visitor. That kind of money buys an awful lot of Guinness.

Closer to home, our neighbor to the north entertained almost as many tourists as we did. Canada has a lot of attractions – great fishing and hunting, spectacular scenery and a common language. You can even watch your favorite T.V. shows. It's a safe bet that a lot of Canada's 14 million tourists are American, and a lot of *our* 17.5 million are Canadian.

Things were looking up for beleagured Brits in 1976 – a record ten million visitors showed up to watch the Changing of the Guard, trek to the Tower of London and to wave at the Queen. That meant a shot in the arm for their ailing economy – to the tune of $2,889 million. And that buys a heap of crumpets. Their reputation for bad weather is obviously counterbalanced by a lot of very splendid British features.

Number of champagne bottles imported (millions)

130		
110		
90		
70		
50		
30		
10		
9		
8		
7		
6		
5		
4		
3		
2		
1		

The sound of popping champagne corks must be almost deafening in France. Frenchmen downed 124½ million bottles in one year, a world record. It's not just "joie de vivre" they're full of.

You probably think of an Englishman with a pint of bitter beer in his hand, not a glass of bubbly. Yet the U.K. tied with Italy as the second most enthusiastic champagne consumer.

Belgium is next, with 6.8 million bottles, followed by the U.S. Americans downed nearly five million bottles, or one bottle for every 40 people. Of course, that's just the figure for imported champagne. A lot of home-grown bubbly goes down the hatch as well.

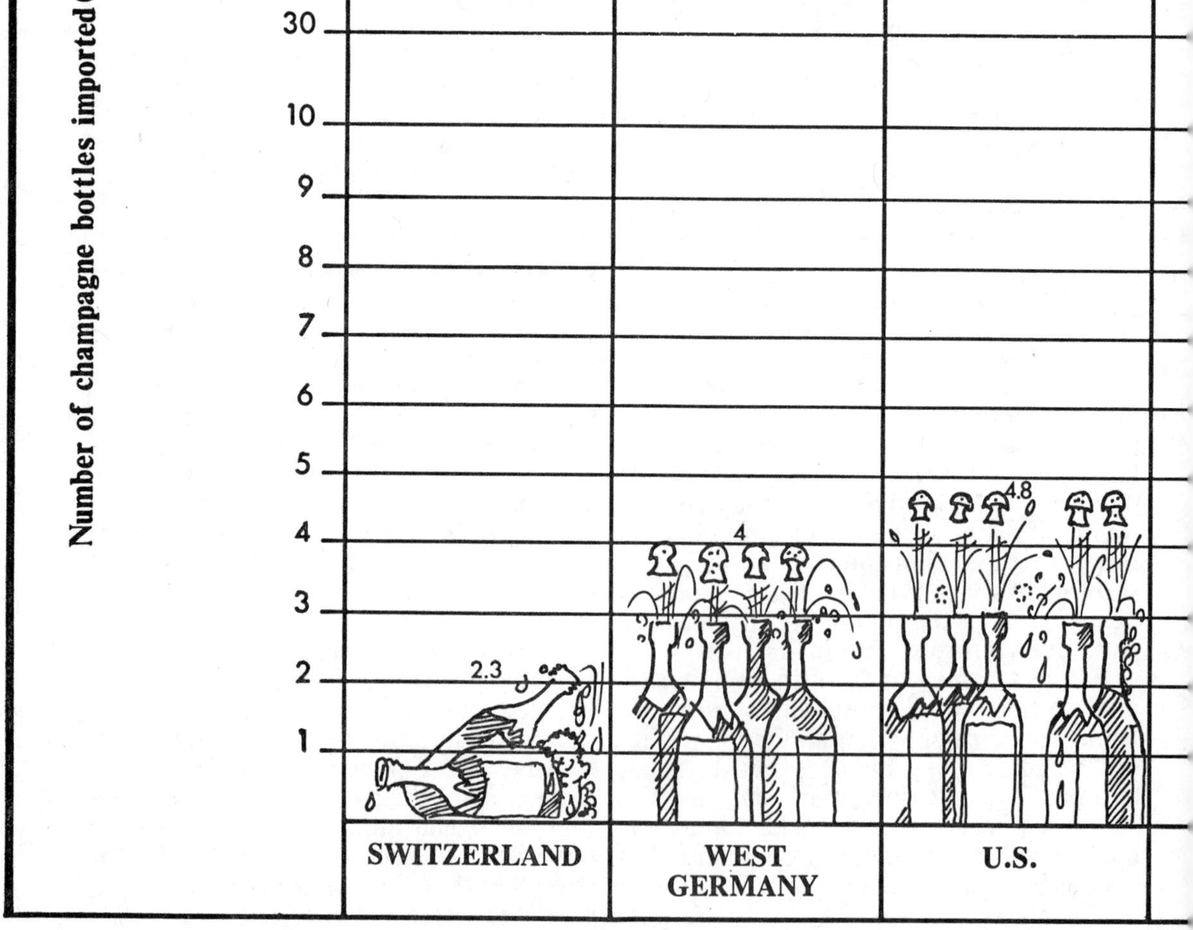

2.3

4

4.8

| SWITZERLAND | WEST GERMANY | U.S. |

CHAMPAGNE

			130
	124.5		
			110
			90
			70
			50
			30
			10
			9
			8
	7.3	7.3	7
6.8			6
			5
			4
			3
			2
			1
BELGIUM	ITALY	U.K.	FRANCE

Underway

We all like to travel. Right from our first faltering footsteps, there's that urge to get somewhere. But nowadays, for most of us, what comes to mind when we think of travel isn't a pair of hiking boots and a backpack, or even a bicycle. It's an automobile.

In this chapter, you'll find some interesting facts and figures on the use and abuse of the automobile. Some of these may come as a surprise. The sheer number of vehicles on the road, for instance, as shown in the first table.

But before you even get your automobile on the road, you'll want to know what it's going to cost you. Well, we've got some facts here too. You might think that people buy more autos in countries where they're cheap and not so many in areas where the prices are high. It just doesn't work out that way. In some countries, people just refuse to do without the convenience of the family automobile, no matter how high the price. And, of course, buying an auto is only the beginning. You've then got the insurance to think about. In most countries this is compulsory. Then you need gasoline. We've got some telling figures on the comparative cost of these in different countries. You might well look at these tables before taking off on your next vacation.

Now you've got your automobile and a tankful of gas. There's just one other thing you're going to need to get very far – a road. Our next table shows you where to go for the wide open highways of the world. You'll be able to see just how driving conditions vary from one country to another. In some countries there's a superb system of roads – but hardly anyone on them. And some of the countries with the most extensive network of roads in the world have one big drawback – you can expect a bumpy ride.

Of course, most of the time it's not pot-holes that make us take it easy on the throttle. It's the dreaded sight of speeding cops in our rear-view mirror. Every country's got speed limits of one kind or another, but they can vary quite a bit from place to place. So if you're planning to do a lot of traveling it could well pay you to take a look at our table which illustrates this. If you intend to take your 140 mile-an-hour Lamborghini on a tour of Japan, for example, you'll have a slow time of it. And you wouldn't want to travel the *autobahns* of West Germany on a motor bike.

If you do any driving at all, you're bound to have some interest in road safety. All the topics we've dealt with so far – number of cars on the road, driving conditions, speed limits – have a great deal to do with that. But if you want to discover the plain facts about the road accident records of different countries, our table will provide you with the information you want.

If the figures on road accidents make you think twice about going on a drive – take heart. There are other ways of getting around. If it's more than a short trip you have in mind, maybe you'll want to fly. If so, take a look at our next set of tables. We've brought together a lot of material here, on all aspects of flying. Where better to start than at the airport. Just how much traffic do the major airports handle? Our table has the answers.

Then we turn to the airlines themselves. From the hundreds of airlines throughout the world, we've chosen a few of the larger ones from each of the major nations. If you want to know just how these different airlines compare with one another – in terms of distances covered and number of flights – our table will help you out. The accompanying text adds quite a lot of interesting information also. You might expect to find the American airlines leading the world's air traffic – and you'd be right. But are you so sure who comes next? Most of the leading countries have just one major national airline. But how about the lesser airlines?

Our tables show that some of these smaller lines do a surprising amount of business – in some cases more than the well known international giants.

There's another aspect of flying that you're going to want to know something about – and that's air safety. The next table in the chapter takes ten different airlines and gives the number of deaths per billion passenger miles. Over the page, there are figures showing at what stage of your plane journey you're most at risk.

You can also find out which airports have the worst safety records – something to bear in mind when you're thinking about your next vacation.

Finally, we have a table of figures for one of the more frightening phenomena of modern times – air transport terrorism. The figures show the number of incidents and deaths there were between 1968 and 1976. One encouraging fact is that successful terrorist acts are getting fewer and fewer.

Whether you're more used to traveling on a pedal bike or a Jumbo, there's something for you in this chapter.

It's no accident that mass-produced Model Ts first rolled off Henry Ford's production-line in the heartland of America. Fast, reliable and cheap transportation has become, along with television, the dominant feature of our culture. We're all in a rush to get there (wherever "there" may be) first and fastest.

Today the Ford Motor Company's annual revenue is greater than the national budget of many small countries. That's not counting General Motors. Or American Motors. Or the billions of dollars spent on imported automobiles. Even the Germans – with over 19 million cars – don't touch us. No one else is in the American league of wheels. Our landscapes and cities are clogged with 110 million cars.

We do have more people. And we have the longest road system in the world. But the proportion of cars to people is still almost ridiculously high. With 500 cars to every thousand of population, there's one to every two people.

With about 3.1 million miles of paved roads in the U.S. (see paved roads table) there are approximately 25 cars to every mile of road. And that's not counting the dumped, wrecked or abandoned cars.

Canada has almost nine million cars. But it comes second in the ratio of cars to population with 386 for every thousand inhabitants or one car for every 2.6 people. That's the same ratio of car to people as Australia's 380 per thousand inhabitants. Canada and Australia are both large countries with comparatively small, young and mobile populations – ideal markets for car salesmen.

Sweden has 350 cars per thousand inhabitants – the highest ratio in Europe. In fact, Sweden is the only comparatively small country that produces enough cars to export to foreign markets. It's production efficiency that counts. The Lutheran Swedes must share some of the Henry Ford Protestant work ethic.

Germany and France, with about 310 cars per thousand population, are the other most densely-wheeled countries on the table. After the U.S., Germany's 19 million cars is the highest. France is just three million behind them.

Britain is well down the table, with 263 cars per thousand population – even less than Italy with 285. In both countries,

	U.S.A.	CANADA
	1976	1975
1. Passenger automobiles on the road (millions)	109.7	8.9
per 1,000 inhabitants[+]	500	386
2. People per automobile[0]	2.0	2.6
	1975	1976
3. Motorcycles/scooters on the road (000s)	4967.0	355.5
per 1,000 inhabitants[+]	2^x	15

	GREAT BRITAIN	AUSTRALIA	AUSTRIA	BELGIUM	DENMARK	FRANCE	(WEST) GERMANY	IRELAND	ITALY	JAPAN	NETHERLANDS	NORWAY	SPAIN	SWEDEN	SWITZERLAND
	1976	1976	1976	1976	1976	1976	1976	1976	1976	1976	1976	1976	1976	1976	1976
	14.4	5.3	1.8	2.7	1.3	16.2	19.2	0.55	15.9	18.5	3.8	0.97	5.3	2.9	1.9
	263	380	243	274	264	306	312	174	285	163	275	240	147	350	291
	3.9	2.6	4.1	3.6	3.8	3.2	3.2	5.7	3.5	6.1	3.7	4.2	6.8	2.9	3.4
	1976	1976	1976	1976	1976	1976	1976	1976	1976	1976	1976	1976	1976	1976	1976
	682.0	304.0	82.2	100.0	36.5	500.0	300.3	36.0	1221.0	750.4	68.0	22.0	1142.0	28.4	93.7
	12	22	11	10	7	9	5	11	22	7	5	5	32	3	15

x Motorcycles only

production has been plagued by costly labor disputes and inflationary spirals. Nevertheless, Italy and the U.K. continue to be the traditional specialists in luxury cars. Rolls Royce, Bentley, Jaguar, Maserati and Ferrari are not hunting for buyers in Italy, the U.K. or the rest of the world.

Spain is the lowest country on the table in terms of cars. Only 147 cars are shared among each thousand of population. But the Spanish take to the road on motorcycles and scooters with a vengeance. There are over 30 per thousand, the highest rate on the table. It seems that the further south you go in Europe, the louder the whine of two-wheeled travelling machines. Italy buzzes with well over a million – the kamakazis of the Mediterranean.

Surprisingly, Japan is second lowest on the table in terms of automobiles. Despite the thousands of Toyotas and Datsuns that roll off the assembly lines, there's only one car for every six or seven people. Most Japanese cars are manufactured for export.

Motorcycles and scooters, generally the main means of transportation in poorer countries, may be the vehicles of the future. They're less expensive. They use less gas. And they aren't as costly to repair as cars. Spain tops the list, followed by Italy and Australia. The U.S. has the fewest motorcycles of all, with only two for every thousand people in the country.

Sources:
International Road Federation
+Heron House estimates
0Society for Motor Manufacturers and Traders, London

The table on the right compares the cost of buying, and running, an automobile in 17 cities. Data has been extracted from information provided by the Union Bank of Switzerland, who've compared purchase and maintenance costs for the most popular, medium-sized (over 1500cc) automobiles in 41 major cities.

An automobile is obviously a luxury in Scandinavia. It costs more to buy one there than anywhere else.

In Norway, the average automobile costs nearly $11,500 – easily the highest price in the table, and more than double the price of our 17-country average. Once a Norwegian has an automobile, though, he only pays $265 a year to maintain it.

Denmark comes next: an average auto costs almost $8,000. Sweden follows at just over $7,000. Despite these high figures, the Scandinavians are above average in automobile ownership. But the real surprises are at the bottom end of the price scale. Spain and Japan are lowest – the average automobile costs just under $3,500 in each country. Both have their own automobile manufacturing industries and plentiful cheap labor. Surprisingly, they're also easily the lowest countries in auto ownership – at around 150 per thousand people.

The U.K. is next in low-price auto production. A Ford Cortina costs just $3,804 – despite all those strikes at Dagenham.

The next country? Unbelievably, it's the U.S. It costs just over $4,142 to buy a Chevy Nova. Little wonder we're way ahead on the ownership table, with 500 automobiles per thousand inhabitants.

Once you've bought your auto and paid the taxes, you have to pay for insurance. "Third party liability insurance" covers the damage you do to someone or something, but not the damage you do to yourself or your automobile.

The highest insurance rates are in Dublin ($308). The Irish are famous for their drinking, and maybe this accounts for the cost of their insurance. Next is Paris; where the French have also been known to favor a glass of wine or three. Madrid ($29) and Tokyo ($57) are cheapest on the table.

London ($127) and New York ($150)

	NEW YORK	TORONTO
	1976	1976
1. Average cost of automobile (US $)	a 4142	b 5457
2. Maintenance cost (US $)[+]	201	306
3. Annual insurance premium[0] (US $)	150	244
4. Average price (US $) of 1 gallon of regular gasoline[x]	0.65	0.65

COST OF DRIVING

	LONDON	SYDNEY	VIENNA	BRUSSELS	COPENHAGEN	PARIS	DUSSELDORF	DUBLIN	MILAN	TOKYO	AMSTERDAM	OSLO	MADRID	STOCKHOLM	ZURICH
	1976	1976	1976	1976	1976	1976	1976	1976	1976	1976	1976	1976	1976	1976	1976
	c	d	e	f	g	h	i	j	k	l	m	n	o	p	q
	3804	6337	5034	5088	7949	5246	5268	4626	5090	3445	6076	11466	3420	7203	5535
	226	174	266	396	305	376	354	464	184	211	506	265	95	345	449
	127	102	181	269	152	287	241	308	145	57	205	158	29	181	268
	1.03	0.69	1.38	1.50	1.42	1.42	1.38	1.34	1.73	1.53	1.50	1.50	1.19	1.38	1.53

a = Chevy Nova Standard   b = Chevy Nova   c = Ford Cortina   d = Holden Kingswood
e = Ford Taunus 1600L   f = Renault 16TL   g = VW Golf   h = Renault 16L
i = VW Passat TS   j = Hillman Hunter DL   k = Fiat 132, 1600   l = Toyota Corona Mark II
m = Peugeot 504L   n = Volvo 244   o = Seat 1430   p = Ford Taunus 1600L
q = Opel Ascona 16S

Source:
Union Bank of Switzerland
+Annual tax, insurance and check up
0For third party automobile liability insurance written for an unlimited amount. In some countries, third party liability is not compulsory and in others, insurance companies grant discounts according to age and the policy holder's accident record.
xHeron House calculations based on UBS data

come roughly in the middle of the insurance cost table, along with Copenhagen ($152) and Milan ($145).

In Milan, gas cost more than $1.73 a gallon in 1976. Fuel prices, like everything else in Italy, have been badly hit by inflation, so you have to update that price accordingly.

Tokyo and Zürich come next on this list, with gas at $1.53 a gallon.

The Scandinavian countries all have high gasoline prices, and Norway is top at $1.50 a gallon. But this will surely change with the development of North Sea oil. The U.K., as the table shows, fares well compared with all other European countries. At $1.03 per gallon (1976 price), gas is 16 cents cheaper than its nearest European rival, Spain. Both Belgium and the Netherlands are high on the table

And who's the lowest? Canada and the U.S. are kings of the road on this score, at 65 cents per gallon. Of course, we have our own oil, but we aren't self-sufficient like the Canadians. Short of new discoveries, the U.S. price will soon rise.

If you drove every mile of paved road in the U.S., you'd travel a distance equal to six round-trip journeys to the moon, or 120 circumnavigations of the earth. No matter how you picture it, Americans have satisfied their love of the automobile with a truly monumental system of roads. We turned the English idea of the turnpike into a way of financing our national obsession. And we've taxed ourselves almost to the breaking point to build miles and miles of freeways.

With more than three million miles of roads, the U.S. has nearly three times as much paved roadway as all the paved roads in France, Germany, the U.K. and Italy put together. That's more than 14 miles of paved roads for every thousand inhabitants. And it's not counting thousands of miles of paved driveways. Only Ireland has a higher ratio of pavement to people – which says more about the small size of the Irish population than about the roads! In fact, more Irish have left Ireland for the U.S. than the current population of the island. Not a few of these immigrants were originally employed laying out the roadways that now serve their descendants in the U.S.

The U.S. has vast open spaces that are still reached by more primitive routes. Only 80.8% of the entire network of roads in the U.S. is paved. Roughly one road in five is unpaved. In countries where road systems have been laid out for centuries, the progress toward paving them all is considerably more advanced compared

	U.S.A.	CANADA
	1975	1975
1. Miles of paved roads (000s)	3100	80.2
per 1,000 inhabitants[+]	14.1	3.4
2. Total road network (miles – 000s)	3837	182.2
3. Paved roads as % all roads	80.8	44.0

to those countries settled more recently.

Naturally, this means that Europeans have a much larger percentage of paved roads than Australia. At 80.8% paved, the U.S. is not doing too badly. But the Dutch and the Austrians claim to have no unpaved roads at all. This must take a lot of the adventure out of camping trips. Except for Norway and Sweden, most of the rest of Europe has virtually eliminated dirt roads.

France has the second highest number of miles of paved roads – nearly 440,000 miles. But Australia's spindly network of outback track gives her a larger total of road miles. Germany – with just over half France's total paved miles – comes third.

But the French and German figures obscure the fact that for decades Germany had the finest and most extensive highway system in Europe – one of Hitler's few praiseworthy legacies. (He built the *autobahns* for military purposes.) Although the *autoroute du soleil* – the turnpike from Paris to the south of France – is one of the best long stretches of highway in Europe, France is one of the few important European countries

	U.K.	AUSTRALIA	AUSTRIA	BELGIUM	DENMARK	FRANCE	(WEST) GERMANY	IRELAND	ITALY	JAPAN	NETHERLANDS	NORWAY	SPAIN	SWEDEN	SWITZERLAND°
	1976	1976	1976	1976	1976	1976	1976	1976	1976	1976	1976	1976	1976	1976	1976
	207.0	139.2	84.7	66.3	39.7	438.8	277.2	50.3ˣ	168.2	234.5	53.7	23.0	78.8	41.1	38.2
	3.6	9.5	11.2	6.7	7.8	8.1	4.5	16.0ˣ	3.0**	2.0	3.9	5.6	2.2	4.9	5.8
	214.4	525.0	84.7	71.3	41.3	494.4	291.7	55.3	180.8	670.0	53.7	48.5	90.3	77.6	38.6
	96.5	26.5	100.0	93.0	96.0‡	89.0	95.0	91.0	93.0+	35.0	100.0	47.3	87.3	53.0	99.0

ˣ1975 figures   ‡Average estimate   **Non-official figure

Source:
International Road Federation
+Heron House estimates
°National statistical office

that is still waiting for a comprehensive highway system.

With over 234,000 paved miles, Japan has an impressive road system. But to serve their massive population, the Japanese rely primarily on a more primitive network of unpaved roads. In this, as in many other ways Japan is a tantalizing mix of the traditional and the modern. In spite of its relatively small size, it has a proportion of unpaved roads exceeded only by the Aussies. And their number of paved miles per inhabitant is the lowest shown – even below that of Spain (whose industrial development is considerably less advanced).

With just over 200,000 miles of paved roads, the British have a very low ratio of just over 3½ miles of paved roads to every thousand population. Only Spain, Japan, Italy and Canada are lower. More than 96% of the entire British network is paved. But the mitigating factor is the unusual density of Britain's population – one of the highest in the world. With less distance between towns and villages – on average, less distance between people – the British simply don't have as far to go.

And when it comes to highways, Britain is one of the best serviced countries in Europe. (Warning : this doesn't apply to highway eating; Britain's service station restaurants are a gourmet's nightmare – *la cuisine anglaise* comes into its own.)

Australia, with massive distances between its territories and cities, obviously needs an extensive road system. Not surprisingly, almost three-quarters of the country's roadways are unpaved, the highest figure in the table. You have only to think of the pot-holed dirt tracks that connect the widely scattered sheep farms of the outback to understand why. Australia's paved and unpaved roads make up the most extensive network of all the countries surveyed with the exception of the U.S. and Japan. We have over seven times Australia's mileage. Japan has 670,000 miles and Australia weighs in with a 525,000.

It used to be that an officer had to walk in front of the traffic waving a red flag. That was one way of limiting the speed of cars. When the red flag went, the number of accidents rose dramatically.

Today speed limits are generally high. Cars are built to go fast. Most new cars cruise comfortably at over 70 miles per hour, the average speed limit for the countries listed. Most drivers are naturally tempted to speed when they see a stretch of clear road ahead.

The speed limits in many countries were reduced during the oil crisis. We all remember when the limit was put down to 50 m.p.h. to improve the gas mileage. Unfortunately, many American cars use least fuel at 55 or 60 m.p.h. A 55 m.p.h. limit is still in effect on the interstate highways, but it's no secret that it's widely ignored. In the Canadian wide open spaces, the speed limit is a more realistic 70 m.p.h. But on secondary roads it's still an old-fashioned 50 m.p.h. In town, it's quite low at 30 m.p.h.

The Australians zip along at a reasonable 60 to 68 m.p.h. on their highways. But the best place for speed demons to roam free is New South Wales, where there's no maximum speed limit at all and you can drive as fast as your car – or nerve – will allow you.

In the U.K., during the oil crisis, speed limits on all roads were temporarily reduced from 70 to 50 m.p.h. The trouble with the British driving laws is that there are so many traffic regulations that the London Metropolitan police estimate that every other time a driver takes his car out on the road he breaks some law. And most of the time he knows he is doing so. Traffic regulations should be sensible as well as enforceable, as much by the driver as by the police. But, surprisingly, the figures for road deaths in the U.K. are only now overtaking the numbers killed 40 years ago. In those days there were fewer regulations and fewer cars. But people weren't educated about the dangers of automobile traffic and consequently drove more recklessly with less regard for other road-users.

The highest speed limits on our table are in Italy. Limits of 56 to 90 m.p.h. are maintained, "depending upon engine c.c.". Italy has excellent *autostradas*. It's also the home of a first-rate sports car manufacturing industry – with cars like Ferrari, Maserati and Lamborghini. Not every Italian can afford an expensive sports car. But in his heart, every Fiat driver sees himself in an Alfa Romeo!

	U.S.A.	CANADA
	1978	1978
Maximum speed (mph):		
on a motorway	55[+]	70
on a secondary road	25-40	50
in a built-up area	0	30

196

U.K.	AUSTRALIA	AUSTRIA	BELGIUM	DENMARK	FRANCE	(WEST) GERMANY	IRELAND	ITALY	JAPAN	NETHERLANDS	NORWAY	SPAIN	SWEDEN	SWITZERLAND
1978	1978	1978	1978	1978	1978	1978	1978	1978	1978	1978	1978	1978	1978	1978
70	60-68 [x]	80	74	68	80	81 [++]	60	56-90 [xx]	49	62	56	62	56-68	80
70	‡	62	56	56	68 [**]	62-75 [00]	40	50-68 [00]	37	49	43	56	43	62
30	37	31	37	37	37	31 [++]	30	31	24	31	31	37	31	37

[+] Interstate [0] Varies from state to state [x] New South Wales has no maximum speed limit
[‡] Criteria for categorising secondary roads and designating special speed limits vary from state to state [**] Dual carriageway [++] Recommended [00] As signposted [xx] Varies according to engine cc

West Germany comes next, with a speed limit of 81 m.p.h. on *autobahns*. Germany has an excellent highway system – the most extensive in Europe. It also has Europe's largest car manufacturing industry. As in Italy, there's a strong lobby against any reduction in speed. People tend not to buy the fastest, most expensive, cars when they're not legally allowed to use their purchases at near capacity.

Austria, France and Switzerland rank after Italy and Germany. All three have a speed limit of 80 m.p.h. on all their highways.

The Japanese figure of 49 m.p.h. is the lowest on the table. From this you'd think that Japan has very safe roads filled with careful drivers. Not so. The automobile accident table shows that Japan heads the list in accidents per number of cars on the road, with an impressive 25 per hundred thousand. The Japanese limit is unrealistically low, and many motorists simply ignore it which defeats the point of having a speed limit.

Sources:
Automobile Association
Department of Motor Transport/Australia
Embassies

The Austrians, also high on the accident table, have generous speed limits. The figure of 62 m.p.h. for secondary roads is higher than for any other country except Switzerland and the U.K.. In general, speed limits on secondary roads have an effect on the accident rate. They're also easier to enforce. In Ireland, which has the lowest limit for secondary roads (except for the unusually low Japanese figure), the accident record is good. Only safety-conscious Sweden has a better record.

Where accidents are concerned, there are undoubtedly many factors besides speed limits. You can make some interesting comparisons if you check the tables on automobile accidents, alcoholism, paved roads, and numbers of cars against each other.

The United States has the largest number of people killed by automobile accidents, with over 45,000 deaths each year. That's the population of Cheyenne, Wyoming, or the average attendance at a major league baseball game. Nearly 120 people are killed every day.

But don't let the gross figures mislead you. The total number of deaths per year says more about the number of drivers than about the safety of the roads. For the countries with the most dangerous drivers, check the line that shows deaths per hundred thousand. Here, in relation to population, the U.S. is nearer the average (21 per hundred thousand).

Canada, Australia and France head the list here, each with 26 per hundred thousand. These figures include people who die within 24 hours of an accident as a direct result of injuries they've received. The high figure in France is no doubt related to their high alcoholism rate.

Belgium and Austria come next on the death toll list, with 25 deaths a hundred thousand, followed by Germany with 24. Highway driving along the country's 6,500 miles of high-speed autobahns probably accounts for much of the German figure.

The British have a comparatively good figure of 12 deaths per hundred thousand – one result of persistent road safety campaigns. The U.K. figure is lower than anyone else's, except Norway's (11 per hundred thousand) and Japan's (eight).

Sweden has by far the lowest rate of accidents – 5.9 per thousand cars. Their strict laws on drinking and driving work.

There's no apparent reason for the low figures for Ireland (8.4 accidents per thousand cars). The Irish authorities introduced breath-tests at one point, but

	U.S.A.	CANADA
	1975	1975
1. Deaths from automobile accidents:[o]		
people killed	45,500	6,061
people killed per 100,000 inhabitants[+]	21	26
2. Injuries from automobile accidents:		
people injured (000s)	2,802.3	220.9
people injured per 1,000 inhabitants[+]	13.1	9.6
3. Automobile accidents:		
accidents (000s)	1,861.0	154.8
accidents in built-up areas as % of number of accidents	69.3	NA
accidents at night as % of number of accidents	NA	31.6
accidents per 1,000 cars[+]	17.4	17.4

DANGEROUS DRIVERS

	GREAT BRITAIN	AUSTRALIA	AUSTRIA	BELGIUM	DENMARK	FRANCE	(WEST) GERMANY	IRELAND	ITALY	JAPAN	NETHERLANDS	NORWAY	SPAIN	SWEDEN	SWITZERLAND
	1976	1975	1976	1976	1976	1976	1976	1976	1975	1976	1976	1976	1976	1976	1976
	6,520	3,694	1,903	2,486	873.0	13,787	14,804	477.0	9,511	9,734	2,440	470.0	4,500	1,168	1,188
	12	26	25	25	17	26	24	15	17	8^X	18	11	12	14	18
	331.6	89.4	62.7	84.0	19.5	357.4	480.5	7.6	229.8	613.9	63.5	10.2	94.0	21.8	28.7
	6.1	6.0	8.3	8.5	3.8	6.7	7.8	2.4	4.1	5.4	4.6	2.5	2.6	2.6	4.5
	253.0	65.7	45.0	62.5	15.9	261.2	359.6	4.6	279.8	471.0	55.4	9.9	62.5	17.0	23.5
	NA	NA	82.1	NA	NA	NA	70.0	NA	NA	NA	72.0	NA	48.0	57.6	67.7
	NA	40.6	42.8	NA	NA	NA	NA	NA	NA	NA	NA	NA	30.0	38.0	28.2
	18.0	12.0	24.6	23.1	11.8	16.0	18.7	8.4	18.5	25.4	14.7	9.7	11.6	5.9	12.6

NA not available ^{X}*Deaths within 24 hours of accident*

they were fought so strongly that they just didn't work. Ireland also has the best record for injuries – 2.4 per thousand of the population.

The U.S. has by far the worst injury rates, 13 injuries per thousand. Canada's not far behind, with nearly 10. Belgium and Austria are Europe's battlegrounds (over eight per thousand). That's higher than France (nearly seven). But in France, an accident is much more likely to be fatal.

Source:
International Road Federation

+ Heron House estimates
o This includes people who died 24 hours after the accident or as a consequence of the accident

Chicago's O'Hare is by far the busiest airport with 714,000 flights in and out every year. That's nearly 2,000 flights a day, and approximately one flight every 45 seconds throughout the entire 24 hours. (That's every day of the year, so don't buy a house near the flight path to O'Hare!) Yet only a tiny 3.5% of O'Hare's traffic is international.

London's Heathrow Airport is a distant second, with 278,000 flights per year. Unlike O'Hare, nearly 75% of these flights are international. This doesn't mean that flights to and from Heathrow are necessarily covering greater mileage. A Chicago to New York plane ride covers about three times the mileage of a London to Paris flight.

Ranking after these two, comes Canada's Toronto International, which handles nearly a quarter of a million flights each year; and Germany's Frankfurt Main Airport which handles over 200,000. Here again the difference in the number of international flights is on the side of the smaller European airport, where distances between countries are so much shorter. Of Frankfurt's flights, 62% are international compared to a mere 26% of Toronto's. But then Frankfurt is within 400 miles of 15 other countries.

After Frankfurt, the main airports in Europe are Amsterdam's Schiphol (176,000 flights per year), Rome's Ciampino/Fiumicino (just under 172,000) and Orly, just outside Paris, with nearly 152,000. Most of these European airports – except for Orly – deal mainly with international flights.

The surprising European figure is the low number of flights out of Madrid's Barajas. With just 122,000 flights each year, they deal with fewer flights than Switzerland's Zürich. Yet Spain is very well-sited for transatlantic traffic.

Australia's largest (Sydney Kingsford International) and Japan's largest (Tokyo Haneda International) both handle as much traffic as the major European airports. Yet they both have a low

	U.S.A.	CANADA
	1[0] 1976	2 1976
Total number of aircraft movements+ (000s)	714.0	244.9
Scheduled airline traffic+ (000s)	661.8	160.7
Scheduled international airline traffic+ (000s)	26.2	64.1

U.K.	AUSTRALIA	AUSTRIA	BELGIUM	DENMARK	FRANCE	(WEST) GERMANY	IRELAND	ITALY	JAPAN	NETHERLANDS	NORWAY	SPAIN	SWEDEN	SWITZERLAND
3 1976	4 1976	5 1976	6 1976	7 1976	8ˣ 1976	9 1976	10 1976	11 1976	12 1976	13 1976	14 1976	15 1976	16 1976	17 1976
278.1	132.8	66.3	102.2	163.7	151.9	208.2	76.1	171.9	168.4	176.4	83.3	122.0	105.1	139.8
256.1	101.6	46.3	74.4	147.7	144.5	193.2	35.8	162.8	165.8	132.2	52.5	117.9	66.1	105.1
206.4	20.5	46.2	74.3	115.9	76.4	129.4	32.1	91.7	55.3	128.8	24.6	49.2	47.6	101.4

ᴼJohn F Kennedy has more international commercial air traffic (95.1) than O'Hare
ˣCharles de Gaulle has more international commercial air traffic (82.0) than Orly

1 Chicago O'Hare
2 Toronto International
3 London Heathrow
4 Sydney Kingsford
   International
5 Vienna Schwechat
6 Brussels National
7 Copenhagen Kastrup
8 Paris Orly
9 Frankfurt Main
10 Dublin
11 Rome Ciampino/
   Fiumicino
12 Tokyo International
13 Amsterdam Schiphol
14 Oslo Fornebu
15 Madrid Barajas
16 Gothenburg Torslanda
17 Zürich

Source:
International Civil Aviation Organisation
+Take-offs and landings

percentage of international flights.

The airport on our table with the lowest volume of traffic is Vienna's Schwechat. It only has 66,000 flights a year, of which just over two-thirds are international. In some ways, Vienna is badly placed for international flights – on the way to nowhere but Eastern Europe. Unless the international situation changes, it doesn't look as if there's much room for expansion in Vienna.

The second lowest on the table is Ireland's Dublin Airport. But then Ireland's steadily built up a large international traffic via Shannon Airport.

There are several other things to keep in mind when studying the table. Paris, for instance, has two main airports: Paris Orly, and the brand new Charles de Gaulle, which in 1976 had almost 100,000 flights. Similarly, London has Gatwick as well as Heathrow – and Gatwick is as busy as some of the smaller European airports. And while Chicago's O'Hare may have the largest volume of air traffic in the U.S., New York's Kennedy Airport handles most of the international traffic. In addition New York has another large terminal at La Guardia.

A national airline is a prestige symbol. Every country that can afford it (along with several that can't) has an airline. It may fly a very limited selection of routes – often only between the national capital and one of the major European capitals or New York. Many of these airlines run at a loss and have to be subsidized by their national government.

Even large airlines like British Airways chalk up losses which have to be subsidized out of government funds. This is principally because of rising fuel prices, unrealistic international price agreements and commitments to maintain an uneconomical number of flights on certain routes. For instance, many airlines that fly the Atlantic are half empty.

U.S. airlines are by far the leaders in total number of passenger miles traveled. The biggest *single* airline in the world is Russia's Aeroflot – not represented in our statistics. Aeroflot is a state monopoly and carries all of the U.S.S.R.'s air traffic, both domestic and international.

Each of the four largest U.S. airlines carries more passengers than the combined airlines of any other country. Together they fly more miles than all the other carriers in our table. While we have a large international network, our domestic route structure is even larger. United Airlines, which has mainly domestic flights, makes up almost 30 billion passenger miles a year. The second largest carrier, American Airlines (23 billion passenger miles) and the third, Eastern are also principally domestic carriers.

The U.S. has heavy internal air traffic making O'Hare Airport in Chicago (not Kennedy, Dulles, Heathrow or Orly) the world's busiest airport in terms of aircraft departures and arrivals. We hop on a plane almost as casually as people in other countries take a bus or subway.

After the American airlines, the next figure is for British Airways Overseas. They cover over 13.5 billion passenger miles – nearly 1.5 billion miles more than their neighboring competitor – Air France – which covers nearly 12 billion passenger miles. J.A.L. of Japan follows closely with a figure of over 11.5 billion passenger miles. Air Canada is eighth in our table (nearly 11 billion passenger miles), and West Germany's Lufthansa is ninth (over nine billion passenger miles). These are easily the largest airlines, shown on the table, outside the U.S.

Passenger miles per airline (scheduled[+] flights)			
Country	Airline	Passenger miles (millions)	Date
U.S.A.	United	29,784	1976
	American	23,069	1976
	Trans World	22,292	1976
	Eastern	19,479	1976
CANADA	Air Canada	10,703	1976
	CP Air	4207	1976
	Pacific Western	530	1976
U.K.	British Airways Overseas Division	13,588	1976
	British Airways European Division	3773	1976
	British Airways Caledonian	920	1976
AUSTRALIA	Qantas	7083	1976
AUSTRIA	AUA	512	1976
BELGIUM	Sabena	2418	1976
DENMARK	SAS	1500	1976
FRANCE	Air France	11,869	1976
	UTA	2230	1976
GERMANY (WEST)	Lufthansa	9308	1976
IRELAND	Aer Lingus	949	1976
ITALY	Alitalia	6003	1976
	Alisarda	64	1976
JAPAN	JAL	11,601	1976
	Japan Asia Airways	275	1976
NETHERLANDS	KLM	6407	1976
	NLM	45	1976
NORWAY	SAS	1695	1976
SPAIN	Iberia	6599	1976
	Aviaco	315	1976
SWEDEN	SAS	2204	1976
SWITZERLAND	Swissair	5276	1976

Source:
ICAO
[+]Scheduled flights chosen according to the greatest passenger-mile records

The last year or so hasn't been a good time for airlines, economically. However, this is almost certainly a temporary state of affairs. Once fares are more rationalized – and more competitive – the airlines that are still in business will almost certainly go on expanding.

Which airlines are the biggest in the world? Which one, for instance, has the most planes in the air? That's what this table is all about.

One glance will tell you that the U.S. airlines are the highest fliers.

There are more scheduled flights in the U.S. than in all the other countries in the table put together. Eastern fastened its seatbelts 534,500 times in 1976. That's 17,000 more flights than its nearest rival – United, another American airline. It's also almost three times more than its closest foreign competitor – Air Canada, who had 194,000 takeoffs that year.

The U.S. is not only one of the world's richest countries, it's also one of the largest. And as people become more wealthy they get itchy feet. From the Texas oil mogul in his private jet to the California-bound super-saver, the U.S. is the land of the long-distance traveler. And much of our traveling is done by air – the fastest form of transportation.

For instance, in 1974, U.S. airlines flew the equivalent of 770 miles for every single American.

Restless jet-setters would also do all right in Canada. Their airlines total was 283,300 flights in 1976. Canada's population is only an eighth of America's, so you can see that Canadians like to have their heads in the clouds.

If you look at the low figures in the departure league, you'll find that the Australians are surprisingly earthbound. Qantas, the main airline "down under", has a mere 19,200 flights – peanuts compared with Canada. However, most Qantas flights are international. And when you consider that most Australians have to fly about 1,000 miles before they reach any other country you can begin to see why these figures are so low. Obviously when you fly Qantas you're really flying somewhere – and there's no question of it being just a short shuttle flight to the big city in the next-door state as it is so often is in the States.

After Canada and America comes the U.K. – home of the R.A.F. handlebar moustache. British Airways, their nationalized airline, got 183,600 planes off the ground in 1976. And that was before they went supersonic and put Concorde into service.

Those efficient West Germans come next with Lufthansa (179,300), followed by Iberia with 162,400. It's rather surprising that Iberia should come so high in the departure league. The answer probably lies partly in their trans-Atlantic flights to South America. And there's all that tourist traffic which keeps Spanish skies buzzing air-traffic controllers permitting.

Air France (160,900) follows hot on Iberia's tail; and if you combine the Scandinavian countries – Norway, Denmark and Sweden – S.A.S. takes fifth place with 152,400.

Austria's A.U.A. (23,000) and Ireland's Aer Lingus (27,100) follow Qantas at the bottom of the country table. The population of Ireland is only around four million, so that's an awful lot of globe-trotting men.

Scheduled aircraft departures by airline

Country	Airline	Takeoffs[+] (000s)	Date
USA	Eastern	534.5	1976
	United	517.4	1976
	Delta	500.2	1976
	American	369.8	1976
CANADA	Air Canada	194.0	1976
	Pacific Western	48.2	1976
	Canadian Pacific Airlines	41.1	1976
UK	British Airways European Division	111.6	1976
	British Airways Overseas Division	42.6	1976
	British Airways Caledonian	29.4	1976
AUSTRALIA	Qantas	19.2	1976
AUSTRIA	AUA	23.0	1976
BELGIUM	Sabena	39.8	1976
DENMARK	SAS	39.9	1976
FRANCE	Air France	160.9	1976
	UTA	14.7	1976
GERMANY (WEST)	Lufthansa	179.3	1976
IRELAND	Aer Lingus	27.1	1976
ITALY	Alitalia	106.0	1976
	Alisarda	5.5	1976
JAPAN	JAL	68.3	1976
	Japan Asia Airways	2.5	1976
NETHERLANDS	KLM	56.9	1976
	NLM	20.1	1976
NORWAY	SAS	56.6	1976
SPAIN	Iberia	162.4	1976
	Aviaco	22.0	1976
SWEDEN	SAS	55.9	1976
SWITZERLAND	Swissair	89.3	1976

Source:
International Civil Aviation Organization
[+]Scheduled flights only. Includes both domestic and international flights.
Figures rounded up or down

During the period from 1950–74, over 30,000 people throughout the world were killed in airplane accidents. For anyone involved in air travel, from management to maintenance, it can be a matter of great importance to look closely at these statistics. They can be of interest to the ticket-buying passenger as well. But there's just one thing to remember – air-safety statistics are notoriously difficult to interpret. So don't go flying off to hasty conclusions.

For one thing, there are many different causes of air accidents. In an extreme case, an airline could be entirely innocent of any kind of neglect, and yet be involved in a number of fatal accidents. In the preparation of these figures the causes of accidents have been ignored. In the end, though, it's the responsibility of each airline to take precautions against all hazards and eventualities. And some lines are indeed better at doing just that, as the figures on our table indicate.

Sometimes the full figures on air accidents just aren't available. Some airlines are much more willing than others to provide this data and give full details and circumstances. Other airlines are particularly unco-operative in this respect, so they've been left out of these tables.

There's another question facing the statisticians. How do you express the accident rate so as to give the fairest comparison? Some airlines carry far more passengers and clock up many more

miles than others. Obviously, a straight comparison of the number of fatalities per airline would not take these factors into account. To cover this the number of deaths per billion passenger miles has been calculated. Even this way, though, is not perfect. Some airlines are predominately involved with short-haul traffic. This involves more takeoffs and landings for miles flown and these are the most hazardous parts of any flight (see table on air deaths – when and how.)

In the second part of the table, we've looked at the very latest available figures in order to see whether there are any changing patterns that might redeem the airlines with the worst records. It's noticeable that while some airlines had recorded deaths, four of the airlines had completely clean records. This should reassure you the next time you have to put out your cigarette and strap yourself in. As you ascend into blue yonder, the music that you hear will almost certainly be pre-recorded and not the angels playing on their harps.

1. Deaths[+] per billion passenger miles, 1950-74	
Country	Airline[0]
CUBA	Cubana
CZECHOSLOVAKIA	CSA (Czechoslovak Airlines)
EGYPT	Egyptair‡
JORDAN	ALIA (Royal Jordanian Airline Corporation)**
NIGERIA	Nigeria Airways
PHILIPPINES	PAL (Philippine Air Lines)
RUMANIA	TAROM (Rumanian Airline)
SPAIN	AVIACO (Aviacion y Comercio SA)
TURKEY	THY (Turkish Airline)[++]
VENEZUELA	VIASA (Venezolana Internacional de Aviacion SA)[00]

Deaths[+] per billion passenger miles	Order[x]	2. Subsequent Deaths[‡‡] 1975-77***		
		1975	1976	1977
24.77	10	0	78	0
27.39	7	126	71	4
48.66	5	0	52	0
191.30	1	188	0	0
38.64	6	0	0	0
25.00	9	32	14	0
60.70	4	0	0	0
66.93	3	0	0	0
77.41	2	42	155	0
26.28	8	0	0	0

Source:
Destination Disaster, by Paul Eddy, Elaine Potter and Bruce Page
© Times Newspapers Ltd
[+]Adjusted to the nearest decimal point. The responsibility for deaths on planes owned by one airline but chartered or leased by another was determined by the authors of *Destination Disaster*.
[0]Only airlines in operation at the time of the writing of *Destination Disaster* are included. Figures are not restricted exclusively to scheduled flights. Aeroflot has been omitted because of lack of comprehensive data.
[x]According to the number of deaths per billion passenger miles.
[‡]Egyptair was known as United Arab Airlines and before that, Misrair.
[**]ALIA began operations in 1963.
[++]THY was formerly known as DHY.
[00]VIASA began operations in 1961.
[‡‡]Crew and passenger deaths; absolute figures. Figures include scheduled, non-scheduled and freight flights, and accidents due to hostile action.
[***]Based on *Flight International* data.

Between 1970 and 1977 more than 12,000 people were killed on scheduled and non-scheduled airline flights. That's more than the entire student population at Yale in 1970.

Is this an appallingly large figure? Or an astonishingly small one? Opinions differ. Yet some experts say we're safer flying in an airplane than we are crossing the road. They say that's as it should be – there are comparatively few flights and endless safety precautions are taken before an aircraft can even taxi out onto the runway.

But most people, as they are strapped in their seats when the plane accelerates down the runway, feel a slight quickening of apprehension at some stage. They only relax when they're finally airborne and are allowed to unstrap their seatbelts while they rise through the clouds. But is an airplane most likely to crash during take off? Is it safer once it's airborne? This table answers these questions.

The total number of fatalities has been broken down into deaths during different phases of flight: take off and climb; *en route;* approach and landing. Deaths as a result of terrorism, and as a result of collisions, are also included.

The figures show that you're right to be apprehensive during take off and climb. That's when 20% of all airline fatalities happened during the last seven years. However, it's still not the most dangerous time of a flight. That comes during the approach – at the end of the flight when the airplane lines up with the runway and descends. Between 1970 and 1977, nearly a third (31%) of all airline fatalities occurred during this stage. Nineteen percent happened during landing.

Another figure is for deaths as a result of collisions. With more and more aircraft flying, and airports getting busier all the time, it's surprising that there aren't more of these. However, safety precautions are extremely thorough and all major airports are equipped with sophisticated equipment designed to avoid this particular possibility.

In the past decade, a whole new hazard has cropped up in flying. That's terrorism, a subject that's dealt with more fully in another section in this chapter. Airlines are particularly vulnerable to the criminal or fanatic with a gun or bomb, and a hijacking virtually guarantees world-wide publicity for a cause. Seven percent of the total airline fatalities between 1970 and 1977 were a result of terrorist activities - that's over 800 deaths. However airline security systems are getting more effective every year.

The only other category – deaths *en route* – accounts for just 14% of all airborne fatalities between 1970 and 1977. However, 14% means 1,716 deaths – that's an awful lot of mourning families.

All the news in this field isn't gloomy – in 1977 only 440 passengers were killed on scheduled airline flights (outside Russia). That's one less than the previous record low and each year more and more flights cover more and more miles. Life in the air seems to be getting safer.

Mention must be made, however, of the 578 deaths in the 1977 collision between two 747s at Tenerife. Both aircraft involved were primarily scheduled carriers but in the particular circumstances of the accident were on non-scheduled flights. As such, they are not included in the 1977 figure for

AIR DEATHS: WHEN AND HOW

Deaths[+] on passenger flights[0], 1970-1977	
1. Total deaths 1970-1977	12,004
2. Deaths during take-off and climb	2,357
as % of total	20
3. Deaths en route	1,716
as % of total	14
4. Deaths during approach	3,682
as % of total	31
5. Deaths during landing	2,242
as % of total	19
6. Deaths as a result of terrorism	804
as % of total	7
7. Deaths as a result of collisions	1,203
as % of total	10

Sources:
Heron House Associates compilation, based on *Flight International* data.
[+]Passengers and crew [0]Scheduled and non-scheduled

scheduled flights mentioned earlier in this section. If it had been, the figures would not look so encouraging.

Some words of comfort for tremulous travelers. According to the experts – and the statistics – more and more airline crashes these days involve elderly aircraft. And hijacking is almost always confined to scheduled flights – many charter flights require a passengers' manifest to be made up well in advance, for security checks by the authorities.

In fact, the answer to the passenger's question "what are my chances of getting killed before I get to my destination?" is about three in a million. That answer takes into account the number of fatal crashes that occur and the number of passengers who survive. Those odds are something to remember the next time you fasten your seat-belt and wave good-bye to *terra firma*.

Each year, the International Federation of Airline Pilots Association (IFALPA) draws up a list of 'black star' airports. These are airports which the association considers to be "difficult". Or, by their own criteria, airports which are considered to be "critically deficient" in safety features. The list is sent annually to all members of this airline association, which considers it confidential and not for publication. For this reason, IFALPA officials were unwilling to release the 1978 list for our use.

However, at the time of the Tenerife accident involving a KLM and a Pan Am plane in April 1977, the 'black star' airports for that year were leaked to the press. We've based our table on this information. The complete 1977 list cites 26 'black star' airports – but the names of two of them weren't released by the press because of negotiations between IFALPA and the authorities concerned. They aren't included in our table.

Which country has the most 'black star' airports? IFALPA considers Columbia to be the world's most undesirable airline destination. Seven airports there qualify for the 'black star'. They're all international airports with modern navigational devices, but there's a shortage of fire and safety equipment. According to a top IFALPA executive: "In the event of a bad accident we don't give very much chance for the pilots', or the passengers', chances of survival".

The U.S. is the next worst country in this table – but there are mitigating circumstances. Two of the airports out of the four listed aren't in the U.S. mainland at all, but in dependencies or outlying territories.

There's no excuse for the other two in the American list. Logan Airport, Boston, and Los Angeles Airport are both big and busy – and carry a lot of traffic. They're considered "difficult" by IFALPA because they both have strict anti-noise rules. These require many incoming and outgoing planes to take a flight path over the ocean – which isn't safe when the wind is high, or blowing from certain directions.

Other major airports on the 'black star' list are Osaka Airport in Japan and Tehran Airport in Iran. The latter has been described as an accident waiting to happen – especially during the winter months which can be very severe. Osaka Airport – is also notorious, mainly because of its slippery runways.

However, all the news on the airport front isn't bad. The general opinion amongst airline pilots is that most international airports are safe. And two of the best – Dulles Airport in Washington D.C. and London's Heathrow – are also among the biggest.

In Europe, particularly in France, the U.K., West Germany and the other industrialized countries, air line technology is fully as sophisticated as in the U.S. and in some aspects the Europeans are more advanced. France, for example, uses a battery of jet engines to blast away fog from Paris' two international airports – De Gaulle and Orly. That technique has not been adopted in the U.S. largely because of the noise and pollution it creates.

No system of airport rating can be foolproof. Before the Tenerife disaster in April 1977 the airport wasn't even on IFALPA's 'black star' list.

'BLACK STAR' AIRPORTS

Black Star[+] Airports: 1977

Country	Number	Name
U.S.A.	$2 + 2^0$	Boston — Logan; Los Angeles; St Thomas, US Virgin Islands[0]; Pago Pago, American Samoa[0]
CHILE	1^0	Mataveri, Easter Island[0]
COLUMBIA	7	Bogota; Barrangvilla; Cali; Cartagena; Leticia; San Andres; Medelling
FIJI	1	Suva/Nausori
GREECE	2	Corfu; Rhodes
INDONESIA	3	Denpasar, Bali; Medan; Ujung, Pandang
IRAN	1	Teheran — Mehrabad
ITALY	2	Alghero, Sardinia; Rimini
JAPAN	1	Osaka
MALAYSIA	1	Penang
TONGA	1	Fua'/Amotu

[0]*Dependency or outlying territory*

Source:
Sunday Times files
[+]The International Federation of Air Line Pilots Association Black Star Airport list was leaked to the press in 1977. A Black Star airport is one that is considered to be "critically deficient" in safety features. The complete 1977 list cites 26 Black Star airports; however, the names of two of the airports were not released by the press due to delicate negotiations between IFALPA and the authorities concerned.

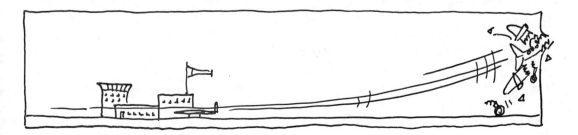

Urban terrorism is one of our modern age's most sensational and unpleasant developments. Anyone can be affected at any time. Aircraft hijacking is only one aspect of this form of terrorism, but for many years it has been the most prevalent.

An aircraft is uniquely vulnerable to this form of terrorism. Hijacking is liable to involve nationalities and airports of many different countries, and so attract the greatest possible amount of publicity. And this, when all's said and done, is what the hijackers are after. Terrorism is usually perpetrated by extremists who're desperate to publicize their cause and will stop at nothing to do so.

From the figures on the table it looks as though hijacking is on the wane. There are many obvious reasons why. All airlines and airports take extremely sophisticated precautions against hijacking – most of which are secret. Anyone who's traveled on an airplane recently will be familiar with security checks like the magnetometer scanning device which each passenger has to pass through to determine if he's carrying metal objects. There are x-ray scanners to check baggage for explosives. And many aircraft carry armed plain-clothes security guards.

The table shows that hijacking was on the increase at the end of the 60s. In 1969 there were 87 hijacking incidents – only 17 of which failed. That means over 80% of attempted hijackings were successful.

From then on the number of incidents decreased – and so did the success rate. In 1970, over 68% of hijackings were successful, but after that the figure barely touched 50%. However, from 1972 onwards, hijacking turned into a fatal business. In 1972 there were 60 attempted hijacks, only half of which were successful. But there were 117 deaths as a result, whereas there had been no fatalities during the preceding four years. As if this wasn't bad enough, the deaths total almost doubled in 1973 – though the number of incidents fell to 22.

Airline security had started to get tough – and so had the terrorists. Hijacking became a very dangerous business – for hijackers, security men and passengers.

During the four years from 1973 to 1976 the number of hijacking incidents for each year stayed in the 20s. In 1973, 50% of these attempts were successful. In 1974 that figure fell to 30.8%. In 1975 it was down to 25%. And by 1976 only just under 17% of all hijacking attempts were successful.

In other words, the odds on a successful hijacking were down – from evens to six to one against – in just four years.

There were only four successful hijackings in 1976. This looks like a success story – but it has a fatal flaw. In 1973, 210 people lost their lives during 22 or so incidents. In 1974, when there were 26 attempts, fatalities dropped to 159. In 1975, with 20 hijacking attempts, there were only 29 fatalities. However, in 1976, with just 24 hijacking attempts (only four of which were successful) a colossal 173 people were killed.

This table shows that hijacking seems to have dwindled to very small proportions. World-wide, in 1976, there was one attempt every 15 days. Fewer and fewer attempts succeed, as precautions become more and more stringent.

TERRORISM

Terrorist incidents and number of deaths caused by air transport terrorism, 1968-1976

Year	Total incidents	Failed attempts	Successful attempts (total)	Successful attempts %	Deaths[+]
1968	35	5	30	85.7	0
1969	87	17	70	80.5	0
1970	82	26	56	68.3	0
1971	59	36	23	39.0	0
1972	60	30	30	50.0	117
1973	22	11	11	50.0	210
1974	26	18	8	30.8	159
1975	20	15	5	25.0	29
1976	24	20	4	16.7	173

Sources:

Heron House Associates compilation based on data from "Security in the Air", Chris Eliot, *Aerospace International*, February/March, 1978 and *Flight International* data.
[+]*Passengers and crew*

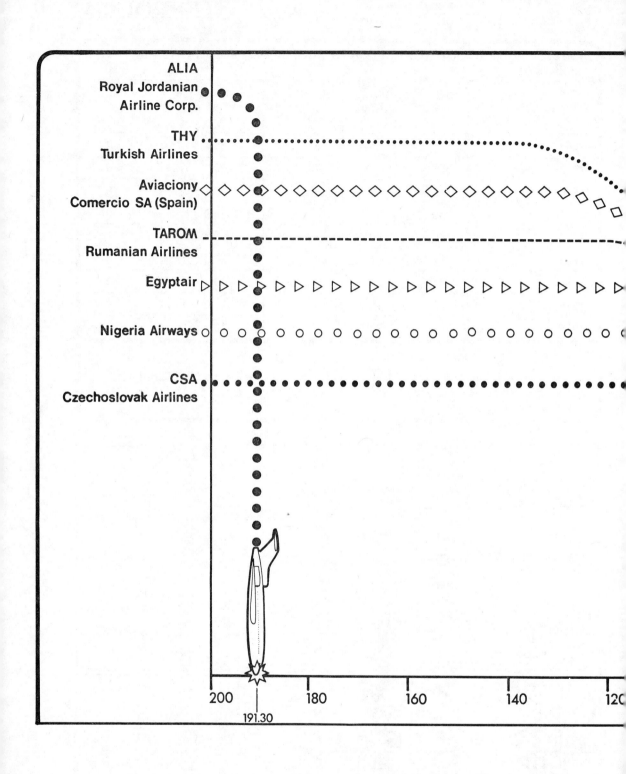

If you're a "white knuckle" flier, you'll be especially interested in these figures. It's often said that traveling by airplane is as safe as crossing the street. True, but some streets are safer than others. For instance, the national Czechoslovakian airline had only around 27 fatalities per billion miles flown. But ALIA lost over seven times as many passengers. If you're heading for the sunny sand dunes of Jordan, maybe you'd better travel by camel.

The Turkish airline THY is the next most hazardous, but their rate of 77 deaths per billion miles is still well under half the Jordanian figure. Spain's AVIACO is next, with nearly 67 fatalities for the same number of miles flown. The airline TAROM records just over 60 deaths — not a terribly high figure, but something to bear in mind the next time you feel tempted to hop a plane for Rumania.

100   80   60   40   20   0

77.41   66.93   60.70   48.66   38.64   27.39

Deaths per billion passenger miles

Diet

Food, glorious food – where would we be without it? Skinnier is what we'd be in the U.S., but you'll find very few people anywhere who don't take a ravenous interest in this subject. Whatever your particular taste, this chapter should stimulate, at least, your intellectual appetite.

First, feast the brain on us Americans, and bite off some food facts from your local supermarket. The cash register checks out our calories as it gobbles up our money and, in cold cash, the table shows that shopping habits boil down to table habits. Whether a chicken in every pot dictates how we dispose of our dollars, or whether the dollar decides the national diet, is a debatable question.

What we *don't* wheel out past the supermarket counter also provides food for thought. The back-to-nature movement has been progressively gaining in the U.S. and more and more people are buying organically grown food, unpolluted by chemical fertilizers. Some people go one step further than this – they grow their own, saving some money while presumably preserving their health. There are specialist foodstores all over the country, from vegetarian delicatessens to lacto-ovarian ice-cream parlors. But this is only an eccentric expenditure in the large amount that we spent on food.

Sinking your teeth into the statistics on American supermarket spending, you'll find some difficult-to-digest surprises. You might not expect that, in a country famed for instant soups, dehydrated ham flakes, Baco-bits and 'man-size' T.V. dinners ad nauseam, what the consumer actually buys are those simple old-fashioned, hard-to-prepare fresh meats, dairy foods and vegetables.

The first section compares the sales of different sorts of foods. Do we carry out more canned juice or canned soup? The article serves up some canny explanations for cold facts.

The thirst for knowledge leads to drink. Liquid libations are a lively selling point in many supermarkets; most shoppers are having more than one can of beer plus the odd bottle of wine. Wet your whistle at a running stream of home truths about our liquor flow in the U.S.

We've got some fresh facts on some changing trends in food buying as well. Some foods are currently out of vogue, but bad taste one year is good taste the next. Don't miss this section if you're opening a food store. You'll notice there's been a striking drop in sugar sales even though prices are now almost normal,

216

perhaps because sugar has suffered lately from a bad press. It seems we can't stomach extra calories these days.

How do our eating habits – and purchasing power – compare with other peoples'? The table provides you with some answers. Meat goes down very well with most Americans, but our meat-eating habits are modest compared with the Australians. They eat more than 20 times as much as the Japanese, which is small wonder, since prime beef (no bones, please) costs over $20 a pound there. We don't know, but perhaps the Japanese compensate by eating 20 times more fish than the Australians.

We've got some tasty tit-bits for dinner-time conversation. Where do they eat the most eggs? The most margarine? Where do we find the sweet-tooths of the world? Did you know that in Canada they eat more than six times as many chickens per capita than we do in the United States?

Maybe you're interested in seeing just what the secret is to that French *haute cuisine*. Well, we can't give you the recipes, but we can certainly tell you just what they're putting into the pot. And the same goes for those other Mediterranean gourmets – the Italians. They top the list twice. They eat more flour than anyone else, and with all that pastas that's probably just what you'd expect.

And after we've eaten, our thoughts naturally turn to other forms of refreshment. If you're interested in knowing who are the world's boozers, our next table has got all the information you can swallow. With all these facts you could be the star of the show at your next cocktail party. You'll see that the favorite tipples vary quite a bit from country to country. And you might find that some popular notions just aren't true. Where do they drink more beer than anywhere else? And are the Australians bigger beer guzzlers than the Americans? We all know about the French taste for wine, but who actually drinks more wine, the French or the Italians?

No figures on drinking would be complete without the Irish. Do they really drink Guinness for breakfast? You'll find that their position in the red-nosed league is surprisingly modest. Perhaps it would look different if we had some figures on Irish moonshine.

Most people shop in supermarkets these days. Which are their favorite items and which are the least popular? This table gives a general idea of what Americans like to eat.

Most of our money is spent on meat – almost one dollar in four, according to the figures. Besides the ever-popular steak and ground round, this category covers bacon, cured ham, frankfurters, sausage products and cold cuts. However, though we all like eating meat, it's the sheer price of it that accounts for much of the high figures shown on the table.

Fresh fruit and vegetables come next. They account for 13.5% of all money spent in supermarkets – around one dollar in every eight. Compare this with the figure for canned fruit and vegetables (just under five percent). The myths about our living on convenience foods and out of cans just aren't true – at least as far as supermarket buying is concerned. Expenditure on *all* canned foods comes to just over eight percent. Add the figure for frozen foods (just over six percent) and you still get only 14.5% – one percent more than the amount spent on fresh fruit and vegetables.

This trend is reinforced by the third highest category. Dairy products – milk, butter, cheese, cream, yoghurt – are all healthy and fresh, and account for nearly eight percent of supermarket spending.

However, the next group of foodstuffs isn't so healthy. Over 7.5% of supermarket spending is on baked goods and snacks, including those tempting cakes, pies and potato chips – all waistline wideners. ''Maybe just one'', you say to yourself – that's how one dollar in 13 gets spent in our supermarkets.

The fifth most popular category is beer and wine. It accounts for over 6.5% of our spending. This figure is confusing. Liquor laws vary from state to state. In some cases supermarkets are allowed to sell a full array of alcoholic drinks. In others they can sell only beer or wine... or only beer... or no alcohol at all... Even so the figure for beer and wine is rising year by year. One explanation is that there's a growing tendency for people to stay at home and drink. Another is that women are drinking more. There could also be a third factor here: more and more men do shopping – and many of them like to make sure the household is well-stocked with ''essential'' items.

Now for the low figures. We're obviously a nation of weightwatchers: of every dollar we spend at the supermarket, only half a cent goes on calorie-rich pasta.

Canned soup comes next lowest. It accounts for just over three-quarters of a percent of supermarket spending – in spite of all the free advertising from Andy Warhol.

The five greatest losers in supermarkets are shown on the table right. We are definitely cutting back on sugar: its sales were down nearly 30% in 1975. The reason for this is obvious: we're calorie-conscious today and sugar is high in calories.

The next greatest drop, 11%, was sales of veal. We still eat as much meat as ever – sales of fresh beef were up over 6.5%, sales of lamb nearly four percent and sales of pork over three percent. The swing away from veal must reflect changing tastes. Or we're beginning to feel sorry for the fatted calf.

One item not shown on the table is coffee. Although the volume of coffee sales has gone down, we're spending more than ever on it today – thanks to the recent huge increases in price.

The other greatest losers were wine, nearly ten percent (since reversed), cooking and salad oils eight percent and margarine, nearly three percent. The last two figures confirm that we're watching our weight these days. The trend here seems to be away from calorie-packed sweets and oily products and towards smaller figures – in every sense of the word "smaller".

Supermarket sales[+]: the five biggest losers		
Decrease in sales[0] since 1975	US $ (millions)	%
Sugar	548.7	29.3
Fresh veal	93.0	11.2
Wine	59.0	9.8
Cooking and salad oils	40.2	8.0
Margarine	32.0	2.8

Source:
Gralla Publications
[+]Excludes health and beauty aids
[0]Ranked according to dollars volume

Average expenditure (%) by shoppers in US supermarkets (1976)[+]	
Baked goods, snacks	7.6
Dairy products	7.9
Frozen foods	6.3
Beer and wine	6.6
Cereals and rice	1.9
Candy and chewing gum	1.4
Canned fruit and vegetables	4.1
Canned juice and drinks	1.1
Canned meat and poultry	1.4
Canned seafood	0.9
Canned soups	0.8
Fresh fruit and vegetables	13.5
Soft drinks	3.3
Fresh meat and provisions	24.0
Fresh fish	0.9
Fresh poultry	2.9
Macaroni, spaghetti, noodles	0.5

[+]Total does not add up to 100 because of other food expenditure

Source:
Gralla Publications

"What is food to one, is to others bitter poison," said Lucretius many years ago. Each country has its own national dishes; yet, just as many of us don't like snails or octopus, many people elsewhere would hate hamburgers.

Many national dishes are really just different ways of cooking the same foods. The main ingredient of spaghetti bolognese, keema curry, Mexican tacos, and Macdonald's hamburgers is the same – ground beef.

But apart from the different methods of preparation, what do people actually eat in different countries?

For most people (with the notable exception of fish-eating Japan) meat is the main ingredient of any meal – if they can afford it. And that's no small consideration these days.

In conjunction with this table, it's worth looking at the foodbasket table showing prices of various foods in the different countries.

While steak is very expensive in Japan, it's comparatively cheap in Australia; so it's no surprise to find the Australians topping the figures for meat consumption. The average Australian chomps his way through over 250 pounds of meat each year. That's 11 ounces of meat for every man, woman and child every day of the year.

This is in surprising contrast to the figures for our steak-loving society. We eat very little meat compared with some other countries on our list – 123 pounds a year per person (less than half the Australian figure).

West Germany is second – the average German consumes 220 pounds of sauerbraten, sausages and other meat each year. Australia and West Germany are the only countries to top the 200 mark, though the French come close at 198. The home of *haute cuisine*, and the originator of the word "*gourmet*" really cares about its food.

With the price of food as high as it is in France, the average Frenchman has to earn a lot of money to buy the meat he

	U.S.A.	CANADA
	1975	1975
Annual per capita consumption (lbs[0]) of:		
butter	4	13
eggs	39	29
cheese	15[+]	NA
margarine	27	11
sugar	92	100
poultry	6	50
fresh fruit	82[+]	NA
fresh vegetables	179[+0]	NA
flour	186	183
meat	123	116

U.K.	AUSTRALIA	AUSTRIA	BELGIUM	DENMARK	FRANCE	(WEST) GERMANY	IRELAND	ITALY	JAPAN	NETHERLANDS	NORWAY	SPAIN	SWEDEN	SWITZERLAND
1975	1975	1975	1975	1975	1975	1975	1975	1975	1975	1975	1975	1975	1975	1975
20	20	11	22	17	20	14	25	18	0.8	9	10	0.6	9	15
31	31	31	24	25	28	37	29	23	35	25	21	35	27	23
13	NA	14	21	21	33	24	7	26	NA	26	23	3	25	23
11	12	17	27	42	7	18	9	2	7	30	44	5	41	15
100	126	97	76	114	90	81	124	71	55	129	55	67	99	74
24	29	19	21	16	31	20	22	36	15	15	4	39	10	13
106	NA	171	164	118	168	278	104[x]	239	NA	188	136	213	111	96
149	NA	161	209	112	242	159	147	341	NA	193	77	210	62	184
135	211	117	163	84	159	98	178	276	80	117	138	161	99	145
135	255	172	198	153	198	220	143	159	10	161	108	132	134	165

NA not available ^{0}*Includes 77lb potatoes* ^{x}*Excludes citrus fruits*

converts into *Boeuf Bourguignonne* and *steak au poivre*.

Equal to the French are their neighbors, the Belgians, who also take great delight in their food. A meal in Belgium can last over three hours.

The roast beef of old England is world famous, but the British can't compare with the really big meat eaters. However, each of them eats ten percent a head more than we do.

The Japanese eat less meat than anyone else: ten pounds per head of population every year. That's less than half a pound a month. If we had the figures for fish consumption, Japan would certainly top the table. They're

Sources:
Euromonitor
$^+$US Department of Agriculture

also fourth lowest when it comes to eating poultry – after Sweden, Norway and America. America's poultry consumption is surprisingly low for the home of Colonel Sanders and Kentucky Fried chicken.

All this adds a new dimension to the words of Brillat-Savarin, the famous gastronome, who wrote, in 1825, in his celebrated "La Physiologie du goût", "Tell me what you eat, and I will tell you what you are."

Bottoms up! Skol! Santé! Here's mud in your eye! If you're a drinker or a liquor salesman, this table will tell you where to find the most convivial company.

Surprisingly the countries with the largest number of alcoholics (see table on alcoholism) don't follow the same order as those which consume the most alcohol. Obviously drinkers in some countries can hold their booze better.

Quantities of alcoholic beverages (pints) per person per year	U.S.A.	CANADA
	1975	1975
beer[+]	188.7	189
wine[+]	14.3	14.7
spirits[o]	16.6	19.0

If you're a beer-oholic, West Germany is the place to go. Seasoned experts claim that German *bier kellers* serve the best beers in the world. The Germans like it anyway. The average German consumes just over 324 pints every year and that's counting all the children and non-drinkers in the picture. When you consider that there are nearly 62 million people in West Germany, it means that more than two billion *gallons* of beer go down the hatch each year.

The lager-loving Aussies are second in this field. They get through just over 312 pints per year per person. No wonder the Aussies have a reputation for drinking the place dry.

The Belgians come next in the beer-drinking stakes. They get through just over 296 pints per head each year. Fourth at 288 pints are the Irish – whose taste for Guinness is legendary.

The Danes are after the Irish. They consume more than 283 pints per person per year. They're world-famous for Tuborg and Carlsberg, two civic-minded companies that sponsor art and science as well as making superb light beers.

The U.K. is about average amongst the beer drinkers of the world. This may come as a blow to the prestige of bitter drinkers – but they should take heart. They still consume over 250 pints per man per year. On average, every Brit drinks over five pints a week.

Americans and Canadians drink over 188 pints of beer a year – mostly while watching baseball and football games.

The Italians drink even less beer. They get through a mere 28 pints per person per year. But they make up for it when it comes to drinking wine. The average Italian downs an extraordinary 236.5 pints of *vino* annually. That translates into about 175 bottles, or around half a bottle of wine a day for every man, woman and child in the land.

The French aren't far behind the thirsty Italians. They drink just over 228 pints of wine per person. The Spanish each drink over 167 pints of wine a year, which puts them third.

Despite all our budding wine connoisseurs, Americans consume only 14

	U.K.	AUSTRALIA	AUSTRIA	BELGIUM	DENMARK	FRANCE	(WEST) GERMANY	IRELAND	ITALY	JAPAN	NETHERLANDS	NORWAY	SPAIN	SWEDEN	SWITZERLAND
	1975	1975	1975	1975	1975	1975	1975	1975	1975	1975	1975	1975	1975	1975	1975
	258.7	312.6	228.3	296.3	283.7	99.6	324.2	288.2	28.1	77.8	173.6	99.2	99.8	129.3	159.8
	11.5	24.6	77.2	37.8	25.2	228.1	51.0	7.75	236.5	1.0	22.5	7.3	167.2	16.8	96.6
	5.2ˣ	6.8	8.7	7.9	9.5	13.7	17.9	10.8	10.5	NA	17.9	9.7	13.7	15.5	10.5

ˣGreat Britain, excluding Northern Ireland   NA not available

pints of wine apiece every year – surprisingly low for a wine-producing country. The Canadian rate is just about the same. But the British rate is lower. In the U.K., people drink only half the amount of wine the Dutch or Australians drink.

Nobody drinks more hard stuff than the Canadians. (Except maybe the Russians with their vodka – but they're not on the table.) They get through 19 pints of spirits per person every year.

The second biggest boozers are the Germans. In addition to all that beer, they imbibe almost 18 pints of hard liquor per person annually. That's a lot, no matter how you sip it.

Where would Carrie Nation find it easiest to keep dry? Big surprise – the U.K. home of Scotch and London Dry Gin. The British drink over five pints of hard liquor per person every year. It's not that they don't like the stuff. It's the tax. This is an insidious device imposed by the government to keep the frugal Scots from drinking all their Scotch – and forfeiting millions of dollars and marks in foreign exchange.

Sources:
+Brewers' Society
0The World Atlas of Wine, revised edition by Hugh Johnson, Mitchell Beazley Ltd, ©1977
   Spirit consumption figures are based on an average strength of 50% alcohol; conversions from metric measures by Heron House.

Annual per capita consumption (lbs) of meat

260 —
240 —
220 —
200 —
180 —
160 —
140 —
120 —
100 —
80 —
60 —
40 —
20 —

Who are the most carnivorous nations in the world? If you expect to find the U.S. at the top of the list, you're wrong. Each year Australians consume a whopping 255lb of meat. Down under's the place for you if you're a steak lover.

The West Germans are close behind — they get through 220lb. That's a lot of wiener schnitzel. In France, the arts of haute cuisine transform 198lb of meat per person into delicious dishes like boeuf bourguignonne.

Finally we get to the U.S., where only 123lb. is consumed annually. Americans are getting more cholesterol – conscious every year, which may have something to do with meat's comparative lack of popularity.

When faced with a choice between steak and raw fish, the Japanese don't hesitate. They each eat only 10lb of meat a year.

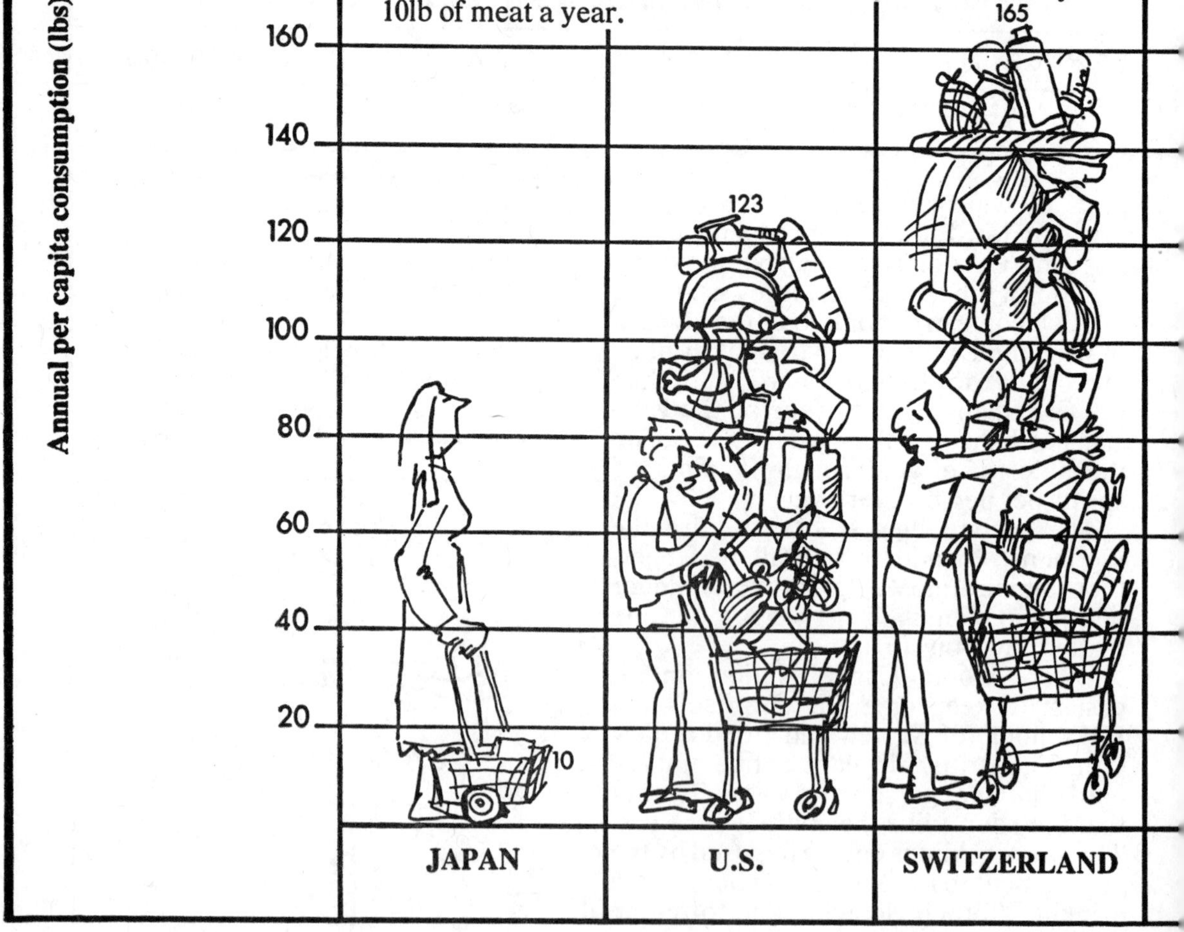

165

123

10

| JAPAN | U.S. | SWITZERLAND |

WHAT PEOPLE EAT

				260
			255	240
		220		220
	198			200
				180
172				160
				140
				120
				100
				80
				60
				40
				20

| AUSTRIA | FRANCE | WEST GERMANY | AUSTRALIA |

Health: Mind and Body

Young or old, rich or poor, black or white, we're all interested in staying healthy. This chapter gives you an insight into the state of the medical profession in different parts of the world, and how much it costs us to maintain our health and cope with illness when it strikes. It also covers which illnesses people suffer from most – the country you live in can make a surprising difference when it comes to meditating on whether you're more likely to suffer from cancer or heart disease, or from self-inflicted illnesses, like alcoholism or narcotics addiction.

We also take a look at an aspect of health that's both painful and inevitable – death. This may be our inevitable end but there are many factors that play a part in determining what form it will take. We've broken down the many horrible causes of death into specific categories and examined how frequently these occur in different countries. For example, why is the average Frenchman less likely to die of a heart attack than the average Swede? Why do the Spanish have less reason to fear cancer than the Dutch? Then there are the aspects of health that are increasingly troublesome today – mental health, suicide, abortion and sexually-transmitted diseases. These are problems that have grown more common – and often increasingly difficult to cope with – in the 20th century. We take a close look at some of the many factors involved – things like changing moral standards and the stress caused by the fast pace of modern life.

So who looks after our health? The first table in this chapter shows how many doctors (and dentists and nurses) there are in the countries we've covered. As you'll learn from the accompanying text, the number of doctors in a country doesn't necessarily reflect the amount of care which patients are getting.

Perhaps a better indicator is the amount of money expended on health care in the individual countries. That's the subject of our next table. Here there are quite a few surprises. Britain, with its famed National Health Service, *isn't* the biggest spender. Swedes shell out more money on health than any one else.

Once again, what does all this government health spending actually produce? A good indicator here is the number of hospital beds available in each country. That's what our next table deals with. It's all very well having all those hospital beds – who's going to fill them? What are the sicknesses and health problems of the people?

To find out about this subject, our next tables are all about illness. So what is the most prevalent form of illness? It's not a very serious one. We all suffer from headaches at some time or another. But who gets the most headaches? Nearly half the people in most European countries seem to regularly suffer serious headaches. But it's the Japanese who have the most surprising figures of all.

All of us have accidents once in a while. It's illuminating to find out what kind of accidents we suffer. The next table shows us how many people die from accidents and what type of accidents they are. The most accident-prone people are our neighbors, the Canadians. Around ten percent of all deaths in Canada are the result of accidents. Unfortunately, we can offer no explanation as to why the Canadians are the people most plagued by accidents. Are they, as a nation, careless – or is it just bad luck?

A lot of our illnesses are self-inflicted. Alcoholism and narcotics addiction come into this category – and these are the subjects of another two tables. And we deal with the sexually transmitted diseases, which have become almost epidemic in some countries. But certainly the worst thing of all we can do to ourselves is to commit suicide. And that's the subject of the next table. Why do people kill themselves? The accompanying text to this table gives us some illuminating insights here.

Certainly one of the reasons people commit suicide is as a result of mental illness. Mental health is much in the news these days. Another controversial and much discussed subject is abortion. As you'll see, the figures in our table on this subject are closely linked with the laws of the countries involved. We've tried to obtain (where possible) figures for both legal and illegal abortions, although this is a notoriously difficult field.

We've all got to die – so it's worth finding out what you're liable to die from. The last tables in this chapter show the principal causes of death in the countries we've covered. Further tables show the incidence of some of the principal causes of death – such as heart disease and cancer – and the age at which you're most vunerable to them.

As the philosophers tell us, our health is more valuable than gold. This chapter will furnish you with at least a few insights on how to look after your most valuable possession.

	U.S.A.	CANADA
	1974	1974
1. Doctors per 10,000 inhabitants	16.5	16.6
people per doctor	610	600
2. Dentists per 10,000 inhabitants	5.1	3.8
people per dentist	1970	2650
3. Nurses (including midwives) per 10,000 inhabitants	63.9	NA
people per nurse	160	NA

In the U.S., the number of doctors per ten thousand population is about average for all the countries covered, at 16.5. It's also virtually identical with that of our neighbor to the north, Canada. In each country there's about one doctor for every 600 citizens.

To a greater or lesser degree, the doctor/population figures overstate the availability of medical help (as you no doubt noticed last time you tried to get a house call). That's because a varying, but sometimes significant, percentage of doctors don't see patients at all (or don't see very many). They may be busy teaching, or in administration or research. What's significant is that they're not busy seeing you. So all of the figures on this table overstate the true doctor to patient (as opposed to people) ratio.

Among the countries shown, Japan is lowest with just one doctor for every 870 citizens. They're also lowest in terms of nurses. One reason for this poor showing is that a large number of companies have medical staff on the premises for their employees. It may not be *personal* but it is *efficient* (and, presumably, a pretty good check on absenteeism).

The U.K., Ireland and Australia are all on the low side when it comes to doctors. How much a doctor can earn – and keep – plays a part in all three cases. Ireland has excellent medical schools but in many ways the nation is still a poor, developing country. So doctors are underpaid and they emigrate, often to the U.K., sometimes to Australia. At the same time Australian and British doctors are heading overseas, often to "greener" pastures in North America.

All the countries shown on the table have far more doctors to tend the population than many other countries in the world. While the U.S. and Canada are about equal, Mexico (not shown on the table) presents a depressingly different story. South of our borders, there's just one doctor per 1,500 inhabitants.

If you're at an airport with a screaming toothache, head for Norway not Spain. When it comes to dentistry, all the Scandinavian countries are way above average for the countries shown.

The U.S. has just over five dentists per

DOCTORS, DENTISTS, NURSES

	U.K.	AUSTRALIA	AUSTRIA	BELGIUM	DENMARK	FRANCE	(WEST) GERMANY	IRELAND	ITALY	JAPAN	NETHERLANDS	NORWAY	SPAIN	SWEDEN	SWITZERLAND
	1973	1972	1974	1974	1972	1974	1974	1972	1973	1973	1974	1974	1973	1973	1974
	15.3	13.9	20.3	17.6	16.3	14.7	17.4	11.8	19.9	11.5	14.9	16.5	14.8[+]	15.5	16.8
	707	720	500	570	620	680	520	850	500	870	670	610	670	650	590
	3.0	4.1[+]	2.0	2.2	7.6	4.8	5.1	2.2	NA	3.6	3.0	9.2	1.0[+]	8.6	4.0
	3270	2460	4950	4550	1310	2090	1960	4570	NA	2740	3290	1090	9650	1160	2510
	49.0	NA	35.3	NA	81.2	55.3	37.0	64.0	NA	32.6	34.5	68.2	NA	69.1	NA
	207	NA	280	NA	120	180	290	160	NA	310	290	150	NA	140	NA

[+]*Number registered — not all working in the country*   *NA not available*

Source:
World Health Organization

ten thousand people – as does West Germany, which has the highest figure for the Common Market countries. In Canada, they have about two-thirds of this figure.

Austria, so big on doctors, is exceptionally poorly off for dentists, with only one for about five thousand countrymen.

The numbers also show that the figures for dentists vary far more between countries than those for doctors.

We've only been able to obtain accurate nursing figures for 11 countries. These reveal Scandinavian concern with the health of their citizens. America does well on the nursing front, compared to most Western European countries, with one nurse for every 160 men, women and children in the population. That means we're roughly equal with Ireland, but that's where most of the similarity ends.

Ireland's nursing figures include midwives, and most babies there are born at home. What's more, with far fewer doctors to look after patients, nurses fill the gap in Ireland; while in the States, they supplement, rather than replace, a doctor's care.

In Austria and Germany, the doctor to population ratios may be better than in the U.S., but the lack of nurses might indicate that their doctors do more of the medical work themselves. This is even more true of the Netherlands, where the number of doctors is below the average for the countries listed. When considered with their low nursing figures, the picture here is fairly bleak.

If you get sick, how much will it cost you to recover and who's going to foot the bill? This table gives the average cost of health care in different countries, and tells how much of that tab the government picks up.

In the U.S. we grumble about our medical and hospital bills. However, the table shows that we have less to complain about than many other people. Total cost of health care in the U.S. is $500 for each inhabitant – a high figure, but not when it's compared to the staggering $803 paid by each West German, or $656 per Frenchman, $593 per Australian or $583 per Swede.

In the U.K., where the National Health Service has provided free health care to the entire population for over 30 years now, the total cost of the program to the government is only $217 a year per person. Twenty four of those dollars are spent by the few Britishers who wish to be private rather than government patients. One reason for these low costs is that it's more efficient to have a central authority running the entire hospital system. Beds can be used at near maximum capacity, and unnecessary duplication of expensive health care machinery and facilities can be kept at a minimum.

The Swedes are the highest government spenders at $460 a person per year, and the Danes are second with $431. These two Scandinavian countries are strenuous supporters of socialized medicine, so it's not surprising they're

	U.S.A.	CANADA
	1974	1973
Annual expenditure on health (US $):		
government expenditure, per person	205	273
private expenditure, per person	295	96
total, per person	500	369

the superspenders. The West Germans and the Australians come next in government outlay ($352 each). There's another very important point. Although you may not have to pay as much directly in one of these countries when you visit your doctor or are admitted to a hospital, the system is being financed by taxation. So indirectly you are shelling out. For example, in the U.K. about $7 billion of taxpayers' money goes towards running their National Health Service. West Germany has the most expensive health care system in the world. In addition to government funds, Germans pay out a whopping $451 a year for private health care. The Australian figure is more modest, $241 is spent privately – $54 a year less than Americans pay. With a huge but sparsely populated land, Australians have had to shoulder the cost of building and maintaining modern hospitals in localities where the population is too small to support them efficiently. This accounts for the high government spending down under.

Costs are lowest in Spain, where the

	U.K.	AUSTRALIA	AUSTRIA	BELGIUM	DENMARK	FRANCE	(WEST) GERMANY	IRELAND	ITALY	JAPAN	NETHERLANDS	NORWAY	SPAIN	SWEDEN	SWITZERLAND
	1975	1975	1974	1974	1974	1974	1974	1975	1975	1975	1972	1973	1974	1974	1974
	193	352	172	222	431	306	352	153	157	171	178	258	74	460	264
	24	241	89	234	NA	350	451	34	181	25	78	NA	69	123	NA
	217	593	261	456	431+	656	803	187	338	196	256	258+	143	583	264^0

NA *not available*   + *Partial total*

total government and private expenditure is \$143 per person per year. Ireland comes next (\$187), followed by Japan (\$196) and the U.K. (\$217). The personal expenditure of the average Japanese is almost as low as that of the average Briton. However, in Japan, fewer tax dollars go towards the cost of subsidizing medicine.

Today every government in the world – including Red China with its squadrons of semi-trained "barefoot doctors" – realizes it has a responsibility to keep its citizens in good physical and mental health. Unlike the U.S., nations like Scandinavia, the U.K., Ireland, Japan and others have opted for a universal health care system in which the state pays everyone's medical bills.

Which system works better – ours or the government-financed health plans? Well, we grumble about the high cost of everything. And in Britain they complain they have to wait months before getting National Health Service treatment for minor, non-emergency ailments. It seems that no system is perfect.

Source:
Organization for Economic Co-operation and Development

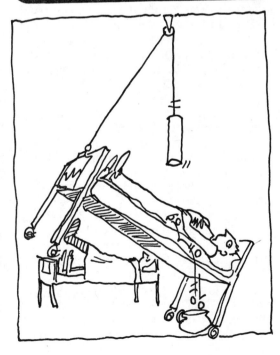

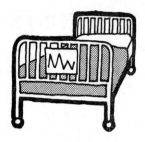

We're all apprehensive about going into hospital. Unless it's for an emergency demanding immediate attention, we don't normally know when we'll be diagnosed, treated or how long we'll stay in.

To patients, beds are just beds. To medical staff and hospital administrators, beds come in different categories. Within a general hospital, set up to care for a wide range of illnesses, there are emergencies, surgical cases, pediatric problems, geriatrics, maternity cases, mentally ill and handicapped people – all with different needs which can't be met without the basic bed.

The staff have to decide how to get the maximum patient turnover without sacrificing health practices. They must have beds for planned deliveries, plus the maternity emergency that could – and will occur, and also keep enough bed space open for a host of other medical demands. Furious would-be patients don't realize that no doctor, nurse or hospital administrator – no matter how skilled, industrious, well-meaning or ambitious – can juggle hospital beds: no more than anyone can consistently predict the next cast of the dice. Today, the birth rate is falling; hospitals have excess maternity places. Could these beds be made available for, say, ophthalmic or geriatric cases? Or will the birth rate suddenly swing again, leaving pregnant women to stand-and-deliver in the hallways?

A hospital has no way of planning ahead...even until tomorrow. People are always going to need hospital care; what type of care and for how long is guess work – luck along with the law of averages. It's even harder for a Washington official to predict the health needs of the entire nation and distribute finances accordingly.

The table shows nine countries that each provide one hospital bed for every 80 to 100 people – seemingly a working average. But the figures don't indicate discrepancies in need, or methods of treatment from country to country. In Europe and Asia, hospitals started as off-shoots of religious orders. Later, benefactors provided infirmaries for the poor. The rich were cared for at home.

The growth of cities and industry in Europe and the U.S. brought with it both epidemics and a big interest in public health. Municipal authorities assumed responsibility for a city water supply, sanitation codes, and public hospitals.

The connection between poverty and hospitals stuck until World War I, when nursing became a respectable profession and being a patient was accepted. As the concept of the welfare state spread, people in some countries came to expect health care to be the responsibility of the national government. Here in the U.S., we rage about high taxes and health insurance premiums, while the individual rages – in time of sickness – about hospital facilities that aren't ready and waiting for him.

Sweden has the most lavish health care facilities. The highly developed state system has one hospital bed for every 60 people – the best ratio in Europe.

In the U.S., there's a bewildering multiplicity of hospitals, some run by the federal state or city governments, others by universities, churches or groups of private citizens. Some are state-funded, others are supported by endowments and charitable contributions, and some are

HOSPITAL BEDS

Number of people to a hospital bed		
Country		Date
U.S.A.	140^x	1974
CANADA	148	1974
ENGLAND/WALES	118	1976
AUSTRALIA$^+$	96	1972
AUSTRIA	90	1976
BELGIUM	152	1974
DENMARK	159	73/74
FRANCE	98	1972
(WEST) GERMANY	84	1976
IRELAND	87	1975
ITALY	94	1974
JAPAN	96	1975
NETHERLANDS	85	1974
NORWAY	131	1976
SPAIN	215	1973
SWEDEN	60	1975
SWITZERLAND	88	1975

^{x}Excludes Alaska and Hawaii; covers hospitals registered by the American Hospital Association

Sources:
National statistical offices
$^+$Hospitals and Nursing Homes, 1972

proprietary – privately owned and run at a profit. All of this adds up to just one hospital bed for every 140 people. In the U.K., where nearly all hospitals are operated by the National Health Service, there's one bed for every 118 people.

How many hospital beds are needed? And do we have enough of them? These are complicated questions, because the answers depend on where the beds are and how they're used. It looks as though the U.S. is less well off than Sweden. Sweden allocates 40 psychiatric beds for every ten thousand people, compared with 12 in the U.S. (see table on mental health.). There are plenty of psychiatrists in both countries, but they treat their patients differently. In the U.S., the aim is to keep people in the community.

Denmark, another country with excellent health and social welfare facilities, has only one general bed for every 159 people. This doesn't seem to be a good ratio, but the Danes have a good reputation for caring for the old, mentally ill and handicapped in small communal homes – or even in their own homes. They want to keep their lives as normal as possible. Therefore they don't need as many geriatric or psychiatric beds.

The really good news is that illnesses which demanded hospital care ten or 20 years ago can now be treated outside – thanks largely to drugs. The average length of hospitalization for all patients is gradually coming down – in Europe it's about 11 days. Some hospitals are even closing down. This is happening in Britain where the Health Ministry is planning to do away with some 50 hospitals in London alone.

Pills, capsules, time-release spanules, even gum. Judging by T.V. commercials, life for the average American is one long headache. But these over-the-counter remedies must have some effect: only 13% of Americans visit their doctor because of headaches. And that number refers to severe pains that are symptomatic of a more serious illness.

The mind-blowing fact is that one person in three throughout the world has a headache regularly. Overall, the figures are complicated and can't be explained by social customs and habits. For instance, the U.K. has had a National Health Service for 30 years. With free medical treatment, Brits have grown accustomed to dash off to their doctor every time their throbbing temples need relief. Forty-two percent of men and women in the U.K. suffer regularly.

However, in Sweden – where health care is as liberal and efficient as in the U.K. – the headache toll is far lower. The stoic, phlegmatic Swedish temperament must make a difference.

In Spain, throbbing guitars pale beside the throbbing temples of 42% of the Spaniards who are afflicted with aching heads. The pain drives them to consume over 7,716 pounds of aspirin every year. Over-the-counter headache remedies may work in America, but in Spain they're obviously less effective.

This tormented nation can't even blame socialized medicine for pampering everybody into hypochondriacal hysterics. There is no national health system. This neglect of basic health needs shows in more pain from minor ailments than in other countries. Fourteen percent of Spanish women suffer from regular period pains; more Spaniards than anyone else endure toothache – 13% of them are in dental pain.

Perhaps the pain threshold varies too. The Spaniards and French (also high on the headache table) are voluble and impassioned. Swagger and braggadocio are expected in their men. A man is expected to complain about a pain, seek a remedy, and then – at the top of his lungs and with pride inviolate – beseech God to send relief.

You'd have thought that the peace and serenity of the Austrian and Swiss mountains would have smoothed the

	U.S.A.	CANADA
	1977	–
1. Percentage of population (men and women) who suffer regularly from:		
headaches	13^x	NA
toothache	NA	NA
2. Percentage of women in the female population who suffer regularly from:		
period pains	NA	NA

U.K.	AUSTRALIA	AUSTRIA	BELGIUM	DENMARK	FRANCE	(WEST) GERMANY	IRELAND	ITALY	JAPAN⁰	NETHERLANDS	NORWAY	SPAIN	SWEDEN	SWITZERLAND
1977	–	1977	1977	1977	1977	1977	–	1977	1977	1977	1977	1977	1977	1977
42	NA	36	40	34	39	28	NA	39	.47‡	38	31	42	27	36
8	NA	6	8	5	6	5	NA	7	NA	5	6	13	4	6
11	NA	9	10	12	12	7	NA	11	NA	9	9	14	6	9

NA not available ˣ*This figure relates to the percentage of the adult population who consult a doctor because of severe headaches ‡Refers only to cases of neuralgia*

most furrowed brow. Not so. Thirty-six percent of Austrians and Swiss suffer from headaches. Belgium, France, Italy and the Netherlands are ahead of them but behind the U.K. and Spain.

Upper lips are stiffer in Sweden and West Germany. To feel pain is a sign of weakness, and to talk about it is contemptible. In these two countries, medicine is taken furtively and not many headaches are reported. Period pains aren't common in Swedish and German women. Six and seven percent respectively suffer with menstrual cramps.

At four percent, the Swedes also have the lowest occurrence of toothache. The West Germans are only just above them at five percent.

The only conclusion is that pain is more a product of expectation and psyche than physique. And mind, once again, triumphs over minor matters.

Source:
Euromonitor
⁺Confidential industry source
⁰*Statistics Year Book,* 1975

Canadians are the most accident-prone people on the table. Over seven out of every hundred Canadians who die, die as a result of some kind of accident. Canadians top the chart in automobile accidents, fatal poisonings and industrial mishaps. Almost twice as many Canadian workers die of job-related causes as Americans – and five times as many die on the job as in France.

The French may have relatively safe factories, but they're second highest when it comes to accidental deaths for every one hundred thousand deaths. For some reason, the French are always falling down. Almost 25 Frenchmen of every thousand who die pass on because of a fatal fall. This would be understandable if they lived in Switzerland, with all those mountains to negotiate.

West Germany is the next highest country on the list in terms of total accident-related deaths per hundred thousand population. Almost seven per cent of all German deaths are caused by mishaps. There are no outstanding figures here, but they all add up. The only areas where Germany is exceptionally low are in the categories of poisoning and death by firearms. Only seven out of every hundred thousand Germans die because of a gun accident – or less than one per ten thousand. Compare that to the American rate of 13 for every thousand – by far higher than any other country in the table.

Austria, Switzerland, Australia and the U.S. come next, with around 5.5% of all deaths caused by accidents.

The Austrian figure is largely due to fatal motor accidents and a high rate of accidental falls. The same applies to Alpine Switzerland.

It's a different story in Australia, where the car accident rate – the main cause of accidental death – is second only to Canada's.

The U.S. figure is also largely made up of road accidents. Its record in most other

	U.S.A.	CANADA
	1974	1974
1. Total number of deaths in accidents per 100,000 deaths	5409	7344
2. Number of deaths per 100,000 deaths:		
in motor vehicle accidents	2399	3792
from accidental poisoning	286	417
from accidental falls	845	1098
by accidents caused by firearm missiles	130	73
by accidents mainly of an industrial nature	289	529
in other types of accident[+]	1459	1853
3. Total number of accidents (000s)	104.6	12.2

	U.K.	AUSTRALIA	AUSTRIA	BELGIUM	DENMARK	FRANCE	(WEST) GERMANY	IRELAND	ITALY	JAPAN	NETHERLANDS	NORWAY	SPAIN	SWEDEN	SWITZERLAND
	1974	1974	1975	1974	1975	1974	1974	1974	1974	1975	1975	1974	1974	1975	1975
	2861	5572	5683	5241	3695	6919	6564	4456	4793	4800	4713	5081	4612	4455	5590
	1126	3294	2585	2181	1677	2139	1958	1609	2287	2023	2033	1391	1609	1401	2212
	142	114	86	226	156	120	66	115	76	125	75	253	115	296	97
	957	1033	1979	1646	1197	2494	1626	1397	1652	674	1800	1847	919	1906	1976
	7	53	11	20	2	23	7	31	24	4	5	30	24	10	13
	125	292	337	122	99	99	175	283	193	379	119	218	200	125	291
	505	1116	684	1045	565	2044	671	1020	560	1595	682	1340	1745	717	1002
	19.0	6.4	5.4	6.0	1.8	38.1	47.7	1.5	25.4	33.7	5.3	2.0	13.6	3.9	3.1

departments is surprisingly good. With two exceptions: accidental deaths by firearms, and the "other types of accident" category, which covers everything from falling through the ice while skating, to choking to death on a chicken bone. With our liberal gun laws, it's not surprising that the U.S. easily heads the list for accidents caused by firearms.

The U.K.'s figures are the lowest on the table. Only 2.8% of U.K. deaths are the result of accidents. The main factor in Britain is the low automobile accident figure. There are over 200 fewer deaths per hundred thousand each year in the U.K. than in any other country listed.

Source:
Heron House estimates based on World Health Organization figures
+This includes deaths in accidents caused by fires, in drowning and transport (excluding motor vehicle) accidents.

Amazingly, fewer people were killed on U.K. roads in 1976 than in 1930.

Spain is high in the "other types of accident" category; a traditional Spanish sport like bullfighting would probably be included in this category. The risk of death in the ring is much higher than it is on the basketball court.

	U.S.A.	CANADA
	1976	1976
1. Narcotic addicts (000s)	540.0⁺	10.8⁺
2. Drug abusers (000s)	92.6⁰	NA

We all take drugs: an aspirin or two for that headache, a couple of barbiturates to get us through that sleepless night, or a tranquilizer to ease us through a lonely day's housework. Then there's the cocktail shaker on hand for those pre-dinner pick-me-ups.

For most people these habits never reach serious proportions but it's clear that abuse of drugs – and even addiction – exists. The ones we mentioned earlier are legal drugs. The late 60s – the era of flower power and psychedelia – saw an increase in the use (or abuse) of illegal drugs. Rock festivals were fragrant with marijuana and hallucinatory drugs such as L.S.D. became widely available. The 60s have gone, but addiction is still with us in the 70s.

Real figures for illegal drug use are hard to obtain. Some countries see drug abuse as more of a health problem than a criminal matter. So many of the statistics won't appear on the crime records.

Also, drug takers – from Naples to New York – are discreet. They prefer to practise their habit in the privacy of their own homes – so who can really estimate how many solid citizens are turning on with something?

This is especially true in the case of marijuana, which has lost a lot of the stigma attached to "drug-taking". Abuse of tranquilizers is also a hidden problem. In countries like the U.S. and the U.K., doctors prescribe literally millions of them each year to help people cope with the stress of modern life. However, its impossible to know just how many people have become dependent on these drugs.

The hard core of drug offenses involves narcotics like heroin and morphine, which are derived from the opium poppy, or cocaine. America tops the list with over half a million known addicts, mainly in the larger cities. Estimates often put this figure much higher, since many addicts have never been arrested. Because most U.S. addicts obtain their supplies on the street, street trafficking is a number one crime problem. Narcotics users also account for a large proportion of violent urban crimes. As heroin addiction increases the user needs larger and larger quantities of the drug. That means he needs more and more money, and often the only way he can get it is by theft, often mugging.

One way the U.S. government tried to tackle the problem was to cut the drug off at its source of supply, by discouraging the cultivation of opium poppies in Turkey and the Far East for example. The U.S. even tried paying farmers in some countries to grow other crops. But the valuable opium crop is vitally important to the economies of some of them. The vast amounts of money that can be made in the international drug market means that controlling the production and sale of opium is very difficult.

In 1977, there were over 131,000

NARCOTICS ADDICTION

	AUSTRALIA	AUSTRIA	DENMARK	FRANCE	(WEST) GERMANY	IRELAND	JAPAN	NETHERLANDS	SWEDEN
U.K.									
1977	1976	1976	1976	1976	1976	1976	1976	1976	1976
131.1ˣ	3.4⁺	0.50⁺	NA	NA	NA	0.30‡	6.4‡	NA	2.0⁺
327.7ˣ	180.0**	NA	5.0⁺	100.0⁺	400.0⁺	0.29‡	9.7‡	10.0⁺	10.0‡

NA *not available*

registered heroin addicts in the U.K. And yet, this year, the number of police convictions for illegal heroin use was under 8,000. This is because British addicts get their supplies from clinics. This way of treating the problem makes for a high addiction figure. However, by keeping most addicts off the streets, it minimizes street peddling and the violent crimes associated with the need to obtain heroin illegally.

The figures for the use of soft drugs in the U.K. is much higher. A total of 327,669 people get high on illegal substances such as cannabis or amphetamines ("speed") or trip out on the hallucinogen, L.S.D. Cannabis, the extract of the marijuana weed, is the most popular and campaigns are underway to legalize it in Britain and also in many other countries.

The use of cannabis has become quite common in many parts of the U.S., especially among the young. Many people, including some in the medical profession, claim that it's not a dangerous drug. Detailed studies have been made of marijuana, but there's no conclusive evidence to prove that it's either harmful or harmless.

The number of people taking LSD or "acid", is much smaller. Most people, including users, agree that it's a far more

Sources:
⁺Commission on Narcotic Drugs
⁰*Annual Abstract of Congression*
⁺*Man Alive*, BBC, April 4th 1978
‡National statistical offices
**Twenty-ninth International Congress on Alcoholism and Drug Dependence, 1970
These are illustrative figures as the definitions of narcotic addiction and drug abuse vary from country to country.

serious drug than marijauna.

The French figures for soft-drug use – cannabis and so on – are much lower than in the U.S. and Britain. That just might have something to do with the cheap free-flowing wine there (see the tables on alcohol consumption and alcoholism).

The sexual revolution has brought the singles' bar, gay liberation movements, integrated college dormitories – and a lot of V.D. The U.S. leads the world in gonorrhea – over 450 cases reported per hundred thousand population. That's nearly one case for every 200 people.

Scandinavia, for so long regarded as the home of sexual freedom, is next worst off. Their figures are in a class of their own compared with the rest of Europe. In Sweden the gonorrhea rate is 313 per hundred thousand, in Norway 248 per hundred thousand, and in Denmark 212. We can see that the Scandinavian countries lead the field in reported cases of the major sexual diseases in Europe. This may not only be due to their sexual revolution – especially in Sweden – but also because of their well-publicized health facilities. The likelihood of catching one of these diseases may be higher, but at the same time there is not the same stigma attached in their treatment.

In Canada where the sixties also speeded up the sexual revolution there is a very high rate for venereal diseases. Canada ranks ahead of Denmark in the incidence of gonorrhea.

The Japanese are the lowest, with a reported rate of only four gonorrhea cases per hundred thousand. The Catholic countries come next lowest – which is no surprise to anybody. Italy and Belgium (with a large Catholic population) have only eight cases per hundred thousand. And in Catholic Ireland they have a mere nine per hundred thousand. These figures are noticeably lower than all the others in the table, with the exception of Japan's.

Doctors use to say that gonorrhea was "no worse than a bad cold" and were usually able to cure the disease with one shot of penicillin. However, new strains, which are resistant to penicillin, have recently appeared. These penicillin-resistant strains originated in south-east Asia and Africa and have migrated to both the U.S. and the U.K. – though thankfully not to any large extent. Researchers are working to find antibiotics that doctors can use to counter this new threat.

America has the dubious distinction of also leading the world in syphilis. The U.S. has about 35 cases annually per hundred thousand people, almost double

	U.S.A.[0]	CANADA
	1976	1975
1. Reported cases of gonorrhea: (000s)	1001	50.7
per 100,000 inhabitants[+]	455	223
2. Reported cases of syphilis: (000s)	76.7	3.9
per 100,000 inhabitants[+]	35	17

VENEREAL DISEASES

U.K.×	AUSTRALIA	AUSTRIA	BELGIUM	DENMARK	FRANCE	(WEST) GERMANY	IRELAND*	ITALY	JAPAN	NETHERLANDS	NORWAY	SPAIN	SWEDEN	SWITZERLAND
1975/6	1976	1976	1976	1976	1972	1974	1976	1975	1976	1976	1973	–	1976	–
26.7	11.4	9.6	0.8	10.8	16.9	78.9	0.3	4.5	5.1++	7.2	10.1	NA	26.4	NA
47	78	126	8	212	31	128	9	8	4	52	248	NA	313	NA
4.0	2.6	1.2	0.3	0.46	4.1‡	5.9	0.06	3.8	3.2++	NA	NA	NA	0.3	NA
4	18	16	3	9	8	9	2	7	3	NA	NA	NA	4	NA

NA not available
++Based on WHO monthly figures minus one month for which an average figure was added

the figure for the next highest country, Australia. Canada is third in syphilis cases with 17 per hundred thousand population.

Sweden – · one of the leaders in gonorrhea – rates extremely low for syphilis with only four cases per hundred thousand inhabitants.

The good news about V.D. is that the rapid rise in cases of venereal disease experienced by a number of countries during the turbulent 1960s has now slowed down. Due to the efforts of governments and private health agencies, more V.D. sufferers are seeking treatment for this condition. They're also encouraged to help trace the partner who gave them the disease and encourage him or her to go in for treatment.

Health authorities in Canada and the U.S. are hopeful that the rise in V.D. will soon be checked and that the figures will go down. However, the situation is not the same in western Europe. In many European countries, the sexual revolution is just beginning to take hold. With the standard of living going up, people moving around more freely, and a greater acceptance of casual sexual contacts, the V.D. rates are expected to rise in the Common Market countries.

This trend could spell bad news for women. If they begin to adopt more relaxed moral standards, their V.D. rate will begin to climb. In the U.K., the figure for contracting gonorrhea is three times greater for men than for women.

Sources:
World Health Organization
+Heron House estimates
0Center for Disease Control
×On the State of Public Health, HMSO
‡Office of Health Economics
*Dept. of Health

About 1,900 years ago, Paul wrote Timothy: "Drink no longer water, but use a little wine for thy stomach's sake."

The operative words here are "a little", because a lot of wine can and often does lead to acoholism.

It's only in comparatively recent times that excessive drinking or a dependence on alcohol has been viewed as anything other than a bad habit or weakness. Today, in many countries, alcoholism is officially classed as a disease, although authorities disagree on what the symptoms are. Some classify any heavy drinker as an alcoholic, while others insist that symptoms such as delirium tremens or cirrhosis of the liver are a surer indication.

The amount of alcohol consumed by an individual is not a very reliable indicator because some people have a low tolerance to drink and can develop signs of alcoholism while ingesting relatively small amounts. Others have a high tolerance and can consume large amount of booze with relative impunity.

In our table, we have established a standard few could argue with: a consumption of 15 centiliters or 6.3 fluid ounces of absolute alcohol per day. That's 12.6 drinks of 100% proof spirit. Not everyone who consumes this amount will be an alcoholic. But then others with a low tolerance for alcohol will show symptoms of alcoholism while drinking less. This figure gives an accurate basis for comparison between countries.

France and Italy, two leading wine-producing nations, also lead the world with the number of alcoholics. In France, almost one drinker out of ten consumes alcohol at or above the alcohol level, while in Italy the figure is slightly more than one in 12. Although the U.S. is also a fairly large wine producer, fewer than one out of 25 exceed the limit.

Just because a country produces a lot of alcohol doesn't mean its population will become drunks. The U.S. and the U.K. – both of which manufacture huge quantities of distilled spirits – are fairly low on the alcoholism tables.

Spain – another wine-producing country, and one that has no legal minimum drinking age – is third highest in the table. The Swiss – with no minimum drinking age – are next, followed closely by West

	U.S.A.	CANADA
	1970	1970
1. People (estimated % of drinkers) who consume over 6.3 fluid oz absolute alcohol per day	3.8	3.1
2. People over the age of 15 (% of population) who drink over 6.3 fluid oz absolute alcohol per day	2.7	2.5
	1978	1978
3. Age at which alcohol may be bought legally	18-21[+]	18-19[0]

	U.K.	AUSTRALIA	AUSTRIA	BELGIUM	DENMARK	FRANCE	(WEST) GERMANY	IRELAND	ITALY	JAPAN	NETHERLANDS	NORWAY	SPAIN	SWEDEN	SWITZERLAND
	1970	1970	1970	1970	1970	1970	1970	1970	1970	1970	1970	1970	1970	1970	1970
	2.8	4.1	3.9	3.8	2.7	9.5	5.1	2.6	8.2	NA	2.1	1.6	5.9	2.5	5.2
	2.1	3.3	3.7	3.6	2.5	9.0	4.8	1.8	7.4	NA	1.9	1.1	5.3	2.0	4.4
	1978	1978	1978	1978	1978	1978	1978	1978	1978	1978	1978	1978	1978	1978	1978
	18	18	16	18[X]	18	‡	18	18	16	20	18**	18	‡	18	‡

NA not available   +Varies from state to state   0Varies from province to province
X14, if accompanied by an adult   ‡No legal age   **16 for any alcohol, 18 for spirits

Germany. Although West Germany is a country that's renowned for wine, there's a minimum drinking age of 18. On the whole, the country isn't known for its addiction to the bottle.

This table totally destroys the popular image of the drunken Irishman. The Irish, despite their reputation, come lower in the table than anyone except the Norwegians, Swedes and Dutch showing up the important difference between drinking a lot of alcohol and actually being an alcoholic. Studies have shown that the Irish are rather allergic to liquor and are affected by comparatively small amounts of it. There's also a strong temperance movement in Ireland.

Sweden has a low figure: it would seem that a few cheering glasses of *aquavit* during those long, winter nights don't lead to alcoholism. In any case the Swedish government makes it difficult to buy liquor, and you can be banned from driving if you're caught behind the wheel with any alcohol in your bloodstream.

Norway – like Ireland – has a strong temperance movement, and whole Norwegian cities often elect to go dry – putting Norway at the bottom of our table.

Australia – with a strict licensing system – is in the middle of the table, despite all those cans of Foster's lager. Overall, the figures indicate that the problem of alcohol really lies in the hands of society. If people can get booze for breakfast, they'll drink it. And if you start that way, that's the way you'll end up.

Sources:
1 & 2 Addiction Research Foundation, Toronto
3 Government sources

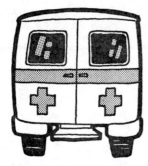

We all have our own ideas about why people commit suicide, and there are plenty of different psychological theories to confirm our particular views. Perhaps suicide is the most difficult subject of all to analyze in terms of figures. Each individual case represents a particular individual tragedy, in which innumerable personal factors have played a part.

It may sound like a truism, but people seldom succeed in killing themselves accidentally. For every successful suicide, there are at least 15 attempted suicides. Some which succeed but are never meant to be successful, could be called accidents. A suicide attempt is often a cry for help. Or it may represent a temporary failure of nerve in the face of overwhelming difficulties. For example, a person might expect to be discovered in the attempt and stopped but, tragically, isn't. Or they underestimate the strength of the pills they take, or suffer from the unforeseen but deadly effect of a mixture of drugs. So the motives and intentions of successful suicide must always remain something of a mystery.

There are many myths about national suicide rates, but these aren't really borne out by the statistics. For example contrary to popular belief, Sweden does not have the highest rate on our table. This doubtful distinction is held by its Scandinavian neighbor, Denmark.

The Danish suicide rate is 26 per hundred thousand inhabitants. That's nearly double the average rate for the countries shown (13.5 per hundred thousand).

Austria comes after Denmark with a rate of 24 per hundred thousand. Then there's a comparatively big drop to the third highest countries on the table: Switzerland and neighboring West Germany (20 per hundred thousand) – looks like the introspective German-speaking people are the ones most prone to suicide, rather than the Scandinavians as a whole. Sweden comes fifth in the table with 19 suicides per hundred thousand people.

It's interesting that the top five countries have affluent, modern societies where wealth is evenly distributed and there's very little poverty. Their high suicide figures indicate that riches and social welfare don't necessarily bring happiness. With the exception of Austria, they have one common revealing factor: they aren't strongly religious countries. However, it's difficult and perhaps dangerous to generalize about superficial resemblances, especially when dealing with a subject as problematic as suicide.

The table shows that suicide can hardly be called a popular practice – even Denmark's figures account for only one in every 4,000 people. Nonetheless, this does mean that in the equivalent of every small country town and every urban neighborhood, there's at least one potential suicide. To say nothing of the other 15 who try and fail. However, suicide is one of the least common causes of death.

There have been societies in which suicide has held a traditional and respected place. The ancient Greeks and Romans both thought it was a perfectly honorable form of death. And in Imperial Japan, suicide was an accepted practice when performed by the traditional method *hara-kiri*: ritual self-disembowelment, more politely known as *seppuka*. Although Japanese society has undergone a great transformation

Suicides per 100,000 inhabitants		Date
U.S.A.	12	1974
CANADA	13	1974
U.K.	8	1974
AUSTRALIA	11	1974
AUSTRIA	24	1975
BELGIUM	15	1974
DENMARK	26	1974
FRANCE	15	1974
(WEST) GERMANY	20	1975
IRELAND	3	1974
ITALY	5	1974
JAPAN	17	1974
NETHERLANDS	10	1975
NORWAY	10	1974
SPAIN	4	1974
SWEDEN	19	1975
SWITZERLAND	20	1975

Source:

World Health Organization

since the old imperial days, their present suicide rate is still high (17 per hundred thousand) – easily the highest outside Western society.

What prevents people from committing suicide? A major factor is, undoubtedly, fear. This probably applies most strongly in religious countries, notably Roman Catholic, where suicide is a mortal sin and brings disgrace to the family of the person who has killed himself. The result is that many suicides are simply hushed up. They're often recorded as accidents to spare the feelings of the bereaved.

This may well be the reason why the lowest figures in our table are all for predominantly Roman Catholic countries. Ireland comes lowest with three suicides per hundred thousand. Perhaps their more easygoing way of life also has something to do with this figure. One of the major contributory causes of suicide is often stress – which is hardly a national characteristic of the Irish. Catholic Spain is next lowest with a figure of four per hundred thousand. The Italians are third lowest with a rate of five per hundred thousand.

The U.S. is about average for the countries on the table, with a figure of 12 per hundred thousand. This blanket figure hides certain facts. For instance, in San Francisco – the city with the highest suicide rate in the U.S. – the figure is a staggering 2,561 per hundred thousand. But in large rural sections of the population – which tend to be heavily religious – it's very much lower than the average. Another surprise is the U.K., with a mere eight per hundred thousand. Maybe the proverbial British "stiff upper lip" has something to do with that low figure.

Psychiatry is big business in the United States. "I'd be lost without my analyst" has become a popular cliché. Many people stay with their analyst for years, even though they are not particularly ill. But in most of the world, psychiatrists are usually referred to only in times of mental illness, or nervous breakdown.

So it's no big surprise to find that the U.S. has the highest ratio of psychiatrists to people – nearly one for every nine thousand. Nor is it any great revelation that in America there are more psychiatrists than anywhere else. But the size of the difference is staggering. With over 23,000 psychiatrists, we have nearly eight times as many as in the next highest country, West Germany.

The Dutch rank second from the top in the ratio of psychiatrists to people. Holland is hardly renowned for its deranged citizens. The familiar image of the solid and dependable Dutch would lead you to expect the very opposite. But it is crowded and lack of room can lead to mental complications. This low ratio also reflects the efficiency of the Dutch health service. The result, in the Netherlands there are less than 13,000 people to every psychiatrist.

Another surprise is that Norway has the third lowest ratio of people to psychiatrists – just over 13,000. Obviously those long gloomy Scandinavian winter nights might have something to do with it. And the post-war transformation of provincial Norwegian society into a modern industrial state may play a role in the need for such services.

Rapid changes in society, with added stresses and uncertainty, apply elsewhere too. Changing values are probably the main factor in the next-ranking country on the list. Japan has just over 14,000 people for every psychiatrist – less than double the ratio in the U.S. In Japan certain national characteristics doubtless also are at work. If you look at the tables on heart disease, which many experts link with stress, you'll find that Japan doesn't have high figures. It's just possible that stress affects the Japanese in a more immediately psychological way.

The U.K. is low down in this category. In Britain there are more than 20,000

	U.S.A.	CANADA
	1970	1970
1. Psychiatrists:		
number of psychiatrists (000s)	23.2‡	1.4**
people per psychiatrist⁺ (000s)	8.9	15.5
	1975	1974
2. Patients:		
mental hospital beds per 10,000 inhabitants	12.8	21.8
admissions per 10,000 inhabitants	30.4	27.7

	U.K.	AUSTRALIA	AUSTRIA	BELGIUM	DENMARK	FRANCE	(WEST) GERMANY	IRELAND	ITALY	JAPAN	NETHERLANDS	NORWAY	SPAIN	SWEDEN	SWITZERLAND
	1970		1970			1970	1970	1970		1970	1970	1970	1970	1970	1970
	2.8‡	NA	.32**	NA	NA	2.1**	3.0**	.13	NA	.74	1.0**	.30	1.2	.46	.32‡
	20.1	NA	23.3	NA	NA	24.4	19.8	24.0	NA	14.1	12.8	13.1	29.2	17.7	20.3
	1975	1972	1976	1974	1970	1974	1975	1976	1975	1975	1975	1975	1974	1975	1975
	30.5	20.7x	35.4o	26.9o	21.1	37.4o	18.2	47.9o	28.9o	18.4	19.2	31.2	12.1	40.5	27.6o
	31.9	21.9x	NA	25.1o	63.8	50.8o	31.6	47.2o	24.9o	13.2	16.9	27.6	13.2	99.7	NA

‡ *Includes child psychiatrists*   ** *Includes neurologists*   *NA not available*

people for every psychiatrist. This must surely have a lot to do with the "stiff upper lip".

What, then, about those countries where psychiatry began? Austria – the fatherland of Sigmund Freud – has a high ratio of one psychiatrist to over 23,000 people. And in Switzerland, birthplace of Carl Jung, there's only one psychiatrist for over 20,000 people.

Spain heads the happy list of countries who seem to have the least need of psychiatry. Here, there's only one psychiatrist for almost 30,000 people. The French come next, followed by the happy-go-lucky Irish.

Let's look at more serious mental problems. One measure – which we've used – is the number of hospital beds per 10,000 population which are allocated to mental patients. Here you can see the

Sources:
World Health Organization

+   Heron House estimates
o   National statistical offices
x   *Hospitals and Nursing Homes*

U.S. is next to last in the table with only 12 beds per 10,000. Ireland, on the other hand, heads the list.

Ireland is also high in the number of admissions per 10,000 population, though France and Denmark are higher. But the highest in this category are the Swedes. One in every hundred Swedes is admitted to a mental hospital every year – an astonishingly high figure. And Denmark's 62 per 10,000 is also high. Neurosis and introspection appear to flourish in northern climes.

	U.S.A.	CANADA
	1976	1976
1. Legal abortions (000s)	114.7[+]	54.0[0]
as % of live births	35	15
2. Estimated illegal abortions (000s)	200[x]	NA

Abortion is a highly controversial subject. Some people regard it as murder, others as a basic human right.

It's defined as the terminating of a pregnancy before the foetus is fully formed. In some countries, Japan for example, abortion is actually one of the main methods of birth control.

There are a number of recognized medical ways of inducing abortion. And there is also a vast mythology of "fringe" methods – all dangerous. One of the chief recognized medical methods includes surgery: the cervix is dilated and the uterus evacuated by scraping, suction or vacuuming. However, terminating pregnancies over 12 weeks is more complicated and another method is used; a strong saline solution is injected into the womb causing a miscarriage within 48 hours.

Most religions have condemned abortion, but at present the Roman Catholic Church's stand on this matter is the firmest. To them abortion is murder. As a result there has been very strong opposition to the introduction of legalized abortion in Roman Catholic countries.

The first country to introduce legalized abortion was the U.S.S.R. in 1920, early in their social experiment. Since the 1940s, most advanced nations have had pro-abortion pressure groups. With the rise of women's lib, the strength of these movements has increased. Feminists demand each woman's "right to choose".

Japan was the next country to legalize abortion. Then it was introduced into some of the Eastern European countries. Scandinavian countries soon followed, so did Switzerland. In these countries, abortion was selective, with certain legal procedures necessary for authorization.

The U.K. and certain states in the U.S. liberalized their abortions laws in the later 1960s. But in France, where there is strong Roman Catholic influence, abortion wasn't made legal until 1975. And this only after a large group of respected female public figures (including Simone de Beauvoir and Simone Signoret) circulated a statement that they had all had abortions, openly inviting a prosecution which would have made a mockery of the law. Abortion has recently been made legal in Italy.

When abortion is legalized, the number of abortions tends to rise dramatically, but only for the first few years. Even so, the percentage of pregnancies terminated by induced abortions can be extremely high.

Even in countries where abortion has been legalized, some criminal abortions do occur. Deaths from criminal abortions are estimated at between 35 and 95 per

U.K.	AUSTRALIA	AUSTRIA	BELGIUM	DENMARK	FRANCE	(WEST) GERMANY	IRELAND	ITALY	JAPAN	NETHERLANDS	NORWAY	SPAIN	SWEDEN	SWITZERLAND
1976	1976	1976	1975	1976	1976	1974	1976	1975	1976	1976	1975	1974	1976	1976
128.0^{0++}	60.0^0	NA	NA	26.8^+	133.6^+	17.8^+	1.8^{+00}	NA	664.1^+	16.0^+	15.1^+	14.1^0	32.4^+	NA
18	26	NA	NA	37	18	3^+	3	NA	36	9	27	2	33	NA
30^{**}	NA	100^{0**}	30^0	$0.4^{0‡‡}$	50^x	NA	NA	500^+	1300^x	NA	NA	NA	0^+	50^x

[++]England and Wales only; includes 26,900 non-residents [00]Abortions obtained in England and Wales [**]Pre-1974 figure [‡‡]1975 figure [***]1966 figure

hundred thousand abortions. Compare this with the rate for legalized abortion – just over one death per hundred thousand pregnancies terminated within the first three months. This figure is slightly misleading – about 40 per thousand die when legal abortions of all kinds are included.

A high proportion of legal abortions are performed on married women. Most illegal abortions are carried out on young, unmarried girls, women who've had previous abortions, and wives who're pregnant when they marry.

The illegal abortion figures on our table show that 1.3 million illegal abortions were carried out in Japan – almost twice the legal figure.

France's legal total is disproportionately high; 1976 was its first year of legalized abortion, and, as mentioned previously, the figures are always high at this stage.

In the U.K., where there have been several proposed amendments to the abortion laws, the figure is under 130 thousand. Proportionately, this is just below average if you compare it with figures for countries of a similar size.

Sources:
[+]Population Council, New York
[0]International Planned Parenthood Federation
[x]National statistical offices and relevant commissions
[‡]British Pregnancy Advisory Service

Arguments for legal abortion

- Women have a right to control their bodies.
- A foetus is not a human being.
- Rather than have a baby, some women will resort to dangerous "back street" abortions.
- Unintended miscarriages and accidents terminate more pregnancies than abortions do.
- There is less physical risk in an abortion than in a completed pregnancy.

Arguments against legal abortion

- No-one should be able to deny a human being's right to live.
- From conception, a foetus has the genetic information that will make it a unique individual.
- Legalized abortion implies society does not consider it wrong.
- Abortions have to be performed quickly and take priority over other gynaecological cases.

Main causes of death (as % of total deaths):	U.S.A. 1974	CANADA 1974
neoplasms/cancer	18.9	20.4
diseases of the circulatory system	53.2	49.3
diseases of the respiratory system	5.6	6.5
diseases of the digestive system	3.8	3.7
ill-defined conditions	1.6	0.9
accidents, poisonings and violence	8.1	10.1

In all the countries shown on the table, the main causes of death are diseases of the circulatory system. These are diseases which affect the tissues of the heart, arteries and veins. Hardened arteries, for instance, which occur when fatty deposits thicken the artery walls, cause the bloodflow to slow down and put strain on the heart. This can lead to coronary thrombosis, in which one or more coronary arteries become blocked and the patient collapses with acute chest pain – the standard "heart attack". If the occlusion of the heart is more gradual, it may produce angina pectoris (painful attacks which are less serious than thrombosis) or cause the heart to degenerate. Deaths from heart attacks during old age are included in our figures.

Cancer is the next biggest cause of death. The medical term for this is neoplasm, which literally means "new growth". This happens when an expanding mass of useless cell tissue accumulates and causes a tumor – which can be either benign or malignant. The cancerous ones are often, but – thanks to the miracles of modern surgery – not always, fatal. A lot of research is being carried out into the prevention and cure of cancer, which – hopefully – will reduce the number of deaths from it.

Pneumonia, pleurisy, bronchitis, 'flu and asthma are the main killer diseases of the respiratory system.

The most striking fact to emerge from the table is that causes of death vary very little in the countries on our table. People tend to die of the same diseases in the same proportions.

Australia is the highest risk country for diseases of the circulatory system: 54% of its inhabitants die from heart or rheumatic complaints. Sweden comes next. The U.S. is third on the list, and in the U.K., Norway and Ireland, the figures in this category are also high.

France comes bottom of this category: at just under 38%, the French suffer the smallest number of deaths from heart attacks. On the other hand, they have the most deaths from digestive complaints, ulcers, and cirrhosis and other diseases of the liver.

The table shows that the Mediterranean countries – where olive oil, low in cholesterol, is the most popular oil for cooking and salads – have fewer deaths.

	U.K.	AUSTRALIA	AUSTRIA	BELGIUM	DENMARK	FRANCE	(WEST) GERMANY	IRELAND	ITALY	JAPAN	NETHERLANDS	NORWAY	SPAIN	SWEDEN	SWITZERLAND
	1974	1974	1975	1974	1975	1974	1974	1974	1974	1975	1975	1974	1974	1975	1975
	20.8	17.4	20.2	21.1	23.8	21.7	21.4	17.6	20.4	20.3	25.8	19.3	17.3	22.3	24.1
	51.9	54.0	49.8	43.2	50.2	37.9	46.4	50.8	47.7	42.8	44.7	51.1	44.2	53.4	47.4
	13.3	7.6	7.0	6.5	6.9	6.6	5.9	13.1	7.4	7.7	6.4	9.1	11.9	4.7	5.9
	2.5	2.6	5.8	3.5	3.1	6.2	5.6	2.2	6.2	5.7	3.1	2.3	5.5	4.2	4.0
	0.6	0.8	1.6	9.1	2.5	8.0	3.8	1.6	3.2	5.4	4.7	4.8	5.6	0.5	1.2
	3.9	7.7	7.8	6.8	6.5	8.9	6.6	5.1	5.5	8.0	5.9	6.2	5.1	6.9	8.3

Source:
World Health Organization

In most countries, cancer accounts for about a fifth of all deaths. The cause of the disease is still one of the great medical mysteries. Theory has it that stress may be a contributory factor. This is certainly backed up by the fact that the highest proportion of cancer deaths is in densely populated Holland. And that the Spanish, followed by the Irish, have the lowest figures. Life in Spain and Ireland is relatively easy-going, and in both countries a relatively high proportion of their population lives in rural areas (30.5% and 44.7% respectively). However, Australia is also low in the cancer league – and a high 86.0% of Australians live in cities.

Spain and Ireland may be low in the cancer figures, but a large number of deaths in both countries are caused by chest complaints. The U.K. is even worse: 13.3% of deaths there are caused by bronchitis, 'flu or some other chest ailment.

Medically mysterious deaths occur with greatest frequency in Belgium where 9.1% of all deaths are reported due to "ill-defined conditions". France is close behind with eight percent deaths undiagnosed. These figures are very high when compared with the 1.6% in the U.S. and the 0.6% in the U.K.

In which countries are we likely to be cut down before completing our expected span? Canada is the leader here with 10.1% of deaths due to accidents, poisonings and violence. The French live dangerously also – 8.9% of their dead succumb in an untimely manner. Switzerland ranks third in violent deaths – just ahead of the U.S. and Japan.

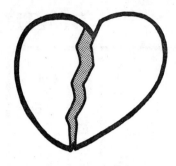

Most of us in the western world lead the good life. But, as with everything, the good life has its price. The main cause of death in affluent urban societies is heart disease. In North America and Europe, far more people die of heart disease and related illnesses than from any other cause.

Heart disease can take many different forms, including inflammatory infections of the membranes, diseases of the valves, enlargement of the heart, degeneration of the tissues and disturbances of the heart's rhythm. All of these forms of disease affect the heart's main function: to keep the blood circulating through the body by pumping blood from the veins through the heart into the arteries.

The percentage of people who died from heart disease is surprisingly uniform in the countries listed on our table – all of which have a high standard of living compared to the rest of the world. With a range of only 16% the figures show a closer correspondence than almost any other statistics in the book.

Australia has the highest percentage of people who die from heart disease and related diseases – over 54%. At first glance, it doesn't seem to be a typical urban affluent society. But if you look at the table showing the percentages of people who live in rural areas (see table

	U.S.A.		CANADA	
	1974		1974	
1. Deaths from heart or related diseases:				
as % of total deaths	53		49	
male as % of total male deaths	51		48	
female as % of total female deaths	56		51	
2. Number of male/female deaths from heart diseases as %+ of all deaths in age groups:	M	F	M	F
0 - 24	.4	.3	.3	.3
25 - 44	3	1	4	1
45 - 54	8	4	8	3
55 - 64	18	10	18	8
65 and over	71	85	70	88

on urban versus rural populations) you'll see that Australians head the list of urban dwellers. More Australians face the stresses of urban life than the rest of us.

The U.S. comes second on the table, with 53% of its deaths due to heart disease or related illnesses. Not surprising when you consider the American passion for beef, and the high tension level of life in many of our cities. Sweden has the same figure as the U.S., and the U.K. comes next, only one point behind these two. In Ireland, one out of every two die of heart disease – approximately the same as Norway and Denmark.

Who is best off on our table in terms of heart disease? In France, only 38% die from heart attacks or related diseases. The French have long been celebrated for

	U.K.	AUSTRALIA	AUSTRIA	BELGIUM	DENMARK	FRANCE	(WEST) GERMANY	IRELAND	ITALY	JAPAN	NETHERLANDS	NORWAY	SPAIN	SWEDEN	SWITZERLAND
	1974	1974	1975	1974	1975	1974	1974	1974	1974	1975	1975	1974	1974	1975	1975
	52	54	50	43	50	38	46	51	48	43	45	51	44	53	47
	50	51	45	42	50	35	43	50	43	40	43	50	40	53	44
	54	58	54	45	50	42	49	52	53	45	46	52	48	54	51

	U.K.		AUSTRALIA		AUSTRIA		BELGIUM		DENMARK		FRANCE		(WEST) GERMANY		IRELAND		ITALY		JAPAN		NETHERLANDS		NORWAY		SPAIN		SWEDEN		SWITZERLAND	
	M	F	M	F	M	F	M	F	M	F	M	F	M	F	M	F	M	F	M	F	M	F	M	F	M	F	M	F	M	F
	.2	.1	.2	.2	.2	.1	.3	.2	.1	.1	.4	.3	.2	.1	.3	.1	.3	.2	.7	.5	.2	.2	.1	.1	1.0	.9	.1	06	.3	.1
	2	.8	3	1	2	.6	2	.9	1	.9	2	.8	2	.8	2	.9	2	1	5	2	2	1	1	.6	3	2	1	.6	2	.9
	8	3	9	4	5	2	6	3	5	2	6	2	5	2	6	3	6	3	7	4	7	2	6	2	6	3	4	2	5	2
	18	8	20	10	11	6	15	7	15	7	12	4	13	6	16	9	14	7	13	9	15	6	16	6	14	8	13	5	13	5
	72	88	68	85	82	91	77	89	79	90	79	93	80	91	76	77	78	89	74	85	76	91	77	91	76	86	82	92	80	92

Source:
World Health Organization

their hedonistic way of life, with its emphasis on enjoyment – so perhaps this figure isn't so bizarre. It appears that one way to avoid heart disease is to be able to relax. This is borne out by the fact that Japan, which still has a stable, traditional way of life, comes after France in the list of "least worse off" countries. The Belgians, who have the same figure as the Japanese, obviously share the Gallic secret of relaxation.

In all the countries listed, except Denmark, women are slightly more likely to die from heart disease. Australian women, not surprisingly, top the list. The average difference between men and women is about four percent – though in Italy it's as high as ten percent, and in Austria it's nine percent. Possibly the

men in these countries have learned how to take life more easily – and pass the burden on to their womenfolk.

The age group sections of the table verify this possibility. As you'd expect, deaths from heart disease soar in the 65-plus age group for both sexes. But in the 45 to 54 age group, the figures for men are over double the figures for the women in most countries. This trend is magnified in the 55 to 64 age group. These figures obviously reflect the fact that more men are in full-time occupations at these ages and at greater risk from heart disease.

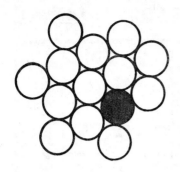

We're all afraid of cancer, but what exactly is it?

Basically, cancer is a malignant growth formed by the patient's own tissues; a collection of cells separate from their neighboring cells, which multiply at a disorderly and uncontrolled rate. Eventually this change becomes so total that, seen under the microscope, they no longer bear any resemblance to their original structure or to the surrounding tissue. They continue to draw on the body's supply of nourishment but cease to perform their original, useful functions.

This is why cancer is so dangerous. Since the cancer cells are no longer under the control of the host body they continue to reproduce themselves. If their growth is not checked, the cancer cells will invade and destroy the adjacent healthy cells. Also, some of the cancer cells may be transported in the bloodstream to distant parts of the body where the process is repeated.

The extent of the problem of cancer can't be exaggerated. In the U.S. and many other countries nearly one in five people die from cancer. And, in some cases, even the treatment is at best destructive. (For instance, if diagnosed early, a high proportion of breast cancers can be cured – but the cure often involves a mastectomy.)

There is amazingly little discrepancy in the figures for the different countries on our table. On average, cancer causes 20% of all deaths. This is a surprising uniformity when you consider the different climates and social conditions in the various countries.

Another general trend is that males are

	U.S.A.	CANADA
	1974	1974
1. Deaths from cancer (000s)		
male	199.2	18.8
female	166.3	15.3
as % of total deaths		
male	18.6	19.5
female	19.3	21.7
2. Male deaths due to various types of cancer+ (as % of male deaths caused by cancer):		
trachea, bronchus, lung	30.9	28.9
prostate	9.6	9.6
stomach	4.6	8.1
oesophagus	2.5	2.3
intestine (excluding the rectum)	9.4	9.2
3. Female deaths due to various types of cancer+ (as % of female deaths caused by cancer)		
breast	19.3	20.4
stomach	3.6	5.8
intestine	12.8	14.3
trachea, bronchus, lungs	10.4	7.7
uterus	3.4	3.1

	U.K.	AUSTRALIA	AUSTRIA	BELGIUM	DENMARK	FRANCE	(WEST) GERMANY	IRELAND	ITALY	JAPAN	NETHERLANDS	NORWAY	SPAIN	SWEDEN	SWITZERLAND
	1974	1974	1975	1974	1975	1974	1974	1974	1974	1975	1975	1974	1974	1975	1975
	75.0	11.4	9.7	14.0	6.3	68.9	77.5	3.3	61.8	80.4	17.1	4.1	28.3	10.5	7.6
	64.3	8.7	9.6	10.6	5.8	50.9	78.3	2.9	46.4	62.4	12.3	3.5	22.7	9.2	5.9
	22.2	17.8	20.8	22.9	22.7	24.1	21.5	17.2	21.9	21.3	26.9	19.0	18.5	21.7	25.4
	19.5	17.0	19.5	19.2	25.2	19.2	21.3	18.0	18.7	19.2	24.6	19.7	15.9	23.0	22.6
	39.8	28.9	27.4	32.9	27.5	17.6	25.0	26.5	24.5	13.3	35.2	14.2	18.7	16.0	26.5
	6.5	9.2	8.4	8.7	8.7	8.7	8.9	9.4	6.6	1.6	9.0	14.5	8.7	16.8	11.2
	10.5	8.2	16.1	10.6	9.5	8.2	14.8	12.9	15.5	37.8	10.7	12.9	17.5	11.2	10.5
	2.8	2.4	1.9	1.8	1.9	7.1	1.9	3.3	2.6	4.8	1.5	1.5	3.6	2.1	4.2
	7.0	9.2	7.2	6.9	7.9	7.0	7.2	9.1	6.2	3.5	6.5	6.1	4.8	8.2	7.3
	19.6	18.8	13.6	17.2	17.6	15.7	14.4	17.9	16.6	5.2	20.2	15.9	12.1	16.1	21.5
	8.9	7.0	13.9	10.4	6.8	8.6	13.0	11.3	14.5	31.2	9.0	10.6	16.9	8.2	9.9
	11.4	14.3	10.5	12.2	10.7	11.8	10.3	12.9	9.1	4.9	11.0	8.5	8.5	9.1	8.6
	11.7	6.5	5.7	4.6	7.9	3.4	3.9	10.8	5.0	6.5	3.5	3.9	4.6	5.4	3.9
	2.9	2.3	6.5	5.0	3.3	6.3	3.8	2.8	9.0	7.3	3.0	2.8	8.0	3.6	4.3

Sources:
World Health Organization
+Main causes of death by cancer

slightly more prone to this disease than females – on average by about two percent. The exceptions here are in the U.S., Canada, Denmark, Ireland, Norway and Sweden, where the women are more prone. The Netherlands suffers most from cancer, the cause of 26% of all deaths there.

Spain has the lowest prevalence of cancer deaths. Here the rate is only just over 17%, a figure closely followed by Australia and Ireland. After this comes the U.S., with a rate of 19%. This is about average for the countries on the table, which incidentally, are the highest group affected in the world.

Over a quarter of a million women die from breast cancer throughout the world each year. In western Europe and the U.S., it's the major cause of death amongst women, a malady that strikes all ages. It is the leading form of death in women between 35 and 54, and is second only to cardiovascular disease in the higher age groups.

However, this pattern doesn't hold true worldwide. The breast cancer death rate is lower in eastern and southern Europe, and drops dramatically in Africa, Latin America and Asia.

Deaths from breast cancer per 100,000 women+	U.S.A.	CANADA
All ages	27.6	25.4
35-44	20.5	21.6
45-54	52.2	56.5
55-64	77.8	83.4
65-74	95.2	99.4
75 and over	132.2	153.8

Experts disagree over the exact causes of the disease, but statistics show that married women are less likely to have breast cancer than unmarried women; and women who have had children are less prone to the disease than those who haven't. Women who have had children in their teens or early 20s are also less likely to suffer from this form of cancer.

What other factors are there? The stresses of contemporary life, emotional pressures, weight problems, environmental and occupational hazards have all been cited as possibly contributing to the disease.

Several trends emerge from our table. On the whole it seems that in the Western countries, those that are densely populated have the worst figures. Overall, the U.K. (population density: 611 per square mile) is the highest, with 39 deaths per hundred thousand, and the Netherlands (1,065 per square mile) and Belgium (851 per square mile) are also high – both have more than 34 deaths per hundred thousand. (On the other hand, why should relatively sparsely populated Denmark be so high?)

At the other end of the scale, Australia and Canada, with their wide open spaces, have relatively "good" figures. But why should Italy (492 per square mile) be lower than either, with only 23 per hundred thousand? It is questions like these that still keep the experts guessing.

Japan (804 per square mile) is obviously a special case. It has far and away the lowest figures in the table – four per hundred thousand deaths overall. We can only speculate as to the reasons for this. Diet, geographical situation, and racial factors may all play their part. Does eating fish and rice help? Is a variable climate useful? Is there more than just beauty in those geisha girls' genes?

There are other factors. Japan is still a highly formalized society, which has only

U.K.	AUSTRALIA	AUSTRIA	BELGIUM	DENMARK	FRANCE	(WEST) GERMANY	IRELAND	ITALY	JAPAN	NETHERLANDS	NORWAY	SPAIN	SWEDEN	SWITZERLAND
38.9	23.6	30.3	34.2	36.8	27.6	30.2	28.9	22.9	4.2	34.3	28.1	–	30.3	33.9
22.0	15.0	13.9	19.3	19.8	13.2	15.9	24.1	16.8	5.4	22.8	15.5	NA	12.2	16.3
57.8	43.5	40.4	51.8	55.0	37.8	41.3	55.5	39.4	11.1	60.7	38.5	NA	41.3	46.4
83.4	64.7	62.0	68.4	83.5	58.0	61.9	69.5	54.9	12.8	87.1	65.9	NA	66.9	76.9
106.8	85.4	81.5	92.3	112.1	77.4	82.6	94.7	71.7	12.3	113.9	83.5	NA	84.6	115.9
161.8	147.3	122.3	156.5	184.6	133.3	135.1	129.9	101.3	17.7	208.2	122.8	NA	134.4	190.2

NA not available

recently become industrialized. It has also been slow to adopt many Western social habits. In several spheres women are still second-class citizens.

But take a closer look at those Japanese figures. They are proportionally very much higher in the lower age groups. For instance, Japan's overall figure is a seventh of the U.S. figure – but the 35 to 44 age group is as high as a quarter of the U.S. figure. Trends like this can be almost as important as the figures themselves. And from this trend it looks as though Japan's days of comparative immunity are sadly coming to a close.

Vast sums are now being allocated to cancer research in all the countries on the table. Indeed, several experts believe that we are on the verge of a major breakthrough in the field. Also, preventative measures are now widely used – screening is available to women in most areas of every country listed in the tables.

Today, breast cancer can be halted if it is treated early on.

Source:
World Health Organization
+Data for years 1965-69

EARLY SYMPTOMS

Breast cancer is a disease that all women fear. However, if it is discovered early enough, it can be cured, so it's important for women to check their breasts for early symptoms. These are a small, painless lump or thickness which can be felt with the flat of the hand; swelling or inflamation; the indrawing of one nipple; roughness and thickening of the skin of the breast; change in the shape of one breast; blood-stained discharge from the nipple; eczema of the nipple.

These symptoms do not necessarily indicate cancer, but, in any case, they should be diagnosed and treated.

To investigate a lump or swelling, the doctor may take a small piece to examine under a microscope. Should it prove to be cancerous, he may advise treatment by X-rays, surgery, or possibly both.

The number of babies who arrive stillborn or die within a few days after birth worries doctors around the world. Figures vary from country to country and within each country from year to year.

It's hard for even an expert to make much sense of these statistics. The U.S., for instance, is eighth on the table in infant mortality: in 22 out of every thousand births, babies are either stillborn or die within six days. Another 16 die in their first year of life. This puts us right in the middle of the pack.

You'd expect the countries with better figures than ours to be ones like Scandinavia and the U.K., who have extensive state-subsidized health care –

	U.S.A.	CANADA
	1975	1975
1. Live births per 1,000 inhabitants	14.7	15.7
2. Infants who died within 6 days of birth per 1,000 total births[x]	21.9	17.6
3. Infants who died in their first year per 1,000 live births	16.1	15.0
	1974	1974
4. Principal causes of infant mortality (as % of male/ female infant deaths):	M/F	M/F
anoxic and hypoxic conditions[‡]	26/21	20[++0]
congenital anomalies[**]	15/17	23[++0]
pneumonia[xx]	4/5	5[++0]
other[oo]	55/57	52[++0]

and that countries that spend less on health would have highest infant mortality rates. This is only partially true. Sweden, Denmark and Norway are more successful than we are in holding down infant mortality, but the U.K. isn't: its death rate is higher than ours. At the other end of the scale, Italy far exceeds us in deaths, but France, not usually renowned for excellence of health care, has fewer (a total of 32.2 per thousand compared with our 38).

The period of greatest danger for babies is the first week of life. The majority of infants who don't survive their first year perish within six days of birth. In the four countries with the best records on infant mortality – Sweden, Norway, the Netherlands and Denmark – the average is 14.6 deaths per thousand within six days of birth.

After the first week, death rates are lower, and more uniform from country to country. Sweden is the lowest with 8.3 deaths per thousand and Austria the highest, 20.8. Compare the difference between these two figures with that between the lowest and highest figures for infant mortality within six days of birth: Sweden at 13.2 per thousand and Italy at 29.2. The younger the infant, the more vunerable he is.

INFANT MORTALITY

	U.K.	AUSTRALIA	AUSTRIA	BELGIUM	DENMARK	FRANCE	(WEST) GERMANY	IRELAND	ITALY	JAPAN	NETHERLANDS	NORWAY	SPAIN	SWEDEN	SWITZERLAND
	1975	1975	1975	1975	1975	1975	1975	1975	1975	1975	1975	1975	1975	1975	1975
	14.1	17.2	12.3	12.3	14.3	14.1	9.7	21.6	14.8	17.2	13.0	14.0	18.2	12.6	12.4
	22.8	22.1	23.0	22	14.5	18.6	23.0	23.2	29.2	16.7	15.4	15.4	NA	13.2	14.1
	17.7	16.1	20.8	16.2	10.7	13.6	19.7	18.4	20.7	10.8	10.6	10.5	13.8	8.3	10.7
	1974	1974	1975	1974	1974	1974	1974	1974	1974	1974	1975	1974	1974	1975	1974
	M/F	M/F	M/F	M/F	M/F	M/F	M/F	M/F	M/F	M/F	M/F	M/F	M/F	M/F	M/F
	22/18	12/10	15/14	8/6	26/20	20/19	21/20	16/15	12/10	23/21	23/19	10/8	NA	20/18	26/24
	21/28	20/26	7/7	23/26	24/31	21/24	18/20	20/26	19/21	14/15	24/29	24/34	19++	28/35	26/27
	8/7	4/4	4/4	3/3	2/1	2/2	2/2	17/13	8/10	8/9	2/1	4/4	13++	3/2	3/5
	49/47	64/60	74/75	66/65	48/48	57/55	59/58	47/46	61/63	55/55	51/51	62/54	10++	49/44	45/44

NA not available   ++*Male and female*

Sources:
1, 2 & 3 Department of Health and Social Services, London
4 World Health Organization
X*Demographic Year Book 1975*
0*Canada Year Book 1976-1977*
‡Absence or deficiency of oxygen. 1974 figures
**Includes spina bifida, congenital anomalies of the heart, other congenital anomalies of the circulatory system, cleft palate and lip, and all other congenital anomalies.
XXViral and other pneumonia
00Includes infective and parasitic diseases, enterilise diarrheal diseases, whooping cough, meningococcal infections, measles, avitominoses and other nutritional deficiencies, diseases of the nervous system, meningitis, acute respiratory infections, influenza, bronchitis, emphysema and asthma, intestinal obstruction and hernia, birth injury and difficult labor, condition of placenta and cord, haemolytic disease of the newborn, other causes of perinatal mortality, symptoms and other ill-defined conditions, accidents.

Percentage of Population

The French really hit the alcoholic jackpot when it comes to hitting the bottle. Nearly one in ten of France's entire population is medically at risk from alcoholism. (The French not only have the greatest wines—they also have the greatest hangovers.) The Italians aren't much better off. In Italy one out of twelve adults has a drinking problem. It can't be a coincidence that the top five countries on the chart all have large wine industries. Compared with these, the USA, home of Alcoholics Anonymous, fares comparatively well. But only comparatively, one American out of 30 has a booze problem.

U.S.A.	AUSTRALIA	WEST GERMANY
3.84	4.11	5.07

ALCOHOLISM

9.53

8.21

5.94

5.20

9

8

7

6

5

4

3

2

1

SWITZERLAND SPAIN ITALY FRANCE

Sex

Love and marriage go together like a horse and carriage. Or so the song says. But a lot of things have changed since those lines were written, including the way we run our sex lives. Things really seem to swing in some countries. After reading this chapter, you'll know if you're missing out on the action or leading the sexual revolution.

The first set of tables will give you an idea of just how widely people's views can differ on controversial issues like the double standard, the so-called "permissive society" and the results of changing moral standards. The "Swinging Sixties" have come and gone but the arguments they raised are still raging as fiercely as ever. You'll see how factors like age and nationality make a big difference in the responses to questions like "Are attitudes to sex today too permissive?". And can you guess where 70% of the men think their sex lives are very enjoyable, while under half the ladies are really enjoying their encounters with the opposite sex?

After looking at what people think about sex, there's the equally intriguing question of what they *do* about it. The tables on the frequency of sexual activity among different age groups in four countries may provide some shocks. For instance, there's a country where the 45 to 49-year-olds outdo all the young marrieds and swinging singles.

Pre-marital sex is a particularly explosive topic. What do Americans think of the "new morality"? Does it mean a breakdown in our country's moral standards? This section points out just how attitudes vary from one country to another.

So much for opinions. But if you want to know what your teenage daughter really gets up to when she goes out on a date, have a look at the section on pre-marital sexual experience. Has the permissive society become a reality for American girls in their mid-teens? The tables even break the figures down according to race, so you can see how different cultural patterns affect young people's sexual behavior. Then there's an eye-opening comparison of U.S. pre-marital activities with British and Dutch.

After looking at what the kids are doing, the next section provides some clues about *when* they start doing it. The tables here cover sexual activities from the tender age of under 12 right up to the over 30s. Again, the comparisons range from different age groups and sexes to different countries.

There's another angle to the whole question of pre-marital sex – that's whether increased sexual freedom has led to promiscuity. Are teenagers really "sleeping around"? Is such behavior universal? Or do different countries and cultures produce different sexual standards? These tables deal mainly with young people, but the Swedish figures include 30 to 60-year-olds. Which provides a good yardstick for measuring just how much change there's been in sexual behavior in the last generation.

In the days when love and marriage actually *did* go together, it was quite likely that the first sexual partner would be the one you walked down the aisle with. Have things changed since then? The tables on first sexual partners suggest they have – at least in the two countries surveyed. Who's replaced spouses? You've guessed it – the steady date.

If you're a young single still playing the dating game, you'll be especially interested in the next section on the average age at marriage. And if you're a young single woman, get ready for the good news – you're in the minority in every one of the 15 countries in our table. In one country, there are 2.5 times as many single young men as women. So check the figures here carefully if you have your heart set on a wedding ring – and start making your vacation plans accordingly.

As the section on average age at marriage shows, wedding bells are still pealing for a lot of young couples. The tables here offer some invaluable facts for the marriage-minded.

So much for marriage – what about the other side of the coin? The table on marriage and divorce leads to some inescapable conclusions about the effect of changing moral standards on permanent relationships.

Needless to say, one of the prime causes of broken marriages is infidelity. The next two sections, on people's attitudes towards extra-marital sex and their extra-marital experiences, seem to indicate that a lot of people just aren't practicing what they preach. For instance, while nearly nine out of ten British men *thought* that a husband ought to remain faithful, only six out of ten had actually managed to do so.

In any discussion of sex, there's one area that's especially controversial – homosexuality. The tables here give some revealing insights into people's feelings about homosexuality – and where it might be safest to "come out of the closet".

Other than politics, there's one topic that's absolutely guaranteed to start an argument. That's sex. Do you believe in the "double standard"? How do you feel about pre-marital sex? Has the permissive society gone too far? Are sex crimes increasing because of lower moral standards? Whatever your opinions on these questions, someone's sure to feel exactly the opposite.

So have a look at the tables in this section. You'll get a good idea of who thinks the way you do – and who doesn't. You'll also see how your responses to the above questions and others about sex may well depend on whether you're male or female, or what country you come from.

In West Germany, one thing seems clear. Women have a much more traditional, conservative approach to the issue of permissiveness and its consequences. For example, when asked if greater sexual freedom would not only harm people's bodies but also lead to the loss of spiritual values, 45% of the women said yes. That's 12% more women than men feeling that increased sexual freedom is a threat to the deeper values of society.

Herren and *damen* again disagreed about whether young people are demoralized by sexual freedom. Forty percent of the women thought so, but 12% fewer

	WEST GERMANY	
	1970	1970
	Men	Women
Men/women[+] (%) who agree:		
Sexual freedom leads to demoralization of young people	28	40
Sex has made people freer. People aren't frightened to talk about things that must be discussed	57	51
With sexual freedom going so far, people will not only harm their bodies but lose their spiritual values	33	45
Sexual freedom enables young people to get to know each other better before they marry	41	34
The open attitude to sexual matters must lead to an increase in sex crimes	28	34
Sexual freedom threatens marriage and the family	28	32

Source:
Allensbacher Berichten, 1970, Institut für Demoskopie Allensbach
[+]Aged 16 and over
Percentages do not add up to 100 as more than one answer was accepted.

men were of the same opinion. Forty-one percent of the men thought that sexual contact between young people before marriage was a good way for them to get to know one another. The women, no doubt feeling maternal concern for their nubile young daughters, weren't so quick to agree. Only 34% of them thought that young people needed to know each other *that* well.

There was only one issue where over half of both sexes agreed things had changed for the better. That was the increased freedom people now feel to discuss formerly taboo subjects that should be brought into the open. Just over half (51%) of the females agreed that sex

ATTITUDES TO SEX

	U.K.
	1976
Women[+] (%) who strongly agree that most people's attitudes to sex are now much too permissive	8
slightly agree	19
neither agree nor disagree	34
slightly disagree	21
strongly disagree	17
no answer	1

Source:
Honey magazine, May and June 1977. Survey conducted by the Schlachman Research Organization Ltd. London.
[+]Single women 18-26

has liberated people in this area. But once again the males went further – 57% agreed with this trend. So we can assume that some of the conversation in those *bier kellers* is spicier these days.

What about the question of sexual freedom as a threat to stable marriages and the family? Understandably, more women than men were worried about this possibility. It used to be bad enough worrying about that attractive new secretary. But now temptation for the bored husband abounds on all sides. Nearly a third of the men were also worried about the state of the family in these permissive times.

As if that wasn't enough to worry about, there's the serious social problem of sex crimes. (Take a look at the tables on this subject and you'll see why the West Germans have good reason to worry.) Just under a third of the men (28%), and over a third of the women (34%), were convinced that modern attitudes to sex lead to an increase in sexual offenses. This is an issue that's

been hotly debated in the media for a long time, but a lot of Germans have apparently made up their minds. Sexual deprivation is perhaps felt more keenly in a society where many people are openly permissive. Resentment and jealously are common feelings in sex offenders.

The Germans as a group showed a pretty high degree of concern over the amount of sexual permissiveness in their society. Even though men generally felt less worried than the women, over a third of them were worried about each of the issues raised.

Now let's look at a different set of opinions. In our second table you can see that young, single women in the U.K. hold very different views from those of the West Germans. They were asked if most people's attitudes to sex are now much too permissive. The lowest number on the table (eight percent) was for those who strongly agreed. That's only about one in 12 feeling things have gone too far in the sexual revolution. More than twice as many felt exactly the opposite – 17% strongly disagreed. Of course, youth's views tend to be more extreme than those of society at large. The young women questioned were all 18 to 26 years old, an age group certainly in a position to enjoy the advantages of greater sexual freedom. So it's not so surprising that a majority of them, (38%) disagreed, either strongly or slightly, that there's too much permissiveness, while only 27% agreed. Quite a few – over a third stayed completely neutral on this issue. Why so many? We can only speculate. But maybe they're just too young to remember anything but today's atmosphere of increased sexual freedom. The "Swing-

AUSTRALIA		
Men/women (%) who rate their sex life as:	1974 Men	1974 Women
very enjoyable	70	45
mostly pleasant	18	30
occasionally pleasant	4	14
neither pleasant nor unpleasant	2	3
mostly and/or very unpleasant	0	2
not applicable	6	6

Source:
Cleo magazine, August and September 1974. Survey conducted by Roy Morgan Research Center Ltd

ing Sixties" seem to have left a deep mark.

It's interesting that the responses in this all-female survey were a complete contrast to the attitudes held by the women of West Germany. What accounts for the difference – is it the generation gap? Or could there be a cultural gap? Maybe the British aren't as straitlaced and reserved as legend has it.

Second, a look at what's going on Down Under. Those high-living, fun-loving Aussies were asked to rate their sex lives. The most striking fact about the results is that a whopping 70% of Australian men find their sex lives very enjoyable. That's seven out of every ten Australian males who are contented, at least in this rather vital area of life. Another 18% – just under two out of ten – rated their sex lives as mostly pleasant. That makes a grand total of 88% who don't find much to complain about. No wonder Australia attracts so many immigrants! Four percent found sex pleasant only occasionally, and a minority (two percent) had a distinctly "blah" approach – they said their sex lives were neither pleasant nor unpleasant. Now for the really amazing fact – absolutely *no* Australian men rated their sex lives as unsatisfactory. At this point you may find yourself wondering if their capacity for sexual fulfilment is only equalled by a talent for exaggeration.

So let's turn to the other half of this issue – the women's point of view. It looks as if the men are having a lot more fun than their partners. Under half the ladies (45%) find their sex lives very enjoyable. It seems Australia is faced with a dissatisfaction gap. And compared

to that, the missile gap and the generation gap are nothing. One-quarter of the ladies just aren't having quite such a wonderful time in bed as those euphoric males.

Still, 30% of the women found things "mostly pleasant" in the area of sexual relations. That's a total of 75% of women who are either very or reasonably satisfied with their sex lives.

On the question of whether things were at least occasionally pleasant, more than three times as many women as men made

	1974	1974	1974	1974	1974	1974	U.S.
	Men			Women			
	Agree	Disagree	Not Sure	Agree	Disagree	Not Sure	
Reactions of men/women (%) to:							
One moral standard for men and another for women have existed for many years	74	18	8	75	16	10	
Single women shouldn't enjoy the same kind of freedom as single men	14	77	9	15	74	11	
Pre-marital sex is immoral	44	46	10	53	36	11	

Source:
The Virginia Slims American Women's Opinion Poll, The Roper Organization Inc, 1974

this rather cool assessment. No doubt about it, Australian women are either hard to please or just plain honest. There are even two percent who dare to admit that things are just plain awful in their sex lives.

It's hard to escape the feeling that maybe – just *maybe* – that Australian tendency to hyperbole has crept into some of the men's claims in this table. But since a lot of satisfaction is really just in the mind, does it matter all that much?

In the U.S. there have been big changes in sexual attitudes in the past few decades. The table above shows the responses of American men and women to some very controversial questions on the subject of sex. On the first issue, that of the "double standard", both sexes are in close agreement. Three-quarters of men and women felt that for many years men have been free to live by one moral code, while women were expected to follow another. In other words, the fellows are free to sow their wild oats, but "nice girls don't".

So how do we feel about that situation?

The responses to the next question showed that 77% of the males thought single women should in fact enjoy the same freedom as single men. That's nearly eight out of ten. Maybe our men aren't so chauvinistic after all. Either that or they think the more sexually liberated single girls around, the better off they are. The surprising thing here is that only 74% of the women agreed with the men that they should have equal freedom. Maybe it's just the traditional female fear of being branded a "loose woman" that makes some of them hesitate to claim the same sexual freedoms. Either that, or Women's Lib has done a better job of winning over men.

On the ever-touchy subject of pre-marital sex, the ladies once again appeared to be more conservative than the men. Over half the women (53%) thought it was immoral to have sexual relations before marriage. But considerably fewer men felt the same way. In fact, 46% of them thought it was fine to indulge before that long walk down the aisle.

One of the biggest – and most publicized – upheavals in everyday life has been the so-called "sexual revolution." Almost every newspaper and magazine frequently carries articles on some aspect of the "permissive society". Nonetheless, sexual intercourse is still a pretty touchy subject. People's prejudices and misconceptions often get in the way of an objective assessment of what's really going on. Some would have you believing that all standards of decency and morality have been abandoned in a headlong rush towards decadence. Others maintain that things haven't really changed that much since the earlier part of the century.

Certainly, there are still a lot of powerful fears and taboos that prevent people from freely indulging in sexual activity. Despite the Pill, there's still the fear of unwanted pregnancy. Guilt feelings, moral training and social disapproval are other big factors in many people's minds. Then there's the fear of venereal disease. That's something that's had a resurgence as certain strains have developed resistance to modern drugs.

In this section, we've tried to shed some light on the whole subject of sexual intercourse by looking at just how often people in four countries, of both sexes and differing marital status and ages, indulge in sexual activity.

Our first table shows the results of a survey carried out among over 800

	1974	1974	1974
	By sex		
	M	W	Under 20
People (%) who, on average during the last six months, have had sexual intercourse:			
never	12	15	31
a few times	11	8	21
once or twice a month	11	13	8
one or twice a week	38	34	15
3 or 4 times a week	19	21	13
over 5 times a week	6	7	8
daily or more often	3	1	0

Source:
Cleo, August and September 1974. Survey conducted by Roy Morgan Research Center Pty Ltd.
Totals do not add up to 100 because of a proportion of "no answers".

Australians, both married and single.

If you look at the overall figures for men and women, you'll see that only one man in every eight hadn't had any sexual experiences in the six months preceding the survey. Slightly more women had abstained. The great majority of both sexes – 38% of men, 34% of women – said they had intercourse once or twice a week. The next most common frequency was three or four times a week – here the women were slightly ahead, with about one in five indulging that often. The lowest figures are in response to the question "did you have intercourse daily or more often?". Still, three percent of the men boasted they'd had a very active six months.

Next we looked at how these responses break down according to age groups. In the under-20s, a mere 31% hadn't had sexual intercourse at all. That means about seven in every ten of the Australian young people surveyed *had* had some

FREQUENCY

1974	1974	1974	1974	1974	1974	1974
			By age			
20-24	25-29	30-34	35-39	40-44	45-49	50 & over
13	4	3	1	5	6	28
8	5	4	5	3	7	115
3	15	13	13	9	21	16
29	42	38	41	52	59	31
27	28	29	34	22	3	6
16	6	7	4	6	0	1
4	0	5	2	3	4	0

sexual encounters. But their sexual encounters tended to be sporadic. One-fifth of them had only had intercourse a few times in the whole six-month period. On the other hand, 15% managed to have sex once or twice a week, and 13% three or four times per week on average. That's far less than the overall average, but still a high figure for this age group.

The highest figure for sexual activity by a particular age group is 59%. That's how many 45 to 49-year-olds have sex once or twice a week. One in 25 of those in the same age bracket claimed to indulge daily or more often. That's the second highest average on the table. Maybe life really does begin at 40!

Things seem to cool off rapidly after the half-century mark. Nearly one-third of the over-50s hadn't had any sexual encounters in the six-month period.

If we look at the combined figures for regular weekly sex, both once or twice a week and three or four times, it's the late 30s group that's most active – 75% said they had sex that frequently. Next came the early 40s (74%), then the late 20s (70%). Strangely, the early 20s group, with all those young marrieds and swinging singles, ranks comparatively low on our tables. Only about one in three had intercourse as often as once or twice a week, and about one in eight hadn't had any sexual encounters at all.

So in Australia, one's sex life seems to get increasingly active as the years go on, at least till that daunting half-century.

Here in the United States, young unmarried women were asked how often they had intercourse in the past four weeks. The same question was asked in 1971 and in 1976.

The 1971 study revealed that most unmarried teenage girls had intercourse infrequently. As measured by the frequency of intercourse during the month preceding the study, approximately two in five abstained. Teenagers in 1976 appear even more abstemious. About half of the respondents hadn't had sex during the preceding month, and less than three in ten hadn't had intercourse as many as three times in the month.

In the 15 to 17-year-old group, another ten percent hadn't had sexual relations in 1976 compared to 1971. The same was true of six percent of the 18 to 19s.

But the trend reverses when we come to the question of intercourse six times in a four-week period. The youngest group

		1969	1969
		Married	Separated/divorced
1. People[+] who have never had sexual intercourse		0	0
2. People[+] who, during the past year, have had sexual intercourse:			
0 times		0	1
1-4 times		0	2
5-24 times		13	2
25-50 times		30	1
over 50 times		203	3
don't know		11	1
total		257	10

Source:
Michael Schofield: *The Sexual Behaviour of Young Adults* (Allen Lane, 1973) p., 170. Copyright © Michael Schofield, 1973. Reprinted by permission of Penguin Books Ltd.
[+]Aged 25. The figures are absolute numbers not percentages.

gave the same response – 8·6% in both years. However, the 18 and 19-year-olds who were having relations that frequently in 1971 increased by only six percent in 1976.

Now let's have a look at Sweden, one of the pioneers in the field of sexual liberation. Two groups, one of 18 to 30-year-olds and another of 30 to 60-year-olds, were asked how often they'd had intercourse in the past month.

In both groups, over 70% of both men and women had intercourse either two to four times or five to ten times. The men claimed greater frequency in both age groups, but the women weren't far behind. Interestingly, over 20% of the 18 to 30-year-old women had relations up to 20 times during the four week period, as compared to a mere 12% of the men.

The highest frequency claim by any age group was the 30 to 60-year-old males. Fifty-three per cent said they had intercourse two to four times that month.

Around two percent of the younger age group said they had intercourse over 20 times a month – that's almost once a day.

Finally, what about the U.K., where that famed British reserve supposedly keeps emotions in check? The table shows the responses of nearly 400 Britons, married, unmarried and divorced. The vast majority of married people – 203 out of 257 – had sexual intercourse at least once a week over the preceding year.

Another 30 said they had intercourse 25 to 50 times.

A third of the divorced people questioned claimed to have intercourse over 50 times a year.

Moving on to the unmarried category, we find that about half of those with a steady boy- or girl-friend had intercourse no less than 25 times in the year. About a quarter of them claimed a rate of over once a week. That's a lower percentage of unmarried couples having regular sexual relations than married couples, but it does indicate that it's become a commonplace in Britain for a lot of "steadys" to sleep together regularly.

Singles without a regular partner had sex less frequently. About two out of five had never had intercourse at all. About a quarter had intercourse five to 24 times.

U.K.

With a steady boy/girl-friend (1969)	No steady boy/girl-friend (1969)
7	19
3	6
6	3
8	13
13	5
12	4
3	2
52	52

SWEDEN

	1973 30-60 years old		1973 18-30 years old	
	M	W	M	W
Men/women (%) who, during the last month, have had sexual intercourse:				
once	12.9	13.4	8.1	5.8
2-4 times	53.4	49.6	36.0	36.0
5-10 times	28.6	30.4	41.6	36.0
11-20 times	4.3	6.1	12.0	20.2
over 20 times	0.8	0.4	2.3	2.0

Source:
Riksförbundet für Sexuell Upplysning, Stockholm

U.S.

	1976 15-17	1976 18-19	1971 15-17	1971 18-19
Unmarried women (%) who, during the last four weeks have had sexual intercourse:				
0 times	51.0	43.5	41.5	37.7
once or twice	30.1	19.6	34.5	25.7
3-5 times	10.3	13.4	15.4	19.5
6 times	8.6	23.5	8.6	17.1

Source:
Reproduced, with permission, from *Family Planning Perspectives,* Vol 9, number 2, from "Sexual and Contraceptive Experience of Young Unmarried Women in the USA, 1976-77" by Melvin Zelnik, Ph.D and John F Kantner, Ph.D.

Our attitudes to sex have undergone a profound change during the last decade. The result has been nothing less than a sexual revolution. Or has it? There's been a lot of talk and publicity on this topic – but what are the facts? What really are our attitudes to sex? Perhaps the central issue here is our attitude to pre-marital sex. That's what this table is about. From the look of the figures there hasn't been as much of a revolution in our attitudes as many would have you believe. Here in the U.S. an overwhelming majority of men and women think that the new morality doesn't make for better, more successful marriages. The women are slightly more conservative on this point than the men, but in both cases a majority of over three to one incline to the opinion that the new morality won't help marriage. There's also an almost two to one majority of both sexes in this country who think that the new morality doesn't help people to make a better choice of marriage partners.

Yet does the new morality enable couples to have more honest relationships? It certainly does in the view of the experts in the field. But they look as if they're out on a limb here. Most Americans don't think that the new morality enables people to have more honest relationships, according to our figures. Though opinions are more divided here – around 50% against and 36% for, amongst both sexes. As with the previous ques-

| | | 1974 | 1974 |
| | | Agree | Disagree |
		M	M
Men/women[+] (%) who think the new morality will:			
make for better, more successful marriages		21	68
enable people to make a better choice of marriage partner		33	55
enable couples to have more honest relationships with each other		39	48
encourage more people to live together without marrying		73	19
encourage more people to stay single		53	35
weaken the institution of marriage		61	31
cause the breakdown of the country's morals		49	41

tions, it's the women who are marginally more conservative in their views. In general, you'll see that this is the case in almost all the answers.

American men and women are in accord on the issue of whether the new morality encourages more people to live together without marrying. Seventy-three per cent of both men and women agree that it does, with a mere 19% who disagree. It's interesting to note that this is the question with the most agreement, as well as having the fewest "don't know" answers (a mere eight percent of both sexes). So we seem to be deeply convinced on this matter – and you only have to look around you to see how much this conviction is borne out by the facts. It's not surprising then to find that the next highest majority is of people who think that the new morality weakens the institution of marriage – just over 62% for both sexes.

On the other hand, we are not convinced that the new morality encourages

ATTITUDES: PRE-MARITAL SEX

1974	1974	1974	1974	U.S.
Don't know	Agree	Disagree	Don't know	
M	W	W	W	
10	17	72	11	
13	28	58	14	
13	34⁰	52	14	
8	73	19	8	
11	54	33	13	
8	64	28	9	
10	56	33	11	

Source:
The Virginia Slims American Women's
Opinion Poll, The Roper Organization Inc,
1974
[+]Aged 18-50

CANADA	
	1977
People (%) who think teenage sex without love is:[+]	
absolutely wrong	46
wrong	19
quite wrong	11
quite acceptable	12
perfectly acceptable	2
no answer	10

Source:
Weekend Magazine, Toronto, December 3rd,
1977
[+]The original question asked: "How do you
rate teenage sex without love on a scale of
1 to 7 ranging from "absolutely wrong"
(level 1) to "perfectly acceptable" (level 7)?"
The other levels were undefined and we have
interpreted them so that levels 2-3 = "wrong";
level 4 = "quite wrong"; levels 5-6 "quite
acceptable".

people to stay single. Only around 53% of both sexes think this is the case – with more than a third of the people questioned disagreeing.

So what is the general American view on the new morality? Do people think that it'll cause a breakdown of the country's morals? The opinions of men and women are more divided on this topic than on any other – though even here the difference is only eight percent. In both cases more people thought that the new morality would lead to a breakdown of the country's morals – 56% of the women questioned thought so, and 49% of the men. What does this mean? These answers would seem to reflect widespread American misgivings about the present situation.

It's the same story when you come to Canada the same people were asked what they thought about teenage sex without love. From the look of these figures the sexual revolution is a long way off.

Almost half the people questioned (46%), were of the opinion that teenage sex without love is absolutely wrong. A further one in five, (19%), considered it wrong, and on top of that one in ten, (11%), thought it quite wrong. This means that over three-fourths of the people questioned (76%) were of the opinion that teenage sex without love is, to a greater or lesser degree, wrong. A pretty bleak picture as far as permissive attitudes are concerned. Just one person in eight questioned, (12%), considered teenage sex without love to be quite acceptable, and a mere two percent considered it to be perfectly acceptable. These opinions seem to be out of line with

	FRANCE	
	1970	1970
	M	W
Young men/women[+] (%) who think it is alright for two single people to have sexual relations if: they're engaged	80	74
they've known each other a long time	75	65
they've known each other a short time	48	65

Source:
Rapport sur le Comportement Sexuel des Francais by Dr. Pierre Simon, published by René Julliard, Pierre Charron, 1972. Survey conducted by l'Institut Francais d'Opinion Publique.
[+]Aged 20-29

the facts (as you'll see if you look at some of the other tables in this chapter).

What do people think about pre-marital sex in other countries? What do all those romantic French think about love and sex, for instance? From the look of these figures, they're heavily in favor of sex at least amongst the 20 to 29 age group. Eighty percent of the French men questioned thought that it was all right for two people to have sexual relations if they were engaged. Slightly fewer women (74%) agreed. This looks like being the category of least disagreement amongst the sexes in the French figures. Seventy-five percent of Frenchmen between the ages of 20 and 29 think that it's all right for two single people to have sex if they've known each other for a long time – that's ten percent more than the women. When it comes to opinions on whether it's all right for two people to have sexual relations if they've known each other for a short time, the opinions of the sexes are even more divided. Forty-eight percent of the men think it's all right, but only

25% of the women– a difference of almost two to one. It looks as if there may be a few lovers' quarrels on this score.

Now we come to the attitudes to pre-marital sex in the U.K. The figures here are from a survey of young women between the ages of 18 and 26 who were asked why they didn't have pre-marital sex. In many cases they gave more than one answer, but it's interesting to see that the most popular answer (given by 46%) was that they hadn't met the right man. The second most popular answer (37% gave it) was that they thought they should wait until they got married. Twenty years ago this would almost certainly have been top of the list, followed by the next most popular reply – that they didn't because they were afraid of getting pregnant (26%). This answer will obviously decrease with the increasing availability of contraceptives. Almost a quarter of those questioned (24%) said they didn't have pre-marital sex because they were afraid of letting their parents down, and slightly less (23%) said they didn't as a

NETHERLANDS		
	1968	1968
	M	W
Men/women[+] (%) who agree a girl may have sexual intercourse with a boy if she's in love with him	50	20
disagree	46	80

Source:
"Sexualiteit in Nederland", published in the women's magazine *Margriet*, 1968.
[+]Aged 21-34

U.K.	
	1976
Young women[+] (%) who do not have pre-marital sex because:	
they're not interested in men	7
they're embarrassed at being thought inexperienced	9
they think pre-marital sex is wrong	23
they're scared of being thought promiscuous	7
they've not met the right man	46
they think they should wait until marriage	37
of religious reasons	9
they feel they're letting their parents down	24
they're frightened of getting pregnant	26
they think it would reduce the chances of a happy marriage	3
they're nervous at the thought of it	16
they're scared of catching VD	7
no answer	9

Source:
Honey magazine, May and June 1977. Survey conducted by the Schlachman Research Organization Ltd, London.
[+]Young women 18-26
Percentages do not add up to 100 because more than one answer was accepted.

matter of principle – because they thought pre-marital sex was wrong.

It's also interesting to note the least popular replies to this question. Only three percent said they refrained from pre-marital sex because they thought it would reduce the chances of a happy marriage. This figure would certainly have been higher 20 years ago. So would many of the other less popular replies. Only seven percent replied that they refrained because they weren't interested in men, or because they were scared of being thought promiscuous, or because they were scared of catching V.D.

Now we come to those figures for the Netherlands on how many people agree a girl may have sexual intercourse with a boy if she's in love with him. Here the differences between the sexes are very acute indeed – around 30%. Even so, the men are almost evenly divided (50% for, and 46% against) – but the women are four to one against. However, these Dutch figures are for 1968, and if anything they simply reflect how much our attitudes have changed since then. Though whether they'll go on changing at the same rate over the next decade is anyone's guess.

Gallup International has conducted a ten-nation survey on young people between the ages of 18 and 24 to determine their attitudes towards pre-marital sex.

As the chart shows, love and marriage don't go together like a horse and carriage but love and sex certainly do. With the sole exception of India, well over 50 per cent of all those queried in those ten nations, approve of pre-marital sex.

	U.S.A.	BRAZIL
	1973	1973
Young[+] people's (%) attitudes to pre-marital sex:		
should be avoided under any circumstances	23	40
all right if the parties concerned are in love	57	48
all right even if the parties concerned are not in love	19	12
no answer/no opinion	1	0

The disapproval rate varies wildly between countries. On the question of "wil she or won't she?", the answer in America is just over two out of ten girls **won't**. While up in the land of the endless night, Sweden, 96 out of 100 **will**. In general, it is the more traditional societies which come up with the highest disapproval ratings. In India, almost three out of four people disapprove of pre-marital sex under any conditions. Two heavily Catholic countries follow: Brazil and The Philippines. But in another Catholic country, France, only ten per cent disapprove of sex out of marriage. So, confessions must feature some colorful goings-on.

Japan has a great deal of reverence for tradition, and chastity is apparently regarded as an important part of traditional values.

The Yugoslavs are on the low side when it comes to approving of sex for sex's sake alone – unlike about one out of five American or French women, or about one out of seven in Great Britain.

If you take approval of sex without love as a sign of permissiveness, Sweden lives up to its reputation; almost four out of ten believe sex for sex's sake is okay. That's twice the U.S. rate. Looked at another way, the overall approval rating for non-marital sex in Scandinavia, is condoned by 94 out of every 100 people versus 76 out of every 100 in the States. The staid Swiss are surprisingly in second place with 91% approving of non-marital sex.

On an overall basis, Europe is way ahead of other Continents when it comes to believing that loveless sex out of marriage is perfectly acceptable.

The chart also shows that in virtually all countries, young people have decided points of views on these questions. Only in Germany do over 5 out of 100 have no answer on these important personal matters of choice.

Finally, the entire chart clearly shows that the sexual revolution has arrived, to stay.

YOUTH: PRE MARITAL SEX

U.K.	INDIA	PHILIPPINES	YUGOSLAVIA	FRANCE	(WEST) GERMANY	JAPAN	SWEDEN	SWITZERLAND
1973	1973	1973	1973	1973	1973	1973	1973	1973
14	73	37	18	10	6	27	4	8
68	23	55	75	65	65	68	56	68
15	4	7	7	22	23	4	38	23
3	0	1	0	3	6	1	2	1

Source:
Gallup International affiliated institutes
in the countries concerned

The question asked: "What one
statement best describes your feelings about
pre-marital sexual relations?".

+Male and female, 18-24 years

277

Pre-marital sex is no longer a taboo subject, but it's still a touchy one. That's especially true when it comes to the issue of sexual experience before marriage. So how many people have sex before they get married? That's what this table is all about. And there are a number of surprises.

	THE NETHERLANDS		
		1968 Men	1968 Women
People (%) who have had pre-marital sexual relationships, aged:			
under 21		25	20
21 to 25		21	17

Source:
Sexualiteit in Nederland, published in the women's magazine, *Margriet,* 1968.

If you're wondering what your teenage daughter gets up to when she goes out on a date, here's the answer. This may be the permissive age, but it still comes as something of a shock to find that nearly one in five of all American 15-year-olds have had sexual experience. By the time they hit 16, the figure is one in four.

When the figures are broken out by black girls compared with white girls they show that at 15, 38.4%, or nearly two in five of the black girls have had sex, compared to under 14% of the white girls. By 16, over half the black girls in the U.S. have had sexual experience, while only around one in five of white girls have.

Not surprisingly, the figures go up as the girls get older. But the biggest leap comes between the age of 16 and 17. Only 25% of 16 year old girls have had sex, but it goes up to 40% when they're 17. Amongst the black girls, well over two-thirds have had sex by this age.

These are the figures for 1976. By then, the sexual revolution, begun in the 60s, had resulted in big changes in attitudes and actions. Now look at the 1971 figures. Back then, American teenagers had noticeably tamer sex lives. Only 13.8% of all 15-year-olds had had sexual experience, and almost ten percent fewer

16-year-olds, than five years later. The 17-year-olds are most affected by changing standards: over 14% more 17-year-olds had sexual experience in 1976 than in 1971. That's true both generally and for white girls alone. However, amongst the black girls in that age group, over 12% more were having pre-marital relationships in 1976 than in 1971.

The age group least affected by society's increasingly relaxed attitudes to sex was the white 15-year-olds. In 1971 just under 11% had sexual experience, and in 1976, 13.8% had experienced intercourse — a difference of only 2.9%.

On average between the ages of 15 and 19 about twice as many black girls have had sex as white girls in any given age group. By the time all American girls are 19 well over half of them have had sexual experience. Amongst the black girls, only one in seven *hasn't* had sexual experience by this age!

How does this compare with girls in the U.K.? Sixty-one percent of unmarried women between the ages of 18 and 20 in the U.K. say they have had pre-marital sexual experience. Just 36% claim they haven't. That leaves only three percent who gave no answer. (Does this mean "Mind your own business", or simply

PRE-MARITAL EXPERIENCE

	1976 All	1976 White	1976 Black	1971 All	1971 White	U.S. 1971 Black
Unmarried women (%) who had sexual experience, aged:						
15	18.0	13.8	38.4	13.8	10.9	30.5
16	25.4	22.6	52.6	21.2	16.9	46.2
17	40.9	36.1	68.4	26.6	21.8	58.8
18	45.2	43.6	74.1	36.8	32.3	62.7
19	55.2	48.7	83.6	46.8	39.4	76.2

Source:
Reproduced, with permission, from *Family Planning Perspectives*, Vol 9, number 2, from "Sexual and Contraceptive Experience of Young Unmarried Women in the USA, 1976-71" by Melvin Zelnik, Ph.D. and John F. Kantner, Ph.D.

"Don't know"?) So in 1976 over three out of five British women had experienced intercourse before marriage. These figures suggest that it's now commonplace for young women in the U.S. and the U.K. to have slept with someone before taking marriage vows.

Overall the U.K. figures seem to be on a par with those for the U.S.

Neither set of figures bears much relation to the only Dutch figures we've been able to get, which are for 1968. The sexual revolution obviously hadn't happened in Holland by then. Only 25% of Dutch men under 21 said they'd had pre-marital sexual relationships, and only 20% of the girls. If you look at the American figures, you'll see that they increased by between five and ten percent between 1971 and 1976 – and the Dutch figures have probably followed suit. That would still mean the Dutch figures for both sexes are much lower than the other two countries. As it is, more American 15-year-olds had sexual experience in 1976 than 21 to 25-year-old Dutch women in 1968. Women in the Netherlands have a lot to do to catch up.

	U.K. 1976
Unmarried women[+] (%) who have had pre-marital sexual experience	61
have not had pre-marital sexual experience	36
no answer	3

Source:
Honey magazine, May and June 1977. Survey conducted by the Schlachman Research Organization Ltd, London.
[+]Aged 18-20

Today's children are constantly exposed to advertising, television programs, magazine and newspaper stories that all emphasize sex one way or another. Many schools have begun sex education programs covering everything from conception to venereal disease. So when do young people start making their own discoveries about the birds and the bees?

The first table here deals with unmarried American women from 15 to 19 years of age. Almost one in seven said their first experience of sexual intercourse was at the tender age of 15. If that strikes you as pretty young, remember that teenagers today generally have a lot of freedom, at least here in the U.S. It's often been said that we're a youth-oriented society. Since they have a whole sub-culture of their own, it's not surprising that our adolescents are beginning their sexual activities at an early age. Also, sex is big business. It's used to sell everything from cars to cigarettes. Could heavy exposure to that sort of advertising have the effect of increasing awareness of sex, leading to earlier experimentation?

The highest figure on this table is the one for 19-year-olds in 1971. That year 18% of the girls surveyed of that age had sex. By 1976 the figure had dropped slightly to 17.1%.

The table on Canada will give you some insight about what's going on north of the border. Unmarried students of both sexes were asked what age they were when they first had sexual inter-

		U.S.
	1976	1971
Average age at first sexual intercourse of unmarried women aged:		
15	14.7	14.7
16	15.5	15.9
17	16.4	16.4
18	16.8	17.2
19	17.1	18.0

Source:
Reproduced with permission from *Family Planning Perspectives*, Vol 9, no 2, from "Sexual and Contraceptive Experience of Young Unmarried Women in the USA, 1976-77" by Melvin Zelnik Ph.D. and John F Kantner Ph.D.

	SWEDEN	
	1967	1967
	M	W
Men/women[+] (%) who first had sexual intercourse at the age of:		
under 16	38.0	25.1
17	19.8	18.6
18	17.7	26.2
19	10.8	12.3
20-30	13.7	17.8

Source:
Riksförbundet für Sexuell Upplysning, Stockholm
[+]Aged 18-30 years

course. Apparently things there are steamier than the weather reports might have led you to believe. In fact, 2.1% of the males aged 22 to 24 had begun their sex lives at the startlingly low age of

AGE AT FIRST EXPERIENCE

	CANADA			
	1974	1974	1974	1974
	19-21	19-21	22-24	22-24
	M	W	M	W
Unmarried male/female students (%) who first had sexual intercourse at the age of:				
under 12	2.4	–	2.1	1.3
12-13	2.4	1.7	1.1	0.0
14-15	8.4	4.5	6.3	1.3
16-17	38.6	29.4	20.0	15.8
18-19	39.2	48.0	28.4	39.5
20-21	9.0	16.4	26.3	34.2
22-23	–	–	14.7	6.6
24-25	–	–	1.1	1.3

Source:
Sexual Experience, Birth Control Usage and Sources of Sex Education among Unmarried University Students by Dr M Barrett and Dr M Fitz-Earle, 1974

under 12. About half as many girls had been as adventurous. Even more of the younger males questioned (19 to 21) had engaged in sexual relations before the age of 12 - 2.4%. Around the same numbers had experienced intercourse between the ages of 12 and 13, making a total of nearly five percent of 19 to 21-year-old males and over three percent of 22 to 24-year-olds who had sexual relations by the beginning of their teens.

Eighteen to 19 was definitely the "big year" for most of the Canadians questioned. Nearly half of the 19 to 21-year-old women had their first experience then. The boys who hadn't made their move by then — also took (or seized) the opportunity at that age. So by the age of 20, 57.9% of both male and female members of the older age group had experienced sexual intercourse.

Sweden is a country with a reputation for very liberal views on sex. How has this affected young people there? Well, when it comes to the age of the first sexual encounter, Swedish girls seem even more precocious than their North American counterparts. One-quarter of them first had intercourse before the age of 16, as compared to 14% of the American girls.

But the Swedish boys look like real Casanovas – a whopping 38%, almost two out of five, claimed their first experience had occurred before their 16th birthday.

Obviously there's lots of sexual activity during the teenage years in Sweden. But what about the slow starters? Over 13% of the men questioned hadn't had any amorous adventures until between the ages of 20 and 30. By that time they must have been faced with a lot of competition from those busy 15-year-olds. Considerably more women – nearly 18% – had abstained from sex till over 20 years of age. These over-20s were definitely in the minority.

In fact, 70% of the females and over three-quarters of the men had had intercourse before the age of 19.

So much for North America, and swinging Sweden. Now let's look at the Netherlands. Things are a lot quieter for those Dutch teenagers. It looks as if they spend all their time doing homework. A mere nine percent of the boys and four percent of the girls had had intercourse at the age of 15 to 16. Strangely the number

Single women (%) who first had sexual intercourse at the age of:	**U.K.**		
	1976	1976	1976
	18-20	21-23	24-26
under 16	26	22	3
16	30	20	13
17-19	42	43	47
20-22	1	15	27
23-26	–	–	10
no answer	1	–	–

Source:
Honey magazine, May and June 1977. Survey conducted by the Schlachman Research Organization Ltd, London.

of young boys having sex actually dropped as their ages went up. So at 18, only four percent of the youths in Holland took the plunge for the first time. What can their minds be on? Maybe they've forgotten that all work and no play can make Hans a dull boy.

So by the time they'd reached 20, only one in five Dutch youths had had intercourse. The girls were even shyer. Only 18% had had relations with a man. The Netherlands certainly isn't a land of Lolitas.

In fact it seems to be a real outpost of traditional morality when it comes to adolescent sexual activity. By the age of 21, eight out of ten Dutch youths, and slightly more girls, hadn't yet had sexual relations. In contrast, think of the Swedish figures, where 86.3% of the males and 82.2% of the women had experienced intercourse by the time they were 20. Can it be that those Dutch teenagers just don't know what they're missing? Or maybe parents in that part of the world have discovered a way to keep a tight rein on their children's love lives? If they have, it's a secret that could probably be marketed for a vast profit in a lot of other countries.

In the U.K., young unmarried women of differing ages were asked at what age they'd first had intercourse. It seems the times are definitely changing. Girls who entered their early teens in the 70s began sleeping with someone at an earlier age than their older sisters did. In fact, well over half of the 18 to 20-year-olds had experienced intercourse by 16, compared to only 16% of the 24 to 26-year-olds.

Now a look at the country that's raised "*l'amour*" to the status of an art. French youth has a lot to live up to in the area of loving – so how are they doing? They certainly don't believe in starting too young. Only one French lad in a hundred had begun his amorous adventures before the age of 14. Girls of a comparable age hadn't got around to any sexual activity at all – at least none they were admitting to. Things picked up a year later, though. Then, seven percent and two percent respectively had sexual encounters. In fact, the boys became increasingly bold right on through their 18th year. That's when the highest percentage (17%) of any male age bracket made their first conquests. By that point, nearly half the French youths questioned had experienced intercourse.

But the *mademoiselles* were really playing hard to get. Either that or Gallic parents keep a closer eye on their daughters than on their sons. That wouldn't be too surprising, in such a heavily Roman Catholic country. Whatever the reason, a mere 20% of those

NETHERLANDS		
	1968	1968
	M	W
Young men/women (%) who first had sexual intercourse at the age of:		
15-16	9	4
17	3	5
18	4	6
19-20	4	3

Source:
"Sexualiteit in Nederland", published in the women's magazine, Margriet, 1968.

FRANCE		
	1970	1970
	M	W
Men/women[+] (%) who first had sexual intercourse at the age of:		
under 14	1	–
14-15	7	2
16	10	2
17	11	5
18	17	11
19	8	10
20	13	13
21-24	12	33
25-29	7	11
over 30	2	3
no answer	4	3

Source:
Rapport sur le Comportement Sexuel des Francais by Dr Pierre Simon. Published by René Julliard, Pierre Charron, 1972. Survey conducted by l'Institute Francais d'Opinion Publique.
[+]Aged 20-65

jeunes filles had succumbed to the advances of their more sexually active male counterparts by their 19th birthdays. Of course, young men are traditionally more sexually adventurous than young women. There's the fear of pregnancy which keeps many teenage girls from pre-marital sex. Also society tends to wink at the sexual activities of male adolescents as they "sow their wild oats". However, it still frowns at young girls who follow the same course.

It's after they're 19 that the action really starts for the ladies in France. Over a third of them were initiated into the national pastime between the ages of 21 and 24. Better late than never, as the saying goes. This would suggest that many French women save themselves for marriage. Another 11% put off the big moment until they're between 25 and 29, while three percent are definitely in the "older woman" category, at over 30. Only in their 20th year do an equal number (13%) of young men and women have intercourse for the first time. Before that most of the fellows are busy gaining the experience they need to live up to their reputation as great lovers. After 20, the women are presumably reaping the benefits of all that expertise.

	1976	1976
	15-19 years old	15-17 years old
Young women (%) who have had sexual intercourse with:		
one partner	50.1	54.0
2-3 partners	31.4	31.5
4-5 partners	8.7	8.4
6 partners or more	9.8	6.1

Source:
Reproduced, with permission, from *Family Planning Perspectives,* Vol 9, number 2, from "Sexual and Contraceptive Experience of Young Unmarried Women in the USA, 1976-71" by Melvin Zelnik Ph.D. and John F Kantner Ph.D.

Shock stories of teenage, and even pre-teenage, immorality are the staple diet of sensation-seeking newspapers all over the world. These tables give us a chance to look at the facts. Is it true that young people are becoming more and more ready to go to bed with each other? Has the increased availability of contraception encouraged more youngsters to have sex? And what about the older generation? Are they as pure and moral as they'd like the youngsters to believe? Look at the tables. It's all there for young people in Europe and U.S. – also a revealing glance at the number of partners that Swedes of all ages have had.

The figures dealing with the sex lives of young American women from 15 to 19 appear, at first glance, to show a surprising drop in the number who have had sexual experience – only 50% in 1976 as opposed to 61% in 1971. Yet take another look. In 1976, it's true, there were fewer girls having sex with one partner than there were five years earlier, but it's no cause for celebration among those who are yearning for a return to stricter sexual morality. What the table shows is a great increase in the number of sexual partners the girls are taking. It isn't that over 11% fewer girls are indulging. On the contrary, they are bestowing their favors on a wider range of partners. There was an increase of six percent in the figures of those who are now having sex with two or three partners. One percent more were sleeping with four or five partners. Most staggering of all, though, is the four percent increase among those whose sex lives involved six or more partners. It seems that the rumors and speculation about the snowballing of promiscuous behavior are true.

A closer look at the figures reveals even more alarming news for parents of young girls. The biggest increases in sexual activity were in the age range 15 to 17. A massive 14% more of these youngsters were having brief sexual encounters with a variety of partners. One-night stands are on the increase. And it is the young ones who are leading the way. Their older sisters aged 18 to 19 showed only a four percent increase between 1971 and 1976 in the numbers who had two or three partners. There was even a drop of almost one percent in the numbers of those who had sex with four or five different men. This decrease means that the table shows that almost as many of the younger girls were sleeping with that number of men. The one area where the older girls showed a greater increase in promiscuity was at the top end of the scale. There, the number of girls who, with their six or more different

NUMBER OF PARTNERS

	U.S.		
1976	1971	1971	1971
18-19 years old	15-19 years old	15-17 years old	18-19 years old
45.3	61.5	66.5	56.1
31.3	25.1	22.7	27.7
9.1	7.8	5.9	9.9
14.3	5.6	4.9	6.3

	U.K.
	1969
People (%) who have had sexual experience with:	
one partner	74
one other partner on one occasion	1
one other partner on several occasions	2
several partners, each on one occasion	2
several partners many times	12
none	9

Source:
Michael Schofield: *The Sexual Behaviour of Young Adults* (Allen Lane, 1973), p170. Copyright © Michael Schofield, 1973. Reprinted by permission of Penguin Books Ltd.
[+]Aged 25 years

partners could really be accused of "sleeping around", increased by a stunning eight percent.

The figures in the next table show the sexual habits of 25-year-olds in the U.K. Only nine percent of all this group claimed that they had never had a sexual experience. Of all the rest, nearly three-quarters had remained faithful to one partner. This high rate of fidelity may be a reflection on the higher standard of strict sexual morality in the country famed for its reserve. On the other hand, two factors have to be taken into account. Firstly, this table was compiled in 1969 when the full effect of the sexual revolution was just beginning to be felt. Secondly, the age band in question was less fully exposed to the changing moral standards than their younger brothers and sisters were. Even taking these points into consideration, the figures still show a tendency towards a freedom in sex that would, in all probability, have shocked earlier generations. Over seven percent of the group had indulged in sexual intercourse with more than one partner. Of these, well over half had known "several partners". There's no way of telling from this vague phrase what numbers are involved. It could be that the responses referred to a modest two or three. On the other hand, the phrase also covers those whose "conquests" range well into double figures.

"Toujours l'amour" is one traditional aspect of French life that the young people of France seem determined to keep alive and kicking. Despite pressures from that bastion of morality, the Catholic Church, French men and women have, for centuries, been generally regarded by the world as the premier exponents of the arts of love. From Abelard and Heloise right up to Brigitte Bardot, the French have been associated with racing pulses, tender caresses and the language of love.

This fabled aspect of French life is, as these 1977 figures reveal, in safe hands with the next generation. Well over half of the 15-year-old boys who were questioned had already had their first taste of sex, and well over a quarter of 15-year-old girls were no longer virgins. As could be expected, it's the boys whose sexual activity is most marked and a surprisingly high percentage of them (47%) had experienced sex several times. Only 11% of the girls, on the other hand, had repeated their sexual experimentation. The girls, too, were the ones who had largely chosen their partners from the same age group. An interesting point to note, though, is that 21% of the boys had been initiated into the mysteries of sex by an older partner. This was true for only ten percent of the girls. Perhaps the consideration and encouragement that the boys found in the arms of these more mature and experienced women is one of the reasons why nearly half of these 15-year-old boys had been eager to go back for more of the same. Whether this is the case or not, the overall figures certainly seem to indicate that, along with their other traditional loves, wine and food, the youth of France will keep up the country's reputation as a nation of lovers. Under the bridges of Paris, and everywhere else in the country, love is still in the air.

The final table reveals some interesting statistics about Sweden, the nearest rival for the title, "Land of Love". One of the first things that becomes obvious is that the Swedes must be meticulous record-keepers. Some of them are even able to remember as many as 50 partners with whom they have had sexual intercourse.

Over half of the young men and well over three-quarters of the young women had known only one to five people sexually. Presumably, the majority of these involved their married partner and perhaps one or two affairs. The number of young men who had experienced sex with over five different partners is, however, striking. Over 43% of men aged between 18 and 30 had had sexual

FRANCE		
	1977	1977
	Boys	Girls
1. Boys/girls[+] (%) who have had sexual experience	54	28
2. Boys/girls[+] (%) who have had sexual experience:		
once	33	18
several times	47	11
with a girl/boy their own age	16	26
with an older woman/man	21	10

Source:
Reproduced by permission of *L'Express*, September 5th-11th, 1977.
[+]Aged 15 years

	SWEDEN			
	1967	1967	1967	1967
	M	W	M	W
	18-30 years old		30-60 years old	
Men/women (%) who have had sexual intercourse with:				
1-5 partners	56.3	87.5	52.3	92.3
6-12 partners	18.2	9.1	23.2	6.1
13-19 partners	7.4	1.0	7.3	0.6
20-50 partners	18.0	2.4	17.1	1.0

Source:
Riksförbundet für Sexuell Applysning, Stockholm

intercourse with six or more partners. A phenomenal 18% of Casanovas obviously had their eye on a world record and managed to attract from 20 to 50 people into their beds. The Swedish women, however, seem to be much less energetic and ambitious because only just over 12% of them had experienced sex with more than six partners. An interesting sidelight is that for both men and women the figures in the column listing 13 to 19 partners are lower than any of the others. It's probably a case of all or nothing with no dawdling around in the middle.

There's certainly a generation difference. Even though the 30 to 60-year-olds have had more time to play the field the figures show that they've had fewer sexual encounters. This is particularly true of the women in this age range. Ninety-two percent of them had had sex with five or fewer partners. Less than two percent of women over 30 had entered the major league of 13 or more partners.

These Swedish figures are intriguing because while the other tables give details of the sex lives of young people, this one takes into account men and women up to the age of 60. The other tables *do* show that sex among young people is on the increase. They *do* show that some of the old taboos that kept sexual urges in check are nowadays being ignored. Yet the Swedish figures reveal that the older generation were not averse to hopping on and off love's roundabout when it suited them. For example, over 17% of all Swedish males over the age of 30 claimed to have bedded between 20 and 50 partners. This is only marginally fewer than the 18% of younger men who claim

to be in this Olympic category. Any sexual revolution that is taking place today is only the continuance of the attitudes of the past. One sterotype this table shatters is that of the Swedish *femme fatale* who's so sexually liberated she sleeps with scores of men. Those Nordic women, famed for their cool blonde beauty, simply don't distribute their favors indiscriminately. In fact, more American girls of 15 to 19 had slept with over six partners than the 18 to 20-year-old Swedes. Swedish women of all ages seem to be anything but promiscuous, so who are all those male sexual athletes performing with? Forty-three percent of Swedish men say they've had intercourse with six or more people, but only 12 percent of the women make the same claim. There must be long waiting lines forming outside the doors of some Swedish ladies.

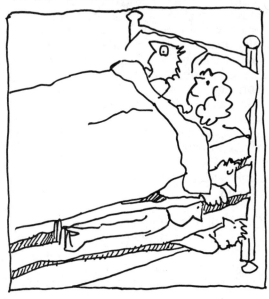

Once upon a time, it was commonly assumed that the first sexual partner should and would be one's husband or wife. But times have changed, especially when it comes to the sexual activity of single women.

Our first table shows the results of a survey conducted among unmarried women in the U.K. Three different age groups were asked who their first sexual partner was. The majority in every group, from the single woman aged 18 to those aged 26, said that their first sexual partner had been a steady boyfriend. In fact, nearly seven out of ten agreed on this. Of course, we haven't got a firm definition here of "steady boyfriend". Is it someone you've been dating for a year, or a month? Nevertheless, that high figure does seem to imply that the majority of single women require a reasonably secure relationship before indulging in the first sexual relationship. It may be the modern day equivalent of "saving yourself for marriage".

It was the women aged between 18 and 20 who were most likely to have first slept with a steady boyfriend. Perhaps this is because women in this age group are in that awkward stage – a bit too young to think seriously about marriage, but old enough to feel ready for the greater personal and sexual freedom of adults. The romantic attachment to a "steady" may seem to provide the security a young girl wants before commiting herself to having sexual relations.

The next highest proportion of women

	U.K.		
	1976	1976	1976
	18-20	21-23	24-26
Single women (%) whose first experience of sexual intercourse was with:			
an acquaintance	5	11	7
a friend	15	13	17
a steady boyfriend	70	65	67
their fiancé	9	11	10
no answer	1	–	–

Source:
Honey magazine, May and June 1977. Survey conducted by the Schlachman Research Organization Ltd, London.

in every age group, said "a friend" was their first sexual partner. That term would seem to indicate a more casual, rather than romantic, relationship. But it is a meaningful connection implying some degree of trust and understanding between the partners.

This is borne out by the number who listed their fiancés as first partners. Fiancés rated third on this table, with about one in ten of the women in each age group saying that their first experience occurred with their intended. (We haven't any figures on whether these women went on to marry those particular males, and subsequently divorced them, but assume that they did intend to marry at the time of first sleeping with them.)

Finally, we come to the more casual sexual encounters. The highest figure here was for the women aged 21 to 23. Eleven percent of them – more than double the number of 18 to 20s – admitted that they first experienced sexual intercourse with an aquaintance. This group may represent young women who had left their parents' home and thus had more opportunity to have casual sexual rela-

AUSTRALIA	
	1974
People (%) whose first experience of sexual intercourse was with:	
their spouse after marriage	23
their fiancé	16
a steady date	26
someone they know	23
a prostitute/relative/stranger/ casual acquaintance	12

Source:
Cleo magazine, August and September 1974. Survey conducted by Roy Morgan Research Center Pty Ltd.

tions. Or it may just be that when questioned, women in a slightly older group feel more free to admit to having initially had intercourse with someone who wasn't a regular boyfriend or fiancé.

Our next table deals with the initial sexual encounters of Australians, and records both men's and women's experiences. Once again, many said it was with a steady date. However it is a smaller proportion than the all-female responses in the first table. (About one in four as opposed to seven in ten.) The next most common experience was either with someone they knew, or with a fiancé. It's an interesting fact that the wedding night, as the time of sexual initiation, has been replaced by a less clear-cut sexual encounter with a boy- or girl-friend. Sixteen percent of the Australians questioned listed their fiancés as the first partner, putting them in fourth place on this table. That's a higher percentage than for any of the three female age-groups in the U.K. So perhaps Australians do set more store by traditional relationships than the British. Either that or they get formally engaged more often.

Least common as a first sexual partner was a prostitute, relative, stranger or a casual acquaintance. Still, 12% of the Australians had been sexually initiated with such a partner – that's about one in eight. It's a higher percentage than in any of the age-groups on the table for British women. One likely reason is that the Australian figures include men. Traditionally, men in all societies have been more free to have casual sexual relations than women, without fear of scandal or social disapproval. In fact, the notorious "double standard" has always implied that men could be experienced lovers on their wedding nights while the blushing bride would have had no previous sexual experience. Undoubtedly, the lingering belief that "nice girls don't" still influences at least some men and women. But the times certainly seem to be changing in this respect. Certainly, single women are now much more free to experiment in sexual activity. As this section shows, a lot of them are doing just that. But even if changing sexual patterns are altering the traditional choice of the first sexual partner, good old-fashioned love and affection seem to be holding their own in 20th century Britain and Australia.

If you're young, single and in search of a partner of the opposite sex, don't expect to find equality: the men outnumber the women wherever you look. On average, there are ten percent more single men aged 25 to 29 in the countries listed on the table below – and in several places the gap is much greater.

Single men fare worst in Japan. In the 25 to 29 age group, 46% are single men, while a mere 18% are unattached women. According to numbers then, each single young kimono-wearer should have two or more male admirers without even trying. But while single women don't suffer from lack of attention, it appears that many young Japanese men will have to devote their energies to business and wait for the next generation of girls to grow up.

Spain is the second best place for a single woman to gather admirers. In Spain, over 46% are single men, while just over 27% are single women. That works out to nearly two young men to serenade each *senorita*.

Almost the same ratio continues in Sweden. Of the 25 to 29 age group, 42% are single men, while only 23% are single women.

Of all the countries on the table, Ireland is remarkable for having the most unmarried people of both sexes in the 25 to 29 age-group. Nearly 50% of the group are unmarried men, and over 31% are unmarried colleens.

So where is romance in the air? In West Germany where, of the 25 to 29 population, less than 20% are single men and fewer than ten percent single women. Whether it's their continuing economic prosperity or simply the *gemütlich* pleasures of the *Bier Keller*, the West Germans meet and marry early. A man in search of a mate won't face huge numbers of competitors in West Germany, but, at the same time, will find precious few available *frauleins*.

Couples in their 20's are almost equally marriage-minded in the U.S. In the 25 to 29 age group, only 21% are unmarried

	U.S.A.	CANADA
	1960	1961
1. Percentage of single men in the male population aged 25-29:[+]	21.0	29.2
urban areas[o]	21.4	27.5
rural areas[o]	19.5	35.5
difference[o]	1.9	-8.0
2. Percentage of single women in the the female population aged 25-29:[+]	10.7	15.6
urban areas[o]	11.8	16.8
rural areas[o]	7.2	11.4
difference[o]	4.6	5.4

U.K.	AUSTRALIA[x]	AUSTRIA	BELGIUM	DENMARK	FRANCE	(WEST) GERMANY	IRELAND	ITALY	JAPAN	NETHERLANDS[x]	NORWAY	SPAIN	SWEDEN	SWITZERLAND
1966	1971	1971	–	1960	1968	1971	1971	–	1970	1975	1970	1970	1970	1970
29.4	25.7	33.6	NA	31.0	32.8	19.6	49.4	NA	46.2	5.4	31.3	46.1	41.6	37.1
29.6	NA	33.2	NA	30.1	30.4	18.7	39.0	NA	47.7	NA	30.4	41.4	38.3	37.4
28.9	NA	34.1	NA	34.5	40.5	24.0	62.3	NA	41.7	NA	32.2	56.8	58.4	36.5
0.7	NA	−0.9	NA	−4.4	10.1	9.8	−23.3	NA	6.0	NA	−1.8	−15.4	−20.1	0.9
15.6	11.6	18.1	NA	15.4	18.1	9.5	31.3	NA	18.0	3.0	16.3	27.5	23.0	21.3
16.4	NA	20.6	NA	18.7	19.0	9.8	30.6	NA	19.1	NA	20.2	25.8	23.1	24.6
12.9	NA	15.4	NA	10.8	15.6	7.9	32.1	NA	14.5	NA	13.1	31.5	22.1	17.0
3.5	NA	5.2	NA	7.9	3.4	1.9	−1.5	NA	4.6	NA	7.1	−5.7	1.0	7.6

NA not available

men, and unmarried women number just over ten percent. The U.S. makes a happy hunting ground for an outsider eager to avoid competition from the resident males, but again, there are comparatively few single women to pick from.

The unattached woman in her 20's has the numerical advantage in all countries. So the single man in search of companionship might do best heading for the countries with the greatest percentage of unattached 25 to 29 year-olds of both sexes – Spain and Ireland. But tread carefully: they may marry late, but Spaniards and Irishmen can't be accused of lacking a passionate temperament.

Source:
[+]Heron House estimates
[0]United Nations
[x]National statistical offices

Who said marriage is going out of style? For the great majority of us, love and marriage still go together like a horse and carriage. What's more we're hitching up earlier – especially in the U.S. American men can hardly wait to get to the altar. They're the youngest bridegrooms in the world, marrying at an average age of 23.4 in the cities and even earlier (23.3) in the country. Among women, too, Americans are the youngest newly-weds, averaging 20.8 years of age in the cities and 20.2 in rural areas. It's interesting that in the past 15 years the age gap between American brides and grooms has been narrowing. Perhaps the growing emphasis on equal rights for women has encouraged girls – and boys too – to expect age equality in marriage rather than having a pseudo daddy-daughter relationship. Spanish males hang around in bachelorhood much longer than their peers in other countries. In rural Spain the average groom is nearly 30 (29.4 years) and in the cities 27.2.

The pattern is different among women. Women get married later in the country than in the towns in only three of the 12 countries surveyed.

Overall, American women head the procession to the altar, Canadian, British and West German brides follow – marrying, on average, in their twenty first year. Young American wives also head the rush for a divorce, and remarry early.

If the figures for first marriages are compared with the number of years men and women expect to live unmarried

	U.S.A.	CANADA
	1960	1961
1. Expected years lived in the unmarried state:		
Men aged 15-65 [0]	11.4	14.0
in urban areas	11.4	13.4
in rural areas	11.4	16.0
Women aged 15-65 [0]	8.7	10.9
in urban areas	9.1	11.4
in rural areas	7.3	9.0
	1960	1961
2. Average age at first marriage:		
Men [0]	23.4	25.1
in urban areas	23.4	24.7
in rural areas	23.3	25.4
	1960	1961
Women [0]	20.7	21.7
in urban areas	20.8	21.8
in rural areas	20.2	21.5

U.K.	AUSTRALIA	AUSTRIA	BELGIUM	DENMARK	FRANCE	(WEST) GERMANY	IRELAND	ITALY	JAPAN	NETHERLANDS	NORWAY	SPAIN	SWEDEN	SWITZERLAND
1966	–	1971	–	1960	1968	1971	–	–	1970	–	1970	1970	1970	1970
13.7	NA	13.6	NA	13.7	14.6	10.4	NA	NA	13.0	NA	14.0	15.4	16.2	14.9
13.6	NA	13.2	NA	13.4	13.8	10.2	NA	NA	13.2	NA	14.0	14.4	15.1	14.3
14.0	NA	14.0	NA	15.0	17.3	11.4	NA	NA	12.5	NA	15.5	17.8	21.9	15.6
11.6	NA	11.8	NA	12.3	11.8	9.6	NA	NA	10.8	NA	11.2	14.3	12.4	13.1
11.8	NA	12.0	NA	12.7	12.0	9.7	NA	NA	11.1	NA	12.2	14.3	12.3	13.7
11.1	NA	11.5	NA	10.2	11.3	9.2	NA	NA	10.1	NA	10.4	14.4	12.9	12.3
1966	1975	1971	1975	1960	1968	1971	1971	–	1970	1975	1970	1970	1970	1970
25.5	24.5[+]	26.1	26.1[+]	25.9	26.8	26.0	27.5[+]	NA	24.5	26.6[+]	25.2	28.3	27.5	26.1
25.6	NA	26.0	NA	25.6	25.9	24.5	NA	NA	27.8	NA	25.4	27.2	26.4	26.4
25.3	NA	26.2	NA	26.2	27.7	25.4	NA	NA	27.1	NA	24.9	29.4	28.5	25.7
1966	1974	1971	1975	1960	1968	1971	1971	–	1970	1975	1970	1970	1970	1970
21.8	21.9[+]	22.2	23.5[+]	22.5	23.2	21.9	25.0[+]	NA	25.2	23.9[+]	22.4	24.0	23.8	22.9
21.9	NA	22.4	NA	22.7	23.2	21.9	NA	NA	25.4	NA	22.8	23.8	23.8	23.2
21.6	NA	22.0	NA	21.8	23.0	22.0	NA	NA	24.6	NA	22.1	24.6	24.1	22.5

NA not available

there are some intriguing implications. It's clear that in countries where both sexes tend to marry late, men and women can expect to spend the longest periods single. But they may also expect to spend up to five years longer in the single state than can be accounted for by that teen to 20 waiting time.

Sources:
United Nations
[+]National statistical offices
[0]Heron House estimated averages

One of the biggest changes in recent years has been attitudes towards divorce. "Till death us do part" once meant what it said. Now in many countries divorce is almost as prevalent as marriage.

In the past divorce cost a British king the throne, senators and congressmen their seats and, many think, Adlai Stevenson the U.S. presidency.

	U.S.A.	CANADA
	1974	1974
1. Marriages per 1,000 inhabitants	10.5	8.8
2. Divorces per 1,000 inhabitants	4.6	2.0
3. Ratio of marriages to divorces	2.3:1	4.4:1

Contrast this with the British public's relatively passive acceptance of Princess Margaret's divorce from Lord Snowdon.

The institution of marriage is strongly challenged by the increasingly common tendency of modern couples to set up house together, open joint bank accounts in their own names, invest in property together – and generally carry on in old-fashioned married style, but without benefit of clergy. Even with relaxed laws, people seem to fear the legal obligations and entanglements of dissolving their marriages more than they crave the security of legal wedlock.

But for those who persist in marrying, what shape is holy matrimony in these days? In the U.S., patterns are changing. The table shows that while marriages are flourishing (10.5 people in every thousand got married in 1974), divorce is big business also – with 4.6 people per thousand untying the knot. Nearly half as many people got divorced as got hitched. There's more marrying and unmarrying – marital activity, if you will – in the U.S. than in any other country.

Many American marriages are repeat trips, with brides and grooms who have already been down the aisle before – another example of the popularity of recycling in the U.S.

Divorce laws in the U.S. may also contribute to the high number of divorces. As many alimony-poor ex-husbands can testify, women very often profit handsomely from divorce – though not as often as just a few years ago.

In some states like California, joint property laws require that, in divorce cases, whatever capital or possessions that have accumulated during the years of marriage must be split equally. But in many instances, the ex-wife – particularly when there are children, or when she is considered the wronged party – walks out of the courtroom with all the assets from the past... and a guarantee of a big percentage of any profits in the future.

Canada has 15% fewer marriages than there are next door in the land of the free and the brave. Nearly nine Canadians per thousand get married. Divorces are a mere two per thousand – that's less than half the U.S. break-up rate.

Sweden follows the U.S. in number of divorces. There's one for very 1.7 marriages – leaving 0.7 contentedly married Swedes. Hopefully, contentment is more common in common-law relationships.

U.K.	AUSTRALIA	AUSTRIA	BELGIUM	DENMARK	FRANCE	(WEST) GERMANY	IRELAND	ITALY	JAPAN	NETHERLANDS	NORWAY	SPAIN	SWEDEN	SWITZERLAND
1974	1974	1974	1974	1974	1974	1974	1974	1974	1974	1974	1974	1974	1974	1974
7.5	8.3	6.5	7.5	6.6	7.6	6.2	7.3	7.3	9.2	8.1	6.9	7.7	5.5	6.0
NA	1.2[+]	1.4	1.06	2.6	0.9	1.5[+]	0	0.3	1.04	1.4	1.3	0	3.3	1.6
NA	6.9:1	4.6:1	7.1:1	2.5:1	8.4:1	4.2:1	0	24.3:1	8.8:1	5.8:1	5.3:1	0	1.7:1	3.2:1

NA not available   [+]*1973 figures*   [0]*Not applicable as divorce isn't recognized*

For better or for worse, the marriage rate in Sweden is increasing. It's risen in three years from 4.9 to 5.5 marriages per thousand people. Swinging Sweden along with Denmark, porn center of the western world, are two of the few countries to show an increased marriage rate.

Italy and Ireland both have many marriages and few divorces. In Italy, the Roman Catholic Church, which seldom permits or even recognizes divorce, is a big factor in the figures. The situation may begin to change now that abortions are legal.

Perhaps divorce – and the widespread enthusiasm for more easily dissoluble living-together arrangements – is symptomatic of a sort of national speed freakism.. a cultural addiction to change, *rapid* change. In the U.S., instant satisfaction is even more in demand than instant coffee. Toiling along, bearing life's – or love's weary burdens isn't the American way. Most of us are in hot pursuit of some elusive Holy Grail of happiness – a state of bliss that Hollywood and American romanticism has led us to *expect* out of life. *Getting* a mate, getting *rid* of a mate, not having a mate – we try it every which way, trying to be happy, happy...happy.

Sources:
1 & 2 United Nations
3 Heron House estimates based on United Nations figures

How far do people practice what they preach when it comes to sexual fidelity? That's what this first table allows us to check because we can compare it with a table in the previous section.

A high proportion (89%) of men in the U.K. thought that, once married, a man should remain faithful to his partner. According to the earlier statistics, though, only 62% of them actually claimed that they'd done this. True, the seven percent who admitted to extra-marital affairs is matched here by the seven percent who don't think that fidelity is essential. What about the 31%, however, who gave no answer in the previous table? Guilty consciences? U.K. women, also, show a difference between their principles and their actions. Here 94% of them state that a wife should be faithful yet only 82% of them swore blind in the last section that they've remained true to this belief.

There must have been some guilty Dutch men in 1968, because while 11% admitted to having sex outside marriage, only three percent in this table are sure that there's nothing wrong with this. The two percent of Dutch women who said that they'd had sex with someone other than their hus-

	U.K.					
	Yes		No		Don't know	
	1969		1969		1969	
Men/women+ (%) who think:	M	W	M	W	M	W
A husband should be faithful for the rest of his married life	89	90	7	7	4	3
A wife should be faithful for the rest of her married life	93	94	5	4	2	2

Source:
Sex and Marriage in England Today
by Geoffrey Gorer, published in 1971
by Thomas Nelson & Sons Ltd, London.
+Aged 16-45

	SWITZERLAND	
	1977	1977
	Men	Women
Men/women+ (%) who agree totally that fidelity has nothing to do with the true nature of marriage	54.1	57.2
more or less agree	19.0	12.6
disagree strongly	16.0	15.6
disagree more or less	7.5	9.3
don't know	3.2	5.0

Source:
Survey conducted by Isopublic, Zürich, on behalf of Weltwoche.
+Aged 18-24

ATTITUDES: EXTRA-MARITAL SEX

	US[+]	CANADA[0]	NETHERLANDS[x]	
	1977	1977	1968	1968
People (%) who think a married person having sexual relations with someone other than the marriage partner is:	Men	Women	Men	Women
always wrong	72	60	52	65
almost always wrong	13	13	44	32
sometimes wrong	10	14	NA	NA
not wrong at all	3	4	3	2
don't know	1	8	NA	NA
				NA not available

Sources:
[+]The National Opinion Research Center of the University of Chicago
[0]The Canadian Gallup Poll Ltd
"Sexualiteit in Nederland", published in the women's magazine Margriet, 1968.
The original question asked in the Netherlands was: "Do you find extra-marital sexual relationships not permissible, sometimes understandable, sometimes objectionable, or do you have no objections in principle?" We have interpreted the answer "not permissible" as "always wrong", "sometimes understandable" as "almost always wrong", "sometimes objectionable" as "sometimes wrong" and "no objections in principle" as not wrong at all".

bands obviously rested easy in their beds, extra-marital or otherwise, because that figure corresponds with the two percent on this table who thought that there was nothing wrong with such behavior.

It looks as if Europeans are less rigid in their marital morality than we North Americans. What Mom told us still held good in 1977 for 95% of all the men questioned and 87% of all the women. We believe that, to a greater or lesser degree, it's wrong to have extra-marital sex. Perhaps our rigid views on this subject account for much of our high divorce rate. In our society there isn't much acceptance of *extra*-marital sex if the marital state is to remain. Compare these figures with the 73% of Swiss men and over 69% of women who feel that fidelity is not an essential prerequisite to the married state. There must be something in all that mountain air because only 16% of Swiss men and 15.6% of the women are absolutely sure that a true marriage requires total sexual faithfulness. Even way back in 1968 European attitudes were less hardened than American views in 1977. Admittedly, only a small percentage of Dutch men and women thought that there was nothing wrong at all in a married person having affairs, but far fewer agreed with us North Americans that it was always wrong. The Dutch obviously thought that there were sometimes extenuating circumstances.

Is marriage sacred any more? Do people consider it necessary to be faithful to their marriage partner? Are they actually faithful to their marriage partner? These are amongst the oldest questions in the world, and we're still asking them. That's what this table is all about.

What percentage of people in the U.K. have made love to someone other than their marriage partner since marrying. Sixty-two percent of males claim they haven't – and that's their story, and they're sticking to it. Only seven percent of British males admit to infidelity.

British wives are even less promiscuous – 82% of them claim to have been completely faithful since marriage, while only three percent admit that since the wedding bells they made love to someone other than their husband.

It makes you wonder about the 31% of British men and 15% of women who gave no answer. Are they keeping quiet about their indescretions or worried about being behind the times?

This trend towards greater male promiscuity is echoed in the Dutch figures. Though on the whole the Dutch are (or claim to be) a great deal less promiscuous than their British opposite numbers.

Seventy-eight percent of married Dutchmen claim never to have had extra-marital sexual relations. But only 11% admit that they *have* – that's four

		U.K.	
		1969	1969
		Men	Women
People (%) who've made love to someone other than their husband/wife since marriage:		7	3
people who haven't		62	82

Source:
Sex and Marriage in England Today by Geoffrey Gorer, published in 1971 by Thomas Nelson & Sons Ltd, London. Percentages do not add up to 100 because there is a proportion of "no answers".

percent more than the British, who on the whole are admittedly more promiscuous in these matters. This would seem to indicate that perhaps Dutch husbands are a little more honest. But only one percent of Dutch married men admit to having regular extra-marital sexual relations.

With whom do those married Dutchmen have their extra-marital relations? From the look of the figures, certainly not with friends' wives. Eighty-six percent of all Dutch married women claim to have been completely faithful to their husbands. Only two percent admit to having had extra-marital sexual relations. None of them said they had extra-marital sexual relations regularly.

Now we come to the figures on extra-marital experience amongst Australian women. Compared with the women of Holland and the U.K. those

EXTRA-MARITAL EXPERIENCE

AUSTRALIA

	1973
Women (%) with extra-marital experience, aged:	
under 26	25
26-30	37
31-40	45
41-50	46
over 50	17

Source:
Reproduced from *The Sex Survey of Australian Women* by Prof. Robert E. Bell, published in 1974 by Sun Books, Australia.

THE NETHERLANDS

	1968 Men	1968 Women
People (%) who have had extra-marital sexual relations:		
never	78	86
sometimes	10	2
often	1	0

Source:
"Sexualiteit in Nederland", published in the women's magazine *Margriet*, 1968.
Percentages do not add up to 100 because of a proportion of "no answers".

Aussie girls seem to have few qualms about extra-marital sex. No 80% fidelity here – except amongst the over-50s.

The most surprising thing about these Australian figures is how they go up as the age of the women increases. Twenty-five percent of Australian married women under 26 claim to have had extra-marital experience. In the group aged 26 to 30 this rises to 37%. After that things really start to happen. According to these figures nearly half (46%) the Australian married women between the ages of 30 and 50 have extra-marital sex. What does this mean? Either those middle-aged Aussie women have a very active sex life, or they have very active imaginations. And what do their husbands think about all this going on? The figures for married Australian males just aren't available.

A few decades ago, homosexuality was spoken of (if at all) in whispers. Even hinting that someone was sexually interested in members of his or her own sex has long been considered fighting words. Today homosexuality is still one of the most taboo aspects of sexual behavior. But the "sexual revolution" of the recent past has brought some changes in that area. Homosexuals are still frequently the subject of hostility and derision. However the more liberal atmosphere of the 60s and 70s has brought more frank discussion of the whole subject. Many homosexuals have joined militant organizations like "Gay Lib" and started their own newspapers and magazines. They put forward the homosexual point of view and lobby to change discriminatory laws. Many homosexuals, especially in large urban areas, are demanding the right to openly admit their sexual preference without fear of job discrimination or reprisals. In some U.S. cities candidates in local elections have run as "gay" candidates. In others, homosexuals have demanded that candidates for office declare their views on the rights of homosexuals in society.

In some places there's been a backlash from "straight" (heterosexual) members of the community. They're demanding a return to legal penalties for practicing homosexuality and they're demanding that homosexuals be discriminated against in certain ways. For example, by banning them from teaching children. In fact, some states in the U.S. still have legislation on the books prohibiting homosexuality. In the U.K. homosexual behavior between two consenting males over the age of 21 wasn't legal until after

	CANADA
	1977
People (%) who think homosexual behavior in adults is caused by:	
childhood upbringing and other environmental factors	33
mental illness	14
a hereditary/natural trait	10
sexual preference	5

Source:
Weekend Magazine, Toronto, December 3rd 1977
Percentages do not add up to 100 because we have excluded other optional answers which were given in the original survey.

the famous Wolfenden Report in the 60s. There were no laws prohibiting lesbianism because Queen Victoria refused to believe women were capable of such behavior.

Oscar Wilde was one famous victim of legal prosecution for his sexual preferences. "The Ballad of Reading Gaol" was the poetic result. Today in the U.S. some police departments use decoys — officers pose as soliciting homosexuals and then arrest anyone who responds to their advances. During World War II, the Nazis persecuted homosexuals by sending them to concentration camps along with other "undesirable" minorities.

Not all societies have frowned on homosexuality. The ancient Greeks considered it the highest form of love. Women weren't considered men's equals, and therefore only the love of one man for another was thought worthy of being celebrated in poetry and song.

In some American Indian tribes a boy who preferred feminine behavior was simply treated as a female. Eventually he could dress and act as a woman without any stigma being attached to his behavior.

	U.S.[+]	U.K.[o]
	1977	1977
People (%) who think homosexuality is: caused by upbringing/ environment	56	28
inborn	12	31
both	14	21
neither	3	3

Sources:
[+]The Gallup Organization Inc, USA
[o]Social Surveys (Gallup Poll) Ltd, UK
Percentages do not add up to 100 because of a proportion of "don't knows".

	NETHERLANDS	
	1968	1968
	M	F
People (%) who think homosexuality is: an innate affliction	28	24
a sickness	23	22
unnatural	21	25
dirty	5	6
unacceptable sexual behaviour	15	10

Source:
"Sexualiteit in Nederland" published in the women's magazine *Margriet*, 1968.

Despite all the publicity it receives today, homosexuality is still a murky topic for many people. Is the preference for members of your own sex a disease? Is it a crime? Is it the result of upbringing and environment? Or is it just a preferred way of behavior that's nobody else's business?

As you'll see from a look at these tables feelings on the subject vary widely from one country to another. The majority of Canadians (33%) think that family environment can cause homosexual behavior. That reflects the increasingly popular view that childhood and upbringing have a lot to do with how people behave later in life. About one in seven Canadians think homosexuality is such a deviation from normal, heterosexual standards that it's actually a form of mental illness. Both those views are shared by some psychiatrists and behavioral psychologists, who have tried to treat homosexuality as an illness, with varying degrees of success. One in ten Canadians thinks homosexual behavior is "in the blood", an inherited characteristic, like blue eyes. Presumably they don't think there's much that can be done to change such

behavior. Only five percent took the relatively mild view that having sexual relations with members of your own sex is merely a preference.

Turn to the tables on the U.S. and on the U.K. and you'll see that there's a big difference of opinion about the issue. In the U.S. well over half those questioned think upbringing and environment are the determining factors in shaping sexual preferences. Maybe that's not so surprising in the land where "going to see a shrink" is a fairly common practice. Modern psychology has given us the idea that children exposed to certain family patterns — for example a dominant mother and inefficient father — become homosexuals. Only 12% think homosexuality is an inborn trait. Their British counterparts disagree. Only 28% think early family surroundings are significant, while the majority feel homosexuality is an inborn trait. In fact, over 2½ times as many Britons as Americans think being homosexual is "just the way you are" from birth. Perhaps the British would be less enthusiastic about having so many single sex schools if they shared the American point of view.

	U.S.[+]	CANADA[0]
	1977	1977
Men/women (%) who think that sexual relations between two adults of the same sex are:		
always wrong	68	60
almost always wrong	5	7
wrong only sometimes	7	9
not wrong at all	14	13
don't know	5	12

Sources:
[+]The National Opinion Research Center of the University of Chicago.
[0]Canadian Gallup Poll Ltd.
[+]*Double Sexuaileit in Nederland*, published in the women's magazine *Margriet*, 1968.
The original question asked in the Netherlands was, "Do you think one should let the homosexual live his life as he wants to?" We have interpreted the answer "Yes" as "Not wrong at all" and "No" as "always wrong".

So much for opinions on the causes of homosexuality. How do people feel about actual homosexual behavior? Those ancient Greeks may have thought it was the highest form of love, but they'd run into some disagreement in present-day Holland. A quarter of Dutch women feel homosexuality is contrary to nature, and over one in five of the men agreed. An even greater number of Dutch men (28%) think it's an affliction the homosexual is born with. Almost the same number of men and women consider sexual activity with your own sex a sickness.

All these views are generally negative, but not as stern as the one held by ten percent of women in the Netherlands. They find homosexual behavior completely unacceptable in society. Around one in 20 people in the Netherlands think such actions are "dirty".

So it's surprising to see that only about half as many people in the Netherlands as in North America think sexual relations between two adults of the same sex is always wrong. Sixty-eight percent of those polled in the U.S. felt that way, while 60% of their northern neighbors agreed. If you include the number who think homosexuality is almost always wrong, 73% of Americans and 67% of Canadians are strongly disapproving. Not a fact to gladden the hearts of "Gay Lib" members. It looks as if the so-called permissive society doesn't extend its liberal views as far in the field of homosexual behavior as in other areas.

Only around one in seven North Americans thinks homosexual behavior is absolutely O.K. But in the Netherlands, there's much more tolerance.

Homosexuals complain that once out of the closet (that is, after they've admitted their sexual preference) they're the victims of discrimination.

The table on the question of hiring homosexuals as elementary school teachers certainly gives weight to their argument. In the U.S. an overwhelming majority of 65% think known homosexuals should be barred from holding this type of job. That's about the same number as those who think sexual relations between members of the same sex are always wrong. Since the majority of people in the U.S. think that homosexual behavior is a result of the early environment, it's not surprising.

NETHERLANDS[x]			U.S.[+]	U.K.[+]	CANADA[0]
1968	1968		1977	1977	1977
M	W				
32	30	People (%) who agree, homosexuals shouldn't be hired as elementary school teachers	65	68	35
NA	NA	disagree	27	22	14
NA	NA	don't know	8	10	8
58	55				
10	15				
NA not available					

Source:
[+]The Gallup Organization Inc
[0]*Weekend Magazine,* Toronto, December 3rd 1977
The original question asked in Canada was: "Should self-confessed homosexuals be allowed to hold jobs such as school teaching that involve dealing with children?". People questioned were shown a scale of seven steps ranging from "definitely not" (which in our chart corresponds to "people who agree") and "completely acceptable" ("people who disagree"). Only these two answers have been retained from the Canadian survey.

People in the U.K. feel even more strongly on the subject. Almost seven out of ten Britons are opposed to letting self-confessed homosexuals work with young children. Only around a quarter of those questioned in both countries think sexual preference in a person's private life shouldn't be a factor.

So in the U.S. and the U.K., an overwhelming majority of people are in favor of discriminating against homosexuals.

Canadians take a more moderate view of the issue. Only 35% take a definite stand against hiring homosexuals. That's about half as many as in the U.K. On the other hand, significantly fewer (14%) think that this form of discrimination shouldn't exist. Presumably many Canadians think other factors have to be taken into account before giving judgment.

There are some interesting conclusions to be drawn from this section. One is that in most countries most people still disapprove of homosexuals. Even when the "straight" majority doesn't think homosexual activity is immoral, it looks upon it as a form of deviation or illness. Although the Dutch are much more tolerant than North Americans, even in the Netherlands a third of the population thinks homosexuality is always wrong. When it comes to job opportunities, the message to homosexuals seems to be "keep quiet about your sex life". That's exactly the opposite message to the one put forward by militant homosexual organizations. They're busy urging homosexuals everywhere to "come out of the closet" and demand equal treatment with the rest of society.

It looks like this particular battle of the sexes — or should we say sex — will be fought a while longer.

Ratio of marriages to divorces

25 —

If you're a newly-wed, head for sunny Italy. The bonds of matrimony are more firmly knotted there than anywhere else. There's only one divorce for every 26 marriages. But of course, Italy's the home of the Roman Catholic Church, which frowns on divorce.

Japan has the next-most devoted married couples; there's only one divorce to almost nine marriages. Divorce is really a Western invention, and Japan's traditions are still fairly strong. France runs a close

20 — third, probably because of its large Catholic population. The Frenchman's habit of keeping a mistress may have something to do with the low divorce rate.

There are from 5.8 to 6.5 marriages to every divorce in the Netherlands and Australia. Sweden's rate of divorce seems to confirm its reputation as a really liberal country. The ratio there is a staggering 1.7 to one. In other words, almost one marriage breaks up for

15 — every two couples that walk down the aisle.

10 —

5.8:1

6.9:1

5 —

1.7:1

| SWEDEN | NETHERLANDS | AUSTRALIA |

MARRIAGE AND DIVORCE

Citizenship

Like so many other concepts, our present-day notions of citizenship owe a lot to the ancient Greeks. They were really the first to emphasize the importance of each individual's participation in government. And, of course, the most common form that participation takes is voting. In this chapter, we find that exercising that precious right to vote varies a great deal from nation to nation.

You'll see that in some countries people take voting very seriously indeed. Can you guess which ones? Have a look at our tables on registered voters and see how we in the U.S. rate as staunch defenders of democracy, when it comes to a big turnout at the polling booths compared with, say, the Italians or West Germans. This is especially interesting when you remember that the question of democratic freedoms was one of the reasons why World War II was fought.

Although men have waged many a bloody battle over the right to vote, there's the women's side of the story. Even in bastions of democracy, the ladies often had to fight long and hard to gain an equal say in the running of the country. We have some eye-opening facts about just *how* recently they've acquired that right in some nations. For instance, did you know that in Switzerland the fairer sex didn't get the franchise till 1970? Supporters of Women's Lib will get some useful information – or should we say ammunition? – in this section.

After all those hard-fought battles for equal rights with the men, the ladies in some countries seem to have lost interest. Just like a woman, some might say. But to be fair to the females, interest in voting – or lack of it – varies from country to country. First, we take a look at how various nations place in the voting league. Then, we offer some theories on the results. Of course, you're free to draw your own conclusions, which may not agree with ours. But if *thinking* about voting can interest a few more people in actually *doing* it next election day, it was all worth it.

Some nations have decided not to leave voting up to the whim of the individual conscience. In the U.S., you're free to decide whether or not to make the trek to the polling both come election day. However, there are countries where the government takes a sterner view. So we find countries where voting is compulsory – even in bad weather.

Weather is just one of the factors that affects how many people exercise their democratic right to vote. We've suggested a few more, and given you enough information to draw some conclusions of your own.

The choices made by those who do bother to get out and vote affect all of us – and that includes the foreigners among the native population. In this chapter, we take a look at what's become a very hot topic indeed – immigration.

Foreign immigrants tend to flock to countries where the economy is booming and there are lots of job opportunities. So our figures in this section are also a sort of economic barometer showing how and where the tides of immigration are flowing today. You'll see for yourself where foreigners actually head for in the greatest numbers.

In some countries, citizenship involves another, more demanding form of participation than voting – service in the armed forces. The draft is a thing of the past in the U.S. Along with Ireland, the U.K. and Canada we now have an all volunteer armed forces. In Switzerland, by contrast, every adult male is automatically a member of the militia.

Another requirement of citizenship – and probably the most disliked – is taxation. Armies cost money, so we took a look at the money various governments spend on the military. You can probably guess which nation leads the field here – after all, we coined terms like "arms race" and "missile gap", but what about other countries? Could you state with confidence which European nation spends the most on its defense? Or which one seems least concerned with military might? And what about a country like Japan, with a long history as a militant nation and a prosperous economy? This section may well offer some surprising answers to these questions and others you may have.

The final section gives the number of political prisoners in various countries – a subject which receives a great deal of news coverage these days.

We hope this whole chapter will shed new light on some of those sensational headlines you're constantly confronted with, and help you to pick your way through the thorny political arguments of the day.

When election time rolls round, most of us take our right to vote for granted. It's easy to forget that democracy didn't just happen but was achieved only after long, hard struggles. In some countries, the ideal of equal voting rights for men and women alike has taken a long time to become reality.

The table shows considerable agreement among nations about the minimum voting age. In all the countries shown, you have to wait until you're at least 18 before you can mark your first ballot paper. In Austria and Sweden, you'll have to wait an extra year before officially coming of age, and in Denmark, Japan, Norway and Switzerland it's another two years.

Although women now have the vote in all our countries, in some places, men have hogged the polling booths much longer than in others. In Switzerland, women didn't get the vote until 1971. This is particularly surprising for a country which considers itself the birthplace of European democracy. Switzerland has a Federal government and also a State Council, made up of members from each of the Swiss cantons – a system which has been very effective in running the government in accordance with the wishes of its citizens. Perhaps the very success of the Swiss democratic system made women slow to insist on their right to participate.

	U.S.A.	CANADA
	1978	1978
1. Legal voting age[0]	18	18
2. Year when women could vote for the first time	1920	1920
3. Countries in which voting is compulsory[x]	V	V
	1976	1974
4. People who voted[‡] (000s)	81,556[+]	9672
as % of registered voters	59.2[+]	71.0

In a number of other countries, women also had to wait until after World War II before they could cast their vote. Belgian women were denied suffrage until 1949. Now they *must* vote: Belgium is one of the few countries that makes voting compulsory. Japanese women weren't permitted to vote until 1946. This delay isn't so surprising, Japan didn't adopt a democratic system along Western lines until the country's post-war redevelopment. France and Italy kept their polls closed to women until 1945. But in Australia men and women have had equal voting rights since 1903.

Now that we've all got voting rights, do we use them? The table shows, for each country, the percentage of registered voters who actually turn out on polling day. It's one thing to have a democratic system but quite another for everyone to

	U.K.	AUSTRALIA	AUSTRIA	BELGIUM	DENMARK	FRANCE	(WEST) GERMANY	IRELAND	ITALY	JAPAN	NETHERLANDS	NORWAY	SPAIN	SWEDEN	SWITZERLAND
	1978	1978	1978	1978	1978	1978	1978	1978	1978	1978	1978	1978	1978	1978	1978
	18	18	19**	18	20	18	18	18	18	20	18	20	18	19	20
	1928	1903	1918	1949	1915	1945	1918	1918	1945	1946	1917	1913	1931	1921	1971
	V	C	C	C	V	V	V	V	V	V	C	V	V	V	V
	1974	1977	1975	1974	1977	1978	1976	1977	1976	1976	1977	1973	–	1976	1975
	29189	8128	4663	5712	3106	29142	34064	1603	37600	57236	8314	2156	NA	5457	1956
	72.5	95.0	92.9	90.3	88.7	82.0	90.4	75.6	92.2	73.4	87.5	80.2	NA	91.8	52.4

**On 1st January of the election year   C compulsory   V voluntary
NA not available

take part. Look at Switzerland, for example. Judging from the figures, women still don't participate in any great numbers. Switzerland has the lowest voter turn-out of any of the nations on the table, with only 52% of registered voters actually casting their ballots. Yet Switzerland's parliamentary system is relatively accessible to everyone. Could that possibly explain the figures? In Switzerland, any group of 30,000 citizens can demand a referendum, which has the power to reverse Federal legislation. Perhaps this safeguard encourages the Swiss to take it easy at election time.

In the U.S., fewer than 60% of us voted in 1976, one of the key elections of the century. Most other countries, apart from Switzerland have higher election turn-outs.

Many factors influence voter turn-out.

Sources:
Government documents
[+]Elections Research Center, Washington DC
[x]Where voting is compulsory, a fine is incurred for not voting
[‡]Actual *valid* votes at last elections

For example, the size of the vote – and its results – are often affected by the weather on voting day. Perhaps Australia's good weather partially explains why just about everyone there votes. The figure at 95% is higher than anywhere else. Still, the fact is that their voting is compulsory. The figures tend to be high – over 90% – for the other compulsory countries. Except in the Netherlands, where – law or no law – 12.5% of the population stubbornly refuse to vote.

Which country has the highest number of resident aliens? It's not surprising to find it's the U.S. After all, apart from the Indians – who are the only real native Americans – we were all once immigrants. There are nearly five million aliens residing in the U.S. today – more than two percent of the population.

However, this percentage is well below average. In Switzerland over 12% of the population are registered foreigners, that's nearly one person in eight. Switzerland is a small country with a high standard of living – and consequently a big manpower problem when it comes to the dirtier and lower-paid jobs. Its geographical position also makes it an obvious target for people who come in search of work. Italians, Yugoslavs, Greeks and Turks all try Switzerland first when looking for jobs in the affluent areas of Europe. The construction work of the Simplon Tunnel kept thousands of immigrant workers busy for years. So it's not surprising to find Switzerland topping the list in percentage terms.

France comes next with nearly eight per cent – over four million – as registered foreigners. A lot of these are Algerians or south Europeans working in agriculture, manufacturing, or the service industries. West Germany – which also relies heav-

	U.S.A.	CANADA
	1975	1975
1. Naturalized aliens (000s)	131.6	137.5
2. Naturalized Italians (000s)	8.8	19.8
as % of all naturalized citizens	6.7	14.4
	1977	–
3. Number of registered foreigners (000s)	4964[+]	NA
as % of population	2.3[+]	NA
	1978	1978
4. Initial cost of a passport (US $)	13.00	12.00
validity (years)	5	5

ily on immigrant workers – is also over the four million mark.

In the U.K., only three per cent – or over 1.5 million people – are registered foreigners. Some of them are workers from Ireland, some are from the U.K.'s old colonies in India and the Caribbean.

Who has the fewest foreigners? In Italy, Spain and Japan the figure is well under one per cent of the population. In Italy, they account for only 0.2% – the lowest figure on our table. On the other hand, Italians tend to emigrate more than

U.K.	AUSTRALIA	AUSTRIA	BELGIUM	DENMARK	FRANCE	(WEST) GERMANY	IRELAND	ITALY	JAPAN	NETHERLANDS	NORWAY	SPAIN	SWEDEN	SWITZERLAND
1965/75	1945/75	1976	–	1976/77	1970/74	–	–	–	–	1973/75	1975	–	1975	1974/77
37.5	962.7	7.5	NA	5.3	179.8	NA	NA	NA	NA	14.9	1.1	NA	16.7	32.8
1.3	172.0	0.4	NA	NA	48.9	NA	NA	NA	NA	0.5	NA	NA	0.2	11.9
3.7	17.8	6.2	NA	NA	27.2	NA	NA	NA	NA	3.8	NA	NA	1.5	36.4
1976	1971	1971	1970	1977	1975	1975	–	1971	1975	1975	1975	1976	1975	1976
1684[0]	722[x]	177	696	91[‡]	4128	4089	NA	122	752	345	68	159	410	801[**]
3.0[0]	5.6[x]	2.5	7.7	1.8[‡]	7.8	6.6	NA	0.2	0.7	2.5	1.7	0.4	4.9	12.2[**]
1978	1978	1978	1978	1978	1978	1978	1978	1978	1978	1978	1978	1978	1978	1978
20.68	23.41	6.58	3.38[++]	21.62	21.88	5.45	7.52	7.18	12.22[00]	20.30	4.70	4.32	15,51	4.70[xx]
10	5	5	1-5	10	5	5	10	5	5	5	10	5	10	1-5

NA not available   [+] *Aliens who reported under the Alien Address Program on January 1st 1977*   [0] *Estimate includes Commonwealth citizens and EEC members*   [x] *Excludes Commonwealth citizens*   [‡] *Excludes Scandinavian citizens*   [**] *Excludes foreign dignatories, their families and others*   [++] *One year only*   [00] *For a single trip only; for more than one trip, the price is $24.44*   [xx] *A further $3.25 is payable annually*

most other nationalities. Figures are also given for naturalized Italians in some countries. They show how many of them strike out to make their lives abroad. Australia and Canada attract a steady stream.

The table also shows the cost of passports in various countries. It's interesting to see the wide range – from Australia, where a passport costs $23.41, right down to Belgium, where holidays abroad are no problem; you can get your credentials for just $3.38.

Sources:
1 National statistical offices
2 Relevant government departments
3 & 4 Embassies

The U.S. has over two million men and women in uniform. That's the largest combined armed forces on our table – more than the combined forces of all the E.E.C. countries added together. But the U.S. doesn't have the largest combined forces in the world. That dubious honor goes to China (not on the table). They've got nearly four million servicemen and women. In Russia (also not on the table) there are more than 3½ million people in the military service.

With a military budget of $113 billion, the U.S. places an exceptionally high burden on its taxpaying citizens. Public military expenditure in the U.S. was $523 per person in 1977 – almost double that of West Germany.

	U.S.A.	CANADA
	1977	1977
1. Size of armed forces (000s)	2088	80.0
people per member of the armed forces[+]	104	295
2. Total defence expenditure (US $ – millions)	113,000	3348
per person	523	144
per member of the armed forces (000s)[+]	54.1	41.8
3. Military service compulsory or voluntary	V	V
length (months) of compulsory military service	–	–

The U.S. combined services are not only larger than the others on our table, and more expensive to equip, they also make up a higher proportion of the population. One in 104 people in the U.S. is in military service.

France comes second on the chart, with combined a services figure of just over half a million (almost a quarter that of the U.S.). The average Frenchman pays over 50% less for military expenses than the U.S. citizen. West Germany has just under half a million people in uniform. They spend nearly three billion dollars more than the French on their combined services but only seven dollars more per person.

Japan and Austria are both uncomfortably close to Russia, and you'd expect their military expenditure to be high. In fact they're low on the table. Japan, at $49 a head spends only four dollars more than Ireland (at the bottom of our list) – about the cost of a steak dinner with wine. Austria is fourth lowest ($68 a head). The reason for these low figures? Japan and Austria have their military expenditure limited by treaty.

Neutral Sweden defends its independence with a vengeance. The average

MILITARY MIGHT

	U.K.	AUSTRALIA	AUSTRIA	BELGIUM	DENMARK	FRANCE	(WEST) GERMANY	IRELAND	ITALY	JAPAN	NETHERLANDS	NORWAY	SPAIN	SWEDEN	SWITZERLAND
	1977	1977	1977	1977	1977	1977	1977	1977	1977	1977	1977	1977	1977	1977	1977
	339.2	69.7	37.3	85.7	34.7	502.1	489.0	14.7	330.0	238.0	109.7	39.0	309.0	68.6	18.5
	165	205	201	115	147	106	125	217	172	480	126	105	119	121	335
	11214	2807[0]	534	2476	1103	13740	16602	146	4416	6090	3357	1194	2154	2833	1280
	201	204[0]	68	253	217	256	263	45	78	49	241	295	59	343	204
	33.0	40.2	14.3	28.8	31.7	27.3	33.9	9.9	13.3	25.5	30.6	30.6	6.9	41.2	69.1
	V	V	C	C	C	C	C	V	C	V	C	C	C	C	C
	—	—	8[00]	8-10[x]	9	12	15	—	12-18[‡]	—	14-17[++]	12-15[**]	18	7½-15	4[‡‡]

C compulsory   V voluntary   [0]1976 figures

Sources:
International Institute for Strategic Studies
[+]Heron House estimates
[x]Eight if served in Germany [‡]18 only for naval service [**]15 if navy or airforce
[++]14-17 if navy or airforce [00]Six months followed by 60 days reservist training for 12 years
[‡‡]17 weeks recruit training followed by reservist refresher training of three weeks for eight out of 12 years for Auszug (20-32 years of age) two weeks for three years for Landwehr (33-42 years of age) one week for two years for Landsturm (43-50 years)

citizen pays $343 towards military expenditures. Service is compulsory. And one in every 121 people is in the service. Norway, which shares a border with Russia (Sweden doesn't) spends less than half the amount Sweden spends.

Both France and Germany have compulsory military service.

Amnesty International is an international organization, independent of any governments, whose primary concern is with certain specific human rights. Its objectives are precisely defined: "Considering that every person has the right freely to hold and to express his convictions and the obligation to extend a like freedom to others, the objects of Amnesty International shall be to secure throughout the world the observance of the *Universal Declaration of Human Rights*, by...working towards the release of and providing assistance to persons who...are imprisoned, detained, restricted or otherwise subjected to physical coercion or restricted by reason of political, religious or other conscientiously held beliefs or by reason of their ethnic origin, sex, color or language, provided that they have not used or advocated violence (hereinafter referred to as "Prisoners of Conscience")..."

Amnesty International also opposes "the detention of any Prisoners of Conscience or any political prisoners without trial within a reasonable time, or any trial procedures relating to such prisoners that do not conform to recognized norms to ensure a fair hearing."

It also opposes the "imposition and infliction of death penalties and torture or other cruel, inhuman or degrading treatment or punishment of prisoners or other detained or restricted persons whether or not they have used or advocated violence..."

Amnesty International has National Sections in 35 countries and individual members in 74. Its International Secretariat is in London.

This table (compiled from the *Amnesty International Report 1977*) shows the number of prisoners "adopted" or under investigation by Amnesty International groups in some of the countries mentioned in their report. This "adoption" system is used for Prisoners of Conscience who haven't used or advocated political violence. It means that Amnesty is concentrating particular attention on individual prisoners whose cases have been brought to their attention. Before "adopting" an individual, Amnesty investigates the case in depth. The number of adopted prisoners doesn't necessarily reflect the total number of political prisoners in a given country. In many countries where civil liberties are most restricted, little information is available – hence political prisoners in these countries haven't been adopted by Amnesty International and don't appear on the table. In these countries Amnesty uses other techniques, such as publicity campaigns and fact-finding missions.

One country with a large number of prisoners adopted or investigated by Amnesty International is the U.S.S.R. Even before Solzhenitsyn's devastating *Gulag Archipelago*, the U.S.S.R. had long been notorious for its treatment of political detainees. Increasing international interest has recently been focused on the plight of political detainees in the U.S.S.R. since the Helsinki Agreement. This agreement was intended to guarantee basic human rights to all citizens of the countries that signed it.

Indonesia is another country where civil rights are not always guaranteed. Since Indonesia achieved independence from the Dutch in 1945, several bloody

POLITICAL PRISONERS

political crises have occurred, one of which involved the death of hundreds of thousands throughout the country. There were 294 Indonesian political prisoners adopted by Amnesty International.

Other countries known for severe treatment of those with "unacceptable" views are Brazil and Chile. There were 213 adopted prisoners in Brazil. Chile, whose head of state is General Pinochet, had 145 prisoners under adoption or investigation by Amnesty International groups – a large figure when you compare the size of Chile to that of the other countries on this table.

Next comes South Africa – whose apartheid policy has been officially condemned by many nations. One hundred and thirty prisoners, most of them black, were adopted by Amnesty International.

Two other countries mentioned in this table also had high figures. In Yugoslavia, there were about 100 prisoners, some adopted, more under investigation – amongst them advocates of minority nationalism (the Croatian and Serbian nationalist movements are active) – as well as opponents of the current regime. There were 90 prisoners under adoption or investigation in the Philippines.

Amnesty International also adopts Prisoners of Conscience in Western countries. Fourteen prisoners in the U.S., two in Sweden and in Switzerland, and 43 in France were mentioned in the *Amnesty International Report 1977*.

As a non-political organization, Amnesty International does not concern itself with political systems of any kind, but simply with Prisoners of Conscience, political prisoners and with the abolition of the death penalty.

Prisoners adopted by Amnesty International		
U.S.A.	14$^+$	1977
ISRAEL	18$^+$	1977
YUGOSLAVIA	100^{+0}	1977
MALI	28	1977
CZECHOSLOVAKIA	29	1977
BRAZIL	213	1977
CHILE	145$^+$	1977
FRANCE	43$^+$	1977
POLAND	40$^+$	1977
INDONESIA	294	1977
ITALY	1	1976
THE PHILIPPINES	90	1977
SOUTH AFRICA	130^{+0}	1977
USSR	300	1977
SPAIN	11	1977
SWEDEN	2	1976
SWITZERLAND	2	1977

$^+$*Adoption and investigation cases*
^{0}*At least this number*

Source:
Amnesty International Report, 1977

Total defense expenditure ($-millions)

130		
120		
110		
100		
90		
80		
70		
60		
50		
40		
30		
20		11,214
10	6,090	
1 Billion		
750		
500		
250		
	146	
IRELAND	JAPAN	U.K.

There hasn't been a major global conflict for over 30 years. Nevertheless, some countries spend vast amounts on defense. The U.S.S.R. is the most military-minded nation in the world. It poured a staggering $127 billion into its 1977 defense budget. That's sabre-rattling on a truely grand scale.

It's no surprise to find that the U.S. is Russia's closest rival. America channeled $113 billion into keeping the balance of power at its present level. The defense budgets of these two military superpowers dwarf all the other countries in the world.

West Germany, nervously poised between East and West, earmarks $16 billion for defense, while France isn't far behind with over $13½ billion. The U.K., despite its economic problems, spends $11 billion, nearly as much as its prosperous European neighbors. Even tiny Ireland puts $146 million into defense.

MILITARY EXPENDITURE

			127,000	130
				120
		113,000		110
				100
				90
				80
				70
				60
				50
				40
				30
	16,602			20
13,740				10
				1
				.750
				.500
				.250

FRANCE   **WEST GERMANY**   **U.S.**   **U.S.S.R.**

Education

Are your kids learning all you want them to in school? We all have our own ideas about education. Are the schools getting better or are academic standards falling fast? What should the government be doing about improving the quality of education? Are our classes over-crowded? These are some of the questions which the figures in this chapter will help you resolve. You can see just what sort of education you can expect for your kids.

Education has now become one of the major priorities of almost every government. There are obvious reasons for this. Education gives you a better start in life. A well educated generation is better able to fulfil its role in society. But there are also hard-headed economic reasons for governments to be concerned about education. A country needs an intelligent, informed working population in order to compete successfully in this highly complex technological age. Well qualified engineers, scientists and technicians are not born, they're made – in schools, colleges, and universities.

Educational programs cost money. And that's the problem. Governments also have many other priorities – and the longer a student's course of studies, the more it's going to cost. Which countries really care most about education?

Many modern experts are of the opinion that the most important years of education are the earliest ones. If a child can read by the time he's four or five, he has a head start on the other kids. That's why early education is the subject of our first table. We've split this question up into four categories. These give the figures for the percentage of children who go to school at an early age of three, four, five or six. Then there are figures on the overall percentage of children in school between the ages of three and six.

There's considerable variation in the figures for different countries. In Belgium, nearly all (96%) of children aged between three and six go to school. Whereas in Sweden, which is in many ways one of the world's most socially advanced countries, only 25% of all children between the ages of three and six are in school. The U.S. and the U.K. are closer to the world-wide average – their figure's around 60%.

The first figures in the next table show the percentage of adults who can read and write. This is an indication of how thorough and efficient an educational system is at its most fundamental level. Needless to say, the figures here are all very high indeed. Do remember that while we may have a 99% literacy rate in the U.S., that illiterate one percent accounts for well over two million people. In Canada, surprisingly, only 93% of the population can read and write.

The normal school age enrolment figures are given after those for literacy. Here we give the full time enrolment rates for children aged seven to 14, and the figures for 15-year-olds, 16-year-olds, 17-year-olds and 18-year-olds. Together with this we give figures which show the minimum years of schooling a child is required to have in each of the countries covered; compare these figures with those for literacy.

What's surprising about these figures is the fact, that in all the countries listed, there still appears to be a tiny percentage of children who, in disregard of the laws, simply don't attend school at all.

The next table covers the percentage of men and women enrolled full-time at the third level of education. (The third level is a U.N.E.S.C.O. term, and is meant to include university students – usually people over 18.)

Here we also include figures to show the number of women enrolled full-time. This gives you an idea of how the battle of the sexes is going on the education front. From the look of things, the women are gaining ground rapidly.

Almost everyone can get to some school somewhere, but what happens when you're there? How much do you actually learn? Obviously, there are many factors that will make a difference, but one of the best indications is the pupil-teacher ratio. The fewer students a teacher has to cope with, the more time he has to spend on each individual and the more likely you are to learn. The figures enable you to compare the size of the classrooms in the countries covered.

The figures in this table are broken down into three categories – elementary schools, secondary schools, and colleges and universities. Besides being an indicator of the standard of education, these figures also show where the governments' priorities are. After all, those teachers have to get paid. And if there are cuts to be made in the educational budget, it's interesting to see where the various governments have decided to make them.

"Get an education and you'll get a good start in life." Most people agree on this one. But how early should the start be? Nursery education is a hot issue these days. Do children get more stimulation from being in nursery school? Or do they need to be at home with their mothers? And how soon should a child learn to read and write? The table details what sort of importance different countries place on nursery schooling. There

Children enrolled in school as a % of children aged:	U.S.A.	CANADA
	1970	1970
3	13	5
4	28	20
5	80	85
6	98	98
3 to 6	57	54

are some startling differences. Belgium is top of the table where three-year-olds are concerned. By this tender age 90% of little Belgians are playing with finger paints and learning their ABC's. But across the border, in the Netherlands, there are no three-year-olds in school. The same applies in Ireland. In Canada and the U.K., only one in 20 has started his or her education. Twelve percent of Spanish three-year-olds are at school – just one percent less than in the U.S. The Japanese figure is also low for this age group: just 17%.

The French figure is comparatively high. In France, 61% of three-year-olds are enrolled in school. Figures aren't available for all the other countries on the table. However, the overall enrolment figures for children aged three to six give a fair indication of the number of three-year-olds at school. It certainly looks as though the Scandinavians don't go for early education for young children.

The picture changes rapidly if you look at facilities for four-year-olds. In Holland, for example, 84% of them are in school, which puts the Netherlands in the third highest place after Belgium (95%) and France (87%). And 60% of Irish four-year-olds have started a nursery school education. For one of the poorest countries in the Western world, there's a lot of money going into educating under-fives. The Japanese figure is high too – 61%. Given the large population, that's a lot of nursery classes.

Who's at the other end of the table? The U.S., Canada and the U.K. aren't putting much of their resources into nursery education. Only six percent of British tinies and 13% of American tots are in nurseries. And a mere 28% of American four-year-olds are in school that's the second-lowest figure for this age group, after Canada's 20%.

Many education experts are beginning to re-examine theories about the advantages of starting children's school days at a very early age. Discovering the delights

U.K.	AUSTRALIA	AUSTRIA	BELGIUM	DENMARK	FRANCE	(WEST) GERMANY	IRELAND+	ITALY	JAPAN	NETHERLANDS	NORWAY	SPAIN	SWEDEN	SWITZERLAND
1971	1971	1970	1970	1970	1970	1970	1970	1970	1970	1970	1970	1970	1970	1970
6	NA	NA	90	NA	61	NA	0	NA	17	0	NA	12	NA	NA
35	NA	NA	95	NA	87	NA	60	NA	61	84	NA	43	NA	NA
98	NA	NA	99	NA	100	NA	90	NA	80	96	NA	49	NA	NA
99	100	97	99	NA	100	NA	100	NA	100+	99	NA	98	NA	NA
60	55+	45+	96	9+	88	45	63	62	65+	70	4+	56	25	39+

of finger paints and climbing frames is a lot of fun if you're three years old. But it doesn't necessarily mean you'll learn to read and write more easily. Early starters *do* have an initial advantage over children who've spent their first years at home – but some studies suggest that things seem to even out quickly.

Certainly we have one of the world's most extensive higher education systems. All those crowded colleges seem to suggest that not getting an early start doesn't necessarily mean a lack of bright students later on.

The French, with their intensive education system have virtually all their children in school by the age of five. In the U.K. and Belgium that's also the compulsory starting age. In Spain, however, only 49% of five-year-olds are sitting at their school desks.

Most countries on the table claim around 100% enrolment when it comes to six-year-olds. Most of us believe in starting 'em young.

Sources:
Organization for Economic Co-operation and Development
+OECD estimates

As you'd expect, almost everybody in the countries on our table can read and write. The small percentage that can't includes the educationally subnormal and the mentally deficient.

All the countries listed have a literacy rate of 97% or more, with the exceptions of Spain, Italy and – surprisingly – Canada. In Canada, the rate is just 93%, the same as in Italy. This means that in these three countries, about one adult in 14 has to rely on family or friends in everyday dealings with the printed word.

The 99% figure for the U.S. looks good. In fact, it means that over two million of us are illiterate. Likewise that 97% figure for the U.K. means that more than one million Britons are unable to read the newspaper or write their own letters. No wonder there's recently been a nationwide literacy campaign there.

In most countries listed, children must spend nine years of their lives in school – usually from the age of six to 15, or from seven to 16. The exception to the starting age is the U.K., where children have to trot through the school gates at the tender age of five. The only exceptions to the school leaving age of 15 or 16 are Italy and Belgium. In Italy, children are allowed to leave school at the early age of 13, and in Belgium they need only stay until 14.

	U.S.A.	CANADA
	1970	1970
1. Adults (%) who can read and write	99	93
	1974	1974
2. Age limits of compulsory education	7-16	6/7-15/16
	1970	1970
3. Children enrolled in full time education as % of age groups:		
7–14	99.0	98.2
15	97.7	98.0
16	93.5	89.1
17	86.2	77.2
18	53.8	45.8

However, 75% of Belgian 15 year olds are still at school compared with only 42% of Italians. Italy's early school leaving age could contribute to the low literacy rate there.

Enrolment rate figures for the seven – 14 age group are high but not 100%. This is because many of the national figures on the table don't include special schools like religious schools, or schools for the blind or deaf. There's also the truant problem.

The lowest figure is for Italy. Nearly 13% of Italian children between the ages

U.K.	AUSTRALIA	AUSTRIA	BELGIUM	DENMARK	FRANCE	(WEST) GERMANY	IRELAND	ITALY	JAPAN	NETHERLANDS	NORWAY	SPAIN	SWEDEN	SWITZERLAND
1970	1970	1970	1970	1970	1970	1970	1970	1970	1970	1970	1970	1970	1970	1970
97	NA	99	99	99	99	99	98	93	99	99	99	94	99	99
1974	1974	1974	1974	1974	1974	1974	1974	1974	1974	1974	1974	1974	1974	1974
5-16	6-15/16	6-15	6-14	7-16	6-16	6-15	6-15	6-13	6-15	6-16	7-16	6-15	7-16	6-15
1970	1971	1969	1966	1970	1970	1969	1967	1966	1970	1970	1970	1970	1972	1970
98.5	100.0	99.8	98.0	98.1	98.6	98.0	98.9	87.3	99.9+	99.0	99.0	90.2	98.8	95.4
73.0	81.5	54.8	75.1	85.2	80.5	54.9	82.4	42.1	83.8+	79.7	94.2	35.0	96.7	94.6
41.5	54.2	32.6	61.3	66.8	62.6	30.8	64.3	33.6	79.0+	60.6	74.6	29.6	74.0	61.5
26.2	37.2	23.6	47.0	31.8	45.1	20.4	46.5	27.4	74.8+	41.5	59.8	22.8	60.8	52.7
17.6	23.6	16.4	33.2	23.2	29.1	15.7	31.8	20.2	29.9+	28.4	46.5	19.0	40.8	27.4

+OECD estimates

of seven and 14 are missing from the school roll. Some 13 year olds, of course will already be spending their first wages.

The figures in the higher age groups, largely reflect the national school leaving age. But in Japan, although school pupils can leave at 15, three-quarters of them study until well after that.

In the 18 year old age group, there are some very big surprises. Who would have expected that the lowest figure would be the country of student youth – West Germany – with an enrolment rate of less than 16%? In Austria it's just over 16%.

Sources:
1 World Bank Tables
2 United Nations Educational, Scientific, and Cultural Organization
3 Organization for Economic Co-operation and Development

The U.K. is about equal at 17.6%. One partial explanation is that these countries have extensive apprenticeship schemes and polytechnic courses for this age group. The U.S. is the country with the most striking high school attendance: 54% of boys and girls are still in class at the age of 18.

The U.S. has by far the highest number of students enrolled in colleges and universities. About 50% of our youth are taking some form of higher learning. Only Canada, with 34.7% comes close to our figure.

Although a college degree may be the key to a bet[,] r paid job in the U.S., that isn't necessarily the case elsewhere. Switzerland, for instance, is richer per head of population than we are (see "richest countries" table) yet it has the lowest percentage of both men and women in college universities (13.2%). Industries such as watchmaking, tourism and banking need trained personnel, but they can survive without college graduates.

One reason we have so many college students is that we believe in equality of education. Government-guaranteed educational loans and the policy of "open admissions" have packed our colleges with students – many of whom will flunk out long before graduation.

Denmark comes after the U.S. and Canada, with more than a quarter of college-age men and women enrolled. The Danes ascribe a great deal of importance to higher education.

The Italians also favor admitting as many students as possible and have the fifth highest university enrolment rates. Almost one in four Italians in the 18-22 age group (one in five women) are taking university courses. The University of Rome, for instance, has so many students that classes have to be given in staggered

	U.S.A.	CANADA
	1974	1974
Full-time enrolment in third level[+] educational establishments:		
men and women (as % of population 18-22)	53.6	34.7
women (as % of female population 18-22)	48.7	30.6

shifts. If all the students showed up at once, there'd be no place to put them. Italy has high unemployment (see "employment" table), and at least this high enrolment rate keeps the young people off the unemployment rolls.

France and the U.K. both score fairly low in the percentage of enrolments category – well under 20%. Higher education in both countries is inclined to be selective and geared to the brightest students. In France and the U.K., graduation from a first-rate institution virtually guarantees access to the best jobs.

The Irish come at the bottom of the table, just above the Swiss. In Ireland just over one man or woman in seven attends a college or university. Ireland is a largely rural country with a large working class. Higher education is mostly reserved for the middle classes.

Take a guess which country has the greatest equality, educationally, between the sexes. As expected the North Americans come out on top. The U.S. leads the field by a long way with a healthy 48.7% of young women going on to study in

U.K.	AUSTRALIA	AUSTRIA	BELGIUM	DENMARK	FRANCE	(WEST) GERMANY	IRELAND	ITALY	JAPAN	NETHERLANDS	NORWAY	SPAIN	SWEDEN	SWITZERLAND
1973	1974	1974	1974	1974	1974	1975	1974	1974	1975	1974	1974	1975	1974	1974
16.2	22.0	16.8	21.6	28.0	18.0	20.3	15.5	23.9	24.7	23.5	21.3	NA	21.8	13.2
11.4	17.8	12.5	17.6	25.3	17.3	14.1	11.4	19.0	16.1	14.9	15.8	NA	20.4	7.8

NA not available

higher education. This near one in two ratio makes all other countries look like centers of male chauvinism by comparison. Only Canada, with nearly one in every three going on to third level education, comes anywhere near. The U.K. comes right near the bottom of the list with 11.4%. Only Switzerland with a tiny 7.8% has a worse record.

It seems as if the old attitude that priority should be given to the nurturing of male brains still applies all over Europe. The best figures in Europe are in Scandinavian countries where, at last, there are signs that they are beginning to realize that women, too, have the capacity and need to deal with advanced studies. In Denmark, just over a quarter of young women enrol in third level educational establishments. A short boat trip away, the Swedes are following; there, one in five girls are educated to university level.

In the rest of the countries shown it looks as if women's liberation movements still have a great deal to do before young women are seen as more than just potential mothers and housewives.

Source:
United Nations Educational, Scientific, and Cultural Organization
+Includes college, university, teacher-training colleges

The effectiveness of any educational institution depends to a large extent on the size of its classes. No matter how good a teacher or professor is, he can't give much individual attention in a class of 50 or 100.

This table shows how many students a teacher or university professor has in an average class. Obviously the figures vary according to the subject being taught. Basic compulsory subjects such as mathematics and English are taught in larger classes than a university course in astro-physics. However, these figures can tell us where there is classroom overcrowding.

Where do they have the best student/teacher ratio in elementary schools? The Scandinavians score highly. The best ratio is in Denmark, where there are only 16 pupils to every teacher. They're almost as well off in Norway, with a ratio of 17 to one. The U.S. is sixth on the table – tied with Sweden. We both have an average figure of 20 to one. The French are third, with 18 students to each teacher.

The Irish are worst off as far as primary education is concerned. They have 31 students to one teacher *on average*.

The Spanish are the next most badly off with a ratio of 29 pupils to every teacher – closely followed by the Dutch with 28 to one at the primary level.

There's a definite trend at secondary

	U.S.A.	CANADA
	1975	1970
Number of students to teaching staff in:		
first level schools[o]	20	25
second level schools[x]	19	16
	1975	1974
universities and equivalent institutions	16	16
non-university teacher training institutions	14	7[++]
other non-university institutions	22	14
all third level institutions	17	15

level. In all countries except Spain, the student/teacher ratio is lower. Each teacher has fewer students and can spend more time with individuals.

Secondary or high school students are best off in Belgium. The ratio there is a low seven students to every teacher at the secondary level. Norway is right behind with nine to one, and Sweden is next with ten to one. Spain has an appalling high school situation with a ratio of 39 students to one teacher. The Americans are badly off at 19 to one. And the Japanese follow with 17 to one. All the other nations have lower ratios – and more effective schools.

Why does the U.S. score so badly in secondary education? Chiefly because

GREAT BRITAIN‡	AUSTRALIA	AUSTRIA	BELGIUM+	DENMARK	FRANCE	(WEST) GERMANY	IRELAND	ITALY	JAPAN	NETHERLANDS	NORWAY	SPAIN+	SWEDEN	SWITZERLAND
1974	1976	1974	1975	1974	1976	1974	1975	1975	1975	1975	1974	1974	1975	
25	22	21	19	16	18	23	31	19	25	28	17	29	20	NA
14	14	15**	7++	16	15	14	14	11++	17	16	9^00	39	10	NA
1973	1975	1975	NA	1974	1971	1975	1975	1975	1975	1970	1975	1974	1974	1974
7	14	9	NA	NA	18	8	11	23	12	9	11	NA	NA	9
10	NA	NA	NA	NA	NA	NA	9	NA	NA	NA	9	NA	NA	NA
NA	NA	NA	NA	NA	NA	NA	8	NA	10	NA	9	NA	NA	NA
NA	14	NA	NA	9	NA	8	10	23	12	NA	10	14	12	NA

‡ *Excludes Northern Ireland* **1973 figure* ++*1974 figure* 00*1970 figure* *NA not available*

we make education compulsory through to the 12th grade. Other countries are more selective and allow many students to drop out after the fifth or sixth grades.

At university level, the Scandinavians lose to the West Germans, who have a ratio of eight students to one teacher.

The Danes, at nine to one, are second, with Norway and Ireland third at ten to one. In Ireland the quality of education improves as students climb the ladder.

If you want to study abroad, don't go to Italy, unless you're more interested in spaghetti than in studying. They have 23 students to every professor. Once again the U.S. is second worst: our ratio is 17 to one. Canada is next at 15 to one.

Sources:
United Nations Educational, Scientific and Cultural Organization
+National statistical offices
0Basically primary schools
xBasically secondary schools

These figures don't reveal that we have many excellent and world-renowned institutions of higher learning in the U.S. They do point to the fact that, overall, the quality of college education in the U.S. is declining. This is due in part to the failings of our high schools and in part to the "equal opportunity" policies which have crowded U.S. colleges.

Ratio of students to teaching staff in second level schools

40 —

Secondary school pupils in Belgium had better be sure to do their homework every night. With one teacher for every seven students, each eager scholar stands a pretty good chance of getting called on in class.

35 —

It's a bit easier to get lost in the crowd if you go to school in Canada, Denmark or Holland. All those countries have a student-staff ratio over twice as high as Belgium's.

30 —

Japan's overcrowding isn't as noticeable in its secondary school classrooms as it is in its subways. There's one teacher for every 17 students.

The U.S. ratio is similar — 19 pupils to every teacher. That doesn't sound bad, till you realize it

25 —

means only three minutes of teacher's time for each student in a one-hour period. As any teacher knows, it can take that long just to get someone's attention.

In Spain, with a 39 to 1 ratio, the whole day could be spent on roll call.

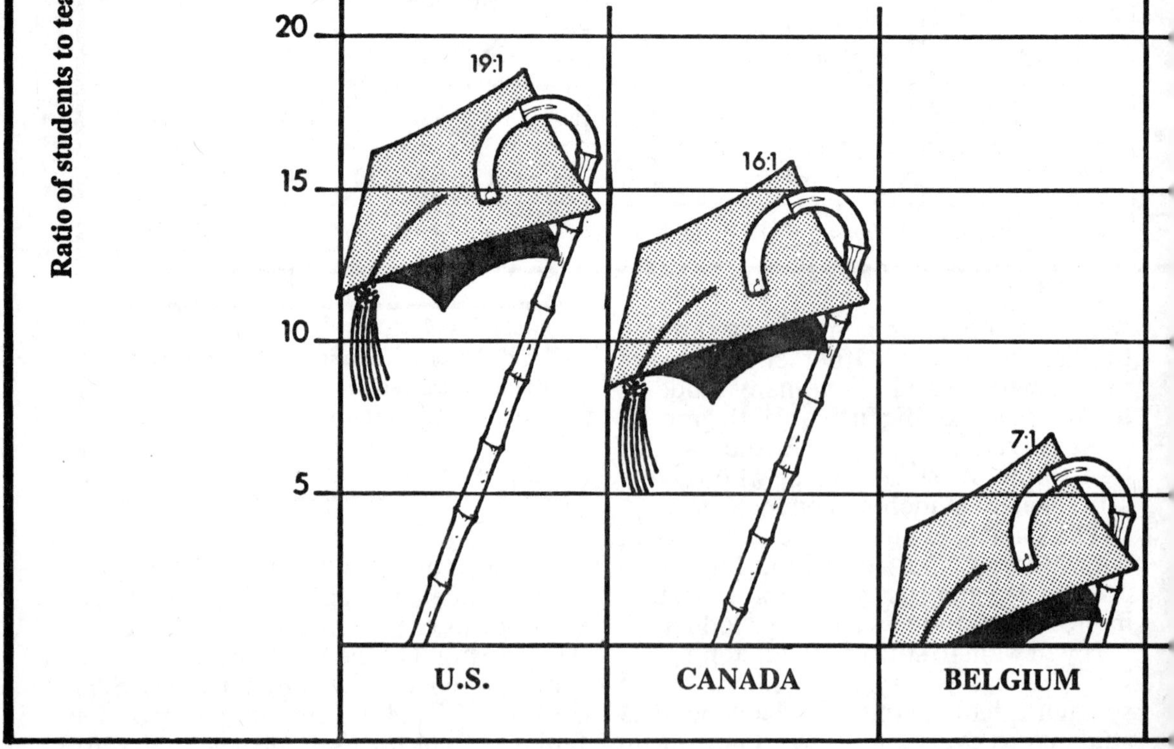

20 —

19:1

15 —

16:1

10 —

7:1

5 —

| U.S. | CANADA | BELGIUM |

PUPILS: TEACHERS

DENMARK	JAPAN	NETHERLANDS	SPAIN
16:1	17:1	16:1	39:1

Crime

In this chapter, we take a look at many aspects of crime. What's the first thing you'd do if you were mugged in the street or found that your home had been burglarized? The answer is obvious – call a cop. But how quickly that call was answered could depend a lot on what nationality you are. There's an enormous variation in the amount of police protection a citizen of France receives compared to, say, Holland.

And the size of a country's police force doesn't necessarily depend on how much protection those citizens need. As you'll see, there are countries where crime is virtually running rampant but there simply aren't enough policemen to match wits with the bad guys. So in some cases, the old saying that "there's never a policeman around when you need one" is true.

But let's be fair to the boys on the beat. They're often faced with almost insurmountable problems. In urban areas in many countries, crime rates have soared sky-high, and they are often unfairly blamed on police inefficiency. There are many social factors beyond the control of the police force – like overcrowding in slums and unemployment among the young – that cause crime rates to be high.

Social factors also help determine what types of crime will be most common in certain countries. Obviously, a heavily urbanized, highly populated nation like Japan will have different problems from those of one like Switzerland.

So, whether you're a prospective master criminal looking for the ideal scene of the crime, or a peaceful law abiding citizen who wants to know where he's least likely to be burglarized or assaulted, there's useful information for you here.

However, a word of warning on all the crime figures contained in the pages which follow. As we've said elsewhere in this book, our facts and figures can only be as reliable as the source data they're taken from. Crime statistics need to be viewed with the same suspicions the police use in quizzing a suspect for several reasons.

The first of these is that an astonishing amount of crime simply goes unreported. There are a variety of reasons for this. One primary one is embarrassment. The man who's had his wallet lifted while visiting a prostitute, or the firm that's suffered embezzlement but doesn't want its reputation to suffer.

Furthermore, much petty crime goes unreported. Many merchants don't prosecute all shoplifters. They build a stock loss factor into the price you pay instead. But these are thefts.

Crime

Finally in many parts of the world law enforcement authorities jiggle the figures to make things look good. Until recent years F.B.I. statistics were a good example. Agents were encouraged to concentrate on interstate auto thefts (an easy crime to solve) and thereby make the overall "case solved" figure look good.

The first table in this chapter shows how many policemen there are in the countries covered – and also gives figures for the number of policemen per thousand population. There are some surprises here. America, where we have so much violent crime, has fewer policemen per thousand population than most European countries. France, where the "flics", as a percentage of the population, outnumber anyone else's police force, has the highest ratio of cops to citizens. The real crime indicator is in the next table. This shows crime rates in the countries we've covered. Here we have figures for the number of sex crimes committed per hour, and the number of larcenies, murders and attempted murders committed per hour.

The next table gives an indication of police efficiency. It gives the number of major and minor larcenies reported and the percentage of them that are solved. Surprisingly, the U.S. fares comparatively well in solving minor larceny offenses – in spite of all those despair stories. So maybe our over-worked cops are pretty efficient after all.

One of the major areas of crime in the U.S. is narcotics offenses. But this isn't just an American problem, as you'll see from the figures in the next table. And the accompanying text comes to some very interesting conclusions on the subject.

Though narcotics offenses are bad, the worse crimes of all are surely rape and murder. Our table gives the gruesome figures here. At a glance one can see why the U.S. has such an appalling reputation for violence. But we're not alone: "peaceful" Holland is obviously not so terribly peaceful after all, and those well-ordered West German *burghers* seem fairly violent too. Not only can you see the number of murders and sex offenses for the countries listed, but also how many the cops manage to solve.

Lastly we have a table which deals with prisoners. It shows just how many there are as a percentage of the population.

	U.S.A.	CANADA
	1976	1976
Number of policemen (000s)	418^X	63.7
per 100,000 inhabitants^0	211^X	280

No surprise to find that the home of Kojak has the most cops. The real story, however, is in the number of police per hundred thousand inhabitants. These figures give an indication of the police capability to deal with the problems that arise on the beat. Here we're way down the list – sixth, to be precise.

France has proportionately the highest number of cops, way ahead of the rest of the field. In the home of gendarmes and "flics", they have more than 450 policemen to every hundred thousand inhabitants – nearly one to every 2,000 people. In spite of this, ten years ago in May, 1968, the Left Bank students took over Paris and paralyzed the entire country for more than a week. Many experts believe that the repressive effect of having so many policemen around helped fan the flames of riot.

Austria comes second, with 328 policemen per hundred thousand people. A hidden factor here is that Austria's army is limited in size by treaty obligations. Given Austria's geographical position this means that those Austrian police are responsible for a comparatively long mileage of frontier with Eastern Europe.

The Italians almost equal the Austrians with 323 policemen per hundred thousand. This is a 1973 figure, and with Italy's recent record of political violence and urban terrorism it has risen considerably. Exact figures aren't yet available, but it's generally accepted that Italy now has the largest force – population-wise – in Europe. They certainly need it.

Italy is followed by Canada – home of the Mounties, the men who always get their man. This boast is no idle one – the Canadian police solve 83% of murders and attempted murders (see murders and sex crimes table).

The Belgians have 263 policemen per hundred thousand inhabitants – 52 more than we have in the U.S. (Not the impression you get from watching T.V. – where half the U.S. population seems to consist of policemen or private eyes.)

The sober, industrious Dutch have proportionately the smallest police force – 136 per hundred thousand inhabitants. But this is a misleading figure. Recently Holland has been something of a target for terrorists. Splinter groups from the West German Baader-Meinhof gang have a habit of going into hiding in Holland, and the Dutch have their own terrorist problem. When South Moluccan terrorists take over a train or a school filled with children, it makes world headlines. But what isn't always so apparent is that it isn't the police who deal with the problem in these cases. It's the army who surround the place, sit out the seige, and finally go in at the end. It's also the army who supervise many of the everyday anti-terrorist counter measures. This means that, strictly speaking, they are in fact taking over police duties

U.K.	AUSTRALIA	AUSTRIA	BELGIUM	DENMARK	FRANCE	(WEST) GERMANY	IRELAND	ITALY	JAPAN	NETHERLANDS	NORWAY	SPAIN	SWEDEN	SWITZERLAND
1977	1976	1973	1973	1973	1973	1973	1973	1973	1976	1973	1973	–	1976	1976
108.2	28.0	24.3+	25.2+	8.2+	233.0+	133.6+	6.5+	174.4+	231.1	19.9	5.5+	NA	14.1	13.0
192	203	328	263	164	452	219	218	323	208	148	137	NA	170	200

NA not available   *x Policemen protecting only 198 million people*

Sources:
Government sources; USA : FBI
+Euromonitor
0Heron House estimates

in these fields. So although the Dutch police force in itself may be proportionately the smallest, many more people are actually involved in what are usually considered as policing duties.

For this reason, Norway really qualifies as the most under-policed nation. Here they have 137 policemen per hundred thousand inhabitants – and here in Norway they're lucky. They don't need the army to help them out with their work, because they haven't yet got a terrorist problem.

The next most underpoliced nations are also both Scandinavian. In Denmark they only have 164 policemen per hundred thousand inhabitants, and in Sweden they have 170. If you look at the tables on crime, you'll see there's comparatively little crime in Scandinavia. So perhaps those Scandinavians are just more law-abiding than the rest of us, although the experts have their own opinions on the matter. They say there's less need for police in Scandinavia and less crime because it's largely rural, with populations spread thinner on the ground than elsewhere. Another contributory factor is that Scandinavian cities are well planned and less crowded. (If you look at the table on green space in cities you'll see what they mean – Oslo and Stockholm are way ahead of the field here).

Next lowest – fifth from the bottom – is the figure for the U.K. In Britain, they only have 195 policemen per hundred thousand. And here it's a different story altogether. In Britain, the police are relatively underpaid and many are leaving the force, while recruitment rates are also dropping.

One significant omission in our table is Spain. The figures are not available. Until recently, Spain was the only permanent police state in Western Europe, and the Spaniards still don't want to talk about that.

Do cops curb crime? Our figures indicate that possibly they do, but not by very much. France and West Germany combined have about the same number of police as we do, but only half the population – and a lower crime rate. At present, 426 major crimes are committed hourly in the U.S. If we were to hire the extra police for our extra population, perhaps we might bring that rate down to the one enjoyed by the French and Germans, 276 per hour (based on population adjustment).

Serious crime occurs with such monotonous regularity that most rapes, robberies or murders aren't even noted in the newspapers in many cities of the world. The table shown here illustrates the extent of serious crime in the countries listed in two ways. The first line of figures is the number of serious sexual offences committed per hour. These include rape, attempted rape or serious molesting (except in the U.S. where only rape figures are given). The second line shows the hourly rate for other serious crimes. These include murder, attempted murder and large-scale robberies. Since the figures give the number of reported incidents on an hourly basis, multiply by 24 to arrive at a daily total and then by 365 for the annual figure.

	U.S.A.	CANADA
	1975	1970
1. Sex offenses per hour[+]	6.4[x]	1.2
2. Major larceny[0], murders and attempted murders per hour[+]	426.6[‡]	1.4

Keep in mind, however, that these figures are only for *reported* crimes. Many crimes remain unreported because the victims are embarrassed or frightened of repercussions. In other cases, they feel it's hardly worth the bother: in some cities, an over-worked police force can't offer much more than sympathy which does little to catch the criminal or lower the crime rate.

The U.S. has the highest number for sex offenses per hour of all the countries listed, with an average of 6.4 – more than one incident every ten minutes, day and night. And that's only the rape figures. West Germany comes second with 5.4. Figures for all sex crimes would be considerably higher. However, these figures (and the others on the table) take no account of differences in comparative populations.

Great Britain follows West Germany with a relatively low rate: 3.1 sex offenses per hour, or about one every 20 minutes.

After Great Britain, the rates drop markedly. Australia and France report 1.5 offences per hour, only about half the British rate. Canada has 1.2 per hour. This rate is low – but so is Canada's population figure.

Those reputedly hot-blooded Italians and Spaniards certainly give the female tourist some embarrassing moments, but it's obviously all in fun – their sex crime rate is very low.

At the crime-free end of the scale, there are a handful of countries where people can walk the streets with virtually no danger of serious sexual offences occuring. In Ireland, on average, such an offense is reported only once every two days. Their rate is a miniscule 0.02 offenses per hour. Also low are Norway (0.11 per hour), Denmark (0.23), Austria (0.25), Sweden (0.37). The Scandinavian countries which have a reputation with the rest of the world for freedom in sexual manners, movies and literature, also have exceptionally low rates of sexual vio-

CRIME RATES

	GREAT BRITAIN**	AUSTRALIA ++	AUSTRIA	BELGIUM	DENMARK	FRANCE	(WEST)⁰⁰ GERMANY	IRELAND	ITALY	JAPAN	NETHERLANDS	NORWAY	SPAIN	SWEDEN	SWITZERLAND
	1974	1974	1974	–	1974	1974	1974	1970	1974	1974	1974	1970	1974	1974	–
	3.1	1.5	0.25	NA	0.23	1.5	5.4	0.02	0.75	1.3	0.86	0.11	0.49	0.37	NA
	65.2	15.3	10.3	NA	9.9	23.5	114.4	1.05	149.8‡‡	0.46	12.4	2.3	14.5‡‡	13.3	NA

ˣ Rape only   ‡ Murders and non-negligent manslaughter; excludes attempted murders.
** Excludes Northern Ireland   ++ Includes Papua New Guinea   ⁰⁰ Includes West Berlin
‡‡ All larceny offenses.

lence. This contradicts the much voiced opinion that an increase of sexual freedom leads to an increase in sex crimes.

The U.S. is undisputed leader in the remaining figures, which report hourly rates of serious crimes including murder, attempted murder, and major larcenies. The American rate, 426.6 per hour, is more than twice that of any other country. This means that, on average, a major crime is committed every hour in every city of any size throughout the U.S. – or six major crimes every hour in every state of the union.

While the U.S. has twice the crime rate of other countries on the table, it also has more than twice the population. Our population is 215 million – the closest contender is Japan with 108 million.

It looks as if crime is also big business in Italy – traditional home of the Mafia. Here, the rate of serious crimes reported is nearly 150 per hour. Obviously the new waves of urban terrorism are an important factor here – not so much in the figures themselves, but in the atmosphere of lawlessness which the (comparatively) few spectacular and well-reported cases help to create. But in these high Italian figures there is a mitigating factor. The

Sources:
Heron House estimates based on figures from the Federal Bureau of Investigation and Interpol.
+ Reported cases
⁰ Robbery, burglary, etc.

Italian rate includes all larcenies reported – both large and small.

After the U.S. and Italy, West Germany weighs in with a still-substantial rate of 114.4 serious crimes an hour. Here again, there are problems with urban terrorism. You only need one Baader-Meinhof gang and the ensuing ripples of lawlessness spread throughout the entire country.

After the preceding high rates, Great Britain registers a rather moderate 65.2 per hour. However, even this modest average means a serious crime occurs more than once a minute, day and night, throughout the year.

Still, the British seem tranquil and pacific compared to Americans. In the minute or so it took to read this page, one major crime occured in Great Britain, but in the same short time span, 50 Americans were attempting to murder or rob their fellow men.

If you're a light-fingered petty thief, hop on the next freighter for Australia. There, less than three percent of all minor larceny offenders are apprehended. But don't go to Japan. If the Japanese police are telling the truth, one out of every two occasions they get their man.

In the countries studied, there are generally twice as many minor larcenies as major thefts.

Austria and West Germany are interesting exceptions. There crooks go for big-time robberies more often than petty robberies.

In the U.S., small-time crime is the order of the day. We have about 5.9 million minor robberies a year. That works out to a hit for about every 30 people. There are also 17 or 18 major thefts for every thousand citizens.

Canada has only 11,600 major thefts for the year shown. Things may have gotten worse during the 70s. Even so, a rate of 55 major robberies per hundred thousand people makes Canada a much safer place to keep your goods than the U.S.

The Canadians don't keep a record of the percentage of the thefts that get solved. Neither does the U.S. where major larcenies are concerned.

The U.S. has a lot of crime. But we don't come near the rate of thefts per unit of population, found in Sweden and Denmark. One in every 25 Danes can expect to be robbed by a petty thief. In Sweden the rate is only slightly less.

When it comes to major larceny, Denmark has 17 major thefts per thousand people. In Sweden, the rate is roughly one for every 70 people. Of the big jobs, only 15% are solved in Sweden, and a quarter in Denmark. With the small fry, 82% get away in Denmark, and 84% in Sweden.

	U.S.A.	CANADA
	1975	1970
1. Major larceny[+] offenses (000s) known to the police	3717	11.6
per 100,000 population	1744	55
2. Major larceny offenses solved (000s)	NA	NA
as % of major larceny offenses known to police	NA	NA
	1975	–
3. Minor larceny[0] offenses known to the police (000s)	5978	NA
per 100,000 population	2804	NA
4. Minor larceny offenses solved (000s)	1177	NA
as % of minor larceny offenses known to police	19.7	NA

GREAT BRITAIN[x]	AUSTRALIA[++]	AUSTRIA	BELGIUM	DENMARK	FRANCE	(WEST) GERMANY**	IRELAND	ITALY	JAPAN	NETHERLANDS	NORWAY	SPAIN	SWEDEN	SWITZERLAND
1974	1974	1974	–	1974	1974	1974	1970	1974	1974	1974	1970	1974	1974	–
570.0	133.8	90.8	NA	86.8	204.6	999.9	9.3	1311 [++]	2.1	108.2	20.5	127.2 [00]	116.7	NA
1047	888	1214	NA	1723	387	1611	308	2355 [++]	1.94	802	524	360 [00]	1427	NA
188.8	26.5	26.7	NA	22.1	37.0	210.3	NA	NA	1.7	31.0	NA	NA	17.4	NA
33	20	29	NA	25	18	21	NA	NA	80	29	NA	NA	15	NA
1973	1974	1974	–	1974	1974	1974	–	–	1974	1974	–	–	1974	–
772	278.2	45.5	NA	200.3	919.9	833.3	NA	–	1013	205.2	NA	NA	288.7	NA
1421	1847	609	NA	3976	1742	1343	NA	–	920	1521	NA	NA	3530	NA
264.8	78.6	116.5	NA	35.7	172.0	348.1	NA	–	517.7	34.5	NA	NA	47.2	NA
34.2	2.8	27.5	NA	17.8	18.6	41.7	NA	–	51.0	16.8	NA	NA	16.0	NA

NA not available ++*All larceny offenses* 00*Includes all types of fraud*

To be fair, the rates of solving crimes of larceny are almost uniformly low except for those efficient Japanese who solve four out of five serious thefts. In fact, Japan is by far the most theft-free country on the table. There's only one major larceny for every 50 thousand people. And only about one petty theft per hundred – not great, but better than anyone else. British bobbies are on their toes too. They solve 33% of all major larcenies committed.

Source:
Interpol
USA: Federal Bureau of Investigation
+Robbery, burglary
0Theft, pickpocketing, shoplifting
xExcludes Northern Ireland
‡Includes Papua New Guinea
**Includes West Berlin

Nearly all human societies use drugs whether it's nicotine, alcohol, opium, hashish, aspirin, caffeine or peyote. According to anthropologists there's a remote Eskimo tribe which is a rare exception – they rely on deep breathing.

All countries have some laws against narcotics. In most industrialized Western countries, narcotics mean derivatives of the opium poppy – opium, morphine and heroin – as well as a number of other naturally occuring drugs. The term also covers a wide spectrum of man-made drugs developed for specific medical purposes. Illegal use or abuse of those drugs can also be a narcotics offense.

In the U.S., the laws vary from state to state. What is termed a "dangerous drug" or "controlled substance" in New York or New Jersey might well be exempt from penalties in Wisconsin or California. Penalties for offenses involving the drug will also vary.

The figures on the table give some idea of the rate of drug abuse in various countries. Exact comparisons can't be made since the definition of "narcotics offenses" differs in each locality.

In some countries, no figures are available. In the 14 where they are, the results are so uneven as to astonish even the most ardent fact-seeker. Rates vary between three offenses per million people (Japan) and one in 356 people (the U.S.).

When it comes to narcotics offenses, some nations are "have's" and others are "have not's". The big three among the have's are the U.S., Sweden and Canada.

	U.S.A.	CANADA
	1975	1975
Narcotic arrests/convictions (000s):	601.4[0]	60.0
per 100,000 inhabitants[+]	281.0	263.0

One out of every 356 Americans is arrested every year for one offense or another against the drug laws. In Sweden the figure is one in 378, in Canada an almost identical 380. Australia follows with one in 869, then Denmark with one in 1,282. Norway (one in 3,448) and the Netherlands (one in 4,545) are next.

Japan, Ireland and Spain have the lowest number of narcotics arrests. All these countries have highly traditional, conservative cultures, which were largely unaffected by the turbulent "protest" movement of the 1960s.

The U.K. figure is also low – 16,000 arrests against over 600,000 in the U.S. This doesn't mean that British society is unusually drug-free. The U.K. figures on this table only show the number of people found guilty of drug offenses and, strangely enough, such offenses are usually to do with "soft" rather than "hard" drugs. The British are more inclined to treat addiction to "hard drugs" like heroin as a medical problem. Addicts are registered with the National Health Service, and they get their drugs from the state free of charge. This may sound like condoning addiction, but it has at least two very practical results. The

NARCOTIC OFFENSES

	U.K.	AUSTRALIA	AUSTRIA	BELGIUM	DENMARK	FRANCE	(WEST) GERMANY	IRELAND	ITALY	JAPAN	NETHERLANDS	NORWAY	SPAIN	SWEDEN	SWITZERLAND
	1976	1975	1976	–	1975	1976	–	1976	1976	1976	1975	1976	1976	1975	–
	16.0‡	15.8[0]	0.7	NA	3.9	3.8	NA	0.03	2.4	0.35[x]	3.0[x]	1.2[x]	0.4	22.0	NA
	3.0	115.0	9.0	NA	78.0	7.0	NA	0.9	4.0	0.3[+]	22.0[+]	29.0	1.0	264.0	NA

[0] All offenses known to the police connected with narcotics, including the sale of narcotics
[x] People charged with any offenses contravening the narcotics laws
[‡] People found guilty of drug offenses   NA not available

drug issue is out of the hands of criminals and policemen, and drug-related crime is minimized. In the U.K., there are fewer addicts who have to steal and traffic narcotics to support their habits.

The French underworld, especially that part of it centered around the port of Marseilles, is a major supplier of heroin to Europe and North America. Yet the figures for France (seven arrests per hundred thousand inhabitants) are low.

Two main factors seem to be involved in the figures on the table: whether or not drugs are wanted by large segments of the population; and whether or not police and other enforcement agencies are aggressive in arresting and prosecuting drug offenders. In the U.S. we have millions of drug-users – and aggressive enforcement of the narcotics laws. As a result, figures for drug offenses are high. The low figures for countries like France and Italy may be due to lack of interest in narcotics on the part of the French and Italians or lack of police interest in prosecuting.

Sources:
Government Departments of Justice
[+] Heron House estimates

If you're an American T.V. addict, it won't come as a surprise to learn that Americans murder each other at a faster rate than any other people shown. There are nearly ten murder attempts – successful and unsuccessful – for every hundred thousand people, or one for every ten thousand. That's the equivalent of one murder a year for every small town and neighborhood in every large town and city. The real rate is even worse than that. Only murders for which somebody is arrested are counted. Unsolved murders, and murders that never get reported, send the true rate of murder sky high.

	U.S.A.	CANADA
	1975	1970
1. Murders and attempted murders known to the police	20510^0	690
per 100,000 population	9.6^0	3.4
2. Solved murders and attempted murders	15998^{x0}	571
as % of cases known to the police	78^{0x}	83
3. Sex offenses[+] known to the police	56093‡	11,025
per 100,000 population	26.3‡	55.0
4. Solved sex offenses	28725^{‡x}	5951
as % of cases known to the police	51.3‡	54.0

On the whole, the Canadians manage to get along together much better than the Americans. Only a third as many Canadians rub each other out as their neighbors south of the border. But that's still fourth highest for all the countries shown.

A big surprise on the murder table is the Netherlands, with its windmills, tulips and pink-cheeked population. Surprisingly, seven in every hundred thousand Dutchmen die at the hands of killers. In Holland, only one in ten murderers gets away.

If you think somebody's after you, board the next flight for Japan. Statistically, at least, you'll get protection. The Japanese murder rate is 400% lower per hundred thousand population than in the U.S., and the efficient Japanese police solve all but four percent of murder-related crimes.

The best places not to get murdered are Norway and Ireland – with probably the most rural economies of any country on the chart. There must be some correlation between lots of elbow room and people living together peacefully without undue violence.

Space to get away from it all doesn't seem to be the determining factor when it comes to sex offenses. Those randy Aussies, with miles of lonely outback to roam in, top the table when it comes to sex crimes (including rape and "traffic in women" – also known as prostitution).

MURDERS AND SEX OFFENSES

	U.K.**	AUSTRALIA++	AUSTRIA	BELGIUM	DENMARK	FRANCE	(WEST)00 GERMANY	IRELAND	ITALY	JAPAN	NETHERLANDS	NORWAY	SPAIN	SWEDEN	SWITZERLAND
	1974	1974	1974	–	1974	1974	1974	1970	1974	1974	1974	1970	1974	1974	–
	1301	411	229	NA	102	1429	2771	24	1643	1912	964	6	233	275	NA
	2.4	2.7	3.1	NA	2.0	2.7	4.5	0.03	3.0	1.7	7.2	0.02	0.7	3.4	NA
	1162	374	216	NA	72	1151	2621	22	NA	1837	875	NA	NA	146	NA
	89	91	94	NA	71	81	95	92	NA	96	91	NA	NA	53	NA
	27028	13674	2274	NA	2068	13828	48075	261	6605	11338	7554	1047	4310	3313	NA
	49.7	90.8	30.4	NA	41.1	26.2	77.5	8.7	11.9	10.3	56.0	27.0	12.2	40.5	NA
	21016	8321	1942	NA	1071	10368	33994	216	NA	10428	3747	476	NA	1574	NA
	77.7	61.0	85.0	NA	52.0	75.0	71.0	83.0	NA	92.0	50.0	45.0	NA	48.0	NA

NA not available 0Murder and non-negligent manslaughter XCrimes cleared by arrest ‡Rape only

Sources:
Interpol
USA figures from the FBI
+Includes rape and traffic in women
**Excludes Northern Ireland
++Includes Papua New Guinea
00Includes West Berlin

And the Aussies don't always have to pay a price for their crimes. Four out of every ten Australian sex offenders manage to get away scot-free.

After the Aussies, West Germany and Holland rank next in the number of sex crimes. Germany is second highest, with nearly 78 per hundred thousand. They have a pretty good success rate – in terms of solving crimes, that is. Almost three in four West German sex offenders get caught. Holland ranks third in sex offenses – with about one sex crime for every two thousand people. Only half of Dutch sex offenders get caught – a rate much lower than for murderers.

Tolerant attitudes towards prostitution may be partially the cause, and "traffic in women" is an offense that perhaps isn't taken very seriously.

The U.S. rate for sex crimes is deceptively low when compared to the other countries but it includes only rape. If prostitution arrests were added, the U.S. might lead the pack – as anyone who has walked around 42nd Street and Broadway in New York City can attest.

341

In every country, there's a small minority that chooses to disobey society's rules. Some get away with it, but most are caught and many of those end up in jail. Our figures here show how the prisoner population varies from one country to another.

Where do we find the most prisoners? Both in terms of overall numbers and percentage of the population, more criminals are under lock and key in America than anywhere else. We have a total of nearly 400,000 jail-birds, that's 189 per hundred thousand of the population – about twice the figure for any other country.

Other countries with well filled jails are Canada, Germany and the U.K. When you recall that Australia was largely colonized by shady characters, you might expect to find quite a few jail-birds there. It's sixth in the table, but there are only 70 prisoners per hundred thousand of the population, so it's a far more law-abiding country than the U.S.

Where do the largest number of people manage to keep out of trouble? They must be well-behaved in the Netherlands, or maybe their police just turn a blind eye. The prison population is only 2,700 – just 21 out of every hundred thousand of the total population.

Dutch women are particularly law-abiding, they make up a smaller proportion of the prison population than in any other country: under two percent. On the other hand, there are a lot of people awaiting trial in the Netherlands. Taken as a percentage of the number already in jail, the figure is higher in Holland than anywhere else except Italy. Nonetheless, even if all of them were eventually jailed, the Dutch prison population would still be the lowest.

There aren't many prisoners in Ireland either – only 35 in every hundred thousand of the population. It also has one of the lowest figures for people

		U.S.A.	CANADA
		1972	1974
1.	Prisoners (000s)	393.7	20.7
	per 100,000 inhabitants[+]	189	95
2.	Female prisoners	28,112	702
	as % of total prison population[+]	7.1	3.4
3.	Male prisoners (000s)	365.6	20.0
		1973	1974
4.	Prisoners under 21	61,794	5608
	as % of prison population[+]	15.7	27.0
5.	Accused persons in prison awaiting trial	NA	2533
	as % of prison population[+]	NA	12.2

	U.K.	AUSTRALIA	AUSTRIA	BELGIUM	DENMARK	FRANCE	(WEST) GERMANY	IRELAND	ITALY	JAPAN	NETHERLANDS	NORWAY	SPAIN	SWEDEN	SWITZERLAND [O]
	1974	1974	1974	1974	1974	1974	1974	1972	1972	1974	1972	1974	1972	1974	1975
	41.7	9.2	7.8	5.6	2.7	27.1	50.5	1.1	27.8	46.0	2.7	1.5	13.8	3.5	4.5
	75	70	104	58	54	52	81	35	51	43	21	39	40	43	69
	1134	275	353	220	82	711	1364	26	1454	1059	49	35	715	94	800
	2.7	2.9	4.5	3.9	3.0	2.6	2.7	2.8	5.2	2.3	1.7	2.3	5.2	2.7	17.7
	40.6	9.0	7.4	5.4	2.6	26.4	49.2	1.0	26.4	45.0	2.7	1.5	13.1	3.4	3.7
	1974	1974	1974	1974	1974	1974	1974	1972	1972	1972	1972	1974	1972	1974	1975
	11912	1554	1007	611	497	4305	NA	428	4560	1161	983	344	1583	831	1000
	28.5	16.8	12.9	10.9	18.3	15.9	NA	40.6	16.4	2.5	35.4	22.3	11.4	23.5	22.2
	3541	1020	2223	1217	840	10731	15942	121	15116	8390	1311	460	5761	520	1200
	8.4	11.0	28.5	21.7	31.0	39.6	31.6	11.5	54.4	18.2	47.2	29.8	41.7	14.7	26.6

NA not available

awaiting trial. But Ireland shares one striking characteristic with the Netherlands – they both have a high number of young offenders. In Ireland, people under 21 account for more than 40% of the jail population. The figure for the U.K. (28.5%) is much less dramatic, although there's plenty of unrest among Britain's youth. In Japan, there's the lowest number of young offenders, which is possibly because of the strict upbringing they receive.

The figures for Italy are interesting. With only about 50 people in jail for every hundred thousand inhabitants, they seem much better behaved than, say, the British. But the number of Italians awaiting trial is over 54% of the number in jail compared to the British percentage of 8.4%. Since these figures were made available, the level of crime in Italy has increased so dramatically that the courts can't keep up.

Sources:
United Nations
[+] Heron House estimates
[O] Department of Justice

Murders and attempted murders known to the police

21,000		
17,500		
16,250		
15,000		
13,750		
12,500		
11,250		
10,000		
7,500		
6,250		
5,000		
3,750		
2,500		
1,250		
10		

The U.S. is famous for its fictional crime-busters like Kojak and Columbo. It needs all of them, fictional or otherwise, with over 20,000 known murders a year. That figure means about one American in every 10,000 will die at the hands of another.

No other country approaches that number of murders. West Germany is next, with 2,771 in one year. You probably associate Japan with tea-drinking ceremonies and flower-arranging. But the Japanese have the third-highest murder figure (1,912) which suggest that modern pressures are changing that gentle image.

Italy's another violent society. There were 1,643 murders in the home of the Mafia. Across the border is France, things are almost as bad: nearly 1,500 Frenchmen met their deaths by foul play.

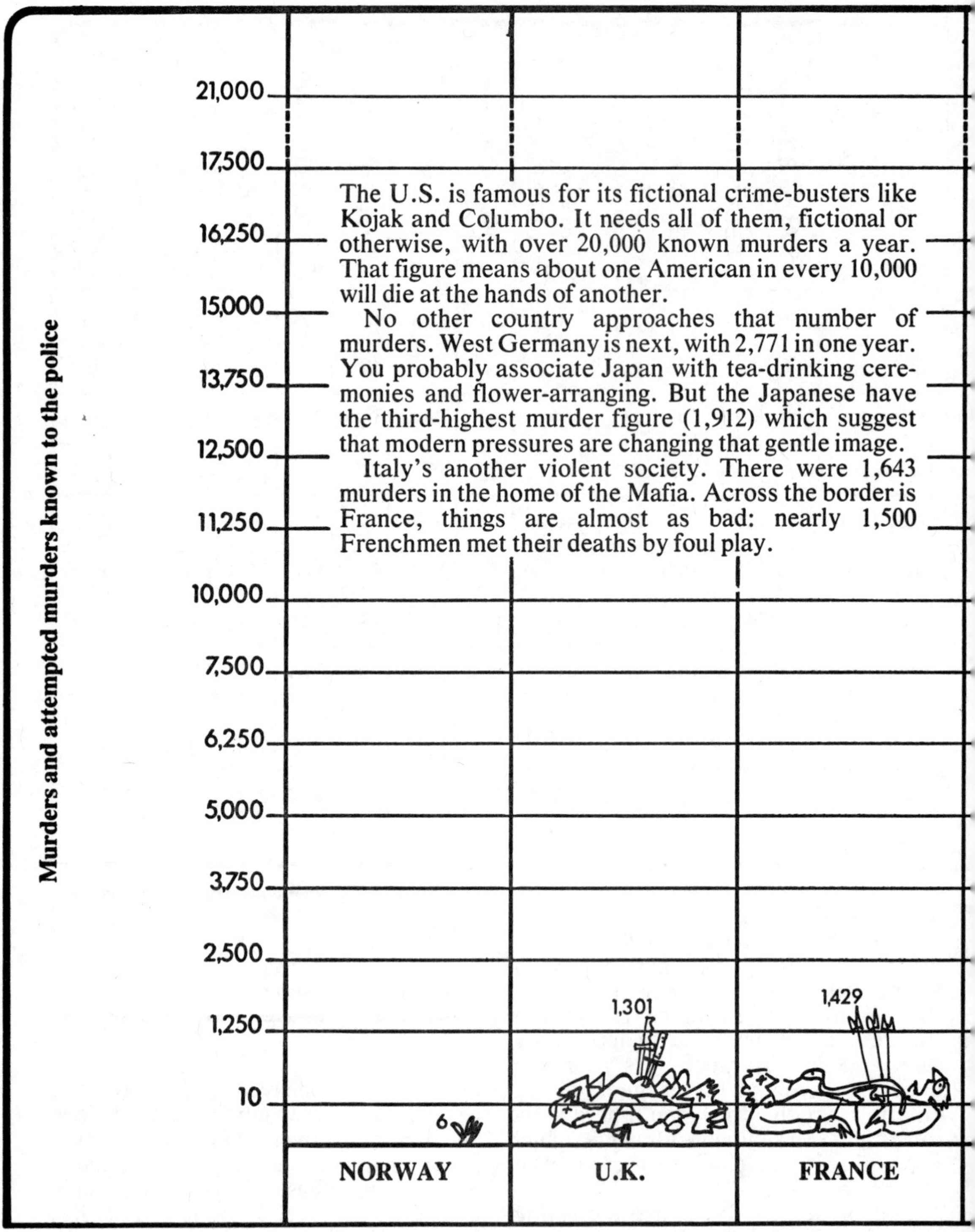

6

1,301

1,429

NORWAY	U.K.	FRANCE

MURDERS

ITALY	JAPAN	WEST GERMANY	U.S.
1,643	1,912	2,771	20,510

What People Use

Have you ever stopped to think how dependent you are on the hundreds of products that modern industry churns out? From the time you stumble out of bed and into the bathroom till you finally switch off the light and call it a day, you'll probably have used most of the products we talk about in the following tables.

As you'll see, nationality plays an important part in determining what people use and what they don't. Of course, most people, regardless of the country they're from, wash up when they get up in the morning. And that involves soap, of course – or does it? Have a look at the section on soap and deodorants to find out who "the great unwashed" really are. While we're on the subject of personal hygiene, let's not forget another important area – your teeth. You might think absolutely everyone owns at least one toothbrush – and uses it. You'd be wrong. Turn to our table on toothbrushes to find out whose teeth are whiter than white – and whose aren't! (This section will be particularly interesting to dentists wondering where to set up shop.)

Then there's a product that only about half our readers have any use for – shaving equipment. According to the figures, there are some shaggy countries around the globe. You may be surprised when you find out which ones. Then there's the eternal male debate over electric shavers versus the old reliable razor. Do you shave wet or dry? This chapter will show you who agrees with your particular preference.

There's lots for the ladies here, too. You'll soon find out the countries to head for if you like the fresh natural look. You'll also see where the girls spend a lot of their time in front of the make-up mirror. But you'll have to decide for yourself if they do it because they actually need to or whether they're just showing an admirable interest in their appearance. There are some areas where even the most intrepid researchers fear to tread.

When it comes to giving nature a helping hand – or whatever – there is some enlightening information on bras. In which countries do most ladies wear them? And, where do most of the female population "let it all hang out"? We also have some eye-opening figures on – well, on eye-opening figures!

Still on the subject of female pulchritude, there is a table on a rather touchy subject – hair colorants. Do blondes really have more fun? It seems a lot of women think so. In some countries about half the women you meet may not be what they seem. Be sure to take a close look at the figures for the Scandinavian countries – some of those blonde Nordic beauties may be pulling the wool over our eyes!

Looking at hair care from the male point of view, can you still get a decent haircut for a reasonable price? Your answer will depend a lot on where you live.

While we're on the topic of hair, there's another vast range of products we rely on to keep us looking good – shampoos. Have a look at the table and see where the shiniest heads are to be found. And find out where they shun commercial hair cleaners and rely on water and old-fashioned elbow grease.

We also tackled the delicate subject of "white shoulders". You may assume there's an obvious connection between shampooing and dandruff – see if you're right.

Even though all the products mentioned so far are useful, you could probably live without them. But there's another product that a lot of people think of as an absolute necessity. That's the controversial weed, tobacco. Our section on smoking sheds some light on just how effective all those anti-smoking campaigns have been. You'll find out which countries you should head for if you're a clean air fan. This section demolishes some of the old stereotypes about who the heavy smokers are. It also points to some interesting trends in the major tobacco-producing nations of the world.

Finally, we come to what's probably the most necessary product of all – energy. Where would we be without oil and electricity? Who are the major consumers of the world's rapidly shrinking energy resources? These questions are especially important ones now, with countries like the U.S. facing a massive energy crisis and screaming headlines about the latest manoeuvres in the Arab world. It's a commonly known fact that North America is greedy when it comes to slicing up the energy pie – so where does that leave the rest of the world? Have a good look at this section and find out. These are just the kind of statistics that come in handy when settling those dinner-table arguments about economics.

In fact this whole chapter is full of facts – and some theories – about products that affect the lives of us all. Things that we take for granted but would be lost without.

When did you last take a bath? If you put that question to a lot of people, you might come up with some distressing answers. This week, last week, sometime, never... People in different countries vary in hygiene habits. Fortunately, at least in the countries surveyed, most people we spoke to did use soap.

If soap-buying is a measure of hygiene, the Scandinavians come out the cleanest of us all. You'd have a job finding a single household up in the Nordic countries without at least a bar or two of soap around the place. And if cleanliness *is* next to godliness, the Scandinavians should have nothing to fear when they're at Valhalla's gates. Unless, of course, they're not next to godliness at all – but are using that soap for waxing skis.

You'd think those bars of soap would be enough to keep them smelling sweet in Scandinavia. Well, they aren't. In Norway and Sweden, about 80% of women use deodorant regularly as extra security. In Denmark, the rate's lower – at 66%. But among Scandinavian men, only one in three bothers to use an anti-perspirant of some kind. Either there's a double standard, or Scandinavian men aren't as sweet as their gorgeous women.

Next in the soap league come Britain and Australia, where 99% of the population buy soap. That's enough to keep just about everyone well scrubbed, except one percent of the British popu-

	U.S.A.	CANADA
	1977	1977
1. Households (%) who buy soap	97	98
	1977	1974
2. People who use a deodorant/ anti-perspirant regularly: men (%)	80	85
	1977	1974
women (%)	90	95

lation – about 560,000 people. That's the entire population of Edinburgh. Come to think of it, in Scotland they call Edinburgh "Auld Reekie."

Forty-one percent of British men use deodorants, compared with 73% of women.

Except for Japan, it's always the women who use deodorants more frequently than the men.

Canada, Italy and the Netherlands come high on the table. Ninety-eight percent of them use soap. That leaves two percent unclean. In Canada, that two percent accounts for about 400,000 people. Maybe they're up in the backwoods of the far north, where it's too cold to take a bath. More Canadian men use deodorant than in any other country – twice as many as Dutch and Italian men. Of course in Italy you can always take a quick dip in the Mediterranean.

SOAP AND DEODORANTS

U.K.	AUSTRALIA	AUSTRIA	BELGIUM	DENMARK	FRANCE	(WEST) GERMANY	IRELAND	ITALY	JAPAN	NETHERLANDS	NORWAY	SPAIN	SWEDEN	SWITZERLAND
1977	1977	1977	1977	1977	1977	1977	1977	1977	–	1977	1977	1977	1977	1977
99	99	83	91	100	91	84	72	98	NA	98	100	94	100	86
1976	–	1976	1975	1975	1975	1975	–	1975	1977	1976	1975	1976	1975	1975
41	NA	31	26	32	29	18	NA	43	25	45	35	39	37	34
1976	–	1976	1975	1975	1975	1975	–	1975	1977	1975	1975	1976	1975	1975
73	NA	51	73	66	70	74	NA	66	21	72	78	63	80	74

NA not available

You might expect the U.S., land of soap operas and soapbox derbies, to top the world in soap sales. Well, it isn't true. Comparatively we're dirty. Three percent, or over six million people, don't touch the stuff. That's almost the population of Chicago or Los Angeles. But both the U.S. men and women make up for soap shortfalls when it comes to deodorants. Eighty percent of the men and 90% of the women use antiperspirants regularly. That's nearly twice as many men as in the U.K.

Let's look at the bottom of the table. Where do soap salesmen have the toughest time? It's a different kind of bar they go for in Ireland. Mention bubbles to an Irishman and he's apt to think of a glass of Guinness stout. According to the study, one in every four Irish doesn't use soap at all. That's about 700,000 people – over 100,000 more than live in Dublin.

Sources:
Confidential industry sources

349

Never look a gift horse in the mouth. Why? Because you can tell its age and general condition by the state of its teeth.

But it's not just horses' teeth we care about. We have doctors to look after the health of our bodies. We have chiropodists to look after our feet. And we have dentists to look after our mouths. In fact, we spend millions every year at the dentist. Filling the cavities. Removing the plaque. Straightening the alignment. We are somewhat obsessed with the need for snow white, cover-girl choppers.

However, an ounce of prevention is better than a gram of novocaine. Toothbrushes! Toothpaste! The real root to healthy root canals is in our hands.

Who buys the most toothbrushes? And how many households use toothpaste among the countries on our table? As we all know, there's practically no such thing as 100% of anything – not even Colgate. But what's surprising is the fact that a considerable percentage of people in each country don't brush their teeth. In the U.S., five percent of the households don't buy toothpaste. That adds up to about ten million people. Maybe they're rubbing their teeth with baking soda. Or salt. Or old-fashioned tooth powder. But they'll never look like Farrah Fawcett-Majors if they keep stinting on their mouths like that.

In which countries do people take the best care of their teeth? First of all, before you buy toothpaste, it's useful to invest in a toothbrush. According to the chart, the Australians buy more toothbrushes than anyone. Nearly two are sold for every person in the country every year. That means the average person buys a toothbrush every six months – or brushes his teeth in half the time using two hands.

The pearly-smiling Aussies are way ahead of the rest of the field. The Japanese are next. They buy an average of one and a half toothbrushes every year – or one every eight months. The Swedes and the Americans buy an average of 1.3 toothbrushes a year – you need that extra third to get in where the ordinary bristles don't reach.

The U.K. is roughly average – one toothbrush bought every fifteen months. If the Brits follow their dentists' advice twice a day, their toothbrushes get worked out almost 1,000 times.

Who are the worst in the clean enamel club? The average Belgian buys a toothbrush less than once every three years. The Irish are just as bad. And the Italians, Spaniards and Austrians use the same brush for 30 months.

	U.S.A.	CANADA
	1977	1977
1. Toothbrushes bought per person per year	1.3	1.0
2. Toothbrushes sold per year (millions)	280	20
3. Households who buy toothpaste (%)	95	96

U.K.	AUSTRALIA	AUSTRIA	BELGIUM	DENMARK	FRANCE	(WEST) GERMANY	IRELAND	ITALY	JAPAN	NETHERLANDS	NORWAY	SPAIN	SWEDEN	SWITZERLAND
1977	1977	1977	1977	1977	1977	1977	1977	1977	1977	1977	1977	1977	1977	1977
0.8	1.9	0.4	0.3	1.0	0.5	0.7	0.3	0.4	1.5	0.7	1.2	0.4	1.3	0.6
44	25	3	3	5	27	42	0.9	22	167	10	5	15	11	4
90	96	85	81	80	86	83	53	94	NA	86	75	87	95	90

NA not available

Getting a toothbrush operating is only half the battle. Now we need to know how many people use toothpaste. Here the Australians come out on top again – along with the Canadians. Ninety-six percent of all Australian and Canadian households use toothpaste. We don't have data on what type of toothpaste they prefer – green, striped, plain, with fluoride or without – and nor do we know whether they press the tube from the bottom or the top.

In any case, the next countries on the list are the U.S. and Sweden. Here 95% of all households use toothpaste. The Italians are marginally less kissable, at 94%. Even though they don't change toothbrushes too often, they get high marks when it comes to paste.

Of all the countries studied, the Irish buy the least amount of toothpaste. Only slightly more than half of all Irish households use the stuff. No wonder the song goes "When Irish *eyes* are smiling..." – they obviously can't afford to flash their teeth too much!

Sources:
Confidential industry sources

Prepare to have an illusion shattered. The stereotype of an American male jumping into his Chevy, headed for work with an electric shaver plugged into his dashboard, is false. Three-quarters of all American men who shave do so with water! So much for the dry shave in the land of "Burma-shave" and "Take it all off." Curiously, of all the countries listed in our table almost the only places in the world where wet shaving is preferred are the English-speaking ones. Could it be compensation for dry gin and that dry Anglo-Saxon brand of humor? Nowhere is there a lower percentage of electric shavers than in the U.S. What's more, bearded Uncle Sam keeps watch over virtually the hairiest male population in our studies. Only Canada – no doubt because of nippy weather, lumberjacks and hirsute trappers – has fewer shaved men. The proportion of shavers to non-shavers, of course, is still heavily on the side of the smoothies. But only 88% of Americans shave, compared to a nearly universal 97% in both Belgium and Japan.

Apparently there's little connection between whether a man shaves, and whether he prefers to shave with a wet blade. It's true that in most places where shaving is practised by 95% or more, the preference is solidly in favor of the electric razor. In Norway, Sweden, West Germany and Belgium, shavers prefer electric about three to two. But in Italy

	U.S.A.	CANADA
	1976	1976
1. Men (%) aged 15 and over who:		
shave regularly	88	87
do not shave regularly	12	13
2. Men (%) aged 15 and over who shave:		
wet	75	60
with an electric razor	25	40

and the U.K. – both big on shaving – the preference is heavily wet, 74% and 72% respectively. Could those stiff-upper-lipped Brits have a secret in common with those devastating wet-lather Latins?

In about half the countries, the preference for electric is very pronounced – about 60% or a bit more. In three places – France, Spain and Japan men are split pretty evenly between wet and dry – perhaps an accurate psychological portrait of their respective climates. But in the U.S., Canada, Australia, Ireland, the U.K. and Italy, there is a very strong preference for the old-fashioned razor blade.

One peculiar fact shown on our table is that though Canadians prefer a blade, they do so to a much smaller degree than men in other non-electric countries. In fact, only 60% of Canadians use soap and blade, while three-quarters of the men in the other "wet" countries do so.

	U.K.	AUSTRALIA	AUSTRIA	BELGIUM	DENMARK	FRANCE	(WEST) GERMANY	IRELAND	ITALY	JAPAN	NETHERLANDS	NORWAY	SPAIN	SWEDEN	SWITZERLAND
	1976	1976	1976	1976	1976	1976	1976	1976	1976	1976	1976	1976	1976	1976	1976
	95	90	91	97	90	94	95	92	96	97+	95	95	90	95	93
	5	10	9	3	10	6	5	8	4	3+	5	5	10	5	7
	72	72	38	40	40	54	41	72	74	51	33	40	48	40	38
	28	28	62	60	60	46	59	28	26	49	67	60	52	60	62

+Aged 18 and over

Maybe Canada's French-speaking population throws off the statistics by shaving dry out of respect for its ancestral country. Canada's shaving habits are remarkably like those of the Americans in terms of whether men shave or not. In fact, these two places are the only ones where more than ten percent don't shave. Yet a full 40% of Canadian shavers have been converted to electric, compared to only 25% in the U.S. Appliance manufacturers looking for growing markets take note!

In conclusion, except for Italy, most of the old-fashioned shavers in the world speak English. Will the sun never set on hot foam and razor? Before any further deductions can be made, we need another set of statistics. Are non-shavers (like Bluebeard) more given to violence? Or more pimples? Or could it be that to shave or not to shave is decided at the whim of fashion as last year's beard gives way to this year's smooth look.

Sources:
Confidential industry sources

353

You can't tell from figures which countries have the most beautiful women. And a good thing too – long may beauty lie in the eye of the beholder. However, we can shed some light on what women use in an attempt to allure.

What do they use most frequently in order to improve upon nature? This table shows that lipstick is the favorite in most countries. Overall, figures for perfume and toilet water are only marginally lower. (Maybe husbands around the world just can't think of anything else to buy their wives at Christmas.) In some countries, such as the U.S. and Switzerland, they're higher than for lipstick.

Women (as % female population over 15) who use:	U.S.A.[+]	CANADA[+]
	1977	1974
make-up base	50	42
face powder	33	NA
lipstick	71	90
rouge; blusher	43	62
mascara	50	67
eye shadow	47	77
perfume; toilet water	85	82

To a large extent the figures for lipstick are reflected in the use of other toiletries. However, there are notable exceptions. For example, Swiss ladies splash on perfume though they're only average users of lipstick. Eye make-up holds little attraction for them and rouge is positively shunned. Swiss women like to complement an outfit with an attractive smell and the fresh-faced look.

Canada is the country of the cupid's bow: 90% of all women wear lipstick. Canadians also wear twice as much eye-shadow as their European sisters. Dutch and English women are Europe's most lavish lipstick-users.

The outdoor girls of Norway are lowest on the list: only 40% of them touch up their lips. Denmark comes next lowest, with a figure of just 43% women who bother to color their lips.

In the U.S., we worry most about keeping those American beauty complexions. One out of two women regularly smoothes on a make-up base whether this is to enhance or improve on their own complexion isn't known.

Overall, the Scandinavian trend is towards the natural look. But the Swedes are the odd women out. They're about average when it comes to the art of the dressing table.

Canadian and American women are the most anxious to improve their looks, with their British and Dutch sisters next in line at the make-up counters.

France's figures are average right across the board. Parisian chic seems to take little more than a pot of make-up base and a dash of lipstick. Clothes obviously play a more important part

U.K.	AUSTRALIA	AUSTRIA	BELGIUM	DENMARK	FRANCE	(WEST) GERMANY	IRELAND	ITALY	JAPAN	NETHERLANDS	NORWAY	SPAIN	SWEDEN	SWITZERLAND
1975	–	1975	1975	1975	1975	1975	1975	–	1975	–	1975	1975	1975	1975
38	NA	30	35	17	47	28	NA	31	NA	28	20	26	48	29
39	NA	29	32	17	28	22	NA	34	NA	29	22	32	43	23
74	NA	57	61	43	68	69	NA	48	NA	76	40	55	67	62
24	NA	21	18	17	17	18	NA	11	NA	14	31	15	14	11
42	NA	28	30	30	39	36	NA	36	NA	42	28	34	46	28
41	NA	26	31	16	37	34	NA	32	NA	43	19	46	44	26
68	NA	63	63	21	58	62	NA	43	NA	76	11	54	62	89

than make-up in creating that famous French look.

More Swiss women wear perfume than any other nationality. In Switzerland, 89% of all women use perfume or toilet water. Americans are second in the sweet-smelling league (85%), and Canadians third with 82%. These are the only exceptionally high figures on the table. The Netherlands are fourth (76%) and the U.K. fifth, with 68%. In France, home of Dior and Chanel, 58% of ladies indulge.

The sporty Scandinavians care least what they smell like. In Norway, only 11% of women use perfume or toilet water. Their neighbors in Denmark come next, with 21%. Those sauna baths must give them confidence.

The figures for Japan, Australia and Ireland just aren't available – we'll never know what really puts the sparkle in those smiling Irish eyes.

Sources:
Euromonitor
+Confidential industry sources

In its efforts to keep abreast of our times *The Book of Numbers* has obtained bra cup sizes on a multinational basis from confidential industry sources. We'd like to maintain that this accurately reflects the female physiognomy on a country by country basis but it just isn't so for a variety of reasons.

In the first place these figures are based on those who buy brassieres, not on the adult female population as a whole – in selected countries a very different matter. Thus, for example, you'll note that in Mexico those with the income to purchase a bra are almost to a woman (91%) in the smaller A or B cup category. The equivalent figure for the United States is 59%. Does this mean American women are that much bustier than their sisters in the South? Hardly, instead it means that in Mexico, with a per capita national income of less than 19% that of the U.S., bra ownership is a decidedly upper income phenomenon. As income increases pulchritude gives way to wellbeing and here the study was conducted amongst bra-owning women. Spain proves the point – 59% of women queried didn't specify their cup size. Modesty, doubtless, is part of the reason (as it is with the secretive Swiss) but another reason is quite simply that many Spanish women don't wear bras.

As you move across the European continent a curious thing happens. The figures show that 14% of French women are C/Ds; across the border to Belgium and the figures jump to 16%, onto the Netherlands and you hit 19%. East Germany and you are up to 23%.

While all of the data on our chart was derived in the same year (1977), the research base isn't comparable in all countries so one has to be careful when drawing conclusions. Given that caveat here are some generalities that do hold true:
* American ladies are substantially bustier than Canadians – about four out of ten U.S. women wear a C or D cup versus three out of ten to the North.
* Australian and Canadian women are almost abreast of one another.
* Japan is the hands down winner in the small cup sweepstakes.
* The French have a firm grip on the B cup category – very nearly seven out of ten are in this group.
* Finally, in the U.S., home of fabled bra burning – 97% of adult females own a bra.

	U.S.A.	CANADA
	1977	1977
Percentage of women who take bra size:		
A cup	15	22
B cup	44	42
C cup	28	22
D cup	10	7

BRA SIZES

U.K.	AUSTRALIA	MEXICO	BELGIUM	DENMARK	FRANCE	(WEST) GERMANY	SOUTH AFRICA	ITALY	JAPAN	NETHERLANDS	NORWAY	SPAIN	SWEDEN	SWITZERLAND
1977	1977	1977	1977	1977	1977	1977	1977	1977	1977	1977	1977	1977	1977	1977
22	23	41	25	4	14	17	26	11	65	32	NA	8	25	17
54	48	50	25	24	69	54	57	29	16	41	NA	13	54	37
17	21	5	16	42	14	23	16	30	NA	19	NA	13	15	12
3	7	4	NA	18	NA	NA	NA	19	NA	NA	NA	7	2	4

NA not available

Sources:

Confidential industry sources

357

If Anita Loos was right, gentlemen prefer blondes. And with that idea in mind, a lot of dark-haired ladies decide to change the color of their hair. On the other hand, a lot of women see themselves as raven-haired beauties – and with the help of a few chemicals, they're able to achieve the desired effect.

From bleach to henna, highlighting to dyeing, hair colorants are big business as both women *and* men strive to improve on what nature gave to them.

Here at home, 45% of women use some sort of hair colorant. This is the highest figure on the table. Bubbling blonde or sultry brunette – the choice is yours, straight from the bottle.

The only country to approach our high figure is Denmark. It's generally assumed that there's an abundance of blondes in the Scandinavian countries. Maybe Danish ladies choose a darker color to stand out from the crowd. Or maybe those natural looks aren't quite as natural as we've been led to believe.

After Denmark, there's a big drop to Austria and Sweden, where 30% of the women use a hair colorant to improve on their crowning glory. In Switzerland and Germany about a quarter of the women change the color of their hair. The U.K. is next at 23%, the same as the Norwegian figure.

That famous French chic obviously isn't the result of the use of chemicals. Only 20% of women dye their hair.

	U.S.A.	CANADA
	1975	–
1. Women (%) who use colorants	45⁺	NA
	1977	1977
2. Average price of a man's haircut (US $)	4.00^0	4.00^0
3. Average price of a shampoo and set (US $)	11.00^0	11.00^0

At 14%, Belgium is right at the bottom of the table. Italy's figure is the same as France's. And Spain's 18% is even lower. It seems that the dark-haired ladies of the Mediterranean countries are quite happy to stay just the way they are. Or perhaps their menfolk don't have that penchant for blondes.

Although you may not feel you need to go as far as to change the color of your hair, you doubtless get your hair done. The next figures show the average price a man pays for a haircut and a woman for a shampoo and set. If you look first at the figures for men, you'll see the Swiss have to pay the most – an average of $7.24. They're followed closely by the Swedes – $7.12. When Delilah sheared Samson's tresses, he lost his strength. Things aren't quite as bad for the men in these two countries, but when they have their hair cut, they sure lose a lot of money.

Japan, where you have to pay $6.95 when you visit the barber, is third. France runs a not very close fourth: Frenchmen pay $1.50 less.

U.K.	AUSTRALIA	AUSTRIA	BELGIUM	DENMARK	FRANCE	(WEST) GERMANY	IRELAND	ITALY	JAPAN	NETHERLANDS	NORWAY	SPAIN	SWEDEN	SWITZERLAND
1975	–	1975	1975	1975	1975	1975	–	1975	–	1975	1975	1975	1975	1975
23	NA	30	14	42	20	24	NA	20	NA	24	23	18	30	26
1977	–	1977	1977	1977	1977	1977	–	1977	1977	1977	1977	1977	1977	1977
5.16	NA	2.12	4.35	5.09	5.44	3.35	NA	3.98	6.95^0	3.99	5.31	1.62	7.12	7.24
5.16	NA	3.54	10.89	7.65	11.08	6.91	NA	7.97	10.20^0	7.39	10.42	4.39	10.70	14.59

NA not available

Sources:
1 Euromonitor
2 & 3 Heron House conversions based on CBI
West European Living Costs, 1977
[+]Industry estimates
[0]Confidential industry sources

Spain is definitely the place to be if your hair needs a lot of attention. There, men only have to pay out $1.62 for a short back and sides or the latest layered look. Here in the U.S., a man pays $4 on average so next time you're on vacation in Spain, pop into the local barber before you head home.

In general, women pay more for a hair-do than men – except in the U.K., where the average prices are identical for men and women: $5.16. Unisex salons are all the rage in London, so maybe the men have to fork out for the privilege of sharing premises with the ladies.

In Switzerland, a woman pays an average of $14.59 for a shampoo and set – double what a man would pay for a haircut. At that price, there can't be all that many regular clients of Swiss hairdressers.

France is the next most costly country in the list. But even so, the French pay about a third less than the Swiss: $11.08. The U.S. and Canada are next. An American or Canadian woman saves only eight cents. A Swedish woman pays $10.70 for a shampoo and set, and a Norwegian $10.42. Of the three Scandinavian countries, women in Denmark get the best deal. They pay an average of $7.65 each.

Austria's the place to go for ladies who want to save money on their hairdressing bills. There a shampoo and set costs just $3.54. Again the Spanish price is cheap: a mere $4.39.

But remember the prices in the table are average. The prices charged in small-town beauty salons are obviously cheaper than those in big cities. If you choose to go to an exclusive salon for your coiffure, be prepared to pay their exclusive prices.

Who's got the squeaky-cleanest hair of all? The best PH factor? The least dandruff? Three leading cosmetics firms provide the information for this earth-shattering study. The main conclusion? In the U.S., Canada, Japan and Sweden, at least 90% of all people use shampoo!

	U.S.A.	CANADA
	1977	1974
1. Adults (%) who use shampoo	90	95
	1976	–
2. Adults (%) with dandruff	14	NA

The Canadians top the list. Only five percent of all Canadians *don't* use shampoo. This gives Canada the shiniest locks in the world. On average, there are twice as many shampoo-shunners in the U.S. as in Canada. (Perhaps, like Telly Savalas and Yul Brynner, they don't *need* shampoo.)

There are some other odd contrasts in these tables. For instance, while 91% of Swedes prefer to use shampoo, only 76% of their Norwegian neighbors lather up. And in spite of their reputation for compulsive cleanliness, the Germans have one of the lower shampoo rates, with only 79%. German frugality may overcome Germanic cleanliness, favoring good old-fashioned water, castile soap and elbow-grease. Who knows? Maybe they wash their hair with beer (long used as a rinse).

In fact, for a fifth of the people in nearly half the places shown, castile soap and elbow grease are the order of the day. But this is much more likely to be true on the European side of the Atlantic. In Ireland, for example, 22% decline to use shampoo. And they're not by any means the lowest on the table.

But before you jump to any snap conclusion about the Irish, take note:

Ireland has less dandruff than any country on our table. In fact, Irish washing habits produce a population that is 90% dandruff-free. Maybe it's all that soft rainwater. Or the therapeutic benefits of Irish Mist.

Like the common cold, and the poor, dandruff is always with us. Unfortunately, there is no sure-fire cure for this perennial blight. Many have been suggested. The Romans used to drink garlic juice to cure the flaky problem.

These days, we stick to external solutions. And our remedies are no longer home-made. We can use one or all of several proprietary treatments. And they all come packaged in shampoos. But how effective is the shampoo solution against the unsightly flaky scalp?

We don't, unfortunately, have dandruff figures for those compulsive Canadian shampoo freaks, or for their equally eager Japanese friends. But in the other heavy shampoo-using countries – the U.S. and Sweden – the dandruff rates are relatively low. The fact is, however, there's no clear-cut correlation between using shampoo and avoiding dandruff.

The Irish are not alone in being able to neglect shampoo without the risk of itchy pates. The Germans also have low dandruff rates. They have the same

SHAMPOOS AND DANDRUFF

	U.K.	AUSTRALIA	AUSTRIA	BELGIUM	DENMARK	FRANCE	IRELAND	(WEST) GERMANY	ITALY	JAPAN	NETHERLANDS	NORWAY	SPAIN	SWEDEN	SWITZERLAND
	1977	–	1976	1976	1976	1976	1976	1976	1976	1977	1976	1976	1976	1976	1976
	84	NA	80	82	87	80	78	79	72	93	89	76	77	91	82
	1976	–	1976	1976	1976	1976	1976	1976	1976	–	1976	1976	1976	1976	1976
	24	NA	21	13	15	30	10	13	21	NA	15	14	20	15	19

proportion of afflicted flakers (13%) as the Belgians, who also place low in the shampoo stakes.

But shampooing habits in countries with moderate dandruff rates (around 15%) vacillate wildly. Of these middling types, over one in four is a non-shampooer. Yet the keen, clean Swedes shampoo at a rate of 91% with almost the same flake figure as Norway.

When we turn the coin over, this discrepancy doesn't quite apply. The scurfier extremes do fall pretty low on the shampoo chart. The worst afflicted places are those where 20% or more of the people admit to a dandruff problem.

Of the countries where a scaly scalp is

Sources:
Confidential industry sources

practically epidemic, the highest suds rate mustered is the 84% in the U.K. Yet the British shoulder snow problem is one of the worst in the world – 24% complain – the second highest rate on the table.

The other flaky four fall even lower in shampoo ratings. Austria has 20% non-shampooers and 21% dandruff sufferers. Spain, with 23% non-soapers, has 20% with itchy scalps. In Italy, only 72% lather up, while 21% scratch. In France, a fifth of all the French surveyed decline to use shampoo – and nearly a third complain of the dreaded dandruff.

Smoking is a worldwide pleasure – or vice, depending on your point of view. We've based the figures in our table on regular smokers, people who smoke three or more cigarettes a day. Our total figures include people who smoke regularly, and that rarer bird – the occasional smoker.

Some of the most interesting figures relate to the U.S. and the U.K. The English and their colonies were among the first smoking enthusiasts in the West.

Today North Americans and the British are the most health-conscious smokers in the world. So it's not completely surprising to find both the U.S. and the U.K. near the bottom of the smoking tables. Just over a third of their populations (37%) smoke. Canada has a higher proportion of smokers – 41%. Something else stands out in the British figures: equality between the sexes. The figures for men and women are exactly equal. In the States, only 34% of women claim to be regular smokers. This trend has been changing over the last ten years. Before tobacco is given up altogether, it's likely that the equality found in the U.K. will apply in the American figures too.

The U.S. is the world's largest single producer of tobacco. This makes it all the more ironic that Americans have lately taken such a puritanical line on smoking. Tobacco is a multi-billion dollar business. Many European governments as well as the Japanese government have state monopolies on the manufacture and sale

Smokers as % of population:[+]	U.S.A.°	CANADA°
	1977	1976
men	41	45
women	34	38
total	37	41

of tobacco products. The tax money that the U.S. government received in taxes on the sale of cigarettes last year is far more than tobacco farmers earned for the sale of the crop!

The French, of course, have a reputation for being great smokers. The cliché is Jean-Paul Belmondo, looking surly, with a Gauloise hanging suggestively from his mouth. And it was a Frenchman – Jean Nicot – who gave his name to the weed in the first place. It's true that the French smoke more than Americans or Britons – but still fewer than half their population, 43%, smoke today. The figure is the same for their neighbors in Germany, though French men, at 57%, have the edge on German men (51%). In both countries, women lag far behind. Are French and German women more sensible – or less liberated?

In Japan it's illegal to smoke before the age of 20. So it's a shock to discover that the Japanese are second on our table. 44% of the total population smoke.

But if you look more closely at the figures you'll see that the sexes are more dramatically split here than anywhere

U.K.×	AUSTRALIA×	AUSTRIA‡	BELGIUM‡	DENMARK‡	FRANCE‡	(WEST) GERMANY×	IRELAND‡	ITALY‡	JAPAN**	NETHERLANDS‡	NORWAY‡	SPAIN‡	SWEDEN‡	SWITZERLAND‡
1976	1977	1976	1977	1974	1975	1976	1977	1977	1977	1974	1977	1974	1977	1977
37	34	49	42	47	57	51	42	45	75	65	46	62	40	37
37	30	26	23	39	30	30	33	19	15	50	39	16	35	28
37	32	37	32	42	43	43	37	32	44	57	42	37	38	33

else. Though an astronomical three out of every four Japanese men smoke, fewer than one in six Japanese women do so.

It's surprising to see that the thrifty Dutch lead in the smoking stakes. They're far ahead of all other countries. Holland is the only country in the world where well over half (57%) of all adults smoke.

It's generally true that more men than women smoke. This applies in Holland too. But Dutch women aren't slow to light up with a higher proportion of smoking women than anywhere else in the world. One out of two Dutch ladies lights up at least three times a day.

They're followed – although not very closely – by Norway, Denmark and Canada, where four out of ten women smoke. In Spain, as in Japan, few women smoke. So if you offer a pack of cigarettes around among the ladies, you're more than three times as likely to have them accepted in Holland as in Spain, and twice as likely in Australia or Canada as in Japan. However, if you're in male company in Japan, you'd better carry plenty of cigarettes with you: they'll go

Sources:

Confidential industry sources

+ *Includes smokers who roll their own cigarettes*

o Aged 18 and over
x Aged 16 and over
‡ Aged 15 and over
** Aged 20 and over

twice as fast as in the U.S. Male smokers from Holland and Spain are the only people who can hope to keep up with the Japanese men.

Overall, the figures on smoking suggest that it is very hard to generalize. The heaviest smokers – Holland and Japan – are utterly different insofar as the habits of their women are concerned. And the places where smoking is least common seem to be wildly different in character. What do Australia, Belgium and Italy have in common? In all three a non-smoker would be happier – less than one third of their populations smokes.

	U.S.A.	CANADA
	1976	**1976**
1. Consumption per person of oil equivalent† (tons)	8.9	9.4
	1975	**1975**
2. Consumption per person of electricity (kw hours⁰)	9.3	11.8

Keeping the world's energy stoked up is a crucial problem. Coal, oil and natural gas are nature's resources – and they run out if exploited too greedily. Industrial nations have all begun to use a newer source of energy – nuclear power, but it isn't without its dangers. In many countries, heavy breeder reactors have met protest.

We all know the chaos that shortages can cause. When the Arab sheikhs stopped the oil flow in 1974, they paralyzed industry and threw governments into disorder. Millions of Europeans faced powercuts and long waits at the gas station. During that bitter winter, many couples discovered that candlelight dinners aren't always so romantic.

The by-products of the oil industry are just as basic to our daily lives as gasoline or fuel oils. Our homes and gardens are full of them: paints, detergents, plastic goods, pesticides.

To estimate energy consumption around the world, the tables use a measurement of a ton of oil equivalent per head. This includes oil, natural gas, solid fuels, water power and nuclear power.

North America is the leading energy user. In 1976, Canada consumed 9.4 tons of oil equivalent per person and the U.S. 8.9 tons per person – nearly twice as much as any other country. In terms of rich natural resources, both Canada and the U.S. are among the world's best-endowed countries. We produce most of our own fuel requirements. But to maintain industrial power in world markets and a high standard of living, we import vast quantities of the world's energy supplies, which we then export as manufactured consumer goods.

Spain, the least industrialized nation in Europe, is at the very bottom of the table. In 1976, each Spaniard got through just two tons of oil equivalent. Ireland and Italy followed with 2.5 and 2.7 tons per person respectively. These countries have remained largely agricultural producers. With few natural energy resources of their own, the road to massive industrialization is a long and expensive one. In the future, there's a possibility of oil off Ireland's Atlantic coast and this could change the picture. As for Spain and Italy, one thing they don't lack is solar energy.

In 1976 Sweden and Norway used more tons of oil equivalent than any other European country. The Swedes used 6.7 tons per person and the Norwegians 5.7, which places them third and fourth overall in the table. The Scandinavians are among the most highly developed industrial European nations and need a lot of power. They were pioneers in the development of hydro-electric power.

ENERGY CONSUMPTION

U.K.	AUSTRALIA	AUSTRIA	BELGIUM	DENMARK	FRANCE	(WEST) GERMANY	IRELAND	ITALY	JAPAN	NETHERLANDS	NORWAY	SPAIN	SWEDEN	SWITZERLAND
1976	1976	1976	1976	1976	1976	1976	1976	1976	1976	1976	1976	1976	1976	1976
4.1	5.2	3.6	5.0	4.2	3.7	4.7	2.5	2.7	3.4	5.2	5.7	2.0	6.7	3.9
1975	1975	1975	1975	1975	1975	1975	1975	1975	1975	1975	1975	1975	1975	1975
4.9	5.2	4.1	4.3	3.5	3.4	5.1	2.6	2.7	4.2	4.0	17.8	2.3	9.6	5.3

And with the North Sea full of Scandinavian oil-rigs, it looks as if they can look forward to an energetic future. Australia is fifth on the table with a consumption of 5.2 tons per person. Yet the country has few natural energy resources of its own. Australians have coal and hydro-electric systems, yes – but oil and natural gas, no. What they do have – and what the rest of the world wants and needs – is vast deposits of essential minerals like lead, zinc, copper and gold. The export of these buys the crude oil and petroleum products which – as with most countries in the world – are Australia's largest single import and essential to its industries and high living standards.

The Norwegians are way ahead in the industrial use of electricity. They used 17.8 hours per person in 1975. Norway has an extensive hydro-electric system, which has been the basis of their industrial prosperity. Canada comes next with 11.8 hours per person and Sweden third with 9.6.

It's interesting that not only does Sweden keep its own lights burning but those of neighboring Denmark as well. Since the Danes have no natural energy

Sources:
1 Organization for Economic Co-operation and Development
2 Euromonitor
+ Includes oil, natural gas, solid fuels, water power, nuclear power.
0 Unit of energy: 1 kilowatt hour = 1000 watts per hour

resources and must import all their fuels, they have to be economical. They're 13th in the table of energy consumption.

Norway and Sweden know how to capitalize on their good luck. They've harnessed those mountain torrents to make electricity and can put fossil fuels to more profitable uses.

The Dutch – high energy consumers with a rate of 5.2 tons per person – are more thrifty when it comes to the industrial use of electricity. In 1975 they used only four kilowatt hours per person. In the energy crisis of 1974, when the rest of Europe was still intent on their family outings, the Dutch banned weekend pleasure motoring and stayed at home. And any ecologist would appreciate all those windmills.

Consumption per person of oil equivalent (tons)

Who are the greediest countries when it comes to consuming the world's energy? North America takes the cake here. Canada tops the list — each Canadian consumes almost ten tons of oil equivalent. No doubt a lot of it goes toward keeping warm during the long cold winters. The U.S. is next. The 8.9 tons per person consumed annually help keep all those television sets, blow-dryers and electric toothbrushes running.

Two Northern nations follow. Sweden and Norway, like Canada, use up a lot of energy just keeping cosy in the winter months. An "odd couple", tiny Belgium and vast Australia, both use about five tons of oil equivalent per person. But there the similarities end.

Consumption is lowest in Spain. The climate is warm and sunny — who wants to consume energy when there's all that free-flowing wine?

10	
9	
8	
7	
6	
5	5.0 5.2
4	
3	
2	2.0
1	

SPAIN	BELGIUM	AUSTRALIA

ENERGY CONSUMPTION

NORWAY	SWEDEN	U.S.	CANADA
5.7	6.7	8.9	9.4

What People Think

In this chapter we're going to look at a wide variety of topics, from a standpoint that probably caused the last argument you got into – personal opinion. Are you in favor of Women's Lib? Do you think most ads are misleading drivel? What do you think about the possibility of a Third World War? These are just three of the topics covered.

Our first sections deal with the most vital area of all – your personal life. Are you the cheerful type who looks on the bright side? Or do you find life a hassle with all those unpaid bills and the rising cost of living as constant worries? You'll be able to see who shares your approach, and whether yours is the majority or minority view.

Then we move into an area of really universal concern – job satisfaction. Let's face it, everybody has gripes about their daily grind. But when you come down to it, a surprising number of people get real satisfaction from their work. That's especially true in certain countries. So have a look at these tables to find out who escapes those Monday morning blues, and who's the most likely to be muttering "Thank God it's Friday," at the end of the week.

But not all jobs are nine to five – ask any housewife. We've devoted part of this chapter to the ladies, taking a look at a very controversial issue – the role of women in society. Obviously, both men and women have strong opinions on this, so we look at polls of both sexes in many countries for a comprehensive view. But bear in mind that these are opinions. What people feel about things isn't necessarily a true reflection of the way things *are*.

Then there's the topic of educational opportunity – do boys stand a better opportunity here than girls? And who has a better chance of succeeding in life – males or females? As you'll see, things are changing rapidly in some societies, while others have remained backward. Where would *you* say that the women are still chained to the sink? Check it out against the table.

That leads us to a particularly argument-provoking section – whether husbands help with household work. Just to make things interesting we show the answers to the same question for both halves of interviewed couples.

Then we move into the larger issue of the community as a whole. Do you think community life is improving? And what about those frightening headlines on crime and civil disorder? Are they accurate reflections of the way *you* feel about life today?

Some say the only solution to the social tensions confronting society is revolutionary extremism. Others favor less drastic reform. Still others think global conflict is the only possible conclusion to it all. In this section, you'll see which views prevail in various nations.

Maybe international tensions would be somewhat eased if we could all communicate with greater ease – so we've looked at how many people in various nations speak a foreign language.

On a less secular note, we've examined the belief in God in the U.S., with results that may well surprise you.

Finally, we have opinions on the opinion-makers. In other words, do you think you're being well-informed by the media, or just led down the garden path?

Everybody regards their own views as important. The sector of society which probably cares most about its opinions is youth. Why? They're just starting out in life, they're filled with idealism and ambition, and they're going to make things work their way.

The last part of this chapter is devoted entirely to the opinions of youth. What they think about the world, what they think about themselves, what they think is wrong with society and how it ought to be changed.

First we profile young people's general outlook on life, and their ideals for happiness – whether they think it's more important to be healthy or rich or intelligent and so on. The next tables deal with satisfaction with society, and then, more practically, how to deal with dissatisfaction in society.

After this, the questions become more specific and searching. There are tables giving figures on attitudes to government, women's role in society, and whether there should be more control of business interests.

Finally, young people tell us about their own problems. What do they consider to be their most vital problems? Finding a job? Deciding which career to take up? Whether they should sleep with their boy/girlfriend? What are their attitudes to education? And are they satisfied with school life?

By the time you've finished this chapter, you should have a pretty good idea of what all sorts of people think about all sorts of things. We're willing to bet it'll change a few of your own opinions – even if they're only opinions about what people think.

If you're searching for happiness, you don't have far to go. The U.S. has more very happy people (40%) than any other country on our table. (After all, the right to happiness is written into our Constitution). Another 50% of Americans, though not quite so contented, describe themselves as fairly happy. That leaves only about ten percent who feel they have cause to grumble. We've been getting steadily happier since the early 1970s. Most of us think things are better than five years ago: we were at the top of the happiness list then.

All in all, we have a lot going for us including the highest standard of living in the world. The U.S. is still the land of opppportunity – there are more careers open to the average American than there are to residents of many other countries.

Obviously things aren't so gloomy over in Britain as we often suppose. Just about as many people in the U.K. as in the U.S. feel that the good times are really rolling.

Fewer people feel completely happy in the Scandinavian countries, though as many people as elsewhere feel fairly content with their day-to-day lives.

Figures for Italy and Japan give a much less rosy picture. In both countries, less than ten percent of people can find much to cheer about. In Italy, nearly a third of the population is unhappy.

Almost without exception, the people who are happiest now are the most optimistic about their lives in five years time. However, it's a cautious optimism. There's no country where people expect times to be as bright in the future as they are now. In general, only about half the people who feel happy now expect future happiness.

	U.S.A.	CANADA
1. People (%) who rate their present personal happiness as:+		
very happy	40	36
fairly happy	50	59
not very happy	9	4
2. People (%) who rate their personal happiness five years ago as:0		
very happy	11	7
fairly happy	43	51
not very happy	38	38
unhappy	4	3
3. People (%) who think their personal happiness five years from now will rate as:x		
very happy	22	20
fairly happy	52	66
not very happy	17	11
unhappy	3	2

U.K.	AUSTRALIA	BENELUX	FRANCE	(WEST) GERMANY	E.E.C.	ITALY	JAPAN	SCANDINAVIA
38	37	34	22	12	22	9	9	28
54	57	58	66	63	60	59	56	67
7	6	8	10	19	16	31	23	4
4	7	5	6	4	5	4	2	10
55	51	41	47	53	49	41	42	59
38	35	48	42	36	41	50	54	28
2	3	6	5	3	4	6	2	2
14	20	7	10	9	11	9	3	12
64	66	55	47	61	56	53	55	73
16	8	29	29	22	25	30	38	8
3	2	4	3	*	2	5	4	*

*0.5 or less

Source:
Gallup International affiliated institutes in the countries concerned
The poll was conducted during winter 1974-75 and spring 1976.
+The question asked: "Generally speaking, how happy would you say you are: very happy, fairly happy, or not very happy?"
0The original question used a mountain card and asked: "On which step would you say you stood five years ago?" We have interpreted the mountain card so that level 1 = "very happy"; levels 2-5 = "fairly happy"; levels 6-9 = "not very happy"; levels 10-11 = "unhappy". Totals do not add up to 100 as there is a small proportion of "don't knows" and "no answers".
xThe original question used a mountain card and asked: "Just give me your best guess on which step you think you will stand in the future, say, about five years from now." We have interpreted the levels in the same way as for the question above.

Scandinavians are the leading optimists on our table. At 61%, that's more than three out of every five people in Denmark, Sweden and Norway who think life has improved over the last five years. Optimism is certainly reflected in the second part of this table. The cost of living (and food) is the biggest problem in that part of the world – yet fewer than three Scandinavians in ten rate it on top of their anxiety list. They're very near the bottom for all the "worry" figures except two: 12% think unemployment is the most important problem facing them today – and 11% aren't satisfied with the way they're governed.

If you take an overall look at the "worry" figures, you'll see that most people in most countries worry most about food prices and the high cost of living.

Just under one American in every two (49%) thinks that conditions are worse today than they were five years ago. And the U.K. follows close behind (43%). In both these countries nearly two-thirds find the cost of living a major concern. Strangely enough, only 15% of Americans gave unemployment as their country's most important problem.

The West Germans are far more equable: 49% believe life has improved, and less than half (42%) find that a visit to the supermarket makes their blood pressure soar. But 39% lose sleep worrying about unemployment.

The French can remember better days: 43% feel that life has gone to the dogs lately. However, less than a third (32%) think the price of a *Boeuf Bourguignonne* cause for serious complaint.

More Italians than any other nationality – 53% – think life has deteriorated over the past few years. But the cost of living and food aren't major worries. Only 35% of Italians complain about the price of pasta. On the other hand, 21%

	U.S.A.	CANADA
1. People (%) who think living conditions are:+		
better than five years ago	33	43
worse than five years ago	49	30
same as five years ago	14	25
don't know/no answer	4	2
2. People (%) who think the most important problem facing their country is:0		
high cost of living/food	63	60
unemployment	15	15
unsatisfactory government	19	10
crime; violence	7	3
energy crisis	4	2
strikes	*	7
environment, pollution	2	1

U.K.	AUSTRALIA	BENELUX	SCANDINAVIA	FRANCE	(WEST) GERMANY	EEC	ITALY	JAPAN	NETHERLANDS
34	54	31	61	24	49	34	28	50	
43	29	34	13	43	18	38	53	22	
18	13	35	24	28	32	25	15	23	
5	4	0	2	5	3	3	3	5	
62	56	39	28	32	42	43	35	64	22
15	19	46	12	34	39	24	14	2	57
6	15	4	11	5	3	9	21	21	15[x]
5	0	5	4	1	5	8	23	*	6
4	*	2	7	11	1	4	1	10	—
17	7	1	0	3	0	5	5	1	—
0	2	4	11	1	5	2	*	8	6

[x] The question referred to the housing shortage   — Question not asked
* 0.5 or less

Source:
Gallup International affiliated institutes in the countries concerned
Polls for both questions were conducted during winter 1974-75 and spring 1976, except
in the Netherlands where the date is spring 1977.
[+] The question asked: "Do you think that living conditions for people like yourself
in this country are better or worse than they were 5 years ago?"
[0] The question asked: "In your opinion, what is the most important problem facing
your country today?" The responses given in our table are taken from a more
exhaustive list.

think crime and violence a cause for concern – the highest scores on the table.

All in all, if you look at the figures on our table the Scandinavians are most contented with their lot and the prize for pessimism goes to the Italians.

The top figures on the table are satisfaction ratings on standard of living. As such, they represent our countries' answers to the most common questions, "How are you doing?"

The answer in Scandinavia is "very well" with over eight out of 10 citizens expressing some degree of overall satisfaction and one out of three saying they're very satisfied compared with a low seven percent in France, eight percent in Japan.

Among English-speaking countries the overall satisfaction order is Australia, U.S., Canada and U.K. So younger societies with room to expand do seem to have special attractions.

Looked at the other way round Japan, Italy and France are all countries where just under six out of ten citizens are unhappy with their present way of life.

A family's standard of living is clearly affected by the number of children sired. That makes the figures shown for desired number of children by country surprising. The concept of zero population growth has a long way to go in many of our countries. In Australia, for example, three out of ten respondents want four or more children. While back here at home about one out of five North Americans is in this category.

Quite clearly there appears to be a correlation between desired children and available space. This cuts both ways. 68% of U.K. citizens and 65% of those in Benelux opt for one or two child families.

Japan is an odd man out here. The country is cramped yet 56% want three or more children.

The Germans' interest in keeping family size down is also notable. It shows in their overall population decline (see population table).

Overall it's surprising how few people want to have just one child or remain childless. Given today's widespread use of planned parenthood methods, this is a realistic alternative. Clearly it often doesn't happen by choice.

	U.S.A.	CANADA
1. Satisfaction with standard of living:[+]		
very satisfied (%)	26	24
satisfied (%)	20	24
quite satisfied (%)	13	19
dissatisfied (%)	30	26
very dissatisfied (%)	10	6
2. Ideal number of children:[0]		
1 (%)	3	3
2 (%)	52	44
3 (%)	19	22
4 - 7 or more (%)	18	22
0 (%)	2	2
don't know/no answer (%)	6	7

U.K.	AUSTRALIA	BENELUX	SCANDINAVIA	FRANCE	(WEST) GERMANY	EEC	ITALY	JAPAN
16	31	19	33	7	18	15	14	8
23	26	17	32	15	26	19	12	19
18	15	26	19	19	21	19	15	14
36	22	28	15	47	33	38	45	32
6	6	6	1	11	2	9	13	7
4	2	6	3	3	7	5	7	*
64	38	59	55	53	67	60	60	41
14	25	18	31	33	17	21	21	41
13	29	5	6	4	5	7	8	15
3	2	7	3	2	2	3	1	*
2	4	5	2	3	2	3	3	3

*0.5 or less

Source:
Gallup International affiliated institutes in the countries concerned
The poll was conducted during winter 1974-75 and spring 1976.
[+]The original question used a mountain card and asked: "Considering everything, how satisfied or dissatisfied are you with your standard of living? Just point to the step that comes closest to how satisfied or dissatisfied you feel. Remember the higher the step the more satisfied, the lower the step the more dissatisfied!" We have interpreted the mountain cards so that levels 1 - 2 = very satisfied; level 3 = satisfied; level 4 = quite satisfied; levels 5 - 7 = dissatisfied; levels 8 - 11 = very dissatisfied. Totals do not up to 100 because there is a small proportion of "don't knows" and "no answers".
[0]The original question asked: "If a young married couple could have as many or as few children as they wanted during their lifetime, what number would you, yourself, suggest?"

The Japanese are the biggest worriers when it comes to facing those monthly bills. Even though Japan's economy is booming, 41% are afraid of not having enough yen in their paycheck to pay for what they need. And well over one family in ten says it can't afford adequate nourishment.

If they suddenly had a lot more money, the majority of Japanese would invest it. Only five percent would spent the extra cash on food and other necessities.

In Italy, things seem to be a bit easier on the pocket, yet three people in ten worry about household bills most of the time. Almost a third of all Italians – more than in any other country – would spend a windfall on improving their housing.

We come third on the list of worry-warts. More than a quarter of all Americans worry about paying their bills. And about twice as many people in the U.S. as anywhere else (except Italy and Japan) are occasionally unable to buy food. We're the worst off nation when it comes to health care too – three out of every 20 of us just can't pay the ever-increasing costs of medical attention and hospitalization.

About a third of all Americans would invest their extra dollars. One out of five would buy necessities, and 28% would squander their windfall on travel and luxuries.

More than one person in five feels the pinch of economic deprivation in the U.K. and France. There's one consolation here: the British have almost no worries about medical expenses, thanks to their comprehensive national health system.

The easy-going Australians worry least about family finances – 57% of them hardly give the matter a thought.

	U.S.A.	CANADA
1. People who worry about money:[+]		
all and most of the time (%)	26	15
some of the time (%)	36	30
almost never (%)	38	51
2. Economic deprivation:[0]		
people (%) who have been unable to buy food	14	6
people (%) who have been unable to pay for medical/health care	15	4
3. What people would do with extra money:[X]		
save; invest in business, farming (%)	32	40
buy essentials (%)	21	10
buy new house; repair present house; move to new home or community (%)	21	23
travel; buy non-essentials (%)	28	48
pay bills (%)	13	5

MONEY WORRIES

U.K.	AUSTRALIA	BENELUX	SCANDINAVIA	FRANCE	(WEST) GERMANY	E.E.C.	ITALY	JAPAN
22	12	9	17	22	10	19	29	41
34	31	34	40	37	33	36	39	44
43	57	56	43	35	55	43	32	14
8	4	4	6	6	7	8	15	14
1	4	6	2	8	1	5	9	5
33	46	32	23	32	41	34	27	61
26	5	11	9	24	16	19	16	5
22	16	22	28	28	20	24	32	17
37	34	29	43	29	34	31	23	20
2	6	*	5	*	2	1	1	*

*0.5 or less

Source:
Gallup International affiliated institutes in the countries concerned
The poll was conducted during winter 1974-75 and spring 1976. The questions asked:
+"How often do you worry that your total family income will not be enough to meet your family's expenses and bills?"
0"Have there been times during the last year when you did not have enough money to buy the food your family needed? When you did not have enough money to pay for medical health care?"
x"Suppose you had more money, say twice as much as you have now. What would you do with it?"
Totals do not add up to 100 as the answers used in this table have been extracted from more extensive questionnaires.

Everyone has family problems. They worry about not having enough money, or losing their jobs; about illness in the family or trouble with the children.

Americans are the biggest worriers of all. We score a total of 86% for all the problems on the table. Family finance is our greatest worry. This means trouble for about 40% of us, compared with 30% in the U.K. and only 12% in Germany. For the entire E.E.C., the figure is 18% of the population who think they have money problems. One reason for the high U.S. figure is that our economy is less stable, and we're protected by fewer social welfare and health care programs than most European countries.

The French are the next biggest worriers (79%), followed by the Japanese (77%) and the Italians (75%) each. The Scandinavians have the fewest family worries (51%), with Benelux citizens (54%) and the Australians (55%) just above them.

When it comes to family illness, the West Germans, who are lowest in financial worries (12%), take top position (24%), closely followed by the French with 20%. Health care costs are extremely high in both countries. There clearly aren't many health worries for the English (nine percent), or for the Scandinavians and the Japanese, both with eight percent. It obviously helps if you have a ubiquitous health service, or a large corporation to care for you.

	U.S.A.	CANADA
1. People (%) who think their most important family problem is:[+]		
finance	40	25
illness in the family	13	10
rearing/disciplining/communicating with children	8	5
unemployment	8	5
family (social/in-laws)	5	4
shortage of food/clothing; others	11	18

What about problems with children? The Italians come top with 23%. It figures. With all the hijacking and bombings they're having in Italy, you'd probably worry too. The Japanese figure is also high (19%); maybe this is one of the problems caused by the country's emergence from centuries of tradition. Sixteen percent of the French have cause for concern over their children. Canadians (five percent) and Americans (ten percent), have few worries about their offspring. Peace and happiness reigns in the family on our side of the Atlantic. Perhaps we're a bit better at communicating with our children. Only three percent of people in Japan and nine percent in France worry about unemployment. Even in Italy – the country with the highest figure for unemployment worries – it's only 11% and for the whole of the E.E.C., it's eight percent. Japan and Australia have the lowest figure here: only three percent worry about unemployment. People in the U.K. – which is supposed to have a very bad unem-

U.K.	AUSTRALIA	BENELUX	SCANDINAVIA	FRANCE	(WEST) GERMANY	EEC.	ITALY	JAPAN
30	23	13	14	19	12	18	17	30
9	10	14	8	20	24	17	15	8
7	7	11	6	16	10	13	23	19
6	3	4	4	9	10	8	11	3
6	3	3	2	5	7	5	7	2
8	9	9	17	10	1	6	2	15

Source:
Gallup International affiliated institutes in the countries concerned
The poll was conducted during winter 1974-75 and spring 1976.
[+]The question asked: "What is the most important problem facing your family at this time?"
Totals do not add up because of a high proportion of "no problems" and "no answers".

ployment problem – don't seem very concerned either: the U.K. figure is only six percent. But then even if you *are* unemployed in the U.K., the state will provide enough money for you to live on.

What about all those mother-in-law jokes? As you can see from the table, in Japan and Scandinavia (two percent) and Benelux countries and Australia (three percent), the in-law problem doesn't really exist. And in West Germany and Italy – the countries with the highest figures – only seven percent admit to family difficulties. In Germany, the father is very much the head of the household and the close-knit Italian family is a well-known concept. Maybe this emphasis on the family unit causes problems for its members.

However, people do worry about feeding and clothing their families. For example, in Canada and Scandinavia, nearly one person in five has difficulty in balancing his budget. Yet these are two of the richest countries in the world. Japan is third here with 15%, followed by the U.S. with 11%. Again, neither Japan nor the U.S. is known for its poverty.

Surprisingly, Italy – generally regarded as a relatively poor country – comes second lowest in this category: only two percent worry about food and clothes. Only West Germany is lower (one percent.) Perhaps this reflects the Italians' priorities – with so much to worry about in society at large, they don't have time to worry about things closer to home.

Worriers are distinctly in the minority these days. In most countries, two out of three people say they take life as it comes and don't spend a lot of time fretting about it. However, this generally cheery state of affairs doesn't prevail equally throughout the world. People living in English-speaking countries – the U.S., Canada, Australia and the U.K. – appear to take life pretty much as it comes. Contrary to all popular mythology, the gloomiest domain is France: a startling 50% of the population questioned admitted that they're habitual worriers. This pervasive dejection sends the average worrying quotient of the E.E.C. up to 39% – several points higher than the scores of most individual member countries.

	U.S.A.	CANADA
1. People (%) who worry a lot[+]	34	36
take life as it comes	64	62
don't know/no answer	2	2
2. People (%) who think their life is:[0]		
very interesting	36	30
fairly interesting	52	59
fairly dull	8	9
very dull	4	2
don't know/no answer	*	*

If Gallic insouciance is at an unexpected low, the dark clouds don't stop at the French border. The Italians are second among the worry-warts in the survey. In the land once known for *la dolce vita*, 45% of people questioned confessed that they worry a lot.

The second category on this table shows whether people find their lives interesting or dull. It correlates with, and perhaps helps to explain, the fretful state of affairs among the French and the Italians. In a sharp blow to conventional stereotypes, about a third of the Italians questioned described life as fairly or very dull, and a quarter of the French felt the same way. Perhaps we must say *au revoir* to the much-vaunted Latin *joie de vivre*.

The other spot on the globe where people find life notably lack-luster is Japan; again, a quarter of the citizens find life fairly dull; and the same number confess that they worry a lot. But a further 27% either didn't know or wouldn't tell whether they worry a lot. (In most other countries, only one to five percent didn't answer the question.)

When you consult the figures for Australia, the U.S. and Canada, the level of worriers goes up to about 35% – but the number of people who find life interesting also takes a mighty leap upwards. Ninety-two percent of Australians fall into this enthusiastic group, while the

	U.K.	AUSTRALIA	BENELUX	E.E.C.	FRANCE	(WEST) GERMANY	ITALY	JAPAN	SCANDINAVIA
	31	35	42	39	50	31	45	25	34
	65	63	57	56	45	62	51	48	64
	4	2	1	5	5	7	4	27	2
	28	30	30	20	14	19	14	6	26
	54	62	55	56	60	57	53	67	65
	16	6	11	20	22	19	28	25	8
	2	2	2	3	3	2	5	2	1
	0	0	2	1	1	3	*	*	*

*0.5 or less

Americans and Canadians are just a few points behind. Perhaps this has something to do with their frontier heritage.

Clearly, the overwhelming majority of people everywhere do find life fairly interesting. The teasing differences – the enigmas – lie at the extreme ends of the spectrum. While approximately the same number of people both in the U.K. and in Italy find their lives fairly interesting, fully twice as many of the British find their lot in life very interesting. And similarly, more than twice as many Italians find things very dull.

The last hurrah definitely comes from the world's younger countries. With unmatched zest, a third of Americans, Canadians and Australians describe their lives as very interesting indeed.

Source:
Gallup International affiliated institutes in the countries concerned
The poll was conducted during winter 1974-75 and spring 1976.
+The question asked: "Would you say you worry a lot or that you take life as it comes?"
0The question asked: "Would you say that your life at this time is very interesting, fairly interesting, fairly dull or very dull?"

The Scandinavians are at the top of the league when it comes to enjoying work. Fifty-five percent find nothing at all to complain about in their jobs. Perhaps it's all that clean fresh air and modern working conditions. In Scandinavia, employers try to keep their workers happy by varying the dull routine of the assembly line. This seems to work. Only three percent of the entire work force are dissatisfied and frustrated with their jobs.

	U.S.A.	CANADA
1. Satisfaction with employment: [+]		
very satisfied (%)	49	46
satisfied (%)	46	45
dissatisfied (%)	5	9
2. Choice of occupation if re-starting working life: [0]		
present job (%)	51	46
different job (%)	41	42

Job satisfaction in Scandinavia isn't unanimous. Forty-eight percent of workers say they'd choose a different kind of job altogether if they had a chance.

Australia is the next most contented country. Exactly half of all Aussies say things are just great at work down under – they have no complaints.

Here in the U.S., most of us also appear to whistle while we work. Only one out of 20 is a grumbler – the other 19 are either satisfied or very satisfied with their jobs. More than half of all Americans want to stay in their present jobs, and only 41% would choose a different one if they were starting out all over again – a rather surprising statistic for our mobile, job-hopping society.

In the U.K. only three percent of workers are grumblers. The other 97% are either satisfied or very satisfied with the way they earn their livings.

Other happy fellows are the Canadians and workers in the Benlux countries. West Germans aren't far behind.

Who has the longest faces when it comes to clocking in on Monday morning? The French are in the lead. Only one Frenchman in four shows enthusiasm for his work. Japan and Italy, where the figure is one out of three, tie for second place. The highest percentages of people stuck in jobs they hate are in France and Canada (nine percent), with Australia (eight percent) coming second and Italy (seven percent) third.

Only 28% of workers in Japan would choose the same job over again. Despite this sign of discontent, the number of workers who'd opt for another line of work is small – a mere 38%. These figures and the large number of "don't knows" and "no answers", probably reflect the fact that in Japan job mobility is virtually nil. If you're Japanese, going to work is almost like joining a family. You sign on with a company when you leave school and stay with it all your life. Evidently, this system doesn't greatly please the average Japanese.

U.K.	AUSTRALIA	BENELUX	SCANDINAVIA	FRANCE	(WEST) GERMANY	E.E.C.	ITALY	JAPAN
49	50	46	55	25	44	41	33	33
48	42	50	42	66	55	55	60	64
3	8	4	3	9	1	4	7	3
45	54	57	46	48	53	50	50	28
45	40	40	48	48	39	43	43	38

Source:
Gallup International affiliated institutes in the countries concerned
The poll was conducted during winter 1974-75 and spring 1976.
[+]The original question used a mountain card and asked: "How satisfied are you with your present work, that is, your main employment? If you are extremely satisfied point to the top of the mountain, if very dissatisfied point to the bottom. If you are satisfied with some parts of it and dissatisfied with others, point to some step that comes closest to how satisfied you are with your job. Remember, the higher the step the more satisfied you are, the lower the step the more dissatisfied." We have interpreted the mountain card so that levels 1-3 = very satisfied; levels 4-8 = satisfied; levels 9-11 = dissatisfied.
[o]The question asked: "If you had the chance to start your working life over again would you choose the same kind of work you are doing now or not?"
Totals do not add up to 100 because there is a small proportion of "don't knows" and "no answers".

Is woman's role in the world really changing? Or are things much the way they've always been – despite all the talk of women's liberation?

It seems that woman's role in society is changing most in the U.S. – according to 63% of American men and women.

There's no doubt that America has a more flexible society than many European nations. Life styles have changed enormously – and frequently – in the last 200 years. That means women's life styles too. Compare this with a country like Spain or Italy, where a woman's place has been in the home for centuries. Here in the U.S., women simply have a less rigid tradition to fight against when they choose to play a more dominant role in society.

U.S. women also have easier access to higher education than many Europeans. That means they're better equipped to take jobs outside the home and so make their influence felt.

The next highest figure is for the Scandinavian countries. In Denmark, Sweden and Norway, nearly half of the population feels that the role a woman plays in society is changing rapidly. If we include those who think things have changed a fair amount, that's 80%. Only one percent feel things haven't changed at all, the identical figure to the U.S. and U.K.. The Scandinavian countries like the British and Americans have an advanced social outlook. Their well-

People (%) who think the part played by women in their country is changing:[+]	U.S.A.	CANADA
	1976	1976
a great deal	63	45
a fair amount	28	42
not much	6	11
not at all	1	1
don't know	2	1

known liberal views obviously include an openness to social change that's reflected in these figures. They also have a high standard of living – and a healthy economy certainly creates more opportunities for women who want to get out of the home and play a more active role in society.

Canada is next: 45% think that things are changing a great deal for women, and nearly as many more think that a fair amount of change is taking place. At a total of 87%, the Canadian figures are close to the American ones. Of course, in many ways the two countries are alike. One difference might be found in the majority of French-speaking Canadians. A clue is that in France only 38% of the population thinks their women's roles have felt the winds of change. But French women play a greater part in the running of society than is often realized.

In the U.K., 82% of the people feel that the position of women has changed. Like

384

	AUSTRALIA	BENELUX	FRANCE	INDIA	ITALY	JAPAN	SCANDINAVIA
U.K.							
1976	1976	1976	1976	1976	1976	1976	1976
39	33	31	38	17	32	23	47
43	49	43	41	29	50	48	33
13	14	21	16	18	9	17	18
1	2	2	1	6	2	4	1
4	2	3	4	30	7	8	1

the U.S., the U.K. has passed legislation to guarantee equal opportunities for women. This alone suggests a readiness for social change even though Britain is not yet in the forefront of the women's liberation movement.

India is one of the few countries which has had a woman prime minister – Mrs. Indira Ghandi led India for over five years. Yet only 17% of Indian citizens think she changed women's role in society to any great extent. Six percent don't think things have changed at all – a higher percentage than in any other country. That's understandable, since a large percentage of the population still lives in villages, where the traditional way of life is slow to change. Isolation from the influences that affect Western society may account for the very large percentage (30%) of Indians who don't really know which way things are going regarding women's roles.

Japan is also quite low in the table.

Source:
Gallup International affiliated institutes in the countries concerned
[+]The question asked: "Do you think that the part played by women in your country is changing a great deal, a fair amount, not much, or not at all?"

Less than a quarter of the population thinks that any dramatic changes have taken place, and four percent are quite sure they haven't. That's surprising when you consider the massive changes that have occured in Japanese society since the end of World War II. The powerful Western influences on the Japanese haven't yet managed to alter the female role of graceful flower-arranger and tea-pourer in favor of something more dynamic. The Japanese have traditionally felt that a woman's place is in the home...and it looks as though that's where she's going to stay.

From the early suffragettes to women's lib, the campaigners for equal rights for women have made themselves a powerful force.

In the U.S. it's illegal to discriminate against women in employment. Here and in Canada, it's illegal even to advertise a job as specifically requiring a man. But is this enough? Do women in most countries have equal job opportunities or not? That's what this table tries to answer. Those who answered "no" were then asked "Do you think women should have equal opportunities or not?"

	U.S.A.	CANADA
	1976	1976
1. People (%) who agree women have equal job opportunities with men[+]	48	44
disagree	48	50
don't know	4	6
2. People who agree women should have equal job opportunities with men[0]	39	42
disagree	8	7
don't know	1	1

It's quite a surprise to find the Italians at the top of the league (at least in their own eyes) for equal job opportunities. Fifty-five percent of those questioned thought that women had equal opportunities. It could be just wishful thinking. Or maybe Italy's fiery women's lib movement has achieved some of its goals. If you look into those Italian figures more closely it seems that the latter is the case.

We're next in line when it comes to satisfaction with the way things are going for women. Forty-eight percent of us thought women have equal job opportunities with men.

Australia (third on the table), like the U.S., is a relatively new society where traditional roles are changing rapidly. Forty-six percent thought that women have equal job opportunities.

The Australian figure of 46% is closely followed by the one for India – 45%.

Many upper caste Indian women are encouraged to enter the professions.

Where do most people think women get a raw deal? In West Germany, 64% of those polled thought they don't get an even break – even though those ladies play a large part in German industry.

The Japanese agree with the Germans. Sixty-two percent are convinced that women don't get equal job opportunities. Japan has traditionally always been a male-oriented society. Things are changing, though. This may in part be due to the strong influence that the U.S. has had on Japanese culture since the end of World War II. The women's lib movement there is fanatical and strong – and it needs to be. Although Japanese business methods are extremely up-to-date, many of the old social attitudes are taking a long, long time to die. A large number of Japanese – 16% – said that they didn't know whether

EQUALITY AT WORK

AUSTRALIA	INDIA	BENELUX	U.K.	FRANCE	(WEST) GERMANY	SCANDINAVIA	ITALY	JAPAN
1976	1976	1976	1976	1976	1976	1976	1976	1976
46	45	40	38	37	31	36	55	22
49	34	58	54	58	64	60	36	62
5	21	2	8	5	5	4	9	16
40	20	48	41	51	57	55	27	34
9	11	8	8	5	6	4	8	22
*	3	2	5	2	1	1	1	6

*Less than 1%

Source:
Gallup International affiliated institutes in the countries concerned
+The question asked: "Do you think that women in your country have equal job opportunities with men?"
0The question asked (of respondents who answered 'no' to the previous question): "Do you feel that women should have equal job opportunities with men?" Figures are expressed as percentages of total original sample.

women have equal job opportunities or not. The same sort of reaction exists in India where 21% of people said they didn't know.

Scandinavians rank third (60%) in believing that men retain the advantage when it comes to job opportunity – though Scandinavian women have seemingly been treated as equals for many years. Maybe it was easy enough to get the basic equalities, but Swedish women (like their German neighbors) now demand *complete* equality in *every* field.

People who thought women didn't get equal job opportunities were also asked whether they thought they should. The most "yes" answers came from countries where a high proportion of people thought women weren't getting a square deal. West Germany heads the list with 57%, and Sweden comes a close second with 55%. France is third with 51%, and the Benelux group is fifth (48%). (Here in the U.S., the vast majority (39%) of those who thought women don't have equal job opportunities felt they should.)

American men were asked whether they'd educate their daughter or their son if the daughter were the better student. Forty-two percent of the men surveyed said they'd give their son the advantage of an education – even if the daughter were brighter. The women didn't stand behind their bright daughters either. Thirty percent of the women surveyed would favor a fair to middling male over a budding Marie Curie. (A breakdown by age group is not available for the U.S. – partly because all people asked were parents.)

The U.K. results were more conservative. Only half the men surveyed thought clever girls should have equal opportunity. And only six percent more of that supposedly enlightened age group of under-25s would send the daughter rather than the son to university. British women voted for the fair sex only three points higher than the men. And the younger British women had an even lower percentage than the men overall!

Italian women had the most liberal ideas of equality of education on the basis of merit. Young Italian women were the most willing to stand up for their right to be educated equally with their brothers. And 63% of Italian men under 25 agreed that the smartest child should be given an education.

	U.S.A.[+]	U.K.
	1976	1975
"Parents who can afford to pay for only one of their children to study should decide in favor of the girl if she does better at school than the boy." Men who agree (%):		
total	58	50
under 25 years	–	56
over 55 years	–	49
Women who agree (%):		
total	70	53
under 25 years	–	48
over 55 years	–	44

West Germany voted primarily for equality. Among young German men, 81% believed education should be given on merit, not sex. Young German women were more conservative than the men, only 69% responded favorably.

The French figures present yet another topsy-turvy result. Sixty-seven percent of men, overall, favor equality – the highest figure, and equal to German men overall. But while the younger men only just matched the total figure, the older French men (those over 55) opted 71% for a fair approach to the education of girls. Similarly, older French women, though with a lower figure than the men, have the highest preference for equality.

EDUCATIONAL EQUALITY

BELGIUM	DENMARK	FRANCE	(WEST) GERMANY	IRELAND	ITALY	NETHERLANDS
1975	1975	1975	1975	1975	1975	1975
51	59	67	67	56	64	50
54	55	67	81	47	63	46
44	57	71	63	60	58	48
46	67	66	68	54	65	48
57	62	60	69	55	72	59
36	58	68	58	51	61	39

Sources:
Commission of the European Communities, 1975
+General Mills Inc, 9200 Wayzata Boulevard, Minnesota, 554400
The original question asked in the US was: "Which children should go to college — the sons or the best students?" The possible responses were "sons", "best students", "not sure". The response, "best students", corresponds to the European response, "favorable" towards the decision to pay for the girl's education if she is better than the boy. Only parents were interviewed in the U.S.; "men" corresponds to "fathers" and "women" to "mothers" for the U.S. only.

France is one of the four places where more men than women opted for equal opportunity. Two others – Holland and Belgium – fall in the middle of the table. Half the Dutch men said yes.

The largest crop of budding male chauvinists belong to the Netherlands and Ireland. At 46% and 47% each voting for equality, over half the fathers of the next generation will favor their sons over their daughters when it comes to educating their children.

This table is a barometer showing how attitudes differ between the sexes. Do people think men or women have more opportunity to succeed in life? It's not a test of the relative "equality" between the sexes, but the *idea* of success as it varies from country to country.

In the U.S., 64% of the women tested think they have at least as much, or more, opportunity to succeed as a man. About 31% of them feel disadvantaged in this respect. American men are less optimistic. Only 53% feel that women are as likely to succeed. Three percent more women than men think women have a better chance. This may be the result of actual changes in opportunity – or a new confidence brought about by increased awareness.

The battle between the sexes is fought more evenly in the U.K. Almost half of both men and women feel that opportunities are about the same. An equal number of men and women surveyed think that women have the advantage. But two percent more men think males have the edge in the success stakes. The Dutch figures are roughly the same as the British ones.

A few more women in the Netherlands than in the U.K. feel that chances are about the same for both men and women. But a little over a third of both sexes feel

	U.S.A.	U.K.
	1974	1975
"Women of between 20 and 30 years of age have as much, more, or less, opportunity than men of the same age to succeed in life?"		
as much opportunity (%) total		48
men	48	47
women	56	49
more opportunity (%) total		8
men	5	8
women	8	8
less opportunity (%) total		35
men	42	36
women	31	34

that women are less likely to succeed than men.

In West Germany, the men think more positively about the opportunities of German women. Fifty-two percent of German men think things are more or less equal, while 47% of German women agree. Forty-three percent of German women actually think men have a better chance.

The least optimistic women are the Irish. Nearly half the Irish women think they're less likely to succeed than their menfolk. And only 43% think they've even got a 50-50 chance. Ironically, a

	BELGIUM	DENMARK	FRANCE	(WEST) GERMANY	IRELAND	ITALY	NETHERLANDS
	1975	1975	1975	1975	1975	1975	1975
	53	55	55	49	44	42	49
	55	56	55	52	45	41	48
	51	55	54	47	43	44	50
	6	3	5	6	6	23	6
	7	2	5	6	10	23	7
	6	3	6	5	4	23	5
	32	32	36	41	47	31	35
	30	31	37	38	44	32	35
	33	32	35	43	49	30	34

Sources:
Commission of the European Communities, 1975
+Roper Organization Inc.
The original question asked in the US was: "Are there more advantages in being a man or a woman?". The possible responses were "more advantages in being a man" (which corresponds here to "women have less opportunity"), "more advantages in being a woman" ("women have more opportunity") and "no more advantages in being one than the other" ("women have as much opportunity") Five per cent each of men and women answered "don't know".

large percentage of Irish men actually think women have a better chance to succeed in life.

The most eccentric figures are those for Italy. A low 42% of all Italians surveyed think the chances are equal between men and women. And 31% believe women are disadvantaged. But a remarkable 23% of both men and women think women are better off.

Compared to the U.S., Europe is the stronghold of male chauvinism. In all the eight nations surveyed, more men would place their confidence in a member of their own sex to represent them in Parliament than in a woman. In the U.S., only a small minority (ten percent) of men would not vote for their party candidate if a woman were nominated. The European preference was most marked in Germany. Over half the German men questioned favored male politicians. (In fact, the Germans were at the top of the list in feeling a woman's place is in the home.)

However, 41% of German men thought there was no difference in the degree of confidence they'd have in a man or a woman politician, over half the French, and English agreed.

Perhaps European men are being falsely accused. Across the board almost as many European women preferred a man to represent them in government, reinforcing a conservative attitude in many families. Yet even in a male-oriented society like Italy's, almost one man in ten said he'd *prefer* a woman to represent him in parliament. This just might reflect the Italian's utter disdain of their government. Or it may be a healthy reflection of growing egalitarian values. Almost 40% of Italian males surveyed agreed that there was no difference

	U.S.A.	U.K.
	1976	1975
Reactions to voting for a woman if she were running for Parliament[+]/ Congress[0]:		
would prefer a man (%)		
men	10	37
women	8	31
would prefer a woman (%)		
men	88	5
women	89	12
no difference (%)		
men	–	53
women	–	52

between a male and a female when it came to representation in government – so much for Italian chauvinism.

Some European women are raising their voices and helping to change values in their societies. In Italy, 15% of the women surveyed felt more enthusiastic about having a female represent them in parliament than a man. Their Irish sisters were even more outspoken: 24% preferred to see one of their own sex in a position of political power. It seems that a female backlash has taken place in countries where women have been traditionally the most domesticated. In the conservative Netherlands, only four percent of the women surveyed thought a

WOMEN IN POLITICS

	BELGIUM	DENMARK	FRANCE	(WEST) GERMANY	IRELAND	ITALY	NETHERLANDS
	1975	1975	1975	1975	1975	1975	1975
	42	20	35	53	42	47	28
	35	15	28	37	33	41	23
	4	4	7	2	10	9	3
	8	6	9	8	24	15	4
	46	70	51	41	45	38	57
	48	73	56	50	40	40	59

— Question not asked

Sources:
[+]Commission of the European Communities, 1975
The original question asked: "In general, would you have more confidence in a man or a woman as your representative in Parliament?"
[0]The Gallup Organization Inc, 1976
The original question asked in the U.S. was: "If your party nominated a woman to run for Congress from your district, would you vote for her if she were qualified for the job?" The response "yes" corresponds here to "would prefer a woman", "no" to "would prefer a man". Totals do not add up to 100 because there is a small proportion of "don't knows".

woman in politics deserved their confidence. Does contentment or apathy account for the striking difference in attitude?

The Danes have the most liberal attitude of all the European countries on the table. The great majority of both Danish men and women don't think sex is an important issue in choosing a political representative.

The Americans are even more liberated. The vast majority of American men and women wouldn't hesitate to vote for a female Congressional candidate.

"A woman's work is seldom done – by her husband" (to rephrase an old saying). Although many men would probably tell a different tale.

The table on the right shows that European couples just don't agree on the touchy subject of how often a husband lends his wife a helping hand. In every country, however many men there are who think they help around the house, fewer women would agree with them.

In the U.K., 65% of men thought that they helped round the house "frequently" or "occasionally". Only 54.5% of British wives agreed. It seems highly likely that 10.5% of British married couples spend a lot of time arguing about labor.

Husbands who help in household work (men's/women's responses):[+]	U.K.
frequently	
male (%)	35.9
female (%)	22.7
occasionally	
male (%)	29.1
female (%)	31.8
never	
male (%)	9.2
female (%)	15.3
no answer	
male (%)	0.6
female (%)	1.3

Italian men obviously believe that housework is a woman's area. Only 9.6% of them claim they help round the house "frequently" and only 8.1% of their wives agree. Over 35% of them say they wield a duster "occasionally", but seeing as just 21% of Italian women would endorse this statement, they must overestimate their usefulness.

Men in Holland are the most industrious when it comes to housework – both in their own eyes and in the eyes of their wives. Over 75% claim to help round the house "frequently" or "occasionally" and over 63% of Dutch women would agree. But that still leaves 12.6% of husbands in the Netherlands who think they work harder than they actually do. Or maybe there's a lot of Dutch ladies who don't fully appreciate their men.

The smallest disparity in the figures comes in Ireland: 46.2% of Irishmen think they're helpful round the house and 41.6% of their wives agree. However, when you consider that apart from the Italians, the Irish men are the most unhelpful in the table, it doesn't necessarily mean that there are fewer arguments about whether or not husbands in Ireland are pulling their weight.

BELGIUM	DENMARK	FRANCE	(WEST) GERMANY	IRELAND	ITALY	NETHERLANDS
26.3	–	30.1	20.5	17.8	9.6	33.3
18.1	28.4	19.6	14.8	14.0	8.1	21.2
30.0	–	34.5	40.9	28.4	35.3	42.4
26.0	25.7	31.4	35.7	27.6	21.0	41.9
11.7	–	8.0	9.3	9.0	19.6	4.7
20.0	15.7	19.2	15.1	13.0	29.6	14.2
1.0	–	3.8	1.3	0.2	0.4	1.0
1.0	3.3	0.5	0.4	0.8	1.5	1.1

—*Question not asked*

Source:
Commission of the European Communities
[+]The question asked (of married women): "Does your husband ever help you with the household work? If yes, frequently or occasionally?" Married men were asked: "Do you help with household work? If yes, frequently or occasionally?"
Percentages do not add up to 100 as the proportion of unmarried respondents has been omitted.

It's just as well we don't have the U.S. figures on the table. In general, Europe doesn't have the many hours of sport on T.V. that act as an excuse for idle American husbands.

Whatever the country, it looks like the men are doing work round the house of which their wives are unaware. Or maybe they think they've done their share every time they wash up a beer glass.

Our house is our home. It's the place where most of us spend most of our time, the place we can relax, the center of our personal and family life. But what makes people satisfied with their "dwelling" and dissatisfied with their home? Whether they live in harmony with the people they share it with? Or whether it's as good as the one next door or opposite?

Satisfaction with housing:[+]	U.S.A.	CANADA
very satisfied (%)	24	21
satisfied (%)	52	62
quite dissatisfied (%)	21	15
dissatisfied (%)	2	2

The Scandinavians are at the top of the table. They're satisfied with the houses they call home. Over nine out of every ten Scandinavians are either very satisfied or reasonably satisfied with their dwellings.

The Japanese aren't as satisfied with their homes as the Scandinavians. Only one percent of the population are very satisfied with their dwellings. And almost half are reasonably dissatisfied. The top one percent may correspond to the well-paid management of Japan's successful industries. Spacious homes, servants, cars, and even homes away from home, are perks the company often takes care of. The 49% who aren't so happy may be victims of chronic over-crowding.

People in the U.S. and Canada generally like the humble castle they call home. In the U.S. almost one in four is very satisfied and two out of three reasonably satisfied – adding up to over three out of every four who like their homes. In Canada one in five is very satisfied and two-thirds generally satisfied – a grand total of 83% who like the place where they live.

In the U.S., however, almost as many people are reasonably dissatisfied as are very satisfied. You can't win 'em all. Maybe the reasons are legitimate – pointing out the discrepancy between rich and poor in the U.S. Or perhaps the reasons are based on subjective feelings that color everyone's appraisal of the place he lives in.

In terms of housing, Australians are a happy lot. A total of 84% are either very satisfied or reasonably satisfied with their homes.

Two out of three people in France are reasonably satisfied with their housing, which is more than any other country in this category. The Germans are just slightly less enthusiastic. Almost a third of Italians are reasonably dissatisfied with their homes. Many Italian cities have become extremely crowded in the past few decades as workers fled north to the cities to find jobs.

In the U.K., 17% feel that their housing is very good and 59% think it's reasonably alright. Some Brits disagree – over one in five think their dwellings are less than great.

In the E.E.C. category, 16% of the people are very satisfied and 60% reasonably satisfied with their homes – a total of 76%. The same as in the U.S.

SATISFACTION WITH HOUSING

U.K.	AUSTRALIA	BENELUX	SCANDINAVIA	FRANCE	(WEST) GERMANY	E.E.C.	ITALY	JAPAN
17	20	15	27	12	19	16	10	1
59	64	63	64	66	62	60	54	45
21	14	17	8	21	17	20	31	49
2	1	5	1	1	1	3	4	5

Source:
Gallup International affiliated institutes in the countries concerned
The poll was conducted during winter 1974-75 and spring 1976.
[+]The original question used a mountain card and asked: "Considering everything, how satisfied or dissatisfied are you with your present housing? Just point to the step on the card that comes closest to how you feel. Remember, the higher the step the more satisfied, the lower the step the more dissatisfied." We have interpreted the mountain card so that level 1 = very satisfied; levels 2-5 = satisfied; levels 6-9 = quite dissatisfied; levels 10-11 = dissatisfied. Totals do not add up to 100 because there is a small proportion of "don't knows" and "no answers".

397

The question of economic growth has crept out of the classrooms and cabinet meetings and into the minds of the common people. Many people have become aware that the whole issue of growth is more than a theoretical or ideological debate. Industry as we have know it for 200 years is based on resources that are fast running out. And soon we may have to decide either to change the material basis of our society, or to gear the system down.

	U.S.A.	CANADA
Increased industrialization is desirable:+		
people who agree (%)	52	71
people who disagree (%)	40	23
don't know/no answer (%)	8	6

This table shows how people feel about this situation – a test of each country's economic optimism.

The first striking difference is the disparity between the American and Canadian view of the future. What does this suggest? Only about half of all Americans want more industry, but over 70% of Canadians do. Many Americans approve of the industrial system at its present level but think additional growth would saturate the market with produce. Or perhaps we're more concerned about ecological balance and protection of the environment than our northern neighbors. Perhaps the Canadians are more enthusastic than us about factories since they have yet to exploit the industrial potential of their vast un-developed areas.

Italians are the only people who're more enthusiastic than Canadians about industrial expansion. Three-fourths of all Italians want more factories. And it's not hard to see why. Of all the countries in Europe, Italy suffers one of the worst unemployment problems.

Italy has also been slower to develop industries than its northern European neighbors, partly due to lack of natural resources. Conversely, it has some of the most lax environmental protection laws of the countries listed and has experienced disastrous industrial accidents.

The French also have a high percentage (71%) of people favoring more industries. Like Italy, France was reasonably slow to industrialize.

About two out of every three Australians (63%) hope for more industry. But they've got a lot of room in which to manoeuvre. Australia has a young and enthusiastic population and they're growing at a vigorous rate. What's more, they have the raw materials to support new industry. So their positive attitude might not be altered by the harsh reality of increased industralization.

The Japanese at 27% are the least enthusiastic about industralization. Since the end of World War II, this country has experienced almost unimaginable growth, and in a mere three decades, has been transformed from a feudal land to a world industrial power. In terms of traditional values, the cost has been high. With crowded, noisy cities, industrial pollution and a pace equal to that of New

U.K.	AUSTRALIA	BENELUX	SCANDINAVIA	FRANCE	(WEST) GERMANY	E.E.C.	ITALY	JAPAN
31	63	49	55	71	34	52	75	27
53	33	47	34	21	50	37	18	57
16	4	4	11	8	16	11	7	16

York, the urban Japanese may be nostalgic for the old order.

The Japanese also fall into another interesting group among the countries on the table. In the U.K., West Germany and Japan, the same number of people weren't sure how they feel about the question of further industrialization. Sixteen percent either didn't know or didn't answer. But industry in the three countries developed at completely different times. By the time Japan started its rocket trip to economic success, British industry had been long established. And in the case of Britain, there's some question of whether or not the old-fashioned forms of industry are still viable. Yet new sources of oil make the U.K. ripe for new and greater industrial development. Perhaps West Germany's indecision is due to a desire to maintain its position in world markets while wishing to avoid more noise, pollution and the other costs of industry.

In the rest of northern Europe, opinion is more evenly divided – much more like the American view. In Scandinavia, the pro-industry figure is 55%. In the Benelux countries, 49% agree and 47% don't. And four percent just don't know or didn't answer.

Source:
Gallup International affiliated institutes in the countries concerned
The poll was conducted during winter 1974-75 and spring 1976.
[+]The original question asked: "Do you wish there were more industries and factories in this country or not?"

	U.S.A.	CANADA
Quality of community life in 1974-76 compared with 5 years previously		
better (%)	33	40
worse (%)	27	22
same (%)	28	22
don't know/no answer (%)	12	16

Worldwide inflation. The oil crisis. Bankrupt cities. Political mayhem. Yet hope springs eternal. People in every country on the table, except the U.K., feel their community life has improved in the last five years. Who would have thought that almost half the Italians could feel this way? Yet they do. It may be their buoyant sense of life keeps them happy. Maybe a high carbohydrate diet is the secret – or centuries of glorious culture to uplift their spirits. Whatever it is, the Italians feel better about their community life than any people on the table.

In the U.K., more people feel community life is declining than think it's improving. This survey was taken at a low ebb in British fortunes. The pound was declining. World-wide, prices were rising. Labor and racial strife were taking their toll. Perhaps now that North Sea oil has begun to lubricate the British life style, people in Britain would vote differently from the way they did when the survey was taken.

In the U.S., one in three of us felt community life was improving. But almost as many felt it was going the other way, or staying the same. The U.S. is far more stable in the late 70s than it was in the 60s. But you can't satisfy everyone. Problems with school, housing developments (or lack of them), and environmental pollution (no improvements) are all factors that influence our feelings about our community.

Japan and Germany both register a strong vote of confidence in feeling better about their communities than they did five years ago. They should, if their community life reflects the success of their international economic positions and the strength of their currencies. They have every reason to feel good about themselves.

But even where the vote is for "better," a large group sometimes opts for the "worse" category. While more Italians feel better about their communities than any other country studied, more Italians also feel *worse* than any other people on the table. This is because fewer Italians voted for "the same" category – a fact consistent with the Italian character. Why give a passive answer when you can vote "for" or "against" and find an opportunity to get really involved?

Only seven percent of the Germans polled felt that community life was declining. But three times as many Japanese were pessimistic. Maybe many people regret the breakdown of the traditional Japanese way of life. Japan's development into a 20th-century industrial nation was made at a much greater

U.K.	AUSTRALIA	BENELUX	SCANDINAVIA	FRANCE	(WEST) GERMANY	E.E.C.	ITALY	JAPAN
24	45	29	37	29	37	33	46	30
27	17	18	12	20	7	20	28	21
35	27	50	44	37	51	38	19	42
14	11	3	7	14	4	9	7	7

cost in terms of cultural disruption than in most western countries. Perhaps this has affected their estimation of their community life.

The Australians come after Italy, with almost half the population feeling that community life had improved. Canada was third, with 40%. It makes sense. Both Canada and Australia are large countries. They're rich in natural resources. They're stable socially and politically, despite a few thorny domestic issues. They have most of the advantages of modern western countries with few of the disadvantages. They certainly deserve to feel satisfied and optimistic.

Other statistics worth comparing are those of the E.E.C. (European Economic Community) and the U.S. In both groups, a third of the population thinks community life is improving. Perhaps this is not a coincidence. With any statistical study, the larger the group involved, the more the irregularities get evened out. Smaller groups show greater variety of opinion. Local opinion in America fluctuates similarly. People in a small town in the Midwest may feel more secure about

Source:
Gallup International affiliated institutes in the countries concerned
The poll was conducted during winter 1974-75 and spring 1976.
+The question asked: "In your opinion is (name of community) a better place or a worse place for people like yourself to live in than it was 5 years ago?"

their community than people in New York or Detroit. But lumped together, the diverse opinions of all those Americans fall out fairly evenly into clear-cut categories. The same happens with a numerically large group like the E.E.C. All the specific opinions of southern Italian farmers and Breton fishermen and Parisian students and workers from a factory in the Ruhr Valley meld together. We're left with a broad overview of the general feelings of the European Community. The majority feels things are the same; one in three thinks things are getting better; and one in five feels community life is worse than it was five years ago.

How frightened are we by crime? And to what degree are our fears justified?

In the U.S., 17% of those questioned had suffered from a burglary or an attempted one in the last five years. The highest rate in the table.

We also have the highest figure for stolen property, with 26% of the people questioned reporting a theft during the last five years.

Australia is second in both categories, Canada third and well below U.S. rates.

In burglaries the U.K. is modestly above her European counterparts, while for stolen property the British are higher than all save Scandinavia.

Only three per cent of Japanese have confronted a burglary or attempt and they're second lowest for stolen property.

Italy at second lowest in the burglary category is a real surprise. The same holds true of physical assaults. You're three or four times more apt to be physically assaulted in the English speaking world than in Italy. Only Benelux has lower assault figures.

However, in all our standard countries assault is low – no more than five of a hundred people need fear assault during any given year. Surprisingly, the placid British are well above all their Common Market counterparts. A careful analysis of the underlying facts and figures shows that this is a Northern Irish and Scottish

	U.S.A.	CANADA
1. People who, during the last five years, have[+]:		
had their home broken into or an attempt made (%)	17	12
had property stolen from themselves or their family (%)	26	21
been physically assaulted (%)	4	5
2. Fear of walking alone at night within about a mile of home[o]:		
afraid (%)	41	31
not afraid (%)	56	66
don't know/no answer (%)	4	3

phenomenon.

Astonishingly, fear of crime doesn't appear to be related very closely to the actuality. The highest fear of crime is in the Benelux countries. There 46% of the people questioned are afraid of being physically assaulted. And, these countries aren't known for their violence.

Next highest comes West Germany where 45% of the people questioned afraid of physical assault. Yet physical assault is comparatively unknown in Germany, as well as in Belgium and Holland.

The least fearful people are the Scandinavians. And here the lack of fear of being attacked hardly seems justified. Second lowest are Canadians, where 66% are not afraid. Third comes Australia where the figures is 64%. Once again lack of fear seems unjustified by figures for actual assault.

U.K.	AUSTRALIA	BENELUX	SCANDINAVIA	FRANCE	(WEST) GERMANY	EEC.	ITALY	JAPAN
9	14	7	8	8	5	7	4	3
16	25	2	18	11	8	11	11	7
5	5	*	4	3	2	3	1	2
34	33	46	26	36	45	39	35	33
62	64	53	71	58	51	57	60	63
4	3	1	3	6	4	4	5	4

*0.5 or less

Source:
Gallup International affiliated institutes in the countries concerned

The poll was conducted during winter 1974-75 and spring 1976.

+ The original question asked: "During the last five years, have any of these happened to you: Had your home broken into or had an attempt made? Had money or property stolen from you or any other household members? Been personally physically assaulted?"

0 The original question asked: "Is there any place around here — that is within 20 minutes walk — where you would be afraid to walk alone for fear of being physically attacked?"

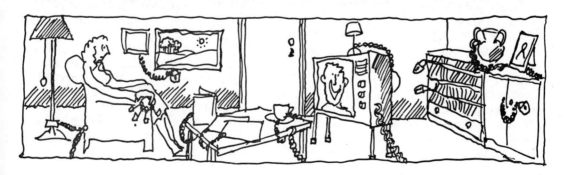

If you believe in revolution, you're an extremist. If you believe in defending your society against "all subversive forces", you're also an extremist. Statistically, you belong on the extreme end of popular o p i n i o n, w h e r e revolutionaries and reactionaries begin to look alike.

Revolutionary extremists tend to be left-wing and are mostly active in right-wing or democratic societies. People in Western countries who believe that society must be changed through revolution incline towards anarchy or extreme Marxism of some kind. Statistics aren't available for Russia. Presumably, revolutionary Soviets are fighting to move their society further to the right. However, in China, considered by some to be the most left-wing country in the world, some "revolutionaries" are pressing to move the government further left. At this point, "left" and "right" as political terms become meaningless.

This table gives a general picture of the political views of eight European countries. Predictably, in the democratic West, moderation takes the day. In 1977, over half those polled in all countries except West Germany voted for improvement through social change. However, fewer people voted for moderation than seven years previously. In West Germany, 30% fewer people voted for social change in 1977 than in 1970,

	U.K.
1. People (%) who thought society should be changed by revolution, in: +	
1977	6
1970	7^x
2. People (%) who thought society should be defended against subversion, in: ^{0}	
1977	28
1970	25^x

throwing their vote to the right – in favor of defending society against "subversive forces".

Italians are responding to their economic and political crisis by turning the other way: ten percent of those polled in 1977 thought that revolution was the only answer – three percent more than in 1970.

So did confidence in the power of gradual social change. The Dutch lost faith by 20% between 1970 and 1977; turning to a conservative standpoint by a dramatic 22%. Right-wing opinion in Italy also increased by 16%. A society under stress always tends to polarize.

After Italy, the French rate of revolutionary thinking is the highest – up by three percent since 1970. The reactionary rate – people who believe in defending society against subversion – went up by ten percent.

BELGIUM	DENMARK	FRANCE	(WEST) GERMANY	IRELAND	ITALY	NETHERLANDS
4	3	8	2	7	10	4
3	4^x	5	2	7	7	6
19	40	22	50	26	27	37
14	38^x	12	20	23	11	15

^{x}1976

Source:
Euro-Barometre 8, 1978
Polls were mainly conducted in February/March 1970 and October/November 1977.
Respondents were shown a card and told: "On this card are basic kinds of attitudes vis-à-vis the society we live in. Please choose the one which best describes your own opinion." The statements on the card read:
+"The entire way our society is organized must be radically changed by revolutionary action."
0"Our present society must be valiantly defended against all subversive forces."

How much real civil tension is there in Europe today? Is it so bad that there's a possibility of the breakdown of civil order within the next ten years?

This table shows that most Europeans would answer "no" to these questions – although there are exceptions.

Over 63% of Italians think that civil disorder in the next ten years is either "certain", "very possible" or "possible" – almost ten percent of them think there's no doubt that it'll happen. But then there's already civil disorder there at the moment: the *Brigate Rosse* and other terrorist groups have nearly paralyzed the country on several occasions.

The Netherlands is the second most pessimistic country: over 37% of the people polled think that the breakdown of civil order is "very possible" in the next ten years and the combined figure for "certain", "very possible" and "possible" is only two percent behind that of the Italians. The Netherlands has recently experienced savage attacks by South Moluccan terrorists in their attempt to gain independence from formerly Dutch Indonesia.

Overall, France is the next most pessimistic country. In 1968 Parisian students took over the capital – something that hadn't happened in Western Europe for decades. In the Pyrenees, also, the Basque nationalists are waging a sporadic war for independence.

	U.K.
	1977
People (%) who think that, in the next ten years, civil disorder is:+	
certain	8.5
very possible	26.4
possible	15.9
unlikely	28.2
impossible	16.3
don't know/no answer	4.6

The U.K. isn't without its problems: Northern Ireland is being torn apart in a tragic civil war. Racial tension between whites and immigrants from India, Pakistan, Africa and the Caribbean also flares up from time to time – especially when the economy's down and competition for jobs is fierce. Nearly 51% think there's a threat of civil disorder.

The Irish are the most confident that they won't have to face the breakdown of order in the next ten years: just over 53% think it's "unlikely" or "impossible". The Danes aren't far behind them at 53%. In fact only 36% of the Danes think there is any risk at all of civil disorder – the lowest figure on the table.

Today's world is changing and complex, so it might be sensible to assess not *whether* various countries will experience civil disorder, but how often it will occur – and whether or not people think that it will be contained.

BELGIUM	DENMARK	FRANCE	(WEST) GERMANY	IRELAND	ITALY	NETHERLANDS
1977	1977	1977	1977	1977	1977	1977
3.1	5.6	3.8	3.7	4.8	9.7	4.0
28.9	14.9	27.8	27.8	19.6	39.3	37.2
14.7	15.5	21.7	17.5	15.1	14.5	20.3
25.0	30.3	30.1	41.0	25.8	26.3	32.2
14.5	22.8	6.1	5.2	27.8	7.7	4.6
13.8	10.7	10.4	4.7	6.7	2.7	1.9

Source:
Euro Barometre 8, 1978
[+]People were shown a card upon which were printed the numbers 100, 90, 80, down to 0 and asked: "Using this scale, could you indicate to what extent you think there is a danger over the next ten years of an increase in tensions in (your country) leading to actual civil disorder."
We have interpreted the card so that level 100 = certain; levels 90-60 = very possible; level 50 = possible; levels 40-10 = unlikely and level 0 = impossible.

War is no longer the romantic charge of the light brigade. It's a grisly, depersonalized prospect – the fingers on the buttons, the intercontinental ballistic missiles, the nuclear devastation of major cities, megadeaths and massive radiation levels – possibly even the extinction of life on the planet. We all know what lies in store for us if the world goes to war again. Even the most hawkish politicians no longer advocate it, recognizing mega – madness for what it is.

But the dangers of war still remain too apparent. The superpowers continue a billion-dollar and billion-rouble arms race. And the arsenals of the world grow larger and more explosive every day. The world is also full of hot spots where the clash of interests between the superpowers may escalate into a major confrontation.

How long can we be sure that there will be no fatal misunderstandings? No major blunder that'll take us all past the point of no return?

From the look of the figures in the table, most Europeans are mildly optimistic about world stability. Nearly half the people questioned in the U.K., Ireland and Denmark feel it's impossible that there will be a world war in the next ten years. The Danes are the most optimistic – nearly 48% of them think war is an impossibility.

Italy, West Germany and France also vote in favor of world sanity. Of all

People (%) who think that, in the next ten years, world war is:[+]	U.K. 1977
certain	3.6
very possible	8.5
possible	10.0
unlikely	27.0
impossible	44.6
don't know/no answer	6.2

Italians polled three-quarters think that a Third World War in the next ten years is either unlikely or impossible. Yet 23% of the Italians feel war is certain, very possible or possible – a few points more than the West Germans.

The West Germans seem surprisingly optimistic, considering their vulnerable geographical position. If war were to break out between East and West, the Germans would be on the front line. But they've got more troops stationed in their country than any other in Western Europe (with large treaty contingents from the U.S., the U.K. and France). Perhaps this accounts for their feeling of optimism and security.

The second highest figure in the unlikely category is for the Netherlands. More than 45% of the Dutch are confident that there will be no war.

The French are also optimistic. Roughly two out of three Frenchmen

THIRD WORLD WAR

BELGIUM	DENMARK	FRANCE	(WEST) GERMANY	IRELAND	ITALY	NETHERLANDS
1977	1977	1977	1977	1977	1977	1977
3.3	3.2	2.3	1.8	2.6	2.7	1.9
14.2	5.6	10.1	10.3	10.1	11.2	14.5
11.5	9.5	14.2	9.3	10.7	8.8	19.0
29.7	19.1	33.3	49.5	25.2	35.7	45.1
26.9	47.9	28.1	21.0	46.1	38.6	16.5
14.5	14.6	11.9	8.0	5.1	3.0	2.9

surveyed doubt that war is in the offing. The Belgians are less positive; over half vote for world stability. But a quarter recognise the possibility of a holocaust and a sixth don't know.

Where are the most people who suspect there'll be a world war in the next ten years? Even in the most pessimistic countries the figures are low. In the Netherlands and Belgium just over 14% are fairly certain there'll be a world war within the next decade.

In all the other countries that gloomy view is shared by an average of about ten percent of people. The striking exception is Denmark, where only one person in 20 thinks disaster is lurking just around the corner.

How many are "absolutely certain" there will be a world war in the next ten years? In the U.K. almost four per-cent talk of the end of civilization, the gloomiest record on the table.

Source:
Euro-Barometre 8 1978
+People were shown a card upon which were printed the numbers 100, 90, 80, down to 0 and asked: "Here is a sort of scale. Would you, with the help of this card, tell me how you assess the chances of a world war breaking out within the next ten years." We have interpreted the card so that level 100 = certain; level 90-60 = very possible; level 50 = possible; levels 40-10 = unlikely and level 0 = impossible

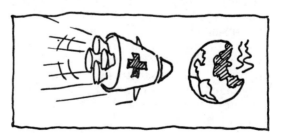

People usually learn to speak a different language because they want to go to a foreign country and be understood, or the foreign land has come to them – in the form of immigrants or neighbors.

In the U.S., both categories maintain. A very large percentage (59%) of Americans speak no second language at all. The land is immense. And unlike Europe, you have to go vast distances to actually need another language. But many Americans have brought a second language with them – from Italy, Puerto Rico, Mexico, Japan, China, Poland and virtually every other place. In some cases, the "mother tongue" is lost by the second generation. But in many families, the Old World language is kept alive in the home, over plates of pasta, *enchiladas* or egg foo yung.

The second language spoken most extensively in the U.S. is Spanish, virtually an official second tongue in Texas, California, New York and other places where Mexican and Puerto Rican immigrants have settled *en masse*.

The British are notorious xenophobes, with something of an island isolationist mentality. Fewer Britons speak a second language than Americans. But when they do, they tend to speak about the weather in French.

In Canada ten percent more people speak a second language than in the U.S.. Mostly French. Five out of six two-language Canadians share French and English. Officially Canada is bilingual, with many French-speaking citizens in Quebec and the Maritime provinces. If the French separatists have their way, Canadian will soon be spelt Québecois!

In Australia, the mix is somewhat wider, although French is still the preferred second language. The Aussies do have a large number in the "all other" category – a reflection of polyglot immigration and the variety of the languages of their Pacific neighbors.

In the Benelux countries, English, French and German are often spoken

	U.S.A.	CANADA
1. People who can speak a foreign language (%):[+]	38	48
2. Number of people (%) who can speak:[+]		
English	2	19
French	9	18
German	9	7
Spanish	12	2
Arabic	1	*
Portuguese	*	0
other	10	8
no answer	1	3
3. People who can't speak a foreign language (%):[+]	59	52

U.K.	AUSTRALIA	BENELUX	SCANDINAVIA	FRANCE	(WEST) GERMANY	E.E.C.	ITALY	JAPAN
32	37	64	64	43	37	40	38	13
1	2	39	48	23	31	20	14	12
22	19	33	10	2	11	17	26	*
7	10	46	34	12	1	10	6	*
2	2	1	3	12	0	4	2	0
0	1	0	0	4	0	1	0	0
0	0	0	*	*	1	*	*	*
6	12	5	13	7	4	5	2	1
2	*	2	12	0	2	2	1	*
68	63	36	36	57	63	59	62	87

*0.5 or less

interchangeably. Though in Flemish-speaking parts of Belgium, it's politically indiscreet to speak French.

In Scandinavia, as in the Benelux countries, multi-lingual speech is the rule rather than the exception. English is most widely spoken there as a second language. And many Scandinavians speak another Scandinavian language, or they speak German.

In terms of *bons mots*, France and Germany have squared off against each other regularly for the last 150 years. Even with peace and the Common Market, only slightly more than ten percent speak each other's language.

The least linguistically adventurous

Source:
Gallup International affiliated institutes in the countries concerned
The poll was conducted during winter 1974-75 and spring 1976.
+The original question asked: "Can you speak or understand any other languages besides your own language? If yes: which languages?"

people in the table are the Japanese, also traditionally xenophobic. A tiny 13% of them know a second language, although trade, the strength of the yen, and the world-wide invasion of Japanese tourists are beginning to bring "Hi" and "O.K." to the Land of the Rising Sun.

If you ever want to open a travel agency, open it in Scandinavia or France – potentially the most profitable countries for such an undertaking. Inside every Scandinavian there is a Viking trying to escape. Given time, opportunity and money, 84% of Norwegians, Swedes and Danes would choose to travel to other countries. The U.S. is their most popular choice.

The French (also 84%) have the same trans-Atlantic inclinations. Spain is their second choice. Maybe they are hoping to avoid all the Canadian tourists who choose France.

Most of us don't think of the U.S. as a tourist country, so it's flattering to see that most nationalities pick the U.S. as their destination.

How do Americans themselves feel about traveling. Only 68% of us want to leave our own shores – the eighth highest figure on the table. Thirty-one percent don't feel any wanderlust at all. That's the next highest number of stay-at-homes after the Japanese. Of those who want to travel, the majority (13%) pick the U.K.

The next most popular choice is Italy (ten percent). No doubt this is because so many of us are of Italian ancestry. Canada is our least favorite destination.

The average Australian is travel-mad. Eighty-three percent said they'd like to travel, preferably to the U.K. or U.S.

	U.S.A.	CANADA
1. People (%) who want to travel[+]	68	79
don't want to travel	31	18
2. People (%) who would like to travel to:[0]		
US	–	12
France	9	18
UK	13	14
Italy	10	4
Spain	5	3
USSR	4	3
Switzerland	5	5
Canada	2	–
Australia	5	9
Japan	8	3

Seventy-nine percent of Canadians want to travel – the fourth highest figure on the table. Their choice of countries is a direct reflection of their origins. Eighteen percent want to visit France and 14% the U.K. The higher figure for France isn't surprising. French is taught as a second language in all Canadian schools. Their third choice is the U.S.. Twelve percent of Canadians feel the urge to explore more of the North American continent.

Twenty-one percent of the British put the U.S. in first place as the nation they would most like to visit. Many British would also like to visit their emigrated friends and relatives in Australia.

U.K.	AUSTRALIA	BENELUX	E.E.C.	FRANCE	(WEST) GERMANY	ITALY	JAPAN	SCANDINAVIA
74	83	70	74	84	67	73	42	84
24	15	30	24	16	30	23	49	14
21	21	9	20	16	25	22	13	23
6	4	8	7	—	8	12	4	8
—	26	2	4	2	4	11	2	12
6	5	8	6	8	9	—	6	9
5	3	13	9	11	11	7	—	13
5	3	3	6	8	5	8	1	9
7	3	9	5	2	5	5	7	6
12	4	2	6	5	5	3	2	3
14	—	2	5	1	3	1	1	5
7	11	2	5	8	4	2	—	7

—Respondents' own country

Source:
Gallup International affiliated institutes in the countries concerned
The survey was conducted during winter 1974-75 and spring 1976.
[+]The question asked: "If you had the time, money and opportunity, would you like to travel to other countries of the world or not?" Totals do not add up to 100 because of a proportion of "don't knows" and "no answers".
[0]The question asked (of respondents who answered 'yes' to the previous question): "To which countries would you like to travel?" Answers have been extracted from a more extensive questionnaire.

A mere five percent of those polled in the U.K. chose Spain as the country they'd most like to visit. Rather surprising when you consider the number of package tours to the Costa del Sol and think how easy Spain is on the battered British pocketbook.

Most Japanese are anti-travel. Only 42% of them want to go anywhere, and 49% say a polite no to foreign travel.

Anyway you slice it, our's is a rich and powerful country. Its influence extends to every corner of the globe. And for millions of people in the world, our way of life has become a standard – the dream people work towards achieving in their own terms.

How do we feel about our country? And which countries do we most admire? In this study, a number of Americans were asked to rate different countries according to how much they liked or disliked them. Not surprisingly the country which tops the popularity charts in America is America.

Despite recent years of intense self-criticism following Vietnam and Watergate, three out of every four Americans polled had high opinions of the U.S. Ninety-six out of every hundred rated the country positively, with 75% giving it a "very favorable" rating.

After home, Canada was the next best for Americans. Ninety-one percent felt favorably towards their neighbor to the north, although only one in three gave Canada a "very favorable" rating.

America's favoritism towards Canada is understandable when you realize that no other country is quite so much like home. What's more, Canada's tourist industry is one of the largest, and almost all her visitors come from the States.

Americans are also fond of Switzerland – a fact borne out by the large number of Yankee tourists who visit there every year. Whether it's because of Swiss

Appraisal of own and other nations:+	U.S.A.	CANADA
	1976	1976
very favorable (%)	75	31
favorable (%)	21	60
don't know (%)	2	7
unfavorable (%)	2	2
overall favorable (%)	96	91

thoroughness and efficiency, or the idea of living among the clear alpine pastures, or just the thought of all that chocolate and all that money – almost nine in ten Americans think Switzerland's got something special.

Nearly as many Americans are fond of England. You'd expect the figure to be higher when you think of the special ties that have always existed between the two countries. On the other hand, remember that our Founding Fathers revolted against the British crown with good reason. Perhaps it's a left-over trace of our original colonial differences.

Australia and Holland get the next highest number of votes. Eighty-five percent of Americans admire these two countries.

Sweden, Germany and Japan were also high on the list. About three-quarters of those polled gave these countries a fairly noble rating. The vote was only slightly lower for Mexico south of the border – many Americans visit Mexico every

	ENGLAND	AUSTRALIA	COMMUNIST CHINA	ISRAEL	CUBA	FRANCE	(WEST) GERMANY	IRAN	ITALY	JAPAN	HOLLAND	MEXICO	RUSSIA	SWEDEN	SWITZERLAND
	1976	1976	1976	1976	1976	1976	1976	1976	1976	1976	1976	1976	1976	1976	1976
	16	16	1	8	1	7	9	2	6	9	12	10	2	11	21
	71	69	19	57	14	67	68	46	62	66	73	64	19	66	67
	7	9	7	10	8	8	9	15	10	8	10	8	7	11	9
	6	6	73	25	77	18	14	37	22	17	5	18	72	12	3
	87	85	20	65	15	74	77	48	68	75	85	74	21	77	88

year, and, as with Canada, familiarity doesn't necessarily breed contempt.

Of all the countries on the table, Iran got the highest number of "don't know" votes. Not too many Americans have ever been there. We like their rings and their oil, but not all their politics. And it never was really clear whether the voting in the poll meant we respected the country – or just wanted to go there as tourists.

But predictably, the least favorite countries according to U.S. opinion were – yes, you guessed – Russia, China and Cuba, with Cuba at the bottom of the list. One percent of all Americans polled gave Cuba a red-star rating of "very favorable". And 14% thought the country was O.K. But 77% thought Cuba was "unfavorable" – four percent more than felt the same way about China. The Russians fared a little better. Seventy-two percent thought they were "unfavorable". Maybe we're getting resigned to Russia, like an ill-fitting but familiar shoe.

Source:
The Gallup Organization Inc.
[+]In the original survey Americans were handed a card with 10 numbered boxes running from plus 5 to minus 5. They were told: ". . . the 10 boxes on this card range from the highest position of plus 5 – something you have a very favorable opinion of – all the way down to the lowest position of minus 5 – something you have a very unfavorable opinion of." We have interpreted the boxes so that plus 5 = very favorable; plus 1 to plus 4 = favorable; minus 1 to minus 5 = unfavorable. The question asked: "How far up the scale or how far down the scale would you rate (name of country)?"

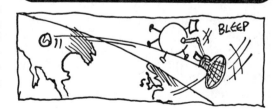

415

Ever since World War II, we've presented ourselves to the world as the number one protector of democracy. This is government policy. But how does the average American feel about playing "big brother" to the rest of the world? If communist-backed forces were to invade one of the nations of the Free World, should we send in the troops – as we did in Vietnam? Send military supplies – as we did in Israel? Or simply refuse to get involved – as in the 1956 Suez Crisis?

Based on the figures in the table, the country that most Americans feel strongly about is Canada.

	CANADA	ENGLAND
If a nation were attacked by communist-backed forces the US should:[+]		
send troops		
1975	57	37
1971	NA	37
send supplies		
1975	19	30
1971	NA	33
refuse to get involved		
1975	14	24
1971	NA	19

Fifty-seven percent of those asked, said we should send in troops if Canada were invaded. Canada is closer to most of us –geographically and socially – than any other country. And it's also close to where that "communist-backed force" might be coming from – across the Polar ice-cap. But only 57%. That figure might come as a real shock to the Canadians. It means that just under half of us don't care enough to send in the Marines. Though, if there were an actual invasion, the figure would almost certainly be a lot higher.

It's not surprising to find Mexico second on the list. Forty-two percent believe that we should fight if those "communist-backed forces" invade Mexico. That's just over four out of every ten Americans. And look at the next set of figures for Mexico: 23% of us appear to believe that we shouldn't react at all if the country were invaded.

The third highest figure is for our so-called "oldest ally" –England. If England were attacked, 37% of us say we should send troops to bail them out. That's just over one in three – while one in four believes we should sit tight and keep our noses clean. Obviously the Vietnam experience has had an effect on the attitude of the man in the street. He's not interested in going to war.

The fourth highest figure is for West Germany. Twenty-seven percent of Americans believe that we should give military assistance if armed conflict were to break out there. And West Germany is one of those places where it's liable to do

BRAZIL	NATIONALIST CHINA	(WEST) GERMANY	INDIA	ISRAEL	JAPAN	MEXICO	PHILIPPINES	SAUDI ARABIA	THAILAND	TURKEY
15	8	27	7	12	16	42	29	7	10	9
16	11	28	7	11	17	45	–	–	11	10
33	27	32	34	42	35	25	34	27	32	29
36	30	41	40	44	34	26	–	–	36	36
39	54	33	47	37	40	23	26	54	46	49
33	45	22	39	33	38	19	–	–	38	37

NA not available   – Question not asked

just that. But you'll see that 33% would prefer to stay home and do nothing at all even if the worst *did* happen.

Turning to the countries about which we are least concerned, we see that only seven percent think we should intervene if either India or Saudi Arabia were attacked. Perhaps this is understandable where India is concerned – it's a remote and relatively unknown country. But what about Saudi Arabia, where more than half our oil comes from?

Only 12% of Americans think we should send troops to Israel if there were a communist invasion. And a mere 16% approve of fighting for Japan – which may be one of our greatest competitors, but, at the same time, is one of the pillars of the Free World's economy.

Source:
The Gallup Organization Inc, 1975
[+]The original question asked Americans: "In the event a nation is attacked by communist-backed forces, there are several things the U.S. can do about it – send American troops; send military supplies but not send American troops; or refuse to get involved".
Totals do not add up to 100 because there is a proportion of "don't knows".

Look at the table and you'll see that God is alive and well and living everywhere – especially in North America. In the U.S. 94% of the people believe in God.

Canadians are next with 89%, closely followed by Catholic Italy with 88%. In Australia 80% of the people believe there's a deity watching over them. The majority of Europeans have held fast to the old traditions: 78% of people in the Benelux countries, and even 76% of the sceptical British admit to believing in a God. However, in Scandinavia, this figure drops down to 65%.

At first sight the Japanese figure of 44% looks low – only four out of ten Japanese believe in God. That doesn't mean they're not religious. Japan is predominantly Buddhist, and Buddhism doesn't require belief in a deity.

Atheists are scarce on the North American continent: only three per cent in the U.S. and seven per cent in Canada – less than one person in ten in both countries. If you're a confirmed non-believer in search of kindred spirits, you'd best go to Scandinavia where 25% of people don't believe in any god; or France, "the eldest daughter of the church," where 23% of the population admit to being unbelievers. Benelux and West Germany are close behind with one person in five (20%) an atheist.

	U.S.A.	CANADA
1. Number of people (%) who:[+]		
believe in God	94	89
don't believe in God	3	7
don't know/no answer	3	4
2. Number of people (%) who think their religious beliefs are:[0]		
very important	56	36
fairly important	30	36
not at all important	5	9
3. Number of people (%) who:[x]		
believe in life after death	69	54
don't believe in life after death	20	29
don't know/no answer	11	17

Although 94% of Americans believe in God, only 56% feel that this belief is very important in their lives. This may seem a low figure, but if you compare it with the 36% scored by Canada and Italy, the runners-up, you'll realize that religion is a stronger influence in the U.S. than in any other country listed. In both the U.K. and France, 20% do not regard religious beliefs as important.

There's another surprise on the table. The many Americans, Canadians and Europeans who believe in God don't all believe they're going to spend any time with Him in heaven when they die. In fact, one in five Americans (20%) are sure that there isn't an afterlife – a figure in

U.K.	AUSTRALIA	BENELUX	SCANDINAVIA	FRANCE	(WEST) GERMANY	EEC.	ITALY	JAPAN
76	80	78	65	72	72	76	88	44
14	15	20	25	23	20	17	7	30
10	5	2	10	5	8	7	5	26
23	25	26	17	22	17	25	36	14
26	33	30	28	33	30	32	42	33
20	13	19	13	20	14	15	6	6
43	48	48	35	39	33	41	46	18
35	40	43	44	48	48	42	36	36
22	12	9	21	13	19	17	18	46

conflict with the high percentage of believers in the same countries. Nearly a third of the Canadians, and just under half the French and Germans agree with them. This suggests that the "god" of their beliefs is a pragmatic sort of god, operative only in the dimension of the present.

The fact that twice as many Japanese don't believe in life after death as do is perfectly consistent. Buddhists believe in reincarnation on this earth.

All in all, this table shows that the U.S. is still "God's own country" – even though many of its citizens may prefer to lay up treasure on this earth rather than bank on the hereafter.

Source:
Gallup International affiliated institutes in the countries concerned
The poll was conducted during winter 1974-75 and spring 1976. The questions on this table were part of a series that dealt with religious beliefs and the existence of a god who observes actions and rewards or punishes accordingly.
The questions asked:
[+] "Do you believe in god as a universal spirit?"
[o] "How important are your religious beliefs?"
Totals do not add up to 100 because some answers have not been used.
[x] "Do you believe in life after death?"

We live in a world of information. The media bombard us with news all the time – but are we getting the information we want? As consumers, we're faced with dozens of decisions every week. Which products, goods or services to buy....how to handle money, credit and taxes... whether to take a vacation now or later. How much help do we get from the media with these matters, and do we believe what they tell us?

Fifty-three percent of West Germans and 50% of the British approve of the consumer information given in their newspapers, and approbation of T.V. is even higher – 63% for the West Germans and 57% for the British.

The French are the most distrustful of newspaper information. Fifty-nine percent thought it either poor or worthless. The Irish (56%), the Italians (53%) and the Belgians (48%) come next. In general, all nationalities feel television gives better consumer information than newspapers.

The table also shows the number of people who feel they have been cheated recently or sold merchandise that wasn't quite what they'd been led to expect. The U.K., has one of the highest numbers of consumers who've felt cheated: 47%. Italy is highest of all: 53% claim to have been cheated at one time or another. Forty-five percent of the Dutch and 41% of the French also say they've been cheated or deceived on a purchase. By contrast, only 21% of Americans say they've been bilked.

Better consumer information from the media would cut down the number of customers (an average of over 37% for all the countries surveyed) who succumb to misleading or deceptive advertising and sales practices.

	U.S.A.
	1976
1. Quality of consumer information provided by newspapers:[+]	
good (%)	NA
poor (%)	NA
none at all (%)	NA
television	
good (%)	NA
poor (%)	NA
none at all (%)	NA
2. People (%) who have been cheated over a purchase[0]	21[+]
3. Reactions to being cheated:	
did nothing; didn't mention any action (%)	NA
complained to sales assistant/asked for a replacement/refund (%)	NA
took legal action (%)	NA

U.K.	BELGIUM	DENMARK	FRANCE	(WEST) GERMANY	IRELAND	ITALY	NETHERLANDS
1975	1975	1975	1975	1975	1975	1975	1975
50	22	42	25	53	38	27	31
34	21	23	35	24	37	30	27
7	27	12	24	14	19	23	19
57	47	63	46	63	35	32	49
29	16	11	29	19	35	29	25
6	13	4	13	7	22	25	8
47	22	25	41	28	38	53	45
32	45	31	24	32	44	35	70
53	40	54	50	42	38	33	27
1	–	2	1	2	1	1	–

NA not available

Sources:
1 European Consumers, Brussels 2 Europe: European Consumers, Brussels USA:
Public Opinion Index, ORC
[+]The question asked: "Do you think that the following information media provide good.
poor or no information at all for consumers?"
[0]The question asked (US): "Have you or your family been cheated or deceived in regard
to any product or service that you have purchased during the past year or so?"
The question asked (Europe): "People sometimes say that they feel they have been cheated
when buying something. Can you remember you or your husband/wife buying something
with which you were not wholly satisfied this year or last year? If yes, did you take any
action? What did you do?"

Are the virtues of thrift and hard work extinct among American youth? By no means. Our young people (in the 18-24 age group) are among the few left in the world who still believe in them. Sixty-three percent disagree with the statement that "money is for spending, not saving" and 58% reject the notion that it's "important in this world to take it easy and not work too hard". The British are in agreement with us – 51% are for saving money and 59% believe in hard work.

In Japan, 57% of the young favor saving their yen – considering they're against hard work by almost three to one, they probably need to. The youth in India take the opposite stand – 58% think money should be spent but 64% approve of hard work.

	U.S.A.
	1973
1. Young[+] people's outlook on life:[0]	
Percentage who agree money is for spending not saving	35
disagree	63
Percentage who agree it's important to take life easy	41
disagree	58
2. Young[+] people's view of the future:[x]	
Percentage who agree human wisdom will avoid world war	53
disagree	46
Percentage who believe society will be better to live in 30 years from now	40
disagree	50

In contrast, nine out of ten young Yugoslavs say they'd rather spend than save. In Sweden this figure is 79%, with 80% deploring hard work. The frugal, diligent Swiss, the fretful, feckless French and the bongo-loving Brazilians also hate work and saving their money.

Moving on to a more serious issue, young people today are generally optimistic about the prospects of avoiding another world war. Those youthful big spenders in Yugoslavia have the highest hopes for world peace, followed by the young Brazilians and Indians.

American youth must be disillusioned by our recent experience in Vietnam. They're less optimistic – only about half of those questioned feel confident that world war can be avoided.

The young Swiss are gloomiest of all: 62% of them feel a war is inevitable.

The question that brings out pessimism in almost everyone is: "Do you believe society will be better to live in 30 years from now?". Only the Yugoslavs (who pin their faith on the future of socialism) feel able to answer "yes" with any confidence.

YOUTH: OUTLOOK ON LIFE

U.K.	BRAZIL	FRANCE	(WEST) GERMANY	INDIA	JAPAN	SWEDEN	SWITZERLAND	YUGOSLAVIA
1973	1973	1973	1973	1973	1973	1973	1973	1973
46	75	71	51	58	41	79	66	90
51	24	20	46	41	57	18	33	10
39	66	72	60	35	72	80	64	58
59	33	20	36	64	27	18	35	42
48	79	52	53	74	64	56	37	80
49	20	31	43	25	34	41	62	20
32	50	20	33	63	29	23	19	83
60	48	48	59	35	68	71	79	17

Source:
Gallup International affiliated institutes in the countries concerned
+Male and female, 18-24 years
0The question asked: "Please state whether you agree or disagree with each of the following statements: money is for spending and not for saving; it is important in this world to take it easy and not to work too hard."
xThe question asked: "Please state whether you agree or disagree with each of the following statements: human wisdom will avoid another world war; we will have a better society to live in 30 years from now."
Totals do not add up to 100 because of a proportion of "don't knows" and "no answers".

Today's youth are strongly idealistic. They believe that happiness is a matter of being healthy – and that wealth and wisdom are far less important than honesty and kindness.

Unfortunately, we don't have figures for U.S. youth. There are some general trends which they would probably fall in with, but there are also some surprising national differences. So just what our young people believe must remain speculative.

However, in all the countries on the table they are unanimous on one point: health tops the list in every country – and in Austria 91% of the youngsters mention it. Even in Finland where it is named least often, health is singled out by 53% of the respondents.

Kindness is almost equally important to the Finns – 51% include it as an ingredient of happiness. The Dutch also put a premium value on kindness. Forty-seven percent of them considered it as an ideal for happiness. These two countries are way ahead of the rest of the field here. The Spanish are the next highest, with a figure of 30% – with the U.K., along with the English Canadians, scoring a slightly above average 26% score for kindness.

However, in the majority of countries honesty was considered the second essential to happiness after health. Though whether this was because the young people questioned thought that a bad conscience would make them

Young+ people (%) whose ideal for happiness is:	CANADA	French
to be healthy	58	61
to be honest	53	60
to be kind	22	11
to have a sense of humor	31	31
to be intelligent and clever	28	36
to be practical and handy	22	37
to be rich	11	10
to be beautiful/handsome	6	5
to be modern	5	4
to be slim	3	2

unhappy, or whether they simply thought that a society which made a practice of dishonesty would be an unhappy one to live in, isn't disclosed. Even so, well over half the Greeks, Italians, Spanish and Canadians questioned thought that honesty was an essential for happiness.

A big surprise – especially considering that those questioned were young people between the ages of 15 and 25 – is to find how unimportant humor is in almost everyone's ideals for happiness. It looks as if only the British – who traditionally pride themselves on their sense of humor – actually consider it to be an essential ingredient of a happy life. Here 56% of the young people questioned considered that a sense of humor is one of their ideals for happiness.

However, if the British enjoy a hearty laugh, the Greeks on the other hand seem

English	U.K.	AUSTRIA	FINLAND	GREECE	ITALY	NETHERLANDS	SPAIN
57	69	91	53	68	60	67	68
51	41	42	36	60	59	38	50
26	26	17	51	18	17	47	30
31	56	25	21	8	15	21	44
24	22	43	15	35	45	37	66
17	18	26	14	20	23	14	20
12	14	13	7	11	16	6	9
6	4	7	4	12	6	13	4
5	6	5	3	8	8	5	8
4	5	6	3	2	2	3	2

Source:
McCann-Erickson Youth Study, 1976-77
+Male and female, 15-25

to take their happiness very seriously indeed. Only eight percent of them considered a sense of humor as one of the ideals for happiness.

Intelligence is uniformly downgraded almost everywhere. In general, only about a third of young people mention it, except in Spain where 66% list it.

Being practical is moderately essential to happiness – mostly to the Austrians (26%). The Dutch and the Finns (both 14%) mention it least.

The old adage that money doesn't buy happiness gets a ringing endorsement from young people. The Italians (16%) include money most often, but across the board just about ten percent of respondents mention being rich as one of the qualities that make for happiness.

Other ideals that are often equated with worldly success – being beautiful or handsome, slim, modern – also seem to be comparatively unimportant to the younger generation. In most cases, fewer than ten percent bother to single out these qualities, though a few more young Dutch have dreams of being beautiful. The Greeks, Italians and Spanish put most value on being modern (eight percent). And Austria puts the highest value on being slim: six percent of the young Austrians believe that happiness is a matter of shedding poundage. This concern isn't too surprising in a country where whipped cream pastries are a central part of the national heritage.

Where are young people most satisfied with their government's protection of people's rights? Two of the most affluent Western European countries head the list. In Switzerland, over one out of every two young people questioned considered that their government was more or less fully protecting their rights and welfare. In West Germany, the rate of full approval was 22%. And 84% of the young people questioned voted "full" and "more or less full" combined – 20% more than in Switzerland.

Somewhat surprisingly the highest and second highest of those who thought the government was fully protecting their rights were in Brazil and India. In India, 23% were fully satisfied. And in Brazil, 29%. High figures when you consider the political oppression perceived by the rest of the world in both huge countries. Brazilians who approved fully or more or less fully total 70% – the second highest after West Germany.

Where are young people most dissatisfied? In Japan, 67% were not fully satisfied. And 22% weren't satisfied at all with the protection of their rights.

In the U.S., predictably, young people stayed middle of the road. Eighty-three percent were more or less fully, or not fully, satisfied with the way Uncle Sam protected their rights. Only 16% felt strongly one way or the other.

Nowhere in the table do even ten percent think the most important task for government is to value traditions and culture.

Promoting industry, enriching the economic life and placing emphasis on social security were the big winners in most countries.

Protecting nature was also a high priority in several countries. This issue ranked highest in Switzerland, the U.S., France, Japan and Sweden, and the least high in India and Brazil.

	U.S.A.
	1973
Young people[+] who think the government is protecting their rights:[0]	
fully (%)	7
more or less fully (%)	44
not fully (%)	39
not at all (%)	9
Young people[+] who think that, above all, their country should:[x]	
value traditions and culture (%)	4
promote industry (%)	12
emphasize social security (%)	17
protect nature (%)	10
earn respect internationally (%)	6

YOUTH: GOVERNMENT PROTECTION

U.K.	BRAZIL	INDIA	YUGOSLAVIA	FRANCE	(WEST) GERMANY	JAPAN	SWEDEN	SWITZERLAND
1973	1973	1973	1973	1973	1973	1973	1973	1973
4	29	23		4	22	1	3	7
39	41	40		27	62	10	54	57
40	19	28		28	10	67	36	29
14	18	8		18	2	22	4	6
3	3	8	7	4	3	3	3	3
35	27	54	23	17	14	8	20	8
21	44	15	50	34	49	57	36	44
4	2	1	5	17	3	11	17	20
6	19	5	0	6	2	1	1	5

Source:
Gallup International affiliated institutes in the countries concerned
+Male and female, 18-24
OThe original question asked: "To what extent do you think that government is protecting the rights and welfare of the people?" Totals do not add up to 100 because there is a small proportion of "don't knows" and "no answers".
XThe original question asked people to choose from the following answers to the question: "What do you think is the one most important thing for our country to do now?"
To value traditions and culture. To promote industry and enrich the nation's economic life. To place extra emphasis on social security and provide a secure way of life for the people. To protect nature. To earn respect in the international community." Totals do not add up to 100 because some other optional answers have not been included.

The young are usually the most discontented in any society. In this report, young people, between 18 and 24, were offered a choice of four means to express dissatisfaction.

Swedish youth appear to be the most docile. More than half of them would vent their displeasure only at the polling booth. More than half the young people in the U.K. and Japan also believe in the power of the vote, with the West Germans only a few percentage points behind.

The most activist youth is right here in the U.S., where 54% believe that active, legal protest is the most effective instrument for social change. The not-so-peaceful Swiss come next on the activist list, followed by Sweden, France, the U.K. and Japan. The fewest demonstrators are in Brazil.

Young French and West Germans are the leading advocates of violence, with six out of every hundred believing that only terrorism can effect reforms. The Swiss are next with five percent, and the U.S., India and Japan follow with four percent. The most peaceful nations are Sweden and the U.K. (two percent) and Brazil (one percent). The Brazilians are probably more disgusted with their society than their figure suggests – 40% of their young people regard dropping out of society as the best solution to national problems. The fed-up French are next, with 17% wanting out, followed by the perennially discontented Swiss, with 12%. Although we invented the term "drop-out", only five percent of young Americans are ready to turn their backs on society.

The young people who said they'd restrict their protest to voting were asked why they chose not to take more active measures. Almost three-quarters of the Japanese and over half the West Germans felt that the individual was ineffective in trying to change society. The most frequent answer for Americans, Swedes, British, Brazilians, Indians and French was that reform should be left to people in the proper positions.

	U.S.A.	U.K.
	1973	1973
1. Measures young[+] people would take if they were dissatisfied with society:[0]		
use their vote (%)	36	54
take active, but legal, measures (%)	54	37
resort to violence and/or other illegal measures (%)	4	2
drop out from society (%)	5	4
2. Reasons why young[x] people would vote, rather than take more active measures to change society:[‡]		
individuals are ineffective (%)	30	30
people in the proper position should cope (%)	46	39
other things are more important (%)	22	28

YOUTH: CHANGING SOCIETY

BRAZIL	FRANCE	(WEST) GERMANY	INDIA	JAPAN	SWEDEN	SWITZERLAND
1973	1973	1973	1973	1973	1973	1973
41	34	49	44	54	55	37
18	37	33	42	37	38	46
1	6	6	4	4	2	5
40	17	4	8	5	4	12
30	16	53	33	73	18	32
48	44	31	45	9	57	30
21	32	11	20	18	23	38

Source:
Gallup International affiliated institutes in the countries concerned
[+]Male and female, 18-24
[0]The question asked: "Suppose you were dissatisfied with society what attitudes do you think you would take: "I will use my voting right but nothing more." "I will actively resort to a variety of measures such as petitions, letters of complaint, demonstrations, strikes etc. so long as the means are premitted by the law." "I will resort to violence and/or other illegal measures if necessary." "I will become a drop-out from society."
[x]Male and female, 18-24; respondents who said they would use their voting right but nothing more in answer to the previous question.
[‡]The question asked: "Why don't you take more active measures as well? Please choose one answer from: "The problems involved are beyond the reach of individuals." "The affairs of society should be handled by persons in the proper position." "There are other things which are more important to me."
Totals do not add up to 100 as there is a proportion of "don't knows" and "no answers".

Everybody's welfare depends on the good of the nation. But the good of the nation also depends on the welfare of the individual. Which should come first is a question of national temperament. And the type of government a people is governed by.

Americans are traditional believers in "rugged individualism". This idea rings out loud and clear from the table. Almost three out of every four young Americans feel that the emphasis on the national good undermines the well-being of the individual. The less government interference, the better, they seem to say.

Nine out of every ten Americans think money reigns supreme in our society. At the same time, the majority feel that their success depends on their own hard work, not on family background.

Traditionally, the West Germans think differently. And the thoughts of young Germans are true to form. Only 44% of them think their individual benefits take back seat to those of the government. A full 49% approves of the government taking priority. This could be interpreted in different ways. It could mean that they think their government doesn't undermine the individual as much as other governments. Or it could be a reflection of deeply rooted, cultural concepts – the notion of the German Fatherland still packs an emotional wallop.

	U.S.A.	BRAZIL
1. "The Government emphasizes benefits to the nation at the cost of the individual"+		
young people who agree (%)	74	55
young people who disagree (%)	25	44
2. "Money reigns supreme in this grossly materialistic society"0		
young people who agree (%)	88	77
young people who disagree (%)	11	21
3. "A person's future is decided by his or her family background"X		
young people who agree (%)	48	61
young people who disagree (%)	51	37

In booming Deutschland, young people aren't at all cynical about the importance of money. Sixteen percent reject the idea that money reigns supreme.

Again, when it comes to the importance of family background, West Germany is odd man out. Nearly three-quarters of all young Germans think a person's success depends largely on the status and wealth of his parents. This is almost twice as high as the percentage in Sweden and France. It's over ten percent higher than in Brazil.

The figures for France are equally interesting. Mammon reigns in the land of luxury and good food. Despite an old guard network, French youth seem more optimistic about the chances of a person making it on his own than any people but the Swedes. Only 38% think you really

YOUTH: ATTITUDES TO GOVERNMENT

U.K.	INDIA	FRANCE	(WEST) GERMANY	JAPAN	SWEDEN	SWITZERLAND
68	71	66	44	88	68	63
28	27	13	49	11	27	35
86	86	90	78	84	82	90
12	13	5	16	16	15	10
42	52	38	72	48	34	57
57	46	53	23	51	63	42

Source:
Gallup International affiliated institutes in the countries concerned. The poll was conducted in 1973.

In the survey young people (male and female, 18-24 years) were told "I am going to read some statements about our national government or society. For each one please tell me if you think it's 'true' or 'false' " The statements:

[+] "The government is placing too much emphasis on the benefits of the nation as a whole at the cost of individuals

[0] "In the present grossly materialistic society, money reigns supreme."

[x] "Man's future is often virtually predetermined by his father's (mother's) profession as well as his family background."

The percentages don't add up to 100 because of the "don't knows" and "no answers".

need a Proustian pedigree to get on in life. Two-thirds of French youth is also on the side of the individual.

The Japanese figures are surprisingly like those for the U.S. Even more young Japanese resent government interference than in America. Eighty-four percent believe in the cult of yen. But most surprisingly their views on the importance of a good background are like ours

	CANADA	French	English
Young⁺ people (%) who agree:			
"A woman's place is in the home"	20	31	16
"If a couple both earn money, both should share the housework"	93	90	94
"Men and women should be paid the same for the same job"	92	91	92
"Washing clothes should still be done by women"	28	46	22
"Cooking should still be done by women"	30	52	23

From this table you can't tell at a glance which country has the most macho males or subservient females because the questions were answered by both men and women. However, we may be able to approach the subject from another direction.

We could ask in which country the macho males would receive most support from dutiful wives.

The answer is Greece, where 80% believe that housework should be shared between men and women if both work, and that women should be paid the same for doing the same job. But there's almost a complete reversal when it comes to the nitty gritty of who should do the washing and cooking. Here, very few believe in sharing the work. By 75% and 72% respectively, the agreement is that women should do both.

The country in which young women appear to be on the most equal footing is Sweden. However, while the Swedes give all the right non-chauvinist answers as to whether a woman's place is in the home, whether she should be paid the same wages as a man, and whether men and women should share housework if they both earn, we don't know what they think about equality in the realm of washing and cooking.

The Finns are consistent supporters of sex equality with only 22% of young people believing that a woman's place is in the home. They're also enthusiastic about sharing the housework (93%) and equal pay (90%). An extremely low percentage of Finns – 13% – believe cooking is solely a woman's job and even fewer – seven percent – think that only she should do the washing.

For a more traditional view of a woman's place, turn to the Austrians, a whopping 57% of whom think women belong in the home. Most of them believe she should do the washing (62%) and the cooking (65%), which puts them almost on a par with the Greeks.

Only 22% of young Spaniards believe a woman belongs at home, and 97% think she should be paid the same money for the same job. They're also fairly liberal about the washing and the cooking, with only about 36% feeling those are solely women's jobs.

The Italians run neck and neck with the British, save that just 37% of Italians

U.K.	AUSTRIA	FINLAND	FRANCE	GREECE	ITALY	NETHERLANDS	SPAIN	SWEDEN
26	57	22	42	39	30	29	22	11
84	96	93	86	80	83	96	92	97
87	87	90	93	81	87	95	97	97
46	62	7	47	75	50	45	35	–
44	65	13	26	72	37	30	37	–

–Question not asked

Source:
McCann-Erickson Youth Study, 1976-77
+Male and female, 15-25

versus 44% of the English believe cooking is a woman's job. It looks like Momma's days of ruling the kitchen are numbered – perhaps to her relief.

Turning to France, we find a country that's not over-enthusiastic about equality: 42% of young people believe that a woman should stay at home – where she belongs.

But there's an interesting 21% gap between whether cooking and washing are woman's sole province. Forty-seven percent vote for women doing the washing, while only 26% feel the same way about cooking.

Overall, one interesting fact emerges: around 90% of youth believe a couple should share the housework and get equal pay for equal work.

Perhaps there's a better future for women's rights than some of our tables indicate.

	CANADA	French	English
Young+ people (%) who agree:			
"Banks and important enterprises should be nationalized"	59	58	61
"Factory workers should have more say in the running of the company"	73	81	71
"There ought to be more government control of products that are put on the market"	88	94	85

Should banks and important industries be nationalized or left in private hands? Should workers have a greater say in running the company they work in? Should there be more government control of products that are put on the market? These are important questions and ones that many 15 to 25-year-olds have strong feelings about. Their opinions on these matters could well affect us all in ten years' time. This table shows what young people in various countries think about these questions.

The two countries which are most resoundingly against nationalization are two welfare states: the U.K. and the Netherlands: only 39% of young people want nationalization. There are already a number of nationalized industries in both countries, so this 39% may just be saying that nationalization's gone far enough.

It does seem that nationalized industries, especially in Britain, just don't function as efficiently as privately owned ones. This may have had some influence on the low figures for these two countries.

The U.K. has often been held up as an example of an economy in which too much control has been given over to the heavy hand of bureaucracy. Undoubtedly, government ministers *do* interfere in the management of nationalized industries for political reasons.

By contrast, Spain and Greece (with 88% and 78% respectively) are most definitely on the side of nationalization.

Until recently, both countries were under dictatorships. The grass is always greener on the other side of the fence – after a long period of strict government control, it's understandable that many of their citizens favor industrial power going to the people.

Austria (73%) is third highest in a desire for increased nationalization, followed by Italy (71%). Italy has the largest Communist Party in the West, so it's no surprise that nearly three out of four young Italians are in favor of more nationalization.

Over 70% of young people in every country except the U.K. (66%) are in favor of the workers having a greater say in running the company they work in. Spain (97%) and Greece (82%) again head the list, with France (81%) and Austria (77%) not far behind.

Remember that in a few years a lot of the youths who took part in this survey will be workers themselves. So it's pretty understandable that they should express strong opinions on worker involvement.

YOUTH: ATTITUDES TO BUSINESS

U.K.	AUSTRIA	FINLAND	FRANCE	GREECE	ITALY	NETHERLANDS	SPAIN	SWEDEN
39	73	53	—	78	71	39	88	48
66	77	77	81	82	74	76	97	—
76	83	67	90	94	96	85	—	75

—Question not asked

Source:
McCann-Erickson Youth Study, 1976-77
+Male and female, 15-25

If they retain these views when they do take their place in the economic system, we could be in for some major adjustments in the way industry is run. So factory owners everywhere: brace yourselves.

For all the countries surveyed, on average, 58% of young people were for increased industralization, and 78% wanted workers to have more say in running their companies,

From these figures, it seems that they'd rather have workers in charge of their companies than the government. At the very least, they'd like management to consult workers on important decisions.

Every country is in favor of more government control of products. The young Finns are lowest with 67%.

The young people of Italy (96%), Greece (94%) and France (90%) are all overwhelmingly for government control.

It seems that some people think that nationalization isn't the answer to improved quality, but that government control of products is. In Canada – a good example of a capitalist, consumer-oriented society – 88% of young people want more product control, but only 59.5% go for nationalization.

Does this indicate a backlash against a lot of present-day advertising, which sometimes promises more than the product actually delivers? Or does it reflect a belief in governments' ability to improve life for its citizens by taking a more forceful role in demanding better quality goods from manufacturers?

Overall there is a strong reaction against *laissez-faire* capitalism. In every case – except the U.K. and Holland in the case of nationalization – the majority of 15 to 25-year-olds favor increased controls, whether through nationalization, worker control of factories or the government monitoring products.

Work takes up a huge chunk of the waking day for most adults in the world. So how do young people today feel about setting out on a lifetime of it? Why are they going to do it? Forget all about the dignity of labor, self-expression and mutual self-help. The majority of 18 to 24 year olds see work as a way to pay those bills.

Young+ people's reasons for working:[0]	U.S.A.	U.K.
	1973	1973
to earn money (%)	59	80
to be a responsible member of society (%)	11	4
to find self-fulfilment (%)	30	14

Top of the list come the young people in the U.K. and France. A massive 80% in both countries are under no illusions as to why they are spending their time in offices or factories – it's to get money. They sweat for eight hours a day to get enough pounds and francs to buy the things they need or just fancy. They don't expect to get satisfaction from their jobs so they hope that their wages will allow them to get it in their private lives.

All the British and French figures are identical. Only four percent believe that work is about keeping the wheels of society rolling and that everybody contributes to the effort. The remaining 14% are the ones who see work as an end in itself. These young people are not looking for any reward other than the satisfaction that their jobs provide. It's a fairly safe bet that the youngsters who opted for this answer are the lucky ones who are not involved in repetitive, mechanical work. Their jobs must give them room to stretch themselves.

The youths in two other Western European countries, West Germany and Sweden, have roughly the same attitudes. The major difference between Swedish young men and women and their French and British counterparts is that twice as many (eight percent) feel that work is their way of being a responsible member of society.

By far the highest percentage of people who believed that work was their way of helping society is found, not unsurprisingly, in Yugoslavia. Twenty-three percent of young Yugoslavs have obviously been deeply influenced by the Communist doctrines that prevail in their country. When one considers the enormous emphasis placed by Communist countries on the importance of the State and the common cause, it's surprising that this figure is not higher. It would be interesting to see the figures for Red China or Russia. As it is, the large majority of Yugoslavs still put their own desire to possess money as their priority. They also returned the lowest number of responses in the "self-fulfilment" column – just eight percent.

There is a great emphasis on spiritual rather than material matters in Eastern philosophies and religions, and it shows in this table. Even in the face of the daily fight for the basics in order to stay alive, a low 56% of Indians believe that their working day is spent only in getting the

YOUTH: MEANING OF WORK

BRAZIL	FRANCE	(WEST) GERMANY	INDIA	JAPAN	SWEDEN	SWITZERLAND	YUGOSLAVIA
1973	1973	1973	1973	1973	1973	1973	1973
43	80	70	56	55	75	63	69
13	4	11	21	11	8	13	23
42	14	15	23	34	15	23	8

daily bread. Forty-four percent of them have their minds on other things. Twenty-one percent forget their own needs and concentrate on working for the general good, while 23% find self-fulfilment in their work.

The Eastern attitude to worldly goods even applies to industrialized, competitive Japan. They may be challenging the markets of the world with cars, motorbikes and electrical goods, but the people who make and sell these products aren't just in it for financial reward. Only 55% of Japanese workers felt that they put the effort in just to earn money. The other 45% had idealistic reasons. Much of the Japanese people's way of thinking and acting is influenced by Shinto, which until recently closely identified religion and state. This may explain the 11% who see work as a duty towards their society. The 34% of Japanese who chose "self-fulfilment" as their reason for work is the second highest response in this category.

Perhaps the possession of wealth eases the desire to earn more by working. Only 59% of Americans and 63% of Swiss put this as their main priority. A high 30% of Americans worked to fulfil themselves and 23% of Swiss workers felt the same.

Source:
Gallup Opinion Index, 100
[+]Male and female, 18-24
[0]The question asked: "Why do you think man works? Please choose one answer closest to your feelings from the following: to earn money; to do his duty as a member of society; to find self-fulfilment."
Totals do not always add up to 100 because of a proportion of "don't knows" and "no answers".

Previous younger generations often had little voice in selecting their careers. Circumstances, social class and parental choice usually dictated which occupations the child could pursue. Today, society is more liberal and its values less absolute. This means greater freedom for young people – freedom to do as they please, freedom to choose what they do. However, this freedom also places a much heavier burden on the individual. Young people have more say in deciding the nature and quality of their lives. They are also aware that these choices can be vitally important. This table is an indication not only of the difficulties that face young people, but also how seriously they take them.

Freedom isn't everything. Unemployment figures (see table on unemployment) show there aren't enough jobs to go round. In some countries the situation is extremely bad, and, in spite of government-sponsored employment programs, the unemployment problem obviously hits young people hard. They're just starting out in life and are very concerned about the opportunities which will or will not be available to them. The first question on the table shows how economic problems have affected the attitudes of young people today. Eighty-six percent of young Spaniards think finding a job is a problem.

Young people (%) who think it's a problem:	CANADA	French	English
finding a job	43	52	40
deciding which job or career to take up	43	46	42
deciding whether to get qualifications or go for a job	30	33	29
deciding whether to live with their girl/boyfriend	6	8	6
deciding whether to sleep with their girl/boyfriend	5	8	4

Italy, where 64% of the young people are worried about getting a job, comes next, followed by France with 59%.

Unemployment is high in Spain and Italy, so these figures are understandable. But why France? The fact that 59% of young French people are undecided about a career reflects increasing discrimination. They don't want any old job but one that will be interesting and well paid. Lack of opportunity in their chosen field is a bitter blow.

When jobs are scarce, dissatisfaction and rebellion are likely to follow. More than half the young people in French Canada, for instance, are worried about finding a job. No wonder there's so much agitation for Quebec Libre.

Two other problems the young people have to cope with are whether to live with their girl or boyfriend and whether to

U.K.	FINLAND	FRANCE	GREECE	ITALY	NETHERLANDS	SPAIN	SWEDEN
27	29	59	46	64	28	86	30
28	42	59	–	49	32	53	40
28	29	38	49	36	19	41	25
6	8	15	24	22	6	28	13
5	6	10	25	19	6	25	–

—Question not asked

sleep with them. These are tough decisions for young people who live in morally rigid societies. For instance, in Roman Catholic Spain more than one out of four young people say that deciding whether to live with their girlfriend (or boyfriend) is a major problem; and exactly a quarter are worried about whether to sleep with her or him. These are the highest figures for both these categories, though the Greek figure is also one in four for the second question. In Greek society, the Orthodox church is still a ruling force.

However, these questions appear to pose hardly any problem in the other countries listed. Less than ten percent considered that sleeping with or living with your girlfriend (or boyfriend) is a problem. If you polled their parents you'd get a very different result.

Source:
McCann-Erickson Youth Study, 1976-77

Most young Americans believe an education is more than reading, writing and arithmetic. It's a way to change social and economic status – and to find a good marriage mate. U.S. students value education as a means of getting ahead. "Go West, young man" has become "Go get a college education". Only five percent think it's a waste of time.

But what about the snob value of education? In this case, we're not as egalitarian as we think. Of all the countries studied, only the Swiss place more emphasis on the prestige of schools than we do. As many as 70% of young Americans surveyed believe that the school name embossed on a diploma means just as much as how well you actually performed. Even the British, with their long tradition of "public school" education, are less snobbish than the Americans. Forty percent of young Brits think a person's actual qualifications are more important than his "old school".

The number of British youth who think higher education is a waste of time is revealing: nearly 20% think it's best to go out to work as soon as possible. In class-conscious Britain, working class youths aren't always encouraged to seek a higher education. Lower school teachers and parents often steer them into trade apprenticeships at an early age.

In conservative Switzerland, the emphasis on higher education shows up markedly. Nearly half the young Swiss go to college to advance their career and marriage prospects. And three-quarters think the name of your school is the name of the game.

The French come close to Americans and Swiss in the value they place on prestige in education. Only 20% of French youth disagree.

School prestige counts for the least in West Germany and Sweden. In Germany, 40% think it's important, in Sweden, only 31%. In fact, two out of every three Swedes disagree with the idea that the prestige of schools is important to future and job.

Young Germans don't all see college as a practical matter. Only 23% go for career reasons. And 14% think it's better to go out to get a job.

	U.S.A.	U.K.
1. Young[+] people who agree a school's social prestige influences job opportunities and future[0]	70	59
disagree	29	40
2. Young[+] people (%) who think higher education:[x]		
improves chances of a good job and marriage	33	32
is a waste of time	5	**19**
3. Young[+] people (%) who would like to stay on at school but have to earn a living[x]	10	17

YOUTH: ATTITUDES TO EDUCATION

BRAZIL	FRANCE	(WEST) GERMANY	INDIA	JAPAN	SWEDEN	SWITZERLAND	YUGOSLAVIA
56	70	40	63	63	31	74	67
42	20	47	34	35	66	24	33
26	21	23	36	25	28	45	18
2	7	14	4	11	11	10	3
18	24	10	9	10	15	12	13

Source:
Gallup International affiliated institutes in the countries concerned.
The survey was conducted in 1973.
[+]Male and female, 18-24
[0]The original question asked whether or not the following statement applied to the experience of the young people questioned: "It is accepted by most people that regardless of your qualifications the social prestige at the school you graduate from will influence your job and future."
[x]The original question asked which of the following statements came closest to the view of higher education of the people questioned: "I have to go to a higher school in order to improve my chances of obtaining a good job and marriage." "It's a waste of time staying on at school or college. I should go out to work as young as possible." "I would like to have stayed on but I have to earn a living." Other options were also offered.

Ironically, the places where college is most valued are also those where the fewest go for practical reasons. In Brazil, India and Yugoslavia, very few people think higher education is a frivolous matter. But only a third of Brazilian youth go on for career reasons. And in spite of the fact that 67% of surveyed Yugoslavians think college is worth the effort, only 18% actually think they'll be advancing themselves in life by getting more education.

School days are supposed to be the happiest days of your life. Indian children couldn't agree more. When the school bell rings on Monday mornings, three-quarters of them can't wait to get behind their desks. Only three percent of Indian pupils say they don't like classroom life.

There's a striking physical contrast between the village schools of India and the modern classrooms of Sweden. Yet children in both countries share a common love of learning. Sixty percent of Swedish pupils are quite satisfied with school. Only one percent hates it.

Brazil is the only other country where over half the children really like school. American kids share the attitudes of their British counterparts, with only about 80% pretty well satisfied with school life.

Compared with French children, American kids are positively enthusiastic. In France 12% can't wait for the bell at the end of the day. French schools are noted for very strict discipline and there's strong pressure on students to do well academically.

Dissatisfaction with school life is greatest in Japan. Almost a fifth of Japanese children loathe school. This is a natural reaction to the enormous pressures imposed by both the educational system and Japanese parents. Success in adult life depends mostly on a really impressive school record.

The next table deals with satisfaction with society among 18- to 24-year-olds. One thing's certain: a high degree of satisfaction isn't necessarily linked to a high level of income. Prosperous young Americans and Swedes are less contented with the status quo than young Indians and Brazilians, who have a lower average income.

French youth leads everyone in self-satisfaction. A substantial 61% of young Frenchmen feel completely satisfied with the way things are, and another 24% feel more or less satisfied.

More surprising, perhaps, is the very high degree of satisfaction shown by young people in Yugoslavia. Overall, 89% are pretty well pleased with their

	U.S.A.	U.K.
	1973	1973
1. Young[+] people's attitudes to school life:[0]		
satisfied (%)	43	47
more or less satisfied (%)	38	33
more or less dissatisfied (%)	12	7
dissatisfied (%)	7	9
2. Young[+] people's attitudes to society:[x]		
satisfied (%)	25	38
more or less satisfied (%)	39	41
more or less dissatisfied (%)	21	12
dissatisfied (%)	14	9

YOUTH: ATTITUDES TO SCHOOL

	BRAZIL	FRANCE	(WEST) GERMANY	INDIA	JAPAN	SWEDEN	SWITZERLAND	YUGOSLAVIA
	1973	1973	1973	1973	1973	1973	1973	1973
	55	38	10	75	17	60	28	44
	32	31	65	19	38	34	46	41
	6	17	17	3	28	5	16	8
	4	12	5	3	17	1	9	7
	47	61	5	52	4	15	33	53
	41	24	55	32	22	49	44	36
	6	9	26	9	46	23	13	6
	6	5	9	7	27	12	10	5

Source:
Gallup Opinion Index, 100
[+]Male and female, 18-24
[0]The question asked: "To what extent are you satisfied with school life? Satisfied; more or less satisfied; more or less dissatisfied; dissatisfied."
[x]The question asked: "To what extent are you satisfied with your society? Satisfied; more or less satisfied; more or less dissatisfied; dissatisfied."
Totals do not always add up to 100 because of a small proportion of "don't knows" and "no answers".

society. Similarly, a wave of contentment prevails in India, where only seven percent of the respondents said they were dissatisfied.

Despite similar problems, there seems to be general contentment in Brazil too; 88% feel fairly satisfied with their society.

At the opposite end of the spectrum, young people from the most prosperous and highly industralized nations in the world seem to be among the least satisfied.

Perhaps the most surprising is the high degree of dissatisfaction expressed in the U.S. and Sweden. In both countries, 36% put themselves in the dissatisfied camp.

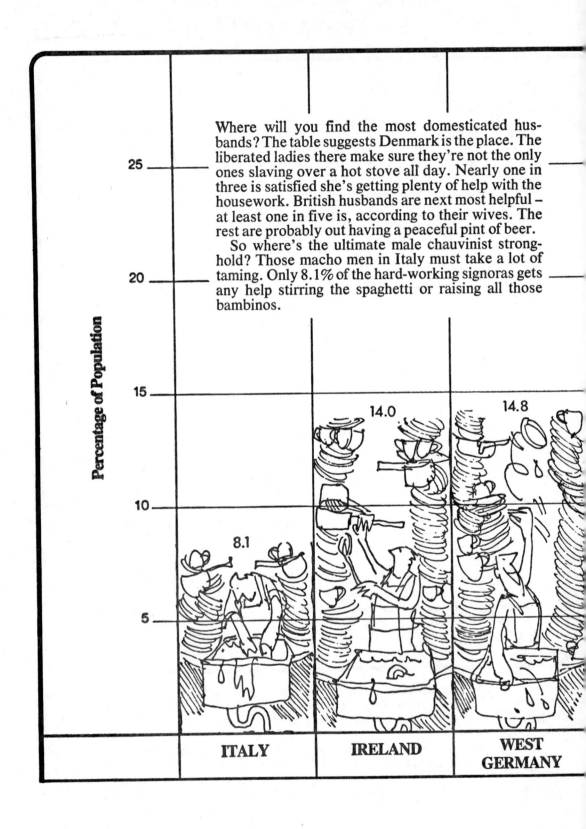

Percentage of Population

Where will you find the most domesticated husbands? The table suggests Denmark is the place. The liberated ladies there make sure they're not the only ones slaving over a hot stove all day. Nearly one in three is satisfied she's getting plenty of help with the housework. British husbands are next most helpful – at least one in five is, according to their wives. The rest are probably out having a peaceful pint of beer.

So where's the ultimate male chauvinist stronghold? Those macho men in Italy must take a lot of taming. Only 8.1% of the hard-working signoras gets any help stirring the spaghetti or raising all those bambinos.

25

20

15

14.0

14.8

10

8.1

5

ITALY | IRELAND | WEST GERMANY

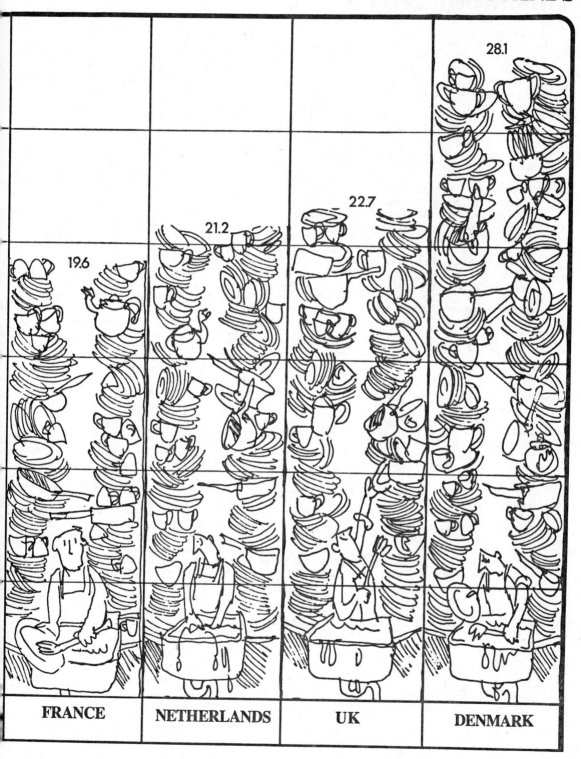

BIBLIOGRAPHY

People
18/19: United Nations; data compiled from document number ESA/P/WP.55, May 28th 1975, "Selected World Demographic Indicators by Country 1950-2000", by the Population Division, Department of Economic and Social Affairs, © United Nations Secretariat, reproduced with their permission. Population Reference Bureau Inc., Washington, D.C.; data calculated by Heron House from 1977 estimates. © Population Reference Bureau Inc., Washington, D.C., reproduced with their permission. 20/21: United Nations; data compiled from medium variant, document number ESA/P/WP.60, February 25th 1976, "Population by Sex and Age for Regions and Countries, 1950-2000", as assessed by the Population Division, Department of Economic and Social Affairs, © United Nations Secretariat, reproduced with their permission. 22/23: United Nations; data compiled from document number ESA/P/WP.56, October 6th 1975, "Single Year Population Estimates and Projections for Major Areas, Regions and Countries in the World, 1950-2000", as assessed by the Population Division, Department of Economic and Social Affairs, © United Nations Secretariat, reproduced with their permission. 24/25: United Nations, data compiled from mediuim variant, document number ESA/P/WP.56, May 28th 1975, "Selected World Demographic Indicators by Country 1950-2000", by the Population Division Department of Economic and Social Affairs, © United Nations Secretariat, reproduced with their permission. 26/27: United Nations, data compiled from document number ESA/P/WP.58, November 21st 1975, "Trends and Prospects in the Population of Urban Agglomerations, 1950-2000", as assessed in 1973-1975, by the Population Division, Department of Economic and Social Affairs © United Nations Secretariat, reproduced with their permission. 28/29: United nations, data compiled from document number ESA/P/WP.55, May 28th 1975, "Selected World Demographic Indicators by Country 1950-2000", by the Population Division, Department of Economic and Social Affairs, © United Nations Secretariat, reproduced with their permission. Population Reference Bureau Inc., Washington, D.C.; data calculated by Heron House using birth and death rates estimated for 1977, © Population Reference Bureau Inc., Washington, D.C., reproduced with their permission.

The Land
34/35: Food and Agriculture Organization, data compiled from *F.A.O. Production Yearbook 1976*, Volume 30, © Food and Agriculture Organization, reproduced with their permission. © 36/37: Food and Agriculture Organization; data compiled from *F.A.O. Production Yearbook 1976*, Volume 30, © Food and Agriculture Organization, reproduced with their permission. 38/39: I.U.C.N.; data compiled from "1975 United Nations List of National Parks and Equivalent Reserves", published 1975, number 33, © I.U.C.N. (International union for Conservation of Nature and National Resources), reproduced with their permission. Vision, data compiled from *Vision* magazine, July/August 1973 issue, © Vision, reproduced with their permission.

Man and the Environment
44/45: "Tables of Temperature, Relative Humidity, Precipitation and Sunshine for the World", H.M.S.O.; data compiled from Parts 1 and 3 and reproduced with the permission of the Controller of Her Majesty's Stationery Office. *World Survey of Climatology*, Elsevier Scientific Publishing Company, reproduced with their permission. 46/47: National Oceanic and Atmospheric Administration, U.S. Department of Commerce. 48/49: World Health Organization, data compiled from "Air Quality in Selected Urban Areas 1973-4", published by W.H.O., Geneva, 1976, reproduced with their permission. 50/51: Overseas Development Council, data compiled from various documents, published by the Overseas Development Council, Washington, D.C. and reproduced with their permission.

People and Money
56/57: United Nations, data compiled from United Nations "Monthly Bulletins" and from "National Accounts", reproduced with their permission. 58/59:*World Bank Atlas 1976*, published by the World Bank, reproduced with their permission. Organization for Economic Co-operation and Development, data compiled from *O.E.C.D. Financial Statistics*, number 11, 1977 and from "Quarterly National Accounts Bulletins", published in Paris in 1977 by O.E.C.D., reproduced with their permission. 60/61: International Monetary Fund, data compiled from the "International Financial Statistics" for years concerned, published by the I.M.F. 62/63: International Monetary Fund, data compiled from "International Financial Statistics" for the years concerned, published by the I.M.F. 64/65: Organization for Economic Co-operation and Development, data compiled from the *O.E.C.D. Financial Statistics Tables* and from "Quarterly National Accounts Bulletins" for the years concerned, reproduced with their permission. 66/67: Bank of England and International Monetary Fund, data compiled from "The Bank of England Quarterly Bulletins" and the "International Financial Statistics Tables", published by the I.M.F. for the years concerned. 68/69: Government sources, data compiled from the various statistical offices concerned and conversions by Heron House. 70/71: Market Research Surveys and Consolidated Gold Fields Ltd., London. Data compiled from their publication "Gold 1977" and reproduced with their permission. 72/73: Aston Martin Lagonda Ltd., Rolls-Royce Motors Ltd. and Panther Cars Ltd., data provided by Public Relations Departments of these three companies. Sojuzpushnina, Moscow,

data provided by their Public Relations Department. All data reproduced with permission of the companies concerned. 74/75: United Nations, data compiled from document number ECSC/ CIRC/PAC/39, June 30th 1978, "Schedule of Post Adjustment Classifications" by International Civil Service Commission. 76/77: International Labor Organization, data compiled from Part III of the "Bulletin of Labor Statistics 1977", 2nd Quarter, © International Labor Organization 1977, converted by Heron House, reproduced with their permission. 78/79: Euromonitor, data compiled from *European Marketing Data and Statistics*, volume 14, 1977/8, London and from © *International Marketing Data Statistics*, volume 3, 1977/8, © Euromonitor Publications Ltd., London, reproduced with their permission. 80/81: International Savings Banks Institute, data compiled from "International Savings Banks' Statistics, 1977 Structural Data", published by the International Savings Banks' Institute in Geneva and reproduced with their permission. 82/83: *Survey of Europe Today*, Reader's Digest 1970. Heron House estimates based on I.L.O. figures; Heron House has interpreted the Table 2b, chapter 1 of the *International Labor Organization Statistics 1977* to match the categories found in *Survey of Europe Today* Reader's Digest, 1970.

Where the Money Goes

88/89: Europa Publications Ltd, data compiled from *The Europa Yearbook, A World Survey 1977*, published by Europa Publications Ltd., London, reproduced with their permission. 90/91: Organization for Economic Co-operation and Development, data compiled from "Development Co-operation, 1977 Review", published by O.E.C.D., Paris, November 1977, reproduced with their permission.

The Taxman Cometh

96/97: Organization for Economic Co-operation and Development, data compiled from *Revenue Statistics of O.E.C.D. Member Countries 1965-1974*, fi O.E.C.D. 1976, reproduced with their permission. 98/99: Organization for Economic Co-operation and Development, data compiled from *Revenue Statistics of O.E.C.D. Member Countries 1965-1974*, © O.E.C.D. 1976, reproduced with their permission. 100/101: Official government documents, data compiled and converted by Heron House based on government data made available to Heron House. 102/103: Government documents, data compiled from various official government documents. 104/105: Organization for Economic Co-operation and Development, data compiled from *Revenue Statistics of O.E.C.D. Member Countries 1965-1974*, © O.E.C.D. 1976, reproduced with their permission. Confidential industry estimates, conversions by Heron House.

Working

110/111: Organization for Economic Co-operation and Development, data compiled from *Labor Force Statistics 1964-1975*, published in Paris in 1977, © O.E.C.D. reproduced with their permission. 112/113: Organization for Economic Co-operation and Development, data compiled from *Labor Force Statistics 1964-1975*, published in Paris in 1977, © O.E.C.D., reproduced with their permission. 114/115: Organization for Economic Co-operation and Development, data compiled from *Labour Force Statistics 1964-1975*, published in Paris in 1977, © O.E.C.D., reproduced with their permission. Organization for Economic Co-operation and Development, January 1978 reprinted from the "O.E.C.D. Observer", data number 90, January 1978. 116/117: International Labor Organization, data compiled from *The Yearbook of Labor Statistics 1977*, © I.L.O. 1977, reproduced with their permission. Heron House estimates were based on I.L.O. figures and converted into a different set of units. 118/119: British Steel Corporation, data compiled from *International Steel Statistics 1976* and converted into the US/UK system of units by Heron House, reproduced with B.S.C.'s permission. 120/121: Union Bank of Switzerland, data compiled from *Prices and Earnings around the Globe*, published in October 1976. 122/123: International Labor Organization, data compiled from *The Yearbook of Labor Statistics 1977*, © International Labor Organization 1977, reproduced with their permission. Heron House estimates based on I.L.O. figures and converted into a different set of units. 124/125: International Labor Organization, data compiled from *The Yearbook of Labor Statistics 1977*, © International Labor Organization 1977, reproduced with their permission. 126/127: International Labor Organization, data compiled from *The Yearbook of Labor Statistics 1977*, © International Labor Organization, 1977, reproduced with their permission. 128/129: International Labor Organization, data compiled from *The Yearbook of Labour Statistics 1977*. © International Labor Organization 1977, reproduced with their permission. 130/131: International Labor Organization, data compiled from *The Yearbook of Labor Statistics 1977*, © International Labor Organization 1977, reproduced with their permission.

At Home

136/137: National statistical offices, data compiled by Heron House based on material provided by statistical offices. Euromonitor, data extracted from *European Marketing Data and Statistics*, volume 14, 1977/8, © Euromonitor publications Ltd., London, reproduced with their permission. 138/139: Euromonitor, data compiled from *European Marketing Data and Statistics*, volume 14, 1977/8, and from *International Marketing Data and Statistics*, volume 3, 1977/8, © Euromonitor Publications Ltd., London reproduced with their permission. National Statistical office, data compiled from the *U.S. Annual Housing Survey 1977* (for the U.S.A.), the *1977 Japan Statistical Yearbook* (for Japan), the *Household Facilities and Equipment 1977* Statistics Canada (for Canada), the *Compendio Statistico Italiano 1977* (for Italy), the *España Anuario Estadístico 1976* (for Spain), the *Official Yearbook of Australia 1975/6* (for Australia). 140/141: Euromonitor, data compiled from *European Marketing Data and Statistics,* volume 14 1977/8, and from *International Marketing Data and Statistics,* volume 3, 1977/8, © Euromonitor Publications Ltd., London and reproduced with their permission. United Nations, data compiled from the *United Nations 1976 Statistical Yearbook,* 28th issue, New York, 1977, © United Nations, reproduced with their permission. 142/143: Euromonitor, data compiled from *European Marketing Data and Statistics,* volume 14, 1977/8, and from *International Marketing Data and Statistics,* London, volume 3, 1977/8, © Euromonitor Publications Ltd., and reproduced with their permission. National Statistical offices, data compiled by Heron House based on documents sent by the statistical offices concerned. 144/145: National statistical offices, data compiled by Heron House based on various publications provided by the statistical offices. Union Bank of Switzerland, data compiled from *Prices and Earnings around the Globe,* published in October 1976 in Switzerland. 146/147: National statistical offices, data compiled by Heron House based on documents sent by the statistical offices concerned. Euromonitor, data compiled from *European Marketing Data and Statistics,* volume 14, 1977/8, and from International *Marketing Data and Statistics,* volume 3, 1977/8, © Euromonitor Publications Ltd., London, reproduced with their permission. 148/149: United Nations, data compiled from the *United Nations Compendium of Housing Statistics 1972-74,* second issue, New York 1976, © United Nations, reproduced with their permission. National statistical offices, data compiled and tabulated by Heron House based on documents sent by the statistical offices concerned. Euromonitor, data compiled from *European Marketing Data and Statistics,* volume 14, 1977/8, and from *International Marketing Data and Statistics,* volume 3, 1977/8, © Euromonitor Publications Ltd., London, reproduced with their permission.

United Nations, data compiled from the *United Nations Compendium of Housing Statistics 1972-74,* second issue, New York 1976, © United Nations, reproduced with their permission. National statistical offices, data compiled and tabulated by Heron House based on documents sent by the statistical offices concerned. Euromonitor, data compiled from *European Marketing Data and Statistics,* volume 14, 1977/8, and from *International Marketing Data and Statistics,* volume 3, 1977/8, © Euromonitor Publications Ltd., London, reproduced with their permission.

At Play
154/155: Roper Organization Inc., "Roper Reports 1978 - 1", © Roper Organization Inc., reproduced with their permission. 156/157: Euromonitor, data compiled from *Consumer Europe 1977* © Euromonitor Publications Ltd., London, reproduced with their permission. Gallup Organization Inc., data reproduced from the "Gallup Opinion Index of March 1974", report number 105, reproduced with their permission. 158/159: Organization for Economic Co-operation and Development, data reprinted from "O.E.C.D. Observer", number 91, March 1978. Heron House estimates, data compiled by Heron House based on *U.N.E.S.C.O. 1975/76 Statistical Yearbook.* 160/161: United Nations, data compiled from *United Nations 1976 Statistical Yearbook,* 28th issue, New York, 1977, © United Nations, reproduced with their permission. United Nations Educational, Scientific, and Cultural Organization, data extracted from the *U.N.E.S.C.O. Statistical Yearbook 1976,* table 14.1, © U.N.E.S.C.O. 1977, reproduced with their permission. 162/163: International Olympic Committee Archives, data compiled from a selection of documents provided by the National Olympic Committee in London. 164/165: Golf Digest Inc., data reprinted from the February, 1975 issue of Golf Digest Inc., U.S.A., © 1975 Golf Digest Inc., U.S.A., reproduced with their permission. 166/167: Euromonitor, data compiled from *European Marketing Data and Statistics,* volume 14, 1977/8, © Euromonitor Publications Ltd., London reproduced with their permission. Government trade offices, data supplied by the respective offices. *Gambling in America,* by the Commission on the Review of the National Policy Toward Gambling, Washington, D.C. 1976. 168/169: Euromonitor, data compiled from *European Marketing Data and Statistics,* volume 13, 1976/7, © Euromonitor Publications Ltd., London, reproduced with their permission. Gallup Organization Inc., data provided by the Gallup Organization Inc., in Princeton, New Jersey, U.S.A., reproduced with their permission. *Leisure Survey of the Secretary of State* published in 1976 by the Secretary of State, Ottawa, Canada. 170/171: United Nations Educational, Scientific, and Cultural Organization, data compiled from *U.N.E.S.C.O. Statistical Yearbook 1976,* © U.N.E.S.C.O. 1977, reproduced with their permission. 172/173: United Nations Educational, Scientific, and Cultural Organization, data compiled from the *U.N.E.S.C.O. Statistical Yearbook 1975,* © U.N.E.S.C.O. 1976, reproduced with their permission. 174/175: United Nations Educational, Scientific, and Cultural Organization, data compiled from *U.N.E.S.C.O. Statistical Yearbook 1975,* © U.N.E.S.C.O. 1976, reproduced with their permission. Library Association, data compiled by the Library Association,

London. 176/177: United Nations, data compiled from the *United Nations 1976 Statistical Yearbook,* 28th issue, New York, 1977, © United Nations, reproduced with their permission. 178/179: E.M.I. Ltd., data compiled from *World Record Markets 1976* published by E.M.I., reproduced with their permission. 180/181: United Nations Educational, Scientific, and Cultural Organization, data compiled from *U.N.E.S.C.O. Statistical Yearbook 1976,* © U.N.E.S.C.O. 1977, reproduced with their permission. 182/183: Euromonitor, data compiled from *European Marketing Data and Statistics,* volume 14, 1977/8, © Euromonitor Publications Ltd., London, reproduced with their permission. Industry estimates. The Australian Tourist Board. 184/185: Organization for Economic Co-operation and Development, data compiled from "Tourism Policy and International Tourism in O.E.C.D. Countries", Paris 1978, © O.E.C.D., reproduced with their permission.

Underway
190/191: International Road Federation, data compiled from *World Road Statistics 1972-1976,* 1977 edition, Geneva, Switzerland. Society for Motor Manufacturers and Traders, London, data supplied by the Society and reproduced with their permission. 192/193: Union Bank of Switzerland, data compiled from *Prices and Earnings around the Globe,* October 1976, reproduced with their permission. 194/195: International Road Federation, data compiled from *World Road Statistics 1972-1976,* 1977 edition, Geneva, Switzerland, data converted by Heron House. 196/197: Automobile Association, London. Department of Motor Transport, Australia. Embassies. Data supplied upon request. 198/199: International Road Federation, data compiled from *World Road Statistics 1972-1976,* 1977 edition, Geneva, Switzerland. 200/201: International Civil Aviation Organization, data compiled from *Civil Aviation Statistics of the World - 1976,* published by I.C.A.O. in Montreal, Canada, reproduced with their permission. 202/203: International Civil Aviation Organization, data compiled from "Digest of Statistics", number 218-A, series T, number 36, "Airline Traffic", volume 1, published by I.C.A.O. in Montreal, Canada, reproduced with their permission. Heron House conversions. 204/205: International Civil Aviation Organization, data compiled from "Digest of Statistics", number 218-A, series T, number 36, Airline Traffic, volume 1, published by I.C.A.O. in Montreal, Canada, reproduced with their permission. 206/207: *Destination Disaster* by Paul Eddy, Elaine Potter and Bruce Page, © Times Newspapers Ltd 1976, reproduced with their permission. *Flight International* magazine, data compiled from January 24th 1976, January 22nd 1977 and January 21st 1978 issues of *Flight International,* ©*Flight International,* reproduced with their permission. 208/209: *Flight Inter-national* magazine, data compiled from January 21st 1971, January 20th 1972, January 18th 1973, January 17th 1974, January 23rd 1975, January 24th 1976, January 22nd 1977 issues of *Flight International,* © *Flight International,* reproduced with their permission. 210/211: *Sunday Times* files, London. 212/213: *Aerospace International* magazine, data compiled from "Security in the Air" by Chris Eliot in February/March 1978 issue of *Aerospace International,* published by Mönch Verlag, Germany, reproduced with their permission. *Flight International* magazine, data compiled from January 21st 1971, January 20th 1972, January 18th 1973, January 17th 1974, January 23rd 1975, January 24th 1976, January 22nd 1977 issues of *Flight International,* © *Flight International,* reproduced with their permission.

Diet
218/219: Gralla Publications, data reprinted by permission of *Supermarketing* magazine, a Gralla Publication, September 1977. 220/221: Euromonitor, data compiled from *European Marketing Data and Statistics,* volume 14, 1977/8, and from *International Marketing Data and Statistics,* volume 3, 1977/8 ©, Euromonitor Publications Ltd., London, reproduced with their permission. U.S. Department of Agriculture, data provided by the Department for reproduction. 222/223: Brewers' Society, data compiled from the *1976 Brewers' Society Statistical Handbook,* London, England, reproduced with their permission. *The World Atlas of Wine,* revised edition by Hugh Johnson published by Mitchell Beazley Publishers, © 1977, data compiled from the above and reproduced with their permission. Heron House conversions.

Health: Mind and Body
228/229: World Health Organization, data compiled from *World Health Statistics Annual, 1977,* © W.H.O. 1977, reproduced with their permission. 230/231: Organization for Economic Co-operation and Development, data compiled from "O.E.C.D. Public Expenditure on Health," July 1977, © O.E.C.D. 1977, reproduced with their permission. 232/233: National statistical offices, data compiled by Heron House based on documents provided by the various government offices. *Hospitals and Nursing Homes 1972,* data compiled from the above source, and Australian government publication. 234/235: Euromonitor, data compiled from *Consumer Europe 1977,* London, © Euromonitor Publications Ltd., London, 1977, reproduced with their permission. Confidential industry source. *The Japanese Statistics Yearbook 1975.* 236/237: Heron House estimates based on World Health Organization figures, data compiled from *World Health Statistics Annual 1977,* © W.H.O. 1977, reproduced with their permission. 238/239: Commission on Narcotic Drugs, data compiled from "Drug Abuse: Extent, Pattern and Trends", Commission on Narcotic Drugs 5th special session. "Annual Abstract of Congression", data compiled from

from "1976 C.I.S. Annual Abstract of Congression Drug Abuse". *Man Alive*, B.B.C. Television, April 4th 1978, reproduced with their permission. National statistical offices, data compiled by Heron House based on documents provided by the various government offices. United Nations, data compiled from documents provided by the 29th International Congress on Alcoholism and Drug Dependence 1970. 240/241: World Health Organization, data compiled from from "World Health Statistics Report", volume 30, number 3, 1977, © W.H.O. reproduced with their permission, Heron House estimates. Centre for Disease Control, data compiled from documents provided by the Centre for Disease Control, U.S. Department of Health, Education and Welfare. H.M.S.O., data compiled from "On the State of Public Health", © H.M.S.O. 1976, reproduced with the permission of the Controller of Her Britannic Majesty's Stationery Office. Office of Health Economics, data compiled from documents provided by the Office of Health Economics, Paris. Department of Health, data compiled from documents provided by the Department of Health, Dublin, Eire. 242/243: Addiction Research Foundation, Toronto, data compiled from "The Epidemiology of Alcoholism: The Elusive Nature of the Problem, Estimating the Prevalence of Excessive Alcohol Use and Alcohol Related Mortality, Current Trends and Issue of Prevention", by J. de Lint, reproduced by permission of the author. Government sources, data compiled by Heron House based on documents provided by the various governemnt offices. 244/245: World Health Organization, data compiled from *World Health Statistics Annual 1977*, © W.H.O. 1977, reproduced with their permission. 246/247: World Health Organization, data compiled from *World Health Statistics Annual 1977*, © W.H.O. 1977, reproduced with their permission. National statistical offices, data compiled by Heron House based on documents provided by various government offices. 248/249: National statistical offices, relevant Commissions, British Pregnancy Advisory Service and International Planned Parenthood Federation files, data compiled from documents provided by the above. 250/251: World Health Organization, data compiled from *World Health Statistics Annual 1977*, © W.H.O. 1977, reproduced with their permission. 252/253: World Health Organization, data compiled from *World Health Statistics Annual 1977*, © W.H.O. 1977, reproduced with their permission. 254/255: World Health Organization, data compiled from *World Health Statistics Annual 1977*, © W.H.O. 1977, reproduced with their permission. 256/257: World Health Organization, data compiled from "World Health Statistics Report", volume 28, number 6, 1975, © W.H.O. 1975, reproduced with their permission. 258/259: Department of Health and Social Security, London. World Health Organization, data compiled

from *World Health Statistics Annual 1977*, © W.H.O. 1977, reproduced with their permission. *Canada Yearbook 1976-77*.

Sex
264/265: "The Virginia Slims American Women's Opinion Poll", The Roper Organization Inc., 1974 (for U.S.A.). *Honey* magazine, May and June issues 1977, survey conducted by the Schlachman Research Organization Ltd., London (for U.K.). *Cleo* magazine, August and September 1974 issues, survey conducted by Roy Morgan Research Centre Pty. Ltd. (for Australia). "Allensbacher Berichten 1970", Institut für Demoskopie Allensbach. All data reproduced with their permission. 268/271: *Cleo* magazine, August and September 1974 issues, survey conducted by Roy Morgan Research Centre Pty. Ltd. (for Australia), reproduced with their permission. "Family Planning Perspectives", volume 9, number 2, 1977, from "Sexual and Contraceptive Experience of Young Unmarried Women in the U.S.A., 1976-71" by Melvin Zelnick Ph.D. and John F. Kantner Ph.D. (for U.S.A.), reproduced with their permission. "Riksforbundet für Sexuel Upplysning", Stockholm (for Sweden). *The Sexual Behaviour of Young Adults* by Michael Schofield, published by Allen Lane, 1973, © Michael Schofield 1973, reproduced with the permission of Penguin Books Ltd. (for U.K.). 272/275: "The Virginia Slims American Women's Opinion Poll", The Roper Organization Inc., 1974 (for U.S.A.). *Rapport sur le Comportement Sexuel des Français* by Dr Pierre Simon, published by Rene Julliard, Pierre Charron, 1972, survey conducted by *l'Institut Français d'Opinion Publique* (for France). *Weekend* magazine, Toronto, December 3rd 1977 issue (for Canada). *Honey* magazine, May and June 1977, survey conducted by the Schlachman Research Organization Ltd., London (for U.K.). All data reproduced with their permission. 276/277: Gallup International Affiliated Institutes in the countries concerned, survey carried out in 1973 sampling attitudes of young people aged 18-24, data compiled from the "Gallup Opinion Index" U.S.A., report number 100, October 1973, reproduced with their permission. A list of the participating institutes is given under Chapter 18 bibliography. 278/279: "Family Planning Perspectives", volume 9, number 2, 1977 from "Sexual and Contraceptive Experience of Young Unmarried Women in the U.S.A., 1976-71", by Melvin Zelnick Ph.D. and John F. Kantner, Ph.D. (for U.S.A.), *Honey* magazine, May and June 1977 issues, survey conducted by the Schlachman Research Organization Ltd., London (for U.K.). "Sexualiteit in Nederland", published in *Margriet*, a women's magazine, 1968. All data reproduced with their permission. 280/283: "Sexual Experience, Birth Control Usage and Sources of Sex Education among Unmarried University Students", by Dr. M. Barrett and Dr. M. Fitz-Earle, 1974 (for

Canada). "Riksforbundet für Sexual Upply-sning", Stockholm (for Sweden). *Rapport sur le Comportement Sexuel des Français by* Dr. Pierre Simon, published by Rene Julliard, Pierre Charron, 1972, survey conducted by *l'Institut Français d'Opinion Publique* (for France). "Family Planning Perspective", volume 9, number 2, 1977, from "Sexual and Contraceptibe Experience of Young Unmarried Women in the U.S.A., 1967-77", by Melvin Zelnik Ph.D. and John F. Kantner Ph.D. (for U.S.A.). *Honey* magazine, May and June 1977 issues, survey conducted by the Schlachman Research Organization Ltd., London (for U.K.). "Sexualiteit in Nederland", published in the *Margriet,* magazine 1968. All data reproduced with their permission. 284/287: "Family Planning Perspectives", volume 9, number 2, 1977 from "Sexual and Contraceptive Experience of Young Unmarried Women in the U.S.A. 1976-71", by Melvin Zelnik Ph.D. and John F. Kantner Ph.D. (for U.S.A.), reproduced with their permission. *L'Express,* September 5th-11th 1977 (for France), reproduced with their permission. Michael Scholfield, *The Sexual Behaviour of Young Adults,* published by Allen Lane, 1973, © Michael Schofield, 1973, reproduced with the permission of Penguin Books Ltd. (for U.K.). "Riksforbundet fur Sexuel Upplysning", Stockholm (for Sweden). 288/289: *Honey* magazine, May and June 1977 issues, survey conducted by the Schlachman Research Organization Ltd., London (for U.K.). *Cleo* magazine, August and September issues, survey conducted by Roy Morgan Research Centre Pty. Ltd. (for Australia). All data reproduced with their permission. 290/291: United Nations, data compiled from document ESA/P/WP.59, January 30th 1976, "Up-dated Study of Urban-Rural Differences in the Marital Status. Composition of the Population", prepared by the Department of Economic and Social Affairs, © United Nations, reproduced with their permission. 292/293: United Nations, data compiled from document ESA/P/WP.59, January 30th 1976, "Up-dated Study of Urban-Rural Differences in the Marital Status Composition of the Population", prepared by the Department of Economic and Social Affairs, © United Nations, reproduced with their permission. 294/295: United Nations, data compiled from the *United Nations 1976 Statistical Yearbook,* 28th issue, New York 1977, © United Nations, reproduced with their permission. 296/297: *Sex and Marriage in England Today* by Geoffrey Gorer, published by Thomas Nelson & Sons Ltd., London, 1971 (for U.K.), reproduced with their permission. Survey conducted by Isopublic, Zurich, on behalf of *Weltwoche* (for Switzerland), reproduced with their permission. The Canadian Gallup Poll (for Canada). The National Opinion Research Centre of the University of Chicago (for U.S.A.). "Sexualiteit in Nederland" published in *Margriet* magazine, 1968 (for Netherlands). 298/299: *Sex*

and Marriage in England Today by Geoffrey Gorer, published by Thomas Nelson & Sons Ltd., London, 1971 (for U.K.). *The Sex Survey of Australian Women* by Prof. Robert E. Bell, published by Sun Books, 1974 (for Australia). "Sexualiteit in Nederland", published in *Margriet* magazine, 1968 (for Netherlands). All data reproduced with their permission. 300/303: *Weekend* magazine, Toronto, December 3rd and 17th 1977 issues and The Canadian Gallup Poll Ltd. (for Canada). The Gallup Organization Inc., U.S.A. and The National Opinion Research Center of the University of Chicago (for U.S.A.). Social Surveys (Gallup Poll) Ltd. (for U.K.). "Sexualiteit in Nederland", published in *Margriet* magazine, 1968 (for Netherlands).

Citizenship

308/309: Government documents, data compiled from documents provided by various government offices. Election Research Center, Washington, D.C. 310/311: National statistical offices. Government departments, data compiled from documents provided by various government offices. Embassies, data pro ided by various embassies in London. 312/313: International Institute for Strategic Studies, London, data compiled from *The Military Balance 1977-78,* © International Institute for Strategic Studies, 1977, reproduced with their permission. 314/315: "Amnesty International Report", 1977, data extracted from the Amnesty International Report 1977, reproduced with their permission.

Education

320/321: Organization for Economic Co-operation and Development, data compiled from *The Educational Situation in OECD Countries,* © O.E.C.D. reproduced with their permission. 322/323: Organization for Economic Co-operation and Development, data compiled from *The Educational Situation in O.E.C.D. Countries,* © O.E.C.D. reproduced with their permission. United Nations Educational, Scientific, and Cultural Organization, data compiled from *U.N.E.S.C.O. Statistical Yearbook 1976,* © U.N.E.S.C.O. 1977, reproduced with their permission. 324/325: United Nations Educational, Scientific, and Cultural Organization, data compiled from *U.N.E.S.C.O. Statistical Yearbook 1976,* © U.N.E.S.C.O. 1977, reproduced with their permission. 326/327: United Nations Educational, Scientific, and Cultural Organization, data compiled from *U.N.E.S.C.O. Stastistical Yearbook 1976,* © U.N.E.S.C.O. 1977, reproduced with their kind permission. Euromonitor, data compiled from *European Marketing Data and Statistics 1977/78,* © Euromonitor Publications Ltd., London, reproduced with their permission. Government statistical offices.

Crime

332/333: Euromonitor, data compiled from *European Marketing Data and Statistics,* volume 12, 1975/76, © Euromonitor Publications Ltd., London, reproduced with their permission. 334/335: Data calculated by Heron House using data provided by the Federal Bureau of Investigation and by the International Criminal Police Organization, Paris. 336/337: Interpol, data compiled from *International Crime Statistics 1975*, published by the International Criminal Police Organization, Paris, reproduced with their permission. F.B.I., data supplied by the Federal Bureau of Investigation. 338/339: Government Departments of Justice, data supplied by the Department of Justice of the countries concerned. 340/341: Interpol, data compiled from *International Crime Statistics 1975*, published by the International Criminal Police Organization, Paris, reproduced with their permission. F.B.I. data supplied by the Federal Bureau of Investigation. 342/343: United Nations, data extracted from document number A/CONF/56/6, New York 1975, presented to the Fifth United Nations Congress on the Prevention of Crime and the Treatment of Offenders.

What People Use
348/349: Confidential industry sources. 350/351: Confidential industry sources. 352/353: Confidential industry sources. 354/355: Euromonitor, data compiled from *Consumer Europe 1976*, © Euromonitor Publications Ltd., London, reproduced with their permission. Confidential industry sources. 356/357: Confidential industry source. 358/359: Euromonitor, data compiled from *Consumer Europe 1977*, © Euromonitor Publications Ltd., London, reproduced with their permission. Confederation of British Industry, data based on *Western European Living Costs 1977*, © Confederation of British Industry, reproduced with their permission. Confidential industry sources. 360/361: Confidential industry sources. 362/363: Confidential industry sources. 364/365: Organization for Economic Co-operation and Development, data reproduced from the *O.E.C.D. Observer*, number 91, March 1978, © O.E.C.D. reproduced with their permission. Euromonitor, data compiled from *European Marketing Data and Statistics 1977/78*, volume 14 and from *International Marketing Data and Statistics, 1977/78*, volume 3, © Euromonitor Publications Ltd., London, reproduced with their permission.

What People Think
370/383: Gallup International Affiliated Institutes in the countries concerned, the surveys were carried out during the fall and winter of 1974/5 and during the spring of 1976, reproduced with their permission. The list of participating institutes is given hereafter. 384/387: Gallup International Affiliated Institutes in the countries concerned, data compiled from "Women in America", U.S.A. Gallup Opinion index 128, March 1976, reproduced with their permission. The list of participating institutes is given hereafter. 388/389: Commission of the European Communities, data compiled from *European Men and Women*, December 1975, Brussels, Gallup International Affiliated Institutes in the countries concerned carried out the survey in May 1975, reproduced with their permission. General Mills Inc., U.S.A., data compiled from *The General Mills American Family Report 1976/77*, "Raising Children in a Changing Society", survey carried out by Yankelovich, Skelly and White in 1976. 390/391: Commission of the European Communities, data compiled from *European Men and Women*, December 1975, Brussels, Gallup International Affiliated Institutes in the countries concerned carried out the survey in May 1975. Roper Organization Inc., data compiled from the "Virginia Slims American Woman's Opinion Poll", volume III, survey carried out by the Roper Organization Inc., during the spring of 1974, reproduced with their permission. 392/393: Commission of the European Communities, data compiled from *European Men and Women*, December 1975, Brussels, Gallup International Affiliated Institutes in the countries concerned carried out the survey in May 1975, reproduced with their permission. Gallup Organization Inc., data compiled from the "Gallup Opinion Index", U.S.A. number 128, March 1976, reproduced with their permission. 394/395: Commission of the European Communities, data reproduced with their permission. 396/403: Gallup International Affiliated Institutes in the countries concerned, the surveys were carried out during the fall and winter of 1974/5 and during the spring of 1976, reproduced with their permission. The list of participating institutes is given hereafter. 404/405: Commission of the European Communities, data compiled from *European Consumers 1976*, Brussels, survey carried out in 1975 by Gallup International Affiliated Institutes in the countries concerned, reproduced with their permission. Opinion Research Corporation, data compiled from "O.R.C. Public Opinion Index", May 1976, survey carried out in 1976, reproduced with their permission. 406/407: Commission of the European Communities, data compiled from *Euro-Barometer* number 8, January 1978, published by the Commission of the European Communities, Brussels, reproduced with their permission, survey carried out by the Gallup International Affiliated Institutes in the countries concerned. The list of participating institutes is given hereafter. 408/409: Commission of the European Communities, data compiled from *European Consumers 1976*, Brussels, survey carried out in 1975 by Gallup International Affiliated Institutes in the countries concerned, reproduced with their permission. Opinion Research Corporation, data compiled from "O.R.C. Public Opinion Index", May 1976, survey carried out in 1976, reproduced with their permission. 410/413: Gallup International Affiliated Institutes in the countries concerned, surveys were carried out during the fall and winter of 1974/75 and during the spring of 1976,

452

reproduced with their permission. The list of participating institutes is given hereafter. 414/415: The Gallup Organization Inc., data compiled from the Gallup Opinion Index, U.S.A. Report number 136, November 1976, survey carried out in September 1976, reproduced with their permission. 416/417: The Gallup Organization Inc., data compiled from the "Gallup Opinion Index", U.S.A. Report number 121, July 1975, survey carried out in April 1971 and April 1975, reproduced with their permission. 418/419: Gallup International Affiliated Institutes in the countries concerned, the survey was carried out during the fall and winter of 1974/75 and during the spring of 1976, reproduced with their permission. The list of participating institutes is given hereafter. 420/421: Commission of the European Communities, data compiled from *European Consumers, 1976*, Brussels, survey carried out in 1975 by Gallup International Affiliated Institutes in the countries concerned, reproduced with their permission. Opinion Research Corporation, data compiled from "O.R.C. Public Opinion Index", May 1976, survey carried out in 1976, reproduced with their permission. 422/423: Gallup International Affiliated Institutes in the countries concerned, the survey was carried out in 1973 sampling attitudes of young people aged 18 to 24, data compiled from the "Gallup Opinion Index", U.S.A., Report number 100, October 1973, reproduced with their permission. The list of participating institutes is given hereafter. 424/425: "McCann-Erickson Youth Study", 1976/77, the survey was carried out between June 1976 and April 1977, the coverage was 10 to 25-year-olds except in Scandinavia and Spain where it was 15 to 25, the survey includes Japan and Brazil and is still being extended, reproduced with their permission. 426/431: Gallup International Affiliated Institutes in the countries concerned, the surveys were carried out in 1973 sampling attitudes of young people aged 18 to 24, data compiled from the "Gallup Opinion Index", U.S.A., Report number 100, October 1973, reproduced with their permission. The list of participating institutes is given hereafter. 432/435: "McCann-Erickson Youth Study", 1976/77, the survey was carried out between June 1976 and April 1977, the coverage was 10 to 25-year-olds except in Scandinavia and Spain where it was 15 to 25, the survey includes Japan and Brazil and is still being extended, reproduced with their permission. 436/437: Gallup International Affiliated Institutes in the countries concerned, the survey was carried out in 1973 sampling attitudes of young people aged 18 to 24, data compiled from the "Gallup Opinion Index", U.S.A., Report number 100, October 1973, reproduced with their permission. The list of participating institutes is given hereafter. 438/439: "McCann-Erickson Youth Study", the survey was carried out between June 1976 and April 1977, the coverage was 10 to 25-year-olds except in Scandinavia and Spain where it was 15 to 25, the survey includes Japan and Brazil and is still being extended, reproduced with their permission. 440/443: Gallup International Affiliated Institutes in the countries concerned, the survey was carried out in 1973 sampling attitudes of young people aged 18 to 24, data compiled from the "Gallup Opinion Index", U.S.A., Report number 100, October 1973, reproduced with their permission. The list of participating institutes is given hereafter.

List of all companies, members of Gallup International Affiliated Research Institutes, who have participated in the surveys quoted above:

Australia: The Roy Morgan Research Centre Pty., Ltd., Melbourne

Brazil: Instituto Gallup de Opiniao Publica, Sao Paulo

Canada: The Canadian Gallup Poll Ltd., Toronto

Denmark: Gallup Markedsanalyse A/S, Copenhagen

Finland: Suomen Gallup O/Y, Helsinki

France: I.F.O.P.-E.T.M.A.R., Paris

Germany: E.M.N.I.D. Institut Gmbh & Co, Bielefeld

India: The Indian Institute of Public Opinion Ltd., Delhi

Ireland: Irish Marketing Surveys Ltd., Dublin

Italy: D.O.X.A., Milan

Japan: Nippon Research Center Ltd., Tokyo

Netherlands: N.I.P.O. het Nederlands Instituut voor de Publieke Opinieen het Marktonderoek B.V., Amsterdam

Norway: Norsk Opinionsinstitutt A-S, Oslo

Sweden: Swedish Institute of Public Opinion Research Ltd., Stockholm

Switzerland: I.S.O.P.U.B.L.I.C., Zurich

United Kingdom: Social Surveys (Gallup Poll) Ltd., London

United States: The Gallup Organization Inc., Princeton, New Jersey

Yugoslavia: Zavod za Trzisna Istrazivanga (Z.I.T.), Belgrade

INDEX

BE A
BOOK OF NUMBERS
CONTRIBUTOR

fill in the questionnaire which follows

QUESTIONNAIRE

Be a Book of Numbers Contributor

While we have scoured the world's resources to come up with the answers contained in this book, there are many other questions we would have liked to answer. This is particularly true since we plan to publish a new *Book of Numbers* in about two years time.

One way to get additional answers is to commission our own research. We are doing that.

Another important way is to ask readers of the first edition for their answers to vital questions. The questionnaire which follows does so.

If you would be good enough to fill in this questionnaire and mail it to us, we would be ever so grateful. If you complete the questionnaire you have the opportunity to be listed as a research contributor in your country's next edition of the work.

As you can appreciate it is difficult to pose questions in an unbiased manner. We have certainly attempted to do so and have no prejudgements on the topics raised below. However, the editors of Heron House take full responsibility for the questions and the way these have been posed. This has not been done in consultation with the many excellent research organisations which have assisted us.

It is possible that in some cases you will disagree with the choices you can circle under a question. Many of these are, after all, complicated topics. In this case we would suggest that you disregard the question rather than circle a view which doesn't accurately reflect your own.

You can complete the questionnaire in one of two ways: either by cutting out the appropriate pages or by taking a separate sheet of paper and writing your answers on it, and then sending them to us.

Thus, for example, if you believe on question 2, that your life is much more satisfactory than it was five years ago, you would put 2.a) on a piece of paper; if on question 5, you believe that police protection is excellent you would list this as 5a)i).

It is vital that you also give us the personal data about yourself at the end of the questionnaire so that we can compare response by sex, age, geographic location, etc. We guarantee that all returned questionnaires will be kept in strict confidence. If you want to be listed as a contributor in the next edition, please give your name.

Here then are the questions:

1 Listed below are a number of personal problems. Would you please list in order the top three which concern you. Thus, if your biggest single problem is a declining standard of living you would put '1' opposite this, if your second biggest problem is 'fear of crime' you would put '2' opposite:
   a) Taxes are too high
   b) Fear of crime
   c) Unhappy family/personal relations
   d) Can't afford children's higher education
   e) Standard of living is declining
   f) Not enough time for family/friends
   e) Other (please specify) ....
   ....

2 Would you say that compared with five years ago your life today is: (please circle)
a) much more satisfactory/ b) more satisfactory/ c) about the same/ d) less satisfactory/ e) much less satisfactory.

3 Would you say that you get from your work: (please circle)
a) a great deal of satisfaction/ b) some satisfaction/ c) indifference/ d) relatively little satisfaction/ e) virtually no satisfaction.

4 Would you say that in your life religion is: (please circle)
a) very important/ b) somewhat important/ c) not very important/ d) not at all important.

5 Would you please rate the following common services by putting the appropriate figure against them:

a) Police protection
b) Mail delivery
c) Public transportation
d) Telephone service
e) Television

i) excellent ii) good iii) average iv) fairly poor v) very bad

6 In recent years a great deal of discussion has centred on racial equality. What are your feelings on this topic: (please circle)
a) far too little has been done/ b) not enough has been done/ c) about the right amount has been done/ d) too much has been done/ e) far too much has been done.

7 In recent years a great deal of discussion has centered on sexual equality at work and elsewhere. What are your feelings on this topic: (please cicle)
a) far too little has been done/ b) not enough has been done/ c) about the right amount has been done/ d) too much has been done/ e) far too much has been done.

8 Under what conditions do you feel your country should intervene in a foreign war: (please circle)
a) to assist a threatened ally/ b) to assist an invaded ally/ c) only if my country is directly threatened/ d) only if my country is invaded/ e) never.

9 Which of the following do you think is the biggest threat confronting the world today: (please circle)
a) terrorism/ b) inflation/ c) unemployment/ d) collapse of world monetary system/ e) population explosion/ f) increased size of government/ g) other (please specify) ....
....

)With respect to couples living together before marriage, do you feel it's alright if: (please circle)
a) the couple are engaged/ b) the couple are in love but not yet engaged/ c) the couple know one another well/ d) they both simply want to/ e) unacceptable under any conditions.

11 Would you please list below in order the three well known living figures whom you respect most:

A. ....

B. ....

C. ....

12 Would you please list below in order the three well known living figures whom you respect least:

A. ....

B. ....

C. ....

13 Listed below are a variety of professions. Would you please circle the number from 1-10 in terms of your respect for and trust in each. Thus, if you think lawyers command 100% of your respect and trust you would give them a '10', whereas if you only think they command 30% of your respect and trust you would give them a '3'.

a) Politician   1 2 3 4 5 6 7 8 9 10
b) Military professional   1 2 3 4 5 6 7 8 9 10
c) Someone in advertizing   1 2 3 4 5 6 7 8 9 10
d) Businessman   1 2 3 4 5 6 7 8 9 10
e) Lawyer   1 2 3 4 5 6 7 8 9 10
f) Government Official   1 2 3 4 5 6 7 8 9 10
g) Doctor   1 2 3 4 5 6 7 8 9 10
h) Teacher   1 2 3 4 5 6 7 8 9 10
i) Minister   1 2 3 4 5 6 7 8 9 10

14 Do you feel abortion should be: (please circle)
a) permitted under all circumstances/ b) permitted when both partners agree/ c) permitted when woman wants/ d) no opinion/ e) not permitted save under exceptional circumstances/ f) totally outlawed/ g) other (please specify) ....

15 In your judgement what is the biggest loss your country has suffered in the last ten years: (please circle)
a) too much welfare state/ b) government corruption /c) lack of economic stability/ d) life far less personalized/ e) problem occasioned by drugs and crime/ f) erosion of traditional values/ g) disintegration of family values/ h) other (please specify) ....

16 Law and Order is a major issue today. Do you feel: (please circle)
a) the police need far more power/ b) the current laws are adequate/ c) we need to do more to protect suspects/ d) other (please specify)...............
....

17 Do you feel unions have: (please circle)
a) far too much power/ b) too much power/ c) the right amount of power/ d) too little power/ e) far too little power.

18 What do you feel is our biggest central problem in the educational system today: (please circle)
a) too discriminatory/ b) pupil to teacher ratio declining/ c) children's reliance on drugs and alcohol/ d) peer group pressure towards lack of discipline/ e) other (please specify) ....
....

19 Tobacco is a controversial issue today. Do you feel that tobacco smoking should be: (please circle)
a) unrestricted/ b) subject to less controls than it is today/ c) allowed to remain as it is/ d) subject to more controls than it is today/ e) prohibited.

20 Some people strongly believe that a family should have no more than two children to keep population at its present level or (given infant mortality) to make it slightly decline. Do you: (please circle)
a) agree/ b) no opinion/ c) disagree.

21 Please circle below your views toward unfaithfulness in marriage:
a) agree/ b) agree when the marriage is patently unhappy/ c) think it's natural/ d) disagree under all but exceptional circumstances/ e) totally disagree.

22 Some people believe that the world is undergoing an "energy crisis". Do you: (please circle)
a) agree/ b) disagree.

23 If you agree, would you be prepared to pay a higher price for gasoline and/or have a less comfortable car to save energy: (please circle)
a) Yes/ b) No.

24 Energy generated by a nuclear power plant is a current issue. What do you think about nuclear power plants: (please circle)
a) approve/ b) disapprove.

25 Illegal aliens are a current issue. Which of the opinions below most accurately summarizes your feelings on this topic: (please circle)
a) they should all be sent home/ b) those who might be undesirable should be sent home/ c) those presently in country should be allowed the opportunity to stay if they have no criminal record/ d) tighter controls should be instituted for the future but existing illegal aliens and their family members should be allowed to stay.

26 Some people feel protecting our environment is important – others feel that our environment should suffer if it would create jobs. Given this stark choice, which do you favor: (please circle)
a) jobs/ b) environment.

27 Do you feel there is too much violence and sex on television and in films: (please circle)
a) yes/ b) no.

28 Do you feel in today's world the United Nations is: (please circle)
a) very important/ b) moderately important/ c) no opinion/ d) moderately unimportant/ e) very unimportant.

29 Most people accept that the third world's standard of living is way below our own. Some people believe we must cut our own standard of living to help with the world's. Do you: (please circle)
a) agree/ b) disagree.

30 Pollution standards are a major issue today. There are many ways of improving pollution standards. Would you please circle below your opinion on these different ways:
a) willing to pay significantly more for gasoline/ b) willing to pay more for my automobile to make it "cleaner"/ c) willing to pay to insulate my home to make it more efficient/ d) willing to pay increased taxes to improve waste disposal/ e) willing to pay more for products to eliminate industrial pollution.

31 Do you believe advertising is: (please circle)
a) misleading and should be eliminated/ b) an area which should be under much tighter control/ c) not important/ d) important to the economy/ e) normally informative and truthful.

32 Do you believe most people cheat on their taxes: (please circle)
a) yes/ b) no.

33 Do you believe that homosexuality/lesbianism amongst consenting adults should remain legal: (please circle)
(a) yes/ b) no.

34 Do you believe that we need: (please circle)
a) more capitalism/ b) to remain at our current level of capitalism versus socialism/ c) more socialism.

35 Do you believe that emphasizing human rights in the Eastern bloc countries is: (please circle)
a) the only proper thing to do/ b) no opinion/ c) not our business.

36 Do you believe that we should recognize Cuba: (please circle)
a) yes/ b) no.

37 At times in the past our space program has cost significant proportions of the total federal budget. Do you believe that it: (please circle)
a) was worth it/ b) wasn't worth it.

38 Do you believe that certain children's products (such as skateboards) should be: (please circle)
a) left to the individual's judgement/ b) no opinion/ c) regulated/ d) totally banned on safety grounds.

39 Do you believe that, with reference to guns, Americans should: (please circle)
a) have the unrestricted right to own guns without registration/ b) be allowed any kind of gun with registration/ c) be allowed only hunting guns if they were proven to be responsible citizens/ d) no opinion/ e) be allowed only hunting guns if they were kept in a central place/ f) all guns should be totally outlawed.

40 With reference to the State of Israel, do you believe we should: (please circle)
a) lend unqualified support whatever the cost/ b) support Israel with some just solution for the Palestinians/ c) only support Israel's current boundaries/ d) no opinion/ e) recognize the obligation to support some form of Israeli State/ f) take no action.

41 With regard to what has become known as "Watergate" do you think that President Nixon: (please circle)
a) was directly responsible/ b) was indirectly responsible/ c) no opinion/ d) was rightly but harshly judged/ e) was far too harshly judged.

42 Do you think that we should have a nationalized health service: (please circle)
a) yes/ b) no.

43 It is just possible that Canada will split into a French versus a non-French speaking geographic section. If this occurred which of the following would you advocate: (please circle)
a) leaving them totally alone/ b) trying to get them to remain together/ c) no opinion/ d) actively supporting a Canadian referendum which made them part of the United States/ e) forcibly taking them over for security reasons.

44 Welfare payments are a source of controversy today. Do you think that, given the complex nature of individual cases, welfare should be: (please circle)
a) left in its present form/ b) adapted to make all able-bodied adults, even with children, work/ c) adapted to make all able-bodied adults without children work/ d) increased/ e) discontinued.

In order to accurately report responses to the questionnaire by different types of people, we would appreciate receiving the following personal information. Dependent upon the degree to which you are willing to tell us these facts, our research will be more accurate: (please tick where appropriate)

1 Male □   Female □
2 Age
3 Income:
        $15,000 or less   □
        $15,000 – $25,000 □
        $25,000 – $35,000 □
        $35,000 –$50,000 □
        Over $50,000   □

4 Married □ Single □ Divorced □ Widowed. □
5 Education
        Didn't complete high school □
        Completed high school   □
        Some college   □
        Completed college   □
        Advanced degree   □
6 Religion:
Protestant □   Catholic □
other (please specify)

7 Name of city and state in which you live:
....
8 Your name if you wish to be included in the credits for the next work.

Please send your completed questionnaire to:
The Research Director
The Book of Numbers
Heron House
Chiswick Mall
London W4 2PR
England